From International to Federal Market

The Changing Structure of European Law

ROBERT SCHÜTZE

OXFORD
UNIVERSITY PRESS

OXFORD
UNIVERSITY PRESS

Great Clarendon Street, Oxford, OX2 6DP,
United Kingdom

Oxford University Press is a department of the University of Oxford.
It furthers the University's objective of excellence in research, scholarship, and education by publishing worldwide. Oxford is a registered trade mark of Oxford University Press in the UK and in certain other countries

First Edition published in 2017

Published in the United States of America by Oxford University Press
198 Madison Avenue, New York, NY 10016, United States of America

British Library Cataloguing in Publication Data
Data available

Library of Congress Control Number: 2017930877

ISBN 978–0–19–880337–9

For Koen Lenaerts,

President of the European Court of Justice—in admiration.

PREFACE

This is the second volume of what will eventually become a trilogy on the 'Changing Structure of European Law'. Dealing with the changing structure of *negative* integration in the past sixty years, it complements my analysis of the changing structure of *positive* integration explored in *From Dual to Cooperative Federalism*.[1] The two volumes should indeed be considered intellectual twins. For not only were they conceived at the same time; thematically, they are meant to form a unity-in-diversity as regards the federal elements within the *substantive* law of the European Union. The third volume will finally explore the formal—constitutional—aspects that have turned the European Union into a federation of States.[2] But considering that it has taken me another eight years to complete this second volume, and in light of the constitutional uncertainty following the British EU referendum, this third volume is again unlikely to be published swiftly in the next few years.[3]

[1] R. Schütze, *From Dual to Cooperative Federalism: The Changing Structure of European Law*.

[2] This third volume will be entitled *From International to Federal Union: The Changing Structure of European Law*. The publishing chronology of the three volumes is thematically inverted when compared to how they should finally be arranged. This 'inversion', while not ideal, results from my—methodological—belief that good constitutional law (and theory) must never start with some lofty ideal but ought to grow from a concrete constitutional 'order' on the ground.

[3] This form of 'slow' publishing is becoming less and less common. Indeed: an ever-greater number of—even the brightest—young scholars feel compelled to publish as quickly (and as much) as possible. And while this may, sadly, be an increasingly necessary strategy in the competition to get a position or a promotion, the long-term effects of these fast-and-furious publications on the individual scholar and on scholarship in general are much less positive. For how can a not-yet-30-year-old scholar in EU law already have a hundred publications? How 'deep' and 'critical' will the analysis be if s/he produces, at this age, ten to twenty articles every year? How much past scholarship has s/he absorbed, reflected on, and criticized? How 'thick' will the intellectual plank be that is being drilled? For an excellent analysis of this dilemma for young scholars 'these days', see: J. Weiler, 'Editorial: On My Way Out—Advice to Young Scholars II: Career Strategy and the Publication Trap'. One cannot today be as selective as Wittgenstein; but the vicious cycle of fast publishing particularly disadvantages, I think, those brilliant—younger—scholars that uncompromisingly insist on quality and a reflective and critical engagement with the past, including their own work. For what is wrong with allowing an article to 'mature' for at least as long as the dust engendered by the creating process has taken to settle? True, the fruits of slow publishing are less immediate than simply 'combining' existing authorities under

Unlike the first book, matters were slightly more entangled with regard to this second volume. For when finalizing the manuscript in the past two years, it became clear to me that since my views on the early jurisprudential period of Article 34 TFEU differ so fundamentally from the (absolutely) dominant view in academic circles, they needed a *very* special treatment. And having combed through the historical archives of the European Commission and those of the European Court, while also immersing myself in the academic journals of the time, the analysis became so long that it filled a monograph on its own! So, instead of integrating a detailed historical and contextual analysis of the jurisprudential period between *Dassonville* and *Cassis de Dijon* here,[4] I have decided to dedicate a—separate—book to this period and the broader methodological question of the relationship between history and philosophy in European law.[5] The concrete results of this 'methodological' project have of course found their way—directly or indirectly, actually or potentially—into Chapter 3. Yet I must nonetheless politely ask the reader for her credit and patience in the absence of a detailed study of the historical context of *Dassonville* and the original meaning of its famous 'formula'.

Leaving these preliminaries aside, much of the first volume's preface still holds true today. Early parts of this book were written in Brussels, Cambridge (United Kingdom), Durham, Florence, Luxembourg, and Zwickau; and I must now add Cambridge (United States), London, Oxford, and Rome. In each of these cities, I was—again—very fortunate to meet a remarkable number of remarkable people. For their advice and encouragement, particularly with regard to this second volume, I wish to single out and thank Karen Alter, Roberta Bassi, Grainne de Búrca, Maria Anna Corvaglia, Claus-Dieter Ehlermann, David Held, Sir Francis Jacobs, Christian Joerges, Camilla Kamrad, Brigitte Leucht, Nicola Lupo,

the fast-publishing mode, but in the long run—I hope and believe—only slow, critical, and matured arguments are likely to pass the test of time. That may however offer little or no consolation for non-tenured academics so long as the collective dynamics of having to compete against 'cheap' outputs are not collectively addressed in the academic world. False civility may here be the greatest enemy of creative and un-orthodox modes of thought. For only through constructive and—sometimes—destructive criticism can quality emerge and be protected.

[4] See Case 8/74, *Procureur du Roi v Benoît and Gustave Dassonville*; and Case 120/78, *Rewe-Zentral AG v Bundesmonopolverwaltung für Branntwein*.

[5] R. Schütze, *Framing Dassonville: Text and Context in European Law*.

Federico Ortino, Ernst-Ulrich Petersmann, Dieter and Isolde Schütze, Hanns Ullrich, and especially Damian Chalmers and Steve Weatherill.[6] Thanks are due to BRILL, Oxford University Press as well as Sweet & Maxwell for allowing me to republish parts of my argument; and grateful acknowledgement is equally made to the European Research Council, whose generous support has allowed me, in the past few years, to reassess the 'federal' dimension behind 'State coordination' in the twenty-first century (EU Framework Programme 2007–13: ERC Grant Agreement No. 312 304).

In addition to the three 'classic' scholars of European constitutionalism that have shaped my early understanding of European law, I wish to warmly declare my admiration for Professor Koen Lenaerts, President of the European Court of Justice. To my mind, no one embodies the much-needed fusion between (academic) theory and (judicial) practice better today.

Durham, December 2016

[6] Many years back, when exploring PhD programmes, both Damian and Steve kindly met me in person to discuss my original proposal (on what was to become this book); and, despite my not taking up the LSE and Oxford offers, both have been extremely supportive ever since—an act of academic generosity that I shall never forget.

SUMMARY CONTENTS

CONTENTS

TABLE AND FIGURES

TABLE OF CASES

European Court of Justice: Judgments

European Court of Justice: Advocate General Opinions

GATT/WTO: Cases

United States: Supreme Court Cases

LIST OF ABBREVIATIONS

CCP	Common Commercial Policy
CEECD	Charge(s) having an Equivalent Effect to Customs Duties
ECJ	European Court of Justice
ECSC	European Coal and Steel Community
EEA	European Economic Area
EEC	European Economic Community
EU	European Union
FTA	Free Trade Area
GATT	General Agreement on Tariffs and Trade
ITO	International Trade Organization
MEEQR	Measure(s) having an Equivalent Effect to Quantitative Restrictions
MFN	Most-Favoured Nation
OEEC	Organization for European Economic Cooperation
OJ	Official Journal
PPMs	Processes and Production Methods
TFEU	Treaty on the Functioning of the European Union
TEU	Treaty on European Union
VAT	Value Added Tax
WTO	World Trade Organization

INTRODUCTION

Coming to Constitutional Terms

'Common markets cannot simply be *opened*, they must be *established*.'[1] The establishment of common markets thereby requires a 'centralizing' will.[2] The *national* will to create a *national* market had first emerged in England where, by the middle of the fourteenth century, '[t]he power of taxation and of trade regulation was beginning to pass from town to state'.[3] For other European States, this national market-building process took much longer: indeed, only by the end of the eighteenth century had the existence of national markets become a part of the economic and constitutional imagination.

How had these national markets been constructed? They were the result of two dialectical processes: internal unification and external demarcation. Internal unification meant that customs duties and regulatory barriers were removed *inside* the national borders. The creation of national markets however also required a second element. For the existence of a 'national' economy depended on the establishment of an external border around it.[4] (This external frontier transformed global trade into inter*national* trade.) The creation of free trade within the national market consequently came at a price: 'foreign' or 'external' trade had to be controlled.

Historically, the classic instrument to 'regulate' international trade is the customs barrier. Customs duties were not solely designed to 'protect' the emerging national industries from foreign competition. They were also a formidable source of revenue for the modern State. In the

[1] P. Reuter, *La Communauté Européenne du Charbon et de l'Acier*, 142 (emphasis added). Thanks go to M. Egan for having unburied this *bonmot* in 'Constructing a European Market', 1.

[2] F. Braudel, *Civilization and Capitalism: 15th–18th Century*, Volume III: *The Perspective of the World*, 287.

[3] J. B. Condliffe, *The Commerce of Nations*, 31.

[4] For a more extensive discussion of this point, see Chapter 1, Section I.

twentieth century, a second instrument of boundary control would gain particular prominence: quantitative restrictions. Quantitative restrictions are—complete or partial—bans on imports into the national territory. They 'regulate' competition between foreign and domestic goods by limiting the 'supply' of the former through an external border to international trade.

How would classic international law respond to the modern State's demand of external—economic—sovereignty? Would it allow States to prohibit trade with one another? By the eighteenth century, the mercantilist idea that States could legitimately restrict international trade had gained ground in international law. While challenged in the nineteenth century, it—sadly—still took two global disasters in the twentieth century before serious steps towards an international economic order were made. The subsequent rise of international economic cooperation was manifested in the 1947 General Agreement on Tariffs and Trade (GATT). The latter legally opened national markets by reducing customs duties and by eliminating quantitative restrictions to imports and exports. Importantly, the philosophical cornerstone of the GATT—and the World Trade Organization today—nonetheless remains the (internal) sovereignty of each State with regard to its own national market.

When founded in 1957, the European Union (EU) embodied the new cooperative economic spirit on a regional international scale. Going beyond a 'free trade area' and a 'customs union',[5] the Union thereby aimed from the very beginning at the creation of a 'common market'.[6] The EU

[5] International trade law typically distinguishes between various 'scales' or 'scopes' of regional economic cooperation. They will briefly be discussed in Chapter 1, Section II(2/d). The important point here is that each form of regional integration builds upon each other. The European Union's choice in favour of creating an internal market thus comprises the choice in favour of a customs union.

[6] Cf. ex-Article 2 EEC. The latter stated: 'The Community shall have as its task, by establishing a common market and progressively approximating the economic policies of Member States, to promote throughout the Community, a harmonious development of economic activities, a continuous and balanced expansion, an increase in stability, an accelerated raising of the standard of living and closer relations between the states belonging to it.' In the following book, the notions of 'common market', 'internal market', and 'single market' are used interchangeably. On the history of each specific expression, see: K. Mortelmans, 'The Common Market, the Internal Market and the Single Market, What's in a Market?'. In the following chapters, I shall—somewhat anachronistically—often refer to the 'common market'. The reason for this semantic preference is that the 'original' formulation not only better corresponds to the international trade law vocabulary. It also seems more 'evocative' of the 'common' nature of the market that the Member States of the Union share.

Treaties here envisaged a *new* form of international economic law: the law of economic *integration*.[7] In the (future) words of the European Court of Justice, market integration would thereby involve 'the elimination of all obstacles to intra-[Union] trade in order to merge the national markets into *a single market bringing about conditions as close as possible to those of a genuine internal market*'.[8] And the creation of this single market constitutes today 'the principal realisation of the European Union'.[9]

How has the Union created a 'common' market out of 'diverse' national markets? To create a common market, the EU Treaties pursued a dual strategy: negative and positive integration.[10] The Union was first charged to 'free' its common market from national barriers to trade in goods, persons, services, and capital. And to establish these 'four fundamental freedoms', the EU Treaties contained four constitutional prohibitions 'negating' illegitimate obstacles to intra-Union trade. This strategy of *negative* integration was—unlike the GATT coordination—complemented by a second strategy: *positive* integration. The European Union was thus charged to adopt European legislation to positively create a 'common law' for its common market by harmonizing the diverse national laws obstructing that market. The problem with this second strategy of market building was, however, that it did depend on the existence of a—centralizing—*political* will among the Member States; and this political will was—at least in the early phases of European integration—not strong enough. With positive integration taken prisoner by protectionist Member States, the construction of the European common market would thus primarily rely on a centralizing *judicial* will.

How far would the European Court of Justice push the boundaries of negative integration? Would it follow the (international) coordination approach adopted by the GATT; or would it venture into the province of legislation? Early on, the Court clarified its belief that the scope of negative integration should not depend on the degree of positive integration within the internal market. But would the—unlimited—forces

7 P. Pescatore, *The Law of Integration: Emergence of a New Phenomenon in International Relations, Based on the Experience of the European Communities*.

8 Case 15/81, *Gaston Schul Douane Expediteur BV v Inspecteur der Invoerrechten en Accijnzen, Roosendaal*, para. 33.

9 C. Blumann et al., *Commentaire Mégret. Introduction au marché intérieur—Libre circulation des marchandises*, 9.

10 J. Pinder, 'Positive and Negative Integration: Some Problems of Economic Union in the EEC', 88.

of negative integration not 'establish a market without rules'?[11] What, in fact, was the purpose behind the four fundamental freedoms: were they 'intended to liberalise intra-[Union] trade or [were they] intended more generally to encourage the unhindered pursuit of commerce in individual Member States'?[12] The following study wishes to answer this question by analysing the structure of the European common market by reference to three ideal-types. These three market models do not concern the *scope* but the *intensity* of economic integration.[13] The three market models are: the 'international' model, the 'federal' model, and the 'national' model (see Figure 1).[14]

[11] Advocate General Tizzano, Case C-442/02, *CaixaBank France v Ministère de l'Économie, des Finances et de l'Industrie*, para. 63.

[12] Advocate General Tesauro, Case C-292/92, *Hünermund and others v Landesapothekerkammer Baden-Württemberg*, para. 1.

[13] This is an important point. The international economic (law) literature classically distinguishes between four scopes or scales of regional economic cooperation—depending on the thematic scope of the cooperation effort. These will be discussed in Chapter 1, Section II(2/d).

[14] For a different construction of economic ideal-types within the internal market, see: M. Maduro, *We The Court: The European Court of Justice and the European Economic Constitution*, esp. Chapter 4. Maduro distinguishes three *non*-descriptive models that he characterizes as 'alternative[s]' (!) to the existing jurisprudence on the free movement of goods. The three models are: a decentralized model, a competitive model, and a centralized model. The author defines them as follows (ibid., 109): 'The centralised model reacts to the erosion of national regulatory powers through Article [34] by favouring a process of market regulation by means of the replacement of national laws with [Union] legislation. The competitive model promotes "competition among national rules", notably through the principle of mutual recognition of national legislation. In the decentralised model, States will retain regulatory powers, but are, at the same time, prevented from developing protectionist policies.' This *Introduction* cannot be the place to provide an in-depth critique of Maduro's descriptive analysis of Article 34 and his suggested normative theory (but see the *Epilogue* in this volume). Suffice to say here that there are at least three disadvantages linked to his terminological choices. First, unlike my 'national' model, Maduro's centralized model is not exclusively constructed out of the Union's approach to negative integration but depends on the existence of Union legislation and positive integration. (It seems that Maduro originally tried to get away from this by also considering his judicial majoritarianism within this model, see: ibid., 109 (emphasis added): 'The centralised model can be linked to those supporting harmonisation of national legislation *either through a majoritarian use of Article [34]* or through [Union] legislation following deregulation at national level.' However, in subsequent descriptions of the centralized model the judicial harmonization aspect is silently dropped.) The problem with identifying the centralized model with Union legislation, however, is that the Court might adopt a decentralized approach under Article 34 and yet follow a centralized approach under Article 114. For unlike Maduro suggests, there is no direct link between the scope and intensity of negative and positive integration. Secondly, Maduro's competition model remains ill-defined and obscure throughout

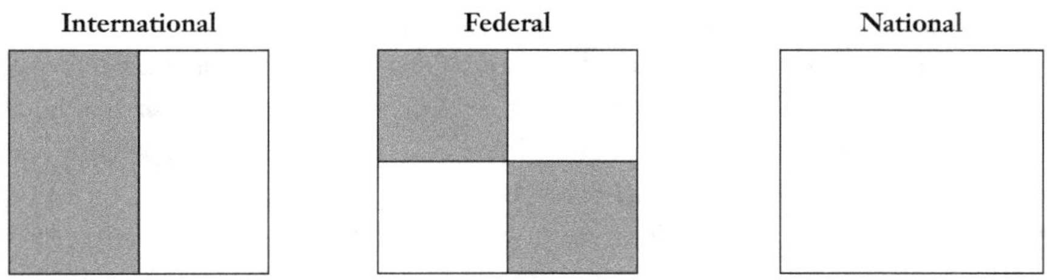

Figure 1. Integration intensity: three market models

Under the (modern) international model,[15] each State contractually commits itself to limiting its *external* sovereignty by opening its *external* borders to foreign goods, while it fully retains internal sovereignty over 'its' national market. This principle has become known as the principle of 'host State' control. It allows the importing—that is, the host—State to impose its domestic laws on foreign goods; yet the State must not discriminate against imports. The prohibition of discrimination quintessentially requires States not to establish a set of rules that *distinctly* apply to imports. (But discrimination may equally be prohibited whenever indistinctly applicable measures materially discriminate against *imports*.) Within the international model, the frame of reference for discrimination is always the 'host State'. Discriminatory effects must flow from the *national measure adopted by the host State*; whereas a 'discrimination' flowing from a diversity of national regulations is not covered. The philosophical demand behind the international model is thus the full assimilation of foreign goods under host State rule. They are entitled to 'national treatment' in all respects—but nothing more. Within this market model, national markets are *coordinated* but *not integrated*.

his work. For instead of relating it to the *Cassis*-line of cases and the principle of mutual recognition based on home State control (cf. N. Reich, 'Competition between Legal Orders: A New Paradigm of EC Law', 861), Maduro prefers to identify it with the (US American) idea of 'economic due process'. But this—I think—is a philosophy that would have much better suited his 'centralized' model—albeit one in which a Court constructs a unitary market philosophy based on economic laissez-faire. Finally, as Maduro admits, there is little distinction between his 'competitive' and 'decentralized' models for in both will there be competition between legal orders (ibid., 143); the only difference between the two models is that in the former it is directly the 'market' that decides, whereas in the decentralized model the decision is left to the national legislatures.

[15] On the distinction between the 'classic' and the 'modern' international model, see Chapter 1 in this volume.

The 'federal' market model, on the other hand, is based on the principle that within a 'common market' States must also lose a part of their *internal* sovereignty over 'their' national market. In line with the Union principle of mutual recognition, goods are generally entitled to move freely within the common market once they comply with the law of their home State. (The host State is thus, in principle, no longer allowed to impose its internal sovereignty over imports because they already have been regulated by another 'sovereign'.) The transition from host State to home State control within the federal model thus signifies a dramatic loss of regulatory power for the host State. The federal model is thereby not concerned with the question whether or not the host State discriminates against imports; it rather examines whether *the extension of host State laws to imports imposes a 'restriction' or 'obstacle' to intra-Union trade.* Such a restriction or obstacle is seen to arise because the good is subject to two—or, in the worst-case scenario, twenty-eight—different national 'sovereigns'.

Finally, according to the 'national' market model, all trade restrictions that are above a—legislative or judicial—Union standard must be removed. The constitutional regime of the 'common market' is here completely assimilated to that of a 'national market'. Where a State adopts rules that are higher than the Union standard, this higher national standard will violate the free-movement provisions—even when this standard is applied to a State's own 'home' production. The philosophical rationale within this third model is thus not one that identifies obstacles to trade resulting from disparities between different national legislations. It is not a relative test that balances the jurisdictional claims of the home State against those of the host State. On the contrary, it is based on an absolute economic criterion: *where a State law reduces the volume of trade within the internal market disproportionately*, it will—in principle—violate the free-movement provisions. The free-movement provisions are here no longer concerned with liberalizing *intra*-Union trade, they aim 'to encourage the unhindered pursuit of commerce in individual Member States'.[16]

[16] Cf. Advocate General Tesauro, *Hünermund* (see n. 12), para. 1. The Advocate General continued, in warning words, as follows (ibid., para. 27): 'Article [34] would otherwise come to be relied on and used, not for its proper purposes but in order to enable certain traders to avoid the application of national provisions which, in regulating a given activity, restrict freedom to trade, whether by imposing opening hours on shops, or by requiring prior authorization in order to carry on a given activity (why not, even a simple trading licence), or else by imposing professional requirements (sometimes technical as well) on those intending to sell certain classes of goods. In that context, I cannot refrain from pointing out that such a use of Article

Which one of these three market models has the European Union adopted? The wording of the free-movement provisions within the EU Treaties offers contradictory suggestions. Some articles are based on an international model.[17] Others seem neutral as to which model is to apply.[18] The general internal market provision in Article 26 of the Treaty on the Functioning of the European Union (TFEU) is—by contrast—textually close to the national model. For in demanding that '[t]he internal market shall comprise an area *without internal frontiers* in which the free movement of goods, persons, services and capital is ensured',[19] it appears to outlaw all trade barriers within the European Union. Was it consequently the aim of the European Treaties 'to unite national markets in a single market *having the characteristics of a domestic market*';[20] or do the Treaties impose a lower degree of market integration on the Member States?

What, in other words, is the legal structure of the European internal market? The answer to this question has changed over time. And serving—again—my personal solution on the silver plate of its title, this book argues that the Union's common market philosophy has moved from an international to a federal philosophy.[21] How can we detect this change?

[34] would ultimately render nugatory the Treaty provisions on the free movement of goods and on establishment, or in any event devalue them.'

[17] Article 110(1) TFEU states: 'No Member State shall impose, directly or indirectly, on the products of other Member States any internal taxation of any kind in excess of that imposed directly or indirectly on similar domestic products.'

[18] Article 34 TFEU states: 'Quantitative restrictions on imports and all measures having equivalent effect shall be prohibited between Member States.'

[19] Article 26(2) TFEU. See also: Advocate General Jabobs, Case C-412/93, *Société d'Importation Edouard Leclerc-Siplec v TF1 Publicité SA and M6 Publicité SA*, para. 39 (emphasis added): 'The central concern of the Treaty provisions on the free movement of goods is to prevent unjustified obstacles to trade between Member States. *If an obstacle to inter-state trade exists, it cannot cease to exist simply because an identical obstacle affects domestic trade.*'

[20] Case 207/83, *Commission v United Kingdom*, para. 17 (emphasis added). And see also: Case 270/80, *Polydor Limited and RSO Records, Inc. v Harlequin Records Shops Limited and Simons Records Limited*, para. 16: 'As the Court has had occasion to emphasize in various contexts, the Treaty, by establishing a common market and progressively approximating the economic policies of the Member States, seeks to unite national markets into a single market having the characteristics of a domestic market'; as well as *Gaston Schul* (see n. 8).

[21] The thesis advanced in this book is—again—not absolute. It does not claim that there were no elements of a federal market model in the early phases of the Union, nor that there are no elements of an international market model in the present. The book also does not deny that there exist counter-currents to the general move from international to federal market structure. The book—like its predecessor—makes a relative claim: the predominant market philosophy underlying the structure of European law has changed from one philosophy to the other. However, it is also important to keep in mind that the Court—even at one particular

The change in the underlying constitutional philosophy is reflected in the changing dogmatic structure of the fundamental freedoms, and here in particular: the free movement of goods.[22]

The book is organized as follows. It is divided into a 'General Part' and a 'Special Part'. The General Part will attempt to clarify two things by means of a comparative legal analysis. It starts by offering a historical overview of the (inter)national instruments governing foreign trade. We shall see there that international economic law has moved from bilateral free trade agreements towards a multilateral free trade system that is today administered by the World Trade Organization. A second chapter subsequently explores the constitutional creation of the 'American' market in the nineteenth and twentieth century. We shall explore whether the 1787 US Constitution completely merged the diverse State markets into a common 'national' market, or whether we still find elements of an international or federal market philosophy in the structure of US free-movement law.

Having analysed the history and structure of the 'international' and the 'American' market, the Special Part of the book then explores the legal structure of the European common market. Chapter 3 investigates the 'international' origins of that market. Starting out from an international market model, the scope of negative integration was originally limited by the fundamental idea that each State exercised (internal) sovereignty over its national market. This dramatically changed with the arrival of a new—federal—philosophy symbolized by *Cassis de Dijon*. This federal trade philosophy was still based on the idea of a 'plurality' of national legislators; yet, States are no longer seen as 'sovereign' *within* their markets. National markets are henceforth 'integrated' into a common market. Chapters 4 and 5 explain this federal market model in greater detail. But the move from

period of time—may not always be consistent with itself. Indeed, as an empirical study of chamber decisions of the Court in the context of the free movement of goods has shown, there exists a significant degree of incoherence in the formal reasoning and the substantive outcomes depending on which chamber of the Court is involved, see L. Woods, 'Consistency in the Chambers of the ECJ: A Case Study on the Free Movement of Goods'. On the question of coherence within free-movement law generally, see: N. Nic Shuibhne, 'The Coherence of EU Free Movement Law: Constitutional Responsibility and the Court of Justice'.

[22] The free movement of goods has long been the vanguard freedom within the common market, see: C. Blumann et al., *Commentaire Mégret. Introduction au marché intérieur—Libre circulation des marchandises*, 7: 'Celle-ci constitue en effet le socle sur lequel s'est fondée non seulement la construction européenne, mais aussi les autres libertés.'

an international to a federal market nonetheless finds one exception: fiscal measures. This 'fiscal exception' is discussed in Chapter 6.

A *Conclusion* will finally provide a summary of the results; and it will also try to generalize them beyond the free movement of goods. Reading the *Conclusion* immediately after this *Introduction* may—again—be profitable in order to avoid the pitfalls of the hermeneutic circle and to install—from the beginning—a feeling for the unity in the diversity of the arguments presented in this book.

GENERAL PART

International and Federal Markets

1

International Law and Market Coordination

Introduction

'Nothing seems so self-evident ... as the classical notion of the *national market*'; and yet, the great modern historian of capitalism tells us, 'the move from the regional to the national market ... had nothing spontaneous about it'.[1] National markets were 'often constructed against all the odds'—having to fight 'against the over-powerful cities with their own policies, against the provinces which resisted centralization, against foreign intervention which breached frontiers'.[2] Not being natural but artificial phenomena, national markets needed to be constructed; and '[n]ot surprisingly then, there was inevitably behind the national market a centralizing *political* will'.[3]

This political will was first and foremost tasked 'to remove the internal customs barriers and tolls' that 'hindered the circulation of goods'.[4] The—national—unification of the customs territory is thereby relatively recent.[5] Leaving the precocious England

[1] F. Braudel, *Civilization and Capitalism: 15th–18th Century*, Volume III: *The Perspective of the World*, 277.

[2] Ibid., 287. [3] Ibid. (emphasis added).

[4] Ibid., 289. For an analysis of the numerous impediments to national trade, see: M. Postan, 'The Trade of Medieval Europe: The North', 182: 'The scope of medieval trade is all the more remarkable for the various obstacles which beset the merchant. It is perhaps true that medieval commerce could not have functioned as it did, had the obstacles in its way been quite as formidable as their history might suggest. Yet formidable they doubtless were, and none more so than the innumerable payments on the frontiers, along the rivers and roads, on two markets and in sea ports[.]'

[5] B. Nolde, 'Droit et technique des traités de commerce', 329–30: 'La souveraineté douanière—expression la plus simple de cette faculté—est une conquête relativement récente de l'évolution historique. Pendant de longs siècles, parfois jusqu'au commencement du xix siècle, les Etats européens vivaient sous l'empire d'un système de morcellement de la souveraineté douanière. Les droits de douane étaient perçus par des provinces, des villes, des seigneurs

aside,[6] it only became a constitutional commonplace by the end of the eighteenth century. In France, this occurred in 1790, when the (revolutionary) 'Constituent Assembly' adopted a 'unification law' that 'created' the—French—national market by outlawing all internal customs duties.[7] The creation of the German national market would even have to wait until well into the nineteenth century.[8]

The *internal* unification of national markets had pushed customs duties to the *national* border.[9] And here, they would be fortified. For the construction of national markets indeed required a second—external—element: a national customs border.[10] National economic unity was—dialectically—based on international disunity: a 'national' market could only exist if demarcated from 'foreign' trade. With the creation of national markets, *global* trade thus becomes inter*national* trade.[11]

What were the legal instruments regulating this international trade? This chapter answers this question in two steps. Section I explores the

féodaux; à chaque pas à l'intérieur des Etats on rencontrait des barrières douanières et des bureaux de douane agissant pour le compte de ces provinces, villes ou seigneurs et exerçant une influence prépondérante sur les conditions des échanges avec l'extérieur. Parmi les pays européens, seule l'Angleterre parait de tout temps avoir été constituée en un Etat à régime douanier unifié et centralisé.... Dans les autres pays européens, la centralisation douanière est le résultat d'une longue et pénible évolution.'

[6] M. Postan, 'The Trade of Medieval Europe: The North', 183: 'England was perhaps the largest area of northern Europe in which trade was free from any but small tolls.' See also: J. B. Condliffe, *The Commerce of Nations*, 31.

[7] French Constituent Assembly, Decree of 31 October 1790: 'On the Abolition of Internal Trade Barriers'. The need to create a national market had, by the mid-eighteenth century, become a political priority: 'The necessity of reform was indeed apparent, for local imposts had become so numerous that wine coming from the Rhône, on the Loire River, to Paris was subjected in 1755 to eleven customs duties and twelve tolls.' (S. B. Clough, *France: A History of National Economics*, 25–6).

[8] For an overview of German economic unification in the nineteenth century, see: W. O. Henderson, *The Zollverein*. The 1871 Imperial Constitution codified this development in its Article 33: 'Germany forms one customs and commercial territory surrounded by a common customs frontier ... All articles of free trade in any one of the States of the Federation may be introduced into any other State of the Federation, and can only be subjected to a duty in the latter in so far as similar articles produced in that State are subject to a home duty.'

[9] J. Morini-Comby, *Mercantilisme et Protectionnisme. Essai sur les doctrines interventionnistes en politique commerciale du XVe au XIXe siècle*, 92.

[10] In the words of R. C. Snyder, 'The Most Favoured-Nation Clause, 2': 'Tariffs have become synonymous with modern economic life because of their close relation to nation-building.'

[11] The historical symbiosis between local and global trade that had existed prior to the rise of the modern State was thus eliminated in favour of the national market. On this point, see only: F. Braudel, *Civilization and Capitalism*, Chapters 2 and 3.

classic international law model that accommodated the (sovereign) 'mercantilist' State. This State was based on 'the unchallenged assumption' that the national government 'had the right and the responsibility to regulate economic activities in the interest of the common [national] good'.[12] Under classic international law, States were thus sovereignly free to become a 'closed commercial State'.[13] Yet this idea of economic coexistence was gradually replaced by a spirit of economic cooperation in the twentieth century.[14] Section II explores the origins and contemporary structures of the modern international law of economic cooperation. This modern model, while still nominally based on the idea of State sovereignty under international law, nonetheless accepts that national economies mutually benefit from 'opening up' by means of a better division of labour and the economies of scale engendered.

I. The 'Classic' Model: The Mercantilist State and Its National Market

How did the nation State control its economic borders? The two classic tools developed to 'regulate' international trade were the import ban and the external tariff.[15] Tariffs combined the interests of domestic producers in protection from foreign competition with the—great—appetite of the nation State to raise revenue.[16] This alliance between 'merchants' and the State became known as 'mercantilism'. Mercantilism generally stands for economic State-building,[17] in which the 'commercial' State jealously guards its balance of trade with other nations; and by the end of

[12] J. O. Appleby, *Economic Thought and Ideology in Seventeenth-Century England*, 99.

[13] I. Nakhimovsky, *The Closed Commercial State: Perpetual Peace and Commercial Society from Rousseau to Fichte*.

[14] W. G. Friedmann, *The Changing Structure of International Law*.

[15] G. Erler, *Grundprobleme des internationalen Wirtschaftsrechts*, 56.

[16] For an analysis of the English case, see only: J. B. Condliffe, *The Commerce of Nations*, 87: 'By the beginning of the eighteenth century the tariff or duties chargeable on imported goods had come to be both the chief source of revenue and an elaborate instrument of protection to English manufacturing industries. This twofold aspect of tariff development was characteristic of the mercantile age.'

[17] S. B. Clough, *France: A History of National Economics*, 8: 'To the economic state-building of the period from approximately 1500 to 1800, Adam Smith in his Wealth of Nations gave the name "mercantile system".'

the eighteenth century, the central tenet of the mercantile system was 'to diminish as much as possible the importation of foreign goods for home consumption, and to increase as much as possible the exportation of the produce of domestic industry'.[18]

This section analyses the mercantilist (inter)national system of the eighteenth century in a first step. We shall thereafter explore the 'new' economic philosophy of international cooperation, and the rise of international free trade; and, finally, the re-emergence of neo-mercantilism in the period between the First and the Second World War.

1. *International Law and the Mercantilist State: The Eighteenth Century*

Could States prohibit trade with other States under international law? Early modern conceptions of international law were ambivalent towards the idea of economic sovereignty.[19] Yet in the late seventeenth century a gradual change occurred;[20] and this change was completed in the middle of the eighteenth century. Henceforth, the classic justification for the mercantilist State is found in Vattel's *Law of Nations*.[21] This famous eighteenth-century textbook clearly distinguished between 'home trade' and 'foreign trade';[22] and the mercantile State was entitled to prohibit the importation of foreign goods:

[18] A. Smith, *An Inquiry into the Nature and Causes of the Wealth of Nations*, 286. For a classic 'English' mercantilist theorist, see only: T. Mun, *England's Treasure by Forraign Trade* (1664), 7: 'The ordinary means therefore to increase our wealth and treasure is by *Forraign Trade*, wherein wee must ever observe this rule; to sell more to strangers yearly than wee consume of theirs in value.'

[19] Cf. H. Grotius, *The Freedom of the Seas*, 61: 'By the law of nations, the principle was introduced that the opportunity to engage in trade of which no one can be deprived, should be free to all men.'

[20] Cf. S. Pufendorf, *De Jure Naturae et Gentium Libri Octo*, Volume 2. Pufendorf allows each State to restrict trade if it 'would lose a considerable profit, or in some indirect way suffer harm' (ibid., 369). Imports can thus be taxed or prohibited 'either because the state may suffer some loss from its importation, or that our own citizens may be incited to greater industry, or that our wealth may not pass into the hands of foreigners' (ibid., 370). In the view of D. A. Irwin, *Against the Tide: An Intellectual History of Free Trade*, 24: 'Pufendorf almost completely undermined the law of nations case for free trade. From this point on, the cosmopolitanism of the earlier natural law thinkers was largely abandoned in favour of rules that supported the independent sovereignty of the nation state in its right to restrict trade.'

[21] E. de Vattel, *The Law of Nations*.

[22] Ibid., 37: '§ 83. Of home and foreign trade: It is commerce that enables individuals and whole nations to procure those commodities which they stand in need of, but cannot find at home. Commerce is divided into home and foreign trade. The former is that carried on in the state between the several inhabitants; the latter is carried on with foreign nations.'

§ 90. Prohibition of foreign merchandise

Every State has consequently a right to prohibit the entrance of foreign merchandises; and the nations that are affected by such prohibition have no right to complain of it, as if they had been refused an office of humanity. Their complaints would be ridiculous, since their only ground of complaint would be, that a profit is refused to them by that nation who does not choose they should make it at her expense ... [23]

Foreign trade was thus left in the hands of each individual State. In the absence of a perfect right under natural law, States could only create 'contractual' commercial rights between themselves: 'A nation, not having naturally a perfect right to carry on a commerce with another, may procure it by an agreement or treaty.'[24] The mercantilist State would thereby need to keep a jealous eye on its balance of trade:

§ 98. Balance of trade, and attention of government in this respect

The conductor of a nation ought to take particular care to encourage the commerce that is advantageous to his people, and to suppress or lay restraints upon that which is to their disadvantage. Gold and silver having become the common standard of the value of all the articles of commerce, the trade that brings into the State a greater quantity of these metals than it carries out, is an advantageous trade; and, on the contrary, that is a ruinous one, which causes more gold and silver to be sent abroad, than it brings home. This is what is called the balance of trade. The ability of those who have the direction of it, consists in making that balance turn in favour of the nation.

§ 99. Import duties

Of all the measures that a wise government may take with this view, we shall only touch here on import duties. When the conductors of a State, without absolutely

[23] Ibid., 38.

[24] Ibid. 39 (para. 93). The international treaty route was here seen as the only one, because even custom could not create a perfect right to international commerce (ibid., 41 = para. 95): 'Thus, although two nations have traded together, without interruption, during a century, this long usage does not give any right to either of them; nor is the one obliged on this account to suffer the other to come and sell its merchandises, or to buy others:—they both preserve the double right of prohibiting the entrance of foreign merchandise, and of selling their own wherever people are willing to buy them. Although the English have from time immemorial been accustomed to get wine from Portugal, they are not on that account obliged to continue the trade, and have not lost the liberty of purchasing their wines elsewhere. Although they have, in the same manner, been long accustomed to sell their cloth in that kingdom, they have, nevertheless, a right to transfer that trade to any other country: and the Portuguese, on their part, are not obliged by this long custom, either to sell their wines to the English, or to purchase their cloths. If a nation desires any right of commerce which shall no longer depend on the will of another, she must acquire it by treaty.'

forcing trade, are nevertheless desirous of diverting it into other channels, they lay such duties on the merchandises they would discourage as will prevent their consumption. Thus, French wines are charged with very high duties in England, while the duties on Portugal are very moderate,—because England sells few of her productions to France, while she sells large quantities to Portugal. There is nothing in this conduct that is not very wise and extremely just; and France has no reason to complain of it—every nation having an undoubted right to make what conditions she thinks proper, with respect to receiving foreign merchandises, and being even at liberty to refuse taking them at all.

This classic legitimation of the mercantilist State was to become the cornerstone of modern international law.[25] Sovereign States were entitled to choose their commercial policy vis-à-vis other States. Neither were they obliged to treat foreign goods in the same way as domestic goods; nor would they have to treat all imports on an equal footing. The sovereign State could decide to be an 'open' or a 'closed' commercial State;[26] and even if it were to open its domestic market to foreign products, it could freely discriminate between trade channels by preferring one foreign State to another.

We find an excellent illustration of this mercantilist philosophy in the 1703 'Methuen Treaty'.[27] Regulating commerce between England and Portugal, the Treaty took its name from the (then) English Ambassador to Portugal. It allowed the importation and sale of English cloth on the Portuguese market while it granted Portuguese wines a lower tariff than French wines. The two central provisions read:

Article I

His sacred Royal Majesty of Portugal promises, both in his own name, and that of his successors, to admit, for ever hereafter, into Portugal, the woollen cloths, and

[25] Cf. L. Oppenheim, *International Law: A Treatise*, Volume 1: *Peace*, 178: 'In consequence of its internal independence and territorial supremacy, a state can adopt ... any commercial policy it likes[.]'

[26] For the philosophically most radical plead to close off the commercial State, see: J. G. Fichte, *The Closed Commercial State*, esp. 160–3: 'In short, this system, where foreign trade is closed incompletely, without precise calculation of what goods ought to be brought into trade given the nation's needs, not only fails to achieve what it should, but in fact brings about new evils ... The state must close itself off entirely to all foreign trade, forming from this point on an isolated commercial body, just as it had already previously formed an isolated juridical and political body.'

[27] There exist three Methuen Treaties; yet only the third—commercial—Treaty has become famous. For an analysis of its negotiation, see: A. D. Francis, 'John Methuen and the Anglo-Portuguese Treaties of 1703'.

the rest of the woollen manufactures of the British, as was accustomed, till they were prohibited by the law; nevertheless upon this condition:

Article II

That is to say, that her sacred Royal Majesty of Great Britain shall, in her own name, and that of her successors, be obliged, for ever hereafter, to admit the wines of the growth of Portugal into Britain: so that at no time, whether there shall be peace or war between the Kingdoms of Britain and France, any thing more shall be demanded for these wines by the name of custom or duty, or by whatsoever other title, directly or indirectly, whether they shall be imported into Great Britain in pipes or hogsheads, or other casks, than what shall be demanded for the like quantity or measure of French wine, deducting or abating a third part of the custom or duty ... [28]

The Treaty eliminated all 'quantitative restrictions' of English cloth in exchange for a 'preferential' tariff on Portuguese wine. Originally, this connection between English cloth and Portuguese wine was 'somewhat accidental';[29] yet it became a major element of British foreign policy, especially in relation to France. For Britain's trade relations with France were subject to a long-standing trade deficit; and because of this trade imbalance, Britain consciously tried to 'divert' its wine importations from France to Portugal. France soon attempted to neutralize the preferential treatment of Portuguese wines, but the British Parliament failed to ratify the commercial provisions of the Treaty of Utrecht.[30] David Hume famously commented on this victory of passion over reason as follows:

Our jealousy and our hatred of France are without bounds; and the former sentiment, at least, must be acknowledged reasonable and well-grounded. These passions have occasioned innumerable barriers and obstructions upon commerce, where we are accused of being commonly the aggressors. But what have we gained by the bargain? We lost the French market for our woollen manufactures, and transferred the commerce of wine to Spain and Portugal, where we buy worse liquor at a higher price ... But would we lay aside prejudice, it would not be difficult to prove, that nothing could be more innocent, perhaps advantageous. Each new acre

[28] The text is taken from A. Smith, *The Wealth of Nations*, Book IV, Chapter 6. The reference to 'Great Britain', instead of England, takes account of the fact that by the time Smith is writing, the Union of England and Scotland had taken place.

[29] A. D. Francis, 'John Methuen and the Anglo-Portuguese Treaties of 1703', 122.

[30] The 1713 Treaty of Utrecht contained a clause similar to a most-favoured-nation clause in its Article 8. The clause would have allowed French wines to be treated like Portuguese wines.

of vineyard planted in France, in order to supply England with wine, would make it requisite for the French to take the produce of an English acre, sown in wheat or barley, in order to subsist themselves; and it is evident, that we should thereby get command of the better commodity.[31]

This 'jealousy of trade' between Great Britain and France resulted in nearly a century of economic 'warfare'. A first effort to re-establish economic peace was made in the 1786 Eden Treaty;[32] which was the first material expression of a new economic philosophy with regard to the wealth of nations.

2. *A (New) Philosophy: International Trade and the 'Wealth of Nations'*

Should States open their domestic frontiers to foreign goods? The question received a novel—and soon canonical—answer in 1776. Adam Smith's *Wealth of Nations* revolutionized the theoretical discourse on international trade by extending the principles of political economy from the national to the international sphere.[33] His famous critique of the mercantile system can be found in Book IV:

It is the maxim of every prudent master of a family, never to attempt to make at home what it will cost him more to make than to buy. The tailor does not attempt to make his own shoes, but buys them of the shoemaker. The shoemaker does not attempt to make his own clothes, but employs a tailor. The farmer attempts to make neither the one nor the other, but employs those different artificers. All of them find it for their interest to employ their whole industry in a way in which they have some advantage over their neighbours, and to purchase with a part of its produce, or, what is the same thing, with the price of a part of it, whatever else they have occasion for. *What is prudence in the conduct of every private family, can scarce be folly in that of a great kingdom. If a foreign country can supply us with a commodity cheaper than we ourselves can make it, better buy it of them with some part of the produce of our own industry, employed in a way in which we have some advantage.*[34]

This was a plea for an international division of labour. International specialization promised—just like the division of labour within an industry—a

[31] D. Hume, *Essays, Moral, Political, and Literary* (1742), II.V.16 'Of the Balance of Trade'.

[32] On this point, see: R. M. Brace, 'The Anglo-French Treaty of Commerce of 1786: A Reappraisal', 151.

[33] A. Smith, *Wealth of Nations*.

[34] Ibid., 292–3 (emphasis added).

dramatic increase in the overall wealth of nations. If each country exploited its natural (or acquired) advantages in the production of particular goods, an exchange of these—more cheaply produced—goods would always be mutually advantageous.[35] The orthodox belief that the balance-of-trade was always a zero-sum game—the very heart of the mercantilist creed—was consequently wrong.[36] A mercantile system did not protect the wealth of the nation; it only protected the wealth of a part of that nation: 'In the restraints upon the importation of all foreign commodities which can come into competition with those of our own growth, or manufacture, the interest of the home-consumer is evidently sacrificed to that of the producer. It is altogether for the benefit of the latter, that the former is obliged to pay that enhancement of price which this monopoly almost always occasions.'[37]

This attack on the mercantilist State was refined, a few decades later, in the work of another British author: David Ricardo. In his *Principles of Political Economy and Taxation* (1817), we read:

> It is quite as important to the happiness of mankind that our enjoyments should be increased by the better distribution of labour, by each country producing those commodities for which by its situation, its climate, and its other natural and artificial advantages it is adapted, and by their exchanging them for the commodities of other countries, as that they should be augmented by a rise in the rate

[35] Ibid., 294–5: 'The natural advantages which one country has over another, in producing particular commodities, are sometimes so great, that it is acknowledged by all the world to be in vain to struggle with them. By means of glasses, hot-beds, and hot-walls, very good grapes can be raised in Scotland, and very good wine, too, can be made of them, at about thirty times the expense for which at least equally good can be brought from foreign countries. Would it be a reasonable law to prohibit the importation of all foreign wines, merely to encourage the making of claret and Burgundy in Scotland? But if there would be a manifest absurdity in turning towards any employment thirty times more of the capital and industry of the country than would be necessary to purchase from foreign countries an equal quantity of the commodities wanted, there must be an absurdity, though not altogether so glaring, yet exactly of the same kind, in turning towards any such employment a thirtieth, or even a three hundredth part more of either. Whether the advantages which one country has over another be natural or acquired, is in this respect of no consequence. As long as the one country has those advantages, and the other wants them, it will always be more advantageous for the latter rather to buy of the former than to make.'

[36] Ibid., 308. Even the existence of a powerful and wealthy neighbouring State, while dangerous in war, would be advantageous in trade: 'A nation that would enrich itself by foreign trade is certainly most likely to do so when its neighbours are all rich, industrious, and commercial nations.'

[37] A. Smith, *Wealth of Nations*, 377.

> of profits ... Under a system of perfectly free commerce, each country naturally devotes its capital and labour to such employments as are most beneficial to each. This pursuit of individual advantage is admirably connected with the universal good of the whole ... It is this principle which determines that wine shall be made in France and Portugal, that corn shall be grown in America and Poland, and that hardware and other goods shall be manufactured in England.[38]

The famous illustration given to explicate this idea was a (not so) fictitious trade agreement between Portugal and England in which Portuguese wine is exchanged for English cloth, and through which Ricardo shows that it could work in both countries' favour—even if one of them were to enjoy an absolute advantage in the production of *both* products![39] This novel theory of 'comparative advantage' would soon become the solid rock on which the philosophy of free international trade was to be built.[40]

Yet the 'British' free trade philosophy was not without critics. One of the early challengers of the idea of—unlimited—free trade was a founding father of the young American Republic: Alexander Hamilton. Having produced a 'Report on Manufacturers' for the House of Representatives in 1791, Hamilton argued against free trade in some

[38] D. Ricardo, *The Principles of Political Economy and Taxation*, 80–1.

[39] The famous 'thought experiment' goes as follows (ibid., 82): 'If Portugal had no commercial connexion with other countries, instead of employing a great part of her capital and industry in the production of wines, with which she purchases for her own use the cloth and hardware of other countries, she would be obliged to devote a part of that capital to the manufacture of those commodities, which she would thus obtain probably inferior in quality as well as quantity. The quantity of wine which she shall give in exchange for the cloth of England, is not determined by the respective quantities of labour devoted to the production of each, as it would be, if both commodities were manufactured in England, or both in Portugal. England may be so circumstanced, that to produce the cloth may require the labour of 100 men for one year; and if she attempted to make the wine, it might require the labour of 120 men for the same time. England would therefore find it in her interest to import wine, and to purchase it by the exportation of cloth. To produce the wine in Portugal, might require only the labour of 80 men for one year, and to produce the cloth in the same country, might require the labour of 90 men for the same time. It would therefore be advantageous for her to export wine in exchange for cloth. This exchange might even take place, notwithstanding that the commodity imported by Portugal could be produced there with less labour than in England. Though she could make the cloth with the labour of 90 men, she would import it from a country where it required the labour of 100 men to produce it, because it would be advantageous to her rather to employ her capital in the production of wine, for which she would obtain more cloth from England, than she could produce by diverting a portion of her capital from the cultivation of vines to the manufacture of cloth.'

[40] D. A. Irwin, *Against the Tide*, 90.

areas so as to protect the young American industry, then still in its infancy.[41] This 'infant industry' argument was subsequently developed by Friedrich List—one of the founding fathers of German economic unification. List equally felt that a 'boundless cosmopolitanism' in international trade would, in the absence of a 'universal confederation of nations', subject less-developed States to the economic hegemony of 'predominant manufacturing nations'.[42] And since every State would wish to develop from an agricultural to an industrialized State,[43] each State was entitled to protect its infant industrial sectors against foreign competition.[44] The cosmopolitan doctrine of free trade is therefore seen in a hegemonic light:

> It is a very common clever device that when anyone has attained the summit of greatness, he kicks away the ladder by which he has climbed up, in order to deprive others of the means of climbing up after him. In this lies the secret of the cosmopolitical doctrine of Adam Smith ... Any nation which by means of protective duties and restrictions on navigation has raised her manufacturing

[41] A. Hamilton, Report on the Subject of Manufacturers. For a historical analysis of the Report and its consequences, see: D. A. Irwin, 'The Aftermath of Hamilton's "Report on Manufactures"', 800: 'To this day, the report is often heralded as the quintessential American statement against the laissez faire doctrine of free trade and for activist government policies—including protectionist tariffs—to promote industrialization.'

[42] F. List, *National System of Political Economy*, Volume 2: *The Theory*, 77. He explains (ibid., 78): 'In proportion, however, as the principle of a universal confederation of nations is reasonable, in just the same degree would a given nation act contrary to reason if, in anticipation of the great advantages to be expected from such a union, and from a state of universal and perpetual peace, it were to regulate the principles of its national policy as though this universal confederation of nations existed already. We ask, would not every sane person consider a government to be insane which, in consideration of the benefits and the reasonableness of a state of universal and perpetual peace, proposed to disband its armies, destroy its fleet, and demolish its fortresses? But such a government would be doing nothing different in principle from what the popular school requires from governments when, because of the advantages which would be derivable from general free trade, it urges that they should abandon the advantages derivable from protection.'

[43] Ibid., 80: 'As an uncivilised nation, having a barbarous system of agriculture, can make progress only by commerce with civilised manufacturing nations, so after it has attained to a certain degree of culture, in no other way can it reach the highest grade of prosperity, civilisation, and power, than by possessing a manufacturing industry of its own.'

[44] Ibid., 86: 'If the theory will teach the Germans, that they can further their manufacturing power advantageously only by protective duties previously fixed, and on a gradually increasing scale at first, but afterwards gradually diminishing, and that under all circumstances partial but carefully limited foreign competition is really beneficial to their own manufacturing progress, it will render far better service in the end to the cause of free trade than if it simply helps to strangle German industry.'

power and her navigation to such a degree of development that no other nation can sustain free competition with her, can do nothing wiser than to throw away these ladders of her greatness, to preach to other nations the benefits of free trade, and to declare in penitent tones that she has hitherto wandered in the paths of error, and has now for the first time succeeded in discovering the truth.[45]

The view that free trade entailed the danger of 'trade imperialism' was of course directed at Great Britain—the (then) workshop of the world.[46]

3. *Free Trade Bilateralism: The (Long) Nineteenth Century*

a. *The European Continent: The Rise (and Fall) of Free Trade*

The 1786 Eden Treaty represented a first legal manifestation of the new free trade philosophy.[47] Inspired by Smith's *Wealth of Nations*, the Treaty was based on three liberal principles. First, it granted (limited) national treatment to a number of goods and persons;[48] secondly, it lowered customs tariffs for certain goods—especially alcoholic beverages;[49] and, thirdly, it contained a most-favoured-nation (MFN) clause.[50] These principles

[45] F. List, *National System of Political Economy*, Volume 3: *The Systems and The Politics*, 46.

[46] This view has been shared by later historians: Cf. S. B. Clough, *France: A History of National Economics*, 15: 'At all events, Great Britain did not adopt free trade until she had such technological advantages over her competitors that they were unable to sell in her markets. When she did apply this doctrine, she endeavoured to convince other nations of the wisdom of pursuing the same policy in the hope that the removal of trade barriers would allow her to sell to them.' And see also: P. Bairoch and S. Burke, 'European Trade Policy, 1815–1914', 14: 'At the same time as Britain was becoming aware of its industrial lead and drew the logical conclusions from this by adopting a free trade policy, the rest of Europe was becoming conscious of its backwardness and was seeking in a new form of mercantilism—more defensive than offensive, in short in what was from the 1840s to be called protectionism—a way of catching up.'

[47] For a (French) copy of the Treaty, see: A. de Clercq (ed.), *Recueil des Traités de la France*, Volume 1: *1713–1802*, 147. For an analysis of the Treaty, see: R. M. Brace, 'The Anglo-French Treaty of Commerce of 1786: A Reappraisal'; as well as: W. O. Henderson, 'The Anglo-French Commercial Treaty of 1786', 104: 'The Anglo-French commercial treaty of 1786 was one of the most important trade agreements of the eighteenth century. It marked a break in a commercial system which had long been accepted as the only method of regulating international trade. It marked also a serious attempt to end the traditional rivalry between France and Britain.'

[48] Eden Treaty, Articles I, IV, and V.

[49] Ibid., Article VI, especially para. 1: 'Les vins de France, importés en droiture de France dans la Grande-Bretagne, ne payeront, dans aucun cas, pas de plus gros droit que ceux que payent présentement les vins de Portugal.'

[50] Ibid., Article VII: 'Et l'intention des deux Hautes-Parties Contractantes étant que leurs sujets respectifs soient les uns chez les autres sur un pied aussi avantageux que ceux des autres

announced, on the normative level, a revolutionary break with mercantilist philosophy;[51] yet, on a practical level, the Treaty proved unbalanced. Inspired by French 'physiocratic' principles, the Eden Treaty shamefully scarified the (nascent) French industry at the altar of tariff concessions for French agricultural products;[52] and in the aftermath of the French Revolution, the Treaty was quickly renounced in 1793.

Sadly, 'the experience obtained from the treaty made France wary of an international division of labour and turned her again towards a policy of economic self-sufficiency'.[53] But worse: in the aftermath of the Napoleonic Wars, most European States returned to the use of mercantilist tools so as to protect their national economies against an overpowering British competition.[54]

It took the better part of the nineteenth century before the idea of free international trade found a second important expression: the 1860 Cobden–Chevalier Treaty.[55] The latter is justly celebrated as the 'true'

nation Européennes, Elles conviennent que, dans le cas où celles accorderoient dans la suite de nouveaux avantages de navigation et de commerce à quelque autre nation Européenne, elles y feront participer mutuellement leursdits sujet, sans préjudice toutefois des avantages qu'elles se réservent, savoir; la France en faveur de l'Espagne, en conséquence de l'article 24 du Pacte de famille signé le 5 Août 1761; et l'Angleterre, selon ce qu'elle a pratiqué en conformité et en conséquence de la convention de 1703 signée entre l'Angleterre et le Portugal.'

[51] This was especially the case with regard to the most-favoured-nation clause. For an extensive analysis of this point, see: G. Erler, *Grundprobleme des internationalen Wirtschaftsrechts*, 66: 'Der Eden-Vertrag ist gegenüber dem Methuen-Vertrag von 1703 und dem Familienvertrag von 1761 deswegen bedeutsam, weil er das weitgehende Zugeständnis der Inländerbehandlung und der vertraglichen Zollermäßigung nicht mehr als Vorzugsbehandlung stipulierte, sondern als eine vertragliche Vereinbarung die durch die Meistbegünstigungspflichten der beiden Staaten automatisch auch einem weiteren Kreise von Ländern, so etwa Spanien im Verhältnis zu Frankreich aufgrund des Familienvertrages zukommen musste. Das Prinzip einer multilateralen Liberalisierung jener Schranken … wurde damit jetzt materiell zur Wirkung gebracht.'

[52] In the words of S. B. Clough the Treaty meant 'that England, with her superior industrial equipment and cheaper costs of production in many lines, would be able to rout her French competitors in the home markets' (*France: A History of National Economics*, 27). On this point see also: R. M. Brace, 'The Anglo-French Treaty of Commerce of 1786: A Reappraisal', 158: 'Qualitatively superior and cheaply priced manufactured goods from across the Channel soon flooded the French markets. Handicapped by outmoded production methods, monopolies, onerous internal tolls, and the lack of good domestic coal, French industry faced a major crisis by the autumn of 1787.'

[53] S. B. Clough, *France: A History of National Economics*, 28.

[54] G. Erler, *Grundprobleme des internationalen Wirtschaftsrechts*, 67.

[55] Treaty of Commerce between Great Britain and France (Paris, 23 January 1860), in L. Hertslet, *A Complete Collection of the Treaties and Conventions and Reciprocal Regulations at Present Subsisting between Great Britain and Foreign Powers*, Volume XI, 165.

manifestation of an international free trade philosophy.[56] Britain here promised, inter alia, to drastically reduce its duties on French wines (and spirits);[57] and in exchange, France would outlaw all import prohibitions and would reduce its customs duties to a maximum of 30 per cent of the value of the imported goods.[58] Fundamentally, however, the Treaty elevated a new type of clause to centre stage: the unconditional most-favoured-nation clause. It stated:

> Each of the two High Contracting Powers engages to confer on the other any favour, privilege, or reduction in the tariff of duties of importation on the articles mentioned in the present Treaty, which the said Power may concede to any third Power. They further engage not to enforce one against the other any prohibition of importation or exportation, which shall not at the same time be applicable to all other nations.[59]

The importance of this clause for the future of (European) international trade law cannot be exaggerated.[60] It became 'the cornerstone of all modern commercial treaties'.[61] Designed to eliminate bilateral trade preferences, (unconditional) most-favoured-nation clauses prohibited a discriminatory treatment of foreign imports. The name of the clause is thus a serious misnomer. For instead of identifying a 'favourite nation', it achieves the very opposite by insisting on the commercial equality of all foreign States, and it thereby indirectly serves the (constitutional) idea of a universal international order.[62] The 1860 (bilateral) Treaty was indeed a 'treaty with

[56] For excellent and extended discussions of the Treaty, and its background, see: A. L. Dunham, *The Anglo-French Treaty of Commerce of 1860*; and more recently: A. A. Iliasu, 'The Cobden–Chevalier Commercial Treaty of 1860'.

[57] Treaty of Commerce between Great Britain and France (see n. 55), Articles VI and VIII.

[58] Ibid., Article I. [59] Ibid., Article XIX.

[60] Prior to the Cobden–Chevalier Treaty, it was this conditional form that dominated European Treaty practice, see: E. Ustor, 'First Report on the Most-Favoured-Nation Clause'. This conditional form became known as the American version. On the conditional—American—version, see below.

[61] S. Hornbeck, 'The Most-Favored-Nation Clause', 395.

[62] G. Erler, *Grundprobleme des internationalen Wirtschaftsrechts*, 59 and 99: 'Vorschriften, die wie die Meistbegünstigungsklausel die Tendenz einer abstrakten Gleichbehandlung aller Staaten in sich tragen, dienen einer universellen völkerrechtlichen Ordnung … Denn diese Klausel trägt, worauf schon hingewiesen wurde, wie kaum eine andere Vorschrift den Ansatz zu einer internationalen Verfassungsnormierung in sich. Sie hat über die individuelle vertragliche Wirkung hinaus einen ausgesprochenen generellen gesetzlichen Effekt, indem sie die zwischen zwei Staaten vereinbarte Liberalisierung der Zoll- und Kontingentvorschriften wenigstens intentionell zu einer allseitigen macht.'

the whole world'.[63] And it was this 'universality' of the Cobden free trade agreement(s) that marked the opening of a phase of trade liberalization within Europe.[64]

This new phase of free trade, while not without set-backs,[65] lasted up to the beginning of the First World War and is often identified as the first era of free global trade.[66] This era of free trade was however largely confined to the European continent. By contrast, the philosophy of free trade hardly managed to penetrate the commercial consciousness of the United States.

b. *The United States: The Rise (and Stay) of Protectionism*

The birth of American protectionism 'coincide[d] with the formation of the Union' and (partly) originated in 'the need for revenue to finance the Union'.[67] But the appetite for revenue was not the sole source of American protectionism. Eager to protect its infant industry against cheaper British imports, the young Republic dramatically raised its tariff barriers after the Napoleonic Wars. The 'Tariff of 1816' was thus the first in a long series of protective tariffs that separated the United States from the free trade philosophy on the European continent.[68] Indeed: all nineteenth century

[63] A. A. Iliasu, 'The Cobden–Chevalier Commercial Treaty of 1860', 71. The inclusion of most-favoured-nation clauses in (bilateral) treaties encouraged third States to join a network of free trade agreements. In the middle of the nineteenth century, there indeed 'came into existence a European network of treaties resting on the combination of independent tariff treaties and most-favored-nation clauses', which 'worked, in an ingenious way, to reduce the general level of tariff duties in the countries concerned, since every reduction of duties granted to one of these States came into force as regards the others also, owing to the independent operation of the most-favored-nation clause' (S. H. Zebel, 'Fair Trade: An English Reaction to the Breakdown of the Cobden Treaty System', 162.

[64] P. Bairoch and S. Burke, 'European Trade Policy, 1815–1914', 36. For a challenge to this traditional view see: O. Accominotti and M. Flandreau, 'Bilateral Treaties and the Most-Favored-Nation Clause: The Myth of Trade Liberalization in the Nineteenth Century'. For a critical analysis of these critical claims, see: M. Lampe, 'Explaining Nineteenth-Century Bilateralism: Economic and Political Determinants of the Cobden–Chevalier Network'.

[65] For a magisterial account of the rise and fall of free trade in Europe, see: C. P. Kindleberger, 'The Rise of Free Trade in Western Europe, 1820–1875'.

[66] In this sense, see: U. Scheuner, 'Die völkerrechtlichen Grundlagen der Weltwirtschaft in der Gegenwart', 39.

[67] J. B. Condliffe, *The Commerce of Nations*, 242–3.

[68] For a famous analysis of the early US tariff history, see: F. W. Taussig, *The Tariff History of the United States*. The high point was here reached in 1828 with the infamous 'Tariff of Abominations', which created a major constitutional conflict over the question of sovereignty within the United States (cf. R. Schütze, 'Federalism as Constitutional Pluralism: Letter from America').

American policy was protectionist—even if its protectionism knew a soft and a strict version.[69]

Apart from tariffs, there was a second—famous—manifestation of this American protectionism. For from the very beginning, the United States only granted trade concessions on a basis of strict reciprocity. This would become known as the 'American' most-favoured-nation clause.[70] Unlike its (unconditional) European 'sister', it made most-favoured-nation treatment dependent on reciprocal concessions; and even where an international treaty appeared to give unconditional most-favoured-nation status, the United States would unilaterally impose its view as a 'rule of construction'.[71]

A good example of this trade philosophy of bilateralism is offered by *Shaw v United States*.[72] The applicant had imported Scottish whisky into the United States and thereby paid a customs duty of $2.25 per gallon. This was a higher duty than that paid by French brandies. The lower French duty had been the result of the 1898 Agreement between the United States and France, which set the tariff for such spirits to $1.75. Pointing to the 1815 Treaty of Commerce and Navigation between the United States and Great Britain, Shaw invoked most-favoured-nation treatment, which

[69] P. Bairoch and S. Burke, 'European Trade Policy, 1815–1914', 140: '[I]t is possible to divide nineteenth-century American commercial history into three relatively distinct periods. The first, which can be labelled a protectionist phase, lasted from 1816 to 1846. From 1846 till 1861 came a period which is sometimes said to have been liberal, but should more accurately be described as one of very modest protectionism. The last phase, which lasted from 1861 to the end of our period (and in fact to the end of the Second World War), was one of strict protectionism.'

[70] For a general discussion, see: V. G. Setser, 'Did Americans Originate the Conditional Most-Favored-Nation Clause?'. For an early example of the clause, see Article II of the 1778 Treaty of Amity and Commerce between the United States and France: 'The most Christian King, and the United States engage mutually not to grant any particular Favor to other Nations in respect of Commerce and Navigation, which shall not immediately become common to the other Party, who shall enjoy the same Favor freely, if the Concession was freer made, or on allowing the same Compensation, if the Concession was Conditional.'

[71] This rule of construction was apparently suggested by (then) Foreign Secretary John Jay (see: S. B. Crandall, 'The American Construction of the Most-Favored-Nation Clause', 708). The Supreme Court would eventually back up this construction, cf. *Whitney v Robertson*, 124 US 190 (1888).

[72] *United States Court of Customs Appeals Reports*, Volume I: *Cases Adjudged in the United States Court of Customs Appeals* (Reporter: T. H. Clark, Washington, 1911), 426.

appeared to be unconditional within that treaty.[73] But in line with a previous decision by the US Supreme Court,[74] the Court of Customs Appeals held otherwise:

> The reciprocity treaty with France is one founded upon mutual considerations. This country gave considerations for the considerations given in exchange therefor by France. If, therefore, this country should concede to Great Britain *without* consideration what it has conceded to France *for* consideration, it would not be conceding to England a favor it conceded to the other country but it would be conceding to England more than it conceded to the other country, because England in such case gives no consideration for the concession for which France gave a consideration. The extension of the $1.75 rate upon spirituous liquors in this case to England without any mutual concession therefrom would be conceding not what was conceded France, but something more than that which was conceded France, and, therefore, can not be within purview of the most-favored-nation clause of the treaty with His Britannic Majesty without consideration, which has not been given.[75]

This 'American' interpretation of a most-favoured-nation clause thus insisted on a reciprocal bilateralism in all trade relations between the United States and foreign nations. Trade concessions given to one State would *not* automatically be extended to a third State. And while the treaty practice of the American Union was not all about protectionism,[76] its trade

[73] Article II of the 1815 Treaty of Commerce and Navigation between the United States and Great Britain states: 'No higher or other Duties shall be imposed on the importation into the United States of any articles the growth, produce or Manufacture of His Britannick Majesty's Territories in Europe and no higher or other duties shall be imposed on the importation into the Territories of His Britannick Majesty in Europe of any articles the growth, produce or manufacture of the United States than are or shall be payable on the like articles being the growth, produce or manufacture of any other foreign country nor shall any higher or other duties or charges be imposed in either of the two Countries, on the Exportation of any articles to the United States, or to His Britannick Majesty's Territories in Europe respectively than such as are payable on the Exportation of the like articles to any other foreign Country nor shall any prohibition be imposed on the exportation or importation of any articles the growth, produce or manufacture of the United States or of His Britannick Majesty's territories in Europe to or from the said Territories of His Britannick Majesty in Europe, or to or from the said United States, which shall not equally extend to all other Nations.'

[74] *Bartram v Robertson*, 122 US 116 (1887).

[75] *Shaw v United States* (see n. 72), 433–4.

[76] The treaty practice of the young American nation was not all about protectionism. In fact, it gradually cultivated and extended a number of clauses that were to become a staple of modern international trade law. US American treaty practice thus significantly developed the national treatment principle (cf. 1815 Treaty with Britain, and the 1831 Treaty of Amity, Commerce

philosophy remained predominantly mercantilist throughout the long nineteenth century.

4. *The Inter-War Years: The Rise of the 'Autarkic' Commercial State*

By the turn of the twentieth century, the United States had become the greatest economic power of the world.[77] Free trade initiatives would therefore have to be endorsed by her. Yet her new status as an economic superpower did not immediately persuade her of the advantages of free global trade. On the contrary, the United States maintained her protectionist philosophy even after the outbreak of the First World War.[78]

On the other side of the Atlantic, the First World War had brutally ended the long nineteenth century—and with it the first era of free international trade. The economic consequences of the war (and the peace) would leave a terrible mark on the national economies on the European continent.[79]After the war, all European economies thus returned to national protectionist policies. This neo-protectionism originated in their decision to retain some wartime commercial controls so as to stabilize their national markets.[80] And in their search for economic stability, States increasingly moved towards economic autarky.[81] After 1918, the most-favoured-nation clause would 'never regain[] its former firm position as the general foundation of commercial treaty policy'.[82] But worse: in an attempt to 'isolate' national markets from the immanent world economic crisis, [83] many States opted for high tariffs; and '[i]n an effort to insulate

and Navigation between the United States and the United Mexican States), and it also revived the (older) idea of independent arbitration (cf. 1794 Jay Treaty).

[77] P. Bairoch and S. Burke, 'European Trade Policy, 1815–1914', 137.

[78] Ibid., 144–5.

[79] In the words of C. Wilcox, *A Charter for World Trade*, 5: 'The foundations of economic liberalism were shaken by the First World War. The economy of Europe was disorganized; productive facilities were destroyed; channels of trade were broken; heavy debts were incurred. Nationalism and protectionism were stimulated by the revision of boundaries and the creation of new states.'

[80] For an analysis of this point, B. Nolde, 'Droit et technique des traités de commerce', 385–6.

[81] U. Scheuner, *Die völkerrechtlichen Grundlagen der Weltwirtschaft in der Gegenwart*, 40 as well as 45.

[82] E. Ustor, 'First Report on the Most-Favoured-Nation Clause', 163.

[83] For a remarkable account of 1930s economic dilemmas, see: D. A. Irwin, *Trade Policy Disaster: Lessons from the 1930s*, esp. Chapter 1.

themselves from economic depression, and to capture dwindling markets from competitors, foreign nations applied on a wider scale than ever before the most effective device yet invented to diminish trade—*the quantitative restriction on imports*'.[84]

These 'neo-mercantilist' devices ushered in a period of 'beggar thy neighbour' policies, which have been—justly or unjustly—identified with the 1930 US Smoot–Hawley Tariff. The latter indeed offered a fatal signal against free trade during the Great Depression; and, unsurprisingly, the British response to this American affront was swift. Britain equally suspended its historical commitment towards free trade and introduced a general tariff that was complemented by its own 'Imperial Preference System' for trade within the British Empire.[85] And with America and Britain having turned away from global free trade by 1932, the achievements of the nineteenth century appeared to lie in ruins.

Yet there were also positive signs. During these difficult times, the United States had—surprisingly—come to embrace the 'European' version of the most-favoured-nation clause.[86] And of tremendous importance for the post-Second-World-War future, the 1934 American Reciprocal Trade Agreements Act delegated the power to conclude future (reciprocal) liberalization agreements to the President.[87] It was this provision that would—again surprisingly—become the central platform for trade liberalization in the United States. However, the brightest signal of a break with the logic of neo-mercantilism took place at the international level. The emergence and growth of this new institutional multilateralism will be discussed in Section II.

[84] S. D. Metzger, 'United State Foreign Trade: Past, Present and Future', 505 (emphasis added).

[85] G. R. Winham, *The Evolution of International Trade Agreements*, 30: 'Following the Smoot–Hawley tariff, Great Britain ended its historic policy of free trade in 1931 and in 1932 negotiated the Ottawa agreements which resulted in a tariff preference area in the British Commonwealth.'

[86] This change of policy occurs in the mid-1920 and can be seen reflected in the 1923 Treaty of Friendship, Commerce and Consular Rights between the United States and Germany. For an analysis of the changing US practice, see in particular: J. Viner, 'The Most-Favored-Nation Clause in American Commercial Treaties'.

[87] This delegation of power to conclude an executive (presidential) agreement would eventually be the basis on which the United States signed the 1947 GATT. For a discussion of this point, see Section II of this chapter.

II. The 'Modern' Model: The Cooperative State in the Global Market

By the early twentieth century, the idea of an international economic league had—unlike the idea of a military league[88]—hardly any intellectual pedigree. The universally agreed 'common' idea was still this:

> Economic sovereignty reigns supreme. It is for each subject of international law to decide for itself whether and, if so, in which form, it desires to grant equal treatment to other States and their subjects or give privileged treatment to some and discriminate against others.[89]

Nevertheless: the idea that economic cooperation between States was necessary to stabilize the world economy slowly emerged after the First World War. One first expression of this changed mood was the League of Nations. While not designed to directly help in the post-First-World-War economic reconstruction, the League was partially tasked to assist in the recalibration of the world economy.[90] The textual foundations of this task were remarkably weak. Indeed, tariffs and other commercial regulations continued to be seen as 'solely within the domestic jurisdiction' of each State;[91] and the Covenant only modestly asked its Member States, subject to existing and future international conventions, to provide for the 'equitable treatment for the commerce of all Members of the League'.[92]

The League nonetheless managed to organize a series of important economic conferences, which produced a range of interesting (draft) conventions on central problems of international trade. The 1927 Convention on the Abolition of Import and Export Prohibitions and Restrictions, expressly invoking the League of Nations,[93] thus stated:

[88] See famously: C. de Montesquieu, *The Spirit of the Laws*, esp. 131.

[89] G. Schwarzenberger, 'Equality and Discrimination in International Economic Law', 163.

[90] P. Calvin, *Securing the World Economy: The Reinvention of the League of Nations, 1920–1946*, 1. For an analysis of the economic aspects of the League, see also: G. Schwarzenberger, *Economic World Order?*, esp. Chapter 3.

[91] League of Nations Covenant, Article 15(8).

[92] Ibid., Article 23(e).

[93] Ibid., Preambles 1–5 state: 'Having regard to the resolution of the Assembly of the League of Nations dated September 25th [29th], 1924; Being guided by the conclusions of the International Economic Conference held at Geneva in May 1927, and agreeing with the latter that import and export prohibitions, and the arbitrary practices and disguised

Article 2

Subject to the exceptions provided for in the following articles, the High Contracting Parties undertake to abolish within a period of six months from the date of the coming into force of the present Convention, in so far as the respective territories of each of them are concerned, all import and export prohibitions or restrictions, and not thereafter to impose any such prohibitions or restrictions ...

Article 4

The following classes of prohibitions and restrictions are not prohibited by the present Convention, on condition, however, that they are not applied in such a manner as to constitute a means of arbitrary discrimination between foreign countries where the same conditions prevail, or a disguised restriction on international trade:

1. Prohibitions or restrictions relating to public security.
2. Prohibitions or restrictions imposed on moral or humanitarian grounds.

...

4. Prohibitions or restrictions imposed for the protection of public health or for the protection of animals or plants against disease, insects and harmful parasites.
5. Export prohibitions or restrictions issued for the protection of national treasures of artistic, historic or archaeological value.

...

7. Prohibitions or restrictions designed to extend to foreign products the regime established within the country in respect of the production of, trade in, and transport and consumption of native products of the same kind.

But unable to deal with the fervent economic nationalism unleashed by the Great Depression, the League experiment sadly faded away in the inter-war period. Yet the idea that something had to radically change in the organization of the world economy had gained root and—ultimately—germinated after the Second World War. This second section explores the rise of institutional trade multilateralism from the International Trade

discriminations to which they give rise, have had deplorable results, without the grave drawbacks of these measures being counterbalanced by the financial advantages or social benefits which were anticipated by the countries which had recourse to them; Being persuaded that it is important for the recovery and future development of world trade that Governments should abandon a policy which is equally injurious to their own and to the general interest; Being convinced that a return to the effective liberty of international commerce is one of the primary conditions of world prosperity; and Considering that this object may best be achieved by resort to simultaneous and concerted action in the form of an international convention.'

Organization (ITO) to the World Trade Organization (WTO) in a first step. Thereafter, we shall analyse the legal structure of the international market in goods under the 1947 General Agreement on Tariffs and Trade (GATT) regime.

1. *The Rise of Institutional Trade Multilateralism: From the ITO to the WTO*

a. The (Stillborn) International Trade Organization

The 'close connection' between economic disorder and the Second World War had strengthened the belief that a peaceful world order could only be founded on a stable international economic order.[94] The economic unit of the nation State was increasingly seen as 'partly too large and partly too small'. It was too large for a 'genuinely free and neighbourly communal life'; and too small 'for those intellectual, political and economic relations which today can only flourish satisfactorily in an international community'.[95]

The most elaborate and institutionally courageous manifestation of this new belief in international economic order was the Havana Charter for an 'International Trade Organization'. The idea to establish such an international organization dated back to the First World War;[96] yet, serious diplomatic efforts only followed after the end of the Second World War. A draft Charter was completed in 1947,[97] and the envisaged International Trade Organization was designed to become one of the specialized agencies of the United Nations.[98] In light of 'the determination of the United Nations to create conditions of stability and well-being which are necessary for peaceful and friendly relations among nations', the central purpose of the ITO was '[t]o promote on a reciprocal and mutually advantageous basis the reduction of tariffs and other barriers to trade and the elimination of discriminatory treatment in international commerce'.[99] In order to achieve this aim, the Charter contained a 'Commercial Policy' chapter. The latter comprised provisions

[94] R. Stödter, 'Völkerrecht und Weltwirtschaft', 79.

[95] W. Röpke, *International Order & Economic Integration*, 45.

[96] C. Wilcox, *A Charter for World Trade*, 37.

[97] Ibid., 40 et seq. A reproduction of the Charter can be found ibid., 231. On the genesis of GATT, see more generally: T. W. Zeiler, *Free Trade, Free World: The Advent of GATT*, and even more recently: D. A. Irwin, P. C. Mavroidis, and A. O. Sykes, *The Genesis of the GATT*.

[98] C. Wilcox, *A Charter for World Trade*, 153.

[99] ITO Charter, Article 1.

on 'General Most-favoured-nation Treatment',[100] 'Reduction of Tariffs and Elimination of Preferences',[101] 'National Treatment on Internal Taxation and Regulation',[102] and a provision on 'General Elimination of Quantitative Restrictions'.[103]

With over 100 articles, the Charter was a 'ponderous' document,[104] which was deliberately designed to become the 'Magna Carta' of world trade. The world was however not yet ready for its comprehensive and institutional approach.[105] A narrower agreement, drafted in parallel with the ITO Charter, therefore gradually moved from the periphery to the centre stage: the 1947 GATT. [106]

b. The General Agreement on Tariffs and Trade (and the World Trade Organization)

In light of the Havana Charter's uncertain future, the 1947 GATT had emerged as a truncated version that could—provisionally—apply until the final agreement on the ITO Charter was reached. Confined to tariffs and trade, it largely reproduced the 'Commercial Policy' Chapter of the Havana Charter but had dropped its broader economic and social provisions.[107] And most importantly: it had been drafted without any 'institutional' base.[108] The GATT was perceived 'as an interim arrangement, not an organization, until the ITO Charter could be formally approved by [the U.S. American] Congress'.[109] (The reason behind the non-institutional approach was to allow its conclusion as an executive agreement by the President of the United States—that is, a conclusion outside the Article II procedure under

[100] Ibid., Article 16. [101] Ibid., Article 17. [102] Ibid., Article 18.

[103] Ibid., Article 20.

[104] G. Bronz, 'The International Trade Organization Charter', 1091.

[105] The Charter was dead by 1950 when the United States announced that it would not ratify it. The Charter would nonetheless occupy an important place in post-war discussions on global trade, cf. G. Schwarzenberger, 'The Principles and Standards of International Economic Law', 89: 'The Havana Charter of 1948, although it never came into force, is still worth remembering as the high watermark in the post-1945 world of liberal and social democratic thinking in the field of international economic relations.'

[106] On the relationship between the ITO and the GATT drafting history, see R. E. Hudec, *The GATT Legal System and World Trade Diplomacy*, Chapters 1–6.

[107] G. Bronz, 'An International Trade Organization: The Second Attempt', 441.

[108] J. H. Jackson, *World Trade and the Law of the GATT*, 31: 'GATT draftsmen contemplated that GATT would depend on the ITO for its "organizational" base. Thus the General Agreement itself does not mention any organization; indeed, even original references to an "Interim Committee" were changed to "CONTRACTING PARTIES acting jointly".'

[109] D. A. Irwin, P. C. Mavroidis, and A. O. Sykes, *The Genesis of the GATT*, 96.

which the Senate must consent.[110]) But as so many things in life, nothing proves more permanent than the transient; and the 'provisional' GATT was to become the keystone of all post-war universal trade coordination.

What type of economic 'organization' was the GATT? The GATT lacked an institutional apparatus for decision-making;[111] and for conceptual purists, it was therefore 'an article of faith that the GATT is not an organisation'.[112] Decision-making within the GATT was consequently not allocated to a formal 'organ' but to the collectivity of the contracting parties acting jointly. This intergovernmental arrangement also extended to the resolution of interstate disputes with the GATT having made a conscious choice 'to refrain from the adjudicatory approach to dispute settlement'.[113] Unlike the United Nations Charter, there was thus no reference to the International Court of Justice; nor did the GATT establish a special court to adjudicate disputes for its parties. The task of 'adjudication' was left to ad hoc panels of experts that operated at the behest of the collectivity of the contracting parties.[114]

The institutional non-existence of the GATT was remedied in 1994 with the foundation of the WTO. Half a century after the failure of the ITO, the WTO finally offered a 'common institutional framework' for a number of multilateral and plurilateral agreements—including the 1947 GATT.[115] The WTO Agreement thereby established a number of

[110] The (old) 1947 GATT was never submitted to the Senate, nor to Congress. Instead, it rested on the 'Protocol of Provisional Application', which had been signed and proclaimed by President Truman under powers delegated by the 1934 Reciprocal Trade Agreement Act (as amended in 1945). This choice in favour of a 'presidential' executive agreement was highly controversial, especially as it seemed designed to circumvent Senate consent for a treaty creating an 'International Trade Organization'. Nonetheless, for an excellent apologia of the executive route, see: J. H. Jackson, 'The General Agreement on Tariffs and Trade in United States Domestic Law', esp. at 273: 'Thus, in answer to the question whether the President had statutory authority to enter GATT, it seems clear that he did. The wording of the statute, legislative history, and the known precedents of prior trade agreements at the time of the 1945 Act combine to show a delegation of authority to enter into all particular provisions of GATT[.]'

[111] For an overview of the weak 'institutional' elements of the original GATT, see: K. W. Dam, *The GATT: Law and International Economic Organization*, Chapter 19.

[112] Ibid., 335. [113] Ibid., 351.

[114] For a wonderful early history of the GATT adjudicatory system, see: R. E. Hudec, *The GATT Legal System and World Trade Diplomacy*, Chapters 7–10.

[115] The tasks of the WTO were generally defined as follows (WTO Agreement, Article III:1): 'The WTO shall facilitate the implementation, administration and operation, and further the objectives, of this Agreement and of the Multilateral Trade Agreements, and shall also provide the framework for the implementation, administration and operation of the Plurilateral Trade Agreements.'

institutions, including: a 'Ministerial Conference', a 'General Council', and a number of special Councils.[116] And, importantly, the WTO Agreement also established a 'Dispute Settlement Body' with the authority 'to establish panels, adopt panel and Appellate Body reports, maintain surveillance of implementation of rulings and recommendations, and authorize suspension of concessions and other obligations under the covered agreements'.[117] The WTO dispute settlement machinery would 'function very much like a court of international trade'; and with its compulsory jurisdiction, it quickly developed into one of the most important international tribunals. This 'judicialization' has been hailed as the harbinger of a gradual 'constitutionalization' of the WTO; yet the legal nature of GATT law has never been held to demand its direct applicability and effect—and with it the automatic integration of world trade law into the national legal systems of its Member States.

2. *World Trade Today: The Structure of the 'International Market' in Goods*

Three classic 'free trade' principles had developed during the nineteenth century: the most-favoured-nation principle, the national treatment principle, and the liberal principle that prohibited import restrictions generally.[118] The GATT codifies these three legal principles and thereby acknowledges them as three liberal principles of contemporary world trade. In doing so, it nevertheless made a number of specific 'systemic' choices.

First, the GATT makes a fundamental distinction between tariff barriers and non-tariff barriers with only the former being a legitimate instrument of protectionism. A State wishing to limit its international trade with the outside world can therefore, in principle, no longer employ quantitative restrictions or discriminatory national laws but it must channel its 'protectionist' ambitions into tariffs. Behind the special status of tariffs as the sole legitimate instrument of economic boundary control lie historical as well as pragmatic reasons.[119]

[116] Ibid., Article IV ('Structure of the WTO').

[117] Ibid., Annex 2: 'Understanding on Rules and Procedures governing the Settlement of Disputes', Article 2.

[118] G. Erler, *Grundprobleme des internationalen Wirtschaftsrechts*, 74.

[119] K. W. Dam, *The GATT: Law and International Economic Organization*, 25 et seq.

Secondly, within the class of non-tariff barriers, the GATT draws an important distinction. It here distinguishes between two types of national measures, namely: 'internal' measures and 'border' measures. The former are subject to a national treatment principle, which demands that a (host) State must not discriminate against foreign goods. Border measures, on the other hand, follow a different logic because the GATT considers all non-tariff border measures that constitute quantitative restrictions as illegal.

Finally, according to a third choice, not all restrictions of international trade are outlawed. The GATT allows for a number of public policy exceptions; and it also recognizes a special exception for regional (economic) unions.

Let us briefly analyse these three choices in more detail.

a. Tariff Barriers: Most-Favoured-Nation and Bound Tariffs under Articles I and II GATT

The central provisions on tariffs are found in Articles I and II GATT. Article I thereby encapsulates a 'most-favoured-nation' principle and states:

> With respect to *customs duties and charges of any kind* imposed on or in connection with importation or exportation or imposed on the international transfer of payments for imports or exports, and with respect to the method of levying such duties and charges, and with respect to all rules and formalities in connection with importation and exportation, and with respect to all matters referred to in paragraphs 2 and 4 of Article III, *any advantage, favour, privilege or immunity granted by any [Member] to any product originating in or destined for any other country shall be accorded immediately and unconditionally to the like product originating in or destined for the territories of all other [Members].*[120]

The provision imposes on each Member State the obligation to treat all imports from other Member States equally with regard to tariffs (and related charges). Every GATT member will thus have to extend its most favourable tariff to everyone else; and Article I thereby enshrines the unconditional and absolute ('European') version of the MFN clause. It thus automatically prohibits any discrimination with regard to the origin of foreign goods; while discrimination means formal as well

[120] Article I (1) GATT (emphasis added). The provision is qualified in paras. (2) and (3).

as material discrimination.[121] This principle of non-discrimination between imports is indeed 'one of the central pillars of the WTO trading system'.[122]

Importantly, the GATT sees tariff rates not as static but engages its Member States in a process of 'binding' tariff reductions. According to Article II, States should thus periodically bind themselves to certain tariff 'concessions' in regular negotiation rounds. These 'bound' items are then set out in the Schedules of the GATT; and the Schedules are incorporated and form an integral part of the GATT.[123] Once a tariff concession is given, all import duties 'in excess' of that agreed level would be illegal.[124] While not eliminating all customs barriers, Article II GATT fixes them for a particular product in time and space.

b. Internal Measures: National Treatment under Article III GATT

While Articles I and II primarily concern border measures of a fiscal nature, Article III outlaws the discriminatory treatment of imported goods inside the national border. Its focus is therefore on 'internal' measures—that is, measures that *indistinctively* apply to imported as well as domestic products.[125] For these 'internal' measures Article III:1 generally states:

> The [Members] recognize that internal taxes and other internal charges, and laws, regulations and requirements affecting the internal sale, offering for sale, purchase, transportation, distribution or use of products, and internal quantitative

[121] See only: WTO Appellate Body, *European Communities—Regime for the Importation, Sale and Distribution of Bananas* (1997) WT/DS27/AB/R.

[122] WTO Appellate Body, *European Communities—Conditions for the Granting of Tariff Preferences to Developing Countries* (2004) WT/DS246/AB/R, para. 101.

[123] Article II(7) GATT: 'The Schedules annexed to this Agreement are hereby made an integral part of Part I of this Agreement.'

[124] Article II(1)(b) GATT.

[125] Measures that *distinctly* apply to imports when they cross the national border will consequently fall outside the scope of Article III GATT. These distinctly applicable (import) measures will have to be analysed under Article XI GATT. The fact that an indistinctly applicable measure is enforced at the border will thereby not exclude it from the scope of Article III. See Annex I ('Notes and Supplementary Provisions'), Ad Article III: 'Any internal tax or other internal charge, or any law, regulation or requirement of the kind referred to in paragraph 1 which applies to an imported product and to the like domestic product and is collected or enforced in the case of the imported product at the time or point of importation, is nevertheless to be regarded as an internal tax or other internal charge, or a law, regulation or requirement of the kind referred to in paragraph 1, and is accordingly subject to the provisions of Article III.'

regulations requiring the mixture, processing or use of products in specified amounts or proportions, should not be applied to imported or domestic products *so as to afford protection to domestic production.*[126]

The provision targets *internal* taxes as well as regulatory measures that affect the *internal* sale or use of a foreign good. These 'internal' measures are subject to a national treatment principle.[127] The idea behind this is relatively simple:

The broad and fundamental purpose of Article III *is to avoid protectionism in the application of internal tax and regulatory measures.* More specifically, the purpose of Article III 'is to ensure that internal measures not be applied to imported or domestic products so as to afford protection to domestic production'. Toward this end, Article III obliges Members of the WTO to provide equality of competitive conditions for imported products in relation to domestic products. '[T]he intention of the drafters of the Agreement was clearly to treat the imported products in the same way as the like domestic products once they had been cleared through customs. Otherwise indirect protection could be given.'[128]

The central aim of Article III is consequently seen to prevent protectionism inside the national border;[129] and this idea is expressed through a prohibition of discrimination.[130] Imports are entitled to be treated *as if they were domestic products*. Importantly, however, the provision has not been held to prevent a State from all differential treatment for imports.[131] The provision only outlaws the *less favourable* treatment of imports.

[126] Emphasis added.

[127] There are express exceptions to this rule, namely: public procurement (para. 8(a)), subsidies exclusively given to domestic products (para. 8(b)), maximum price control measures (para. 9), and cinematograph firms (para. 10).

[128] WTO Appellate Body, *Japan—Taxes on Alcoholic Beverages* (1996) WT/DS8-11/AB/R, 16 (emphasis added).

[129] Ibid., 18: 'Article III:1 articulates a general principle that internal measures should not be applied so as to afford protection to domestic production. This general principle informs the rest of Article III.'

[130] On the meaning of the discrimination principle in GATT law, especially de facto discrimination, see: L. Ehring, '*De Facto* Discrimination in World Trade Law: National and Most-Favored-Nation Treatment—or Equal Treatment?'.

[131] Cf. WTO Appellate Body, *Korea—Measures Affecting Imports of Fresh, Chilled and Frozen Beef* (2000) WT/DS161/AB/R and WT/DS169/AB/R, para. 135: 'A measure that provides treatment to imported products that is *different* from that accorded to like domestic products is not necessarily inconsistent with Article III:4, as long as the treatment provided by the measure is "no less favourable".'

aa. Discriminatory Taxation: Article III:2 GATT

The second paragraph of Article III concretizes the national treatment principle for fiscal measures. It states:

> The products of the territory of any [Member] imported into the territory of any other [Member] shall not be subject, directly or indirectly, to internal taxes or other internal charges of any kind in excess of those applied, directly or indirectly, to like domestic products. Moreover, no [Member] shall otherwise apply internal taxes or other internal charges to imported or domestic products in a manner contrary to the principles set forth in paragraph 1.

The paragraph contains two distinct but related prohibitions with regard to *internal* and *indirect* taxes.[132] First and foremost, it outlaws all internal taxes (or equivalent charges) that are imposed '*in excess of* those applied, directly or indirectly, to *like* domestic products'. The disadvantageous fiscal treatment of like foreign products is here expressly prohibited; and the rationale behind this is straightforward: a discriminatory internal tax operates like an 'additional' customs duty.[133] But the provision also contains a second—wider—prohibition. For the cross-reference to Article III:1 in the second sentence of Article III:2 clarifies that it extends to internal taxes that apply to imported and 'non-like' domestic products in such a way 'as to afford protection to domestic production'. This prohibition will however only apply where imported and domestic goods are 'directly competitive or substitutable products'.[134]

[132] The Appellate Body has defined internal taxes as an 'obligation to pay a charge [that] must accrue due to an internal event, such as the distribution, sale, use or transportation of the imported product' (WTO Appellate Body, *China—Measures Affecting Imports of Automobile Parts* (2009) WT/DS339–40 and 342/AB/R, para. 162). Direct taxes are consequently not covered by Article III:2 GATT.

[133] J. H. Jackson, *World Trade and the Law of the GATT*, 279–80: 'The evil that the draftsmen sought to proscribe by the first sentence was an internal tax applied discriminatorily to imported products, thus operating as effectively as a tariff to protect local products against foreign competition.'

[134] J. H. Jackson (ibid., 282) has pointed out that the original language of Article III (before the Havana amendments) contained an express reference to the situation where there was no substantial domestic production of 'like' products, and here referred to 'affording protection to the production of directly competitive or substitutable products which are not similarly taxed'. And while this was removed by a 1948 amendment, an 'Interpretative Note' was added in Annex I to the GATT Agreement. See: Ad Article III (2): 'A tax conforming to the requirements of the first sentence of paragraph 2 would be considered to be inconsistent with the provisions of the second sentence only in cases where competition was involved between, on the one hand, the taxed product and, on the other hand, a directly competitive or substitutable product which was not similarly taxed.'

bb. Discriminatory 'Regulatory' Measures: Article III:4 GATT

The national treatment principle in Article III also covers discriminatory *regulatory* measures. These regulatory measures are specifically dealt with in paragraph 4, which states:

> The products of the territory of any [Member] imported into the territory of any other [Member] shall be accorded treatment no less favourable than that accorded to like products of national origin in respect of all laws, regulations and requirements affecting their internal sale, offering for sale, purchase, transportation, distribution or use.

The paragraph extends the equal treatment principle to all regulatory measures that are 'affecting', inter alia, the sale or use of an imported product.[135] The provision was constructed broadly from the start. Article III:4 thus captures 'not only the laws and regulations which directly governed the conditions of sale or purchase but also *any laws or regulations which might adversely modify the conditions of competition between the domestic and imported products on the internal market*'.[136] (The famous exception to this broad scope relates to internal measures on 'processes and production methods' (PPMs), which were in the past held to fall outside the scope of Article III.[137])

Article III:4 thereby only outlaws national laws that negatively affect international trade by *discriminating* against foreign goods,[138] because the provision textually insists that an imported product must be accorded 'no less favourable treatment' than a 'like' domestic product.[139] This covers de

[135] It also extends to transportation but here the second sentence of Article III:4 GATT adds: 'The provisions of this paragraph shall not prevent the application of differential internal transportation charges which are based exclusively on the economic operation of the means of transport and not on the nationality of the product.'

[136] GATT Panel Report, *Italian Discrimination Against Imported Agricultural Machinery* (1958) L/833 BISD 7S/60, 64, para. 12 (emphasis added).

[137] For F. Ortino, *Basic Legal Instruments for the Liberalisation of Trade: A Comparative Analysis of EC and WTO Law*, 86 this restrictive reading of Article III:4 was 'simply incorrect', since Article III:1 expressly refers to measures 'affecting the internal sale, offering for sale, purchase, transportation or use of products'. On PPMs in WTO law generally, see: C. R. Conrad, *Processes and Production Methods (PPMs) in WTO Law: Interfacing Trade and Social Goals*.

[138] E. Reid, 'Regulatory Autonomy in the EU and WTO: Defining and Defending', 895: 'Crucially therefore, a non-discriminatory (product) regulatory measure will not breach Article III, notwithstanding its impact upon access to the market. National regulatory autonomy thus remains relatively free, subject to the limitations in the definition of "likeness".'

[139] For an extensive discussion of the notion of 'likeness', see: M. Melloni, *The Principle of National Treatment in the GATT: A Survey of the Jurisprudence, Practice and Policy*, esp. Chapter 3.

jure as well as de facto discrimination.[140] But again, the national treatment principle does not require formally identical treatment;[141] it merely insists that national measures must not 'modify the conditions of competition in the marketplace *to the detriment of imports*'.[142]

In conclusion, the substantive aim of Article III:4 lies in preventing distortions of competition between imported and domestic products. A good example of this insistence on an equality of competitive conditions can be found in *Canada—Alcohol II*.[143] The case concerned a minimum price requirement that applied to both imported and domestic goods; yet the relevant GATT Panel found that the regulatory measure, even if it applied equally to imported and domestic beer, 'did affect the competitive opportunities of imported beer which could otherwise be supplied below the minimum price'.[144]

c. *Non-Tariff Border Measures: Quantitative Restrictions under Article XI GATT*

When the GATT was negotiated, quantitative restrictions were seen as the most 'evil' trade barrier and one that had to be eliminated at all costs.[145] Yet despite this common view, the negotiations proved very hard; and while a general prohibition was finally agreed upon, it was riddled with exceptions and qualifications.[146]

[140] For de jure discrimination, see: GATT Panel, *United States—Measures Affecting Alcoholic and Malt Beverages* (1992) DS23/R–39S/206, para. 5.32: 'In the view of the Panel, therefore, the requirement that imported beer and wine be distributed through in-state wholesalers or other middlemen, when no such obligation to distribute through wholesalers exists with respect to in-state like domestic products, results in "treatment ... less favourable than that accorded to like products" from domestic producers, inconsistent with Article III:4. The Panel considered that even where Canadian producers have the right to establish in-state wholesalers, as is the case in some states, subject to varying conditions, the fact remains that the wholesale level represents another level of distribution which an in-state product is not required to use.'

[141] GATT Panel, *US—Section 337 Tariff Act* (1989) L/6439–36S/345, para. 5.11 (emphasis added): '[Members] may apply to imported products *different* formal legal requirements if doing so would accord imported products more favourable treatment.'

[142] WTO Appellate Body, *Korea Beef* (see n. 131), para. 137 (emphasis added).

[143] GATT Panel, *Canada—Import, Distribution and Sale of Certain Alcoholic Drinks by Provincial Marketing Agencies* (1992) DS17/R–39S/27.

[144] Ibid., para. 5.30.

[145] C. Wilcox, *A Charter for World Trade*, esp. 81.

[146] J. H. Jackson, *World Trade and the Law of the GATT*, 307: 'The longest and most difficult part of the preparatory negotiations leading to GATT was concerned with the drafting of the four articles relating to quota obligations and these articles are the longest, most detailed set of governing rules for any single subject contained in GATT.' The four articles are Articles XI–XIV GATT with Article XI constituting the general prohibition and Articles XII–XIV

The core prohibition on quantitative restrictions is found in Article XI:1 and states:

> No prohibitions or restrictions other than duties, taxes or other charges, whether made effective through quotas, import or export licences or other measures, shall be instituted or maintained by any [Member] on the importation of any product of the territory of any other [Member] or on the exportation or sale for export of any product destined for the territory of any other [Member].

Unlike the most-favoured-nation clause in Article I and the equal treatment clause in Article III, this provision is formulated as an *absolute* prohibition. Quantitative restrictions (and measures of an equivalent effect) would therefore not be outlawed because they discriminated between foreign goods or between foreign and domestic goods; they were illegal because they hindered *international* trade in goods *as such*.

Importantly, however: the scope of the absolute prohibition within Article XI was strictly circumscribed. It was confined to *border* measures—that is, measures that *distinctly* apply to imports (or exports). A good illustration of this limited scope is provided by *Korea—Beef*.[147] Korea had adopted a dual distribution system in which (small) traders had to choose between selling domestic or foreign beef. Was this regulation of the distribution channels a quantitative restriction of trade? The WTO Panel and Appellate Body dealing with the case rejected this by pointing to the fact that the law indistinctly applied to the sale of domestic beef and it thus had to be analysed under Article III:4 GATT. The prohibition in Article XI is consequently concerned with measures that apply distinctly to imports (or exports) *as such*—that is, border measures that have no internal equivalent applying to domestic goods.[148] (Historically,

listing exceptions and qualifications. But even Article XI GATT itself contained a number of exceptions, and the most important here is the exclusion of agricultural products (para. 2). The latter was controversial from the start (ibid., 318): 'This special exception from the quota prohibition for agricultural goods was particularly resented by the less-developed and primary product-producing countries, who saw themselves prohibited from using quantitative restrictions to protect their fledging industries, while the industrial nations were allowed to use this device to protect their local producers from the very type of imports likely to be produced in the less-developed and primary product-producing nations.'

[147] GATT Panel, *Korea—Measures Affecting Imports*. For the Appellate Body Report, see n. 131.

[148] On this point, see also: GATT Panel, *Canada—Administration of the Foreign Investment Review Act* (1984) L/5504–30S/140, para. 5.14: 'For these reasons, the Panel, noting that purchase undertakings do not prevent the importation of goods as such, reached the conclusion that they are not inconsistent with Article XI:1.' Consequently, minimum price measures that

Article XI therefore distinguished between—distinctly applicable—*import* bans and—indistinctly applicable—*sales* bans.[149])

Article XI is consequently confined to a very particular category of measures; yet within the class of regulatory *border* measures, it is nonetheless comprehensive and 'absolute'. It applies to 'all measures instituted or maintained by a [Member State] prohibiting or restricting the importation, exportation or sale for export of products other than measures that take the form of duties, taxes or other charges'.[150] The scope of the term 'restriction' is thereby very broad; and national measures need only indirectly or potentially restrict or impede trade.[151]

d. General and Specific Exceptions to GATT Obligations

aa. Public Policy Exceptions under Article XX GATT

The GATT accepts that trade barriers that fall within its substantive prohibitions can still be justified by reference to a number of public policy justifications. The general provision dealing with these exceptions can be found in Article XX, which states:

> Subject to the requirement that such measures are not applied in a manner which would constitute a means of arbitrary or unjustifiable discrimination between countries where the same conditions prevail, or a disguised restriction on international trade, nothing in this Agreement shall be construed to prevent the adoption or enforcement by any [Member] of measures:

indistinctly apply to both imported and domestic goods have been held to fall outside the scope of Article XI, see: *Canada—Import, Distribution and Sale of Certain Alcoholic Drinks by Provincial Marketing Agencies* (see n. 143), para. 5.28.

[149] For this excellent point, see: F. Ortino, *Basic Legal Instruments*, 83. This clear historical division between border measures and internal measures was blurred in *United States—Import Prohibition of Certain Shrimp and Shrimp Products* (DS 58), where it was found that the American ban on shrimps harvested with a fishing technology that may negatively affect sea turtles was a prima facie violation of Article XI. Yet this inclusion of non-discriminatory processes-and-production-methods followed a 'dubious approach' (F. Ortino, *Basic Legal Instruments*, 89) to Article XI; and it has rightly been put into question in *European Communities—Measures Affecting Asbestos and Products Containing Asbestos* (DS 135). The latter ruling reconfirmed 'that the dividing line between Article III and Article XI is drawn on the basis of whether or not the measure under review is simply part of a broader regulatory framework applicable to both imported and domestic products, even if not in an identical manner' (Ortino, 91).

[150] GATT Panel, *Japan—Trade in Semi-Conductors* (1988) L/6309–35S/116, para. 104.

[151] GATT Panel, *Japan—Imports of Leather* (1984) L/5623–31S/94, para. 55.

(a) necessary to protect public morals;
(b) necessary to protect human, animal or plant life or health;
...
(d) necessary to secure compliance with laws or regulations which are not inconsistent with the provisions of this Agreement, including those relating to ... the protection of patents, trade marks and copyrights, and the prevention of deceptive practices;
...
(f) imposed for the protection of national treasures of artistic, historic or archaeological value;
...
(j) essential to the acquisition or distribution of products in general or local short supply ... [152]

The structure of Article XX is two-tiered. After a first paragraph (the 'chapeau') sets out general justificatory conditions, subparagraphs (a)–(j) list specific grounds of justification. This list is considered to be exhaustive and legally closed.[153]

Part and parcel of many a public policy ground is the question of 'necessity'; yet the nature of the necessity test has been controversial.[154] The central issue here is which national (or international) standard will apply when assessing necessity. Will a zero-risk public health policy be legitimate—even if that maximum standard is not shared by other WTO members? The traditional GATT answer has been positive and deferential to the national standard of the importing State. The 'sovereign' freedom of each WTO member to choose its own standard of protection was thus clarified in *EC—Asbestos*.[155] The Appellate Body here confirmed that 'it is undisputed that WTO Members have the right to determine the level of protection of health that they consider appropriate in a given situation'.[156]

[152] The provision was modelled on Article 4 of the 1927 International Convention for the Abolition of Import and Export Prohibitions and Restrictions. The text of the provision can be found at the beginning of Section II.

[153] P. Mavroidis, *Trade in Goods*, 329.

[154] For a general analysis of the notion of necessity see: J. Neumann and E. Türk, 'Necessity Revisited: Proportionality in World Trade Organization Law After Korea—Beef, EC—Asbestos and EC—Sardines'; as well as: D. H. Regan, 'The Meaning of "Necessary" in GATT Article XX and GATS Article XIV: The Myth of Cost–Benefit Balancing'.

[155] WTO Appellate Body, *European Communities—Measures Affecting Asbestos and Asbestos Contained Products* (2001) WT/DS135/AB/R.

[156] Ibid., para. 168.

The necessity test under Article XX ought thus only to evaluate 'whether there is an alternative measure that would achieve the *same end* and that is less restrictive of trade'.[157] This less-restrictive means test is centred on each State's sovereign right to determine its own level of protection; and the substantive standard of protection of each State will consequently not be questioned.

The host State's right to invoke its *internal* sovereignty over its 'internal' market is also not undermined by the chapeau to Article XX. For the latter only demands that a State must not arbitrarily discriminate between countries 'where the same conditions prevail'; and, it must not invoke one of the grounds in Article XX so as to create a 'disguised restriction on international trade'. The Appellate Body has explained that the chapeau 'addresses, not so much the questioned measure or its specific contents as such, *but rather the manner in which that measure is applied*'.[158] It is essentially designed to prevent an abusive use of a legitimate policy justification in Article XX; and the chapeau has consequently be characterized as 'but one expression of the principle of good faith'.[159]

bb. 'Regional' Exceptions: Customs Unions (and Free Trade Areas)

The GATT contains a second famous exception in Article XXIV, which states:

> 4. The [Members] recognize the desirability of increasing freedom of trade by the development, through voluntary agreements, of closer integration between the economies of the countries parties to such agreements. They also recognize that the purpose of a customs union or of a free-trade area should be to facilitate trade between the constituent territories and not to raise barriers to the trade of other [Members] with such territories.

[157] Ibid., para. 172. See also: WTO Appellate Body, *Brazil—Measures Affecting Imports of Retreaded Tyres* (2007) WT/DS332/AB/R, para. 156: 'We recall that, in order to qualify as an alternative, a measure proposed by the complaining Member must be not only less trade restrictive than the measure at issue, but should also "preserve for the responding Member its right to achieve its desired level of protection with respect to the objective pursued". If the complaining Member has put forward a possible alternative measure, the responding Member may seek to show that the proposed measure does not allow it to achieve the level of protection it has chosen and, therefore, is not a genuine alternative.'

[158] WTO Appellate Body, *United States—Standards for Reformulated and Conventional Gasoline* (1996) WT/DS2/AB/R, 22 (emphasis added).

[159] WTO Appellate Body, *United States—Import Prohibition of Certain Shrimp and Shrimp Products* (1998) WT/DS58/AB/R, para. 158.

5. Accordingly, the provisions of this Agreement shall not prevent, as between the territories of [Members], the formation of a customs union or of a free-trade area or the adoption of an interim agreement necessary for the formation of a customs union or of a free-trade area; *Provided* that:

(a) with respect to a customs union, or an interim agreement leading to a formation of a customs union, the duties and other regulations of commerce imposed at the institution of any such union or interim agreement in respect of trade with [Members] not parties to such union or agreement shall not on the whole be higher or more restrictive than the general incidence of the duties and regulations of commerce applicable in the constituent territories prior to the formation of such union or the adoption of such interim agreement, as the case may be[.][160]

The GATT here shows a remarkable tolerance towards regional economic 'leagues' in the form of 'customs unions' (CUs) and 'free trade areas' (FTAs). The idea of a customs union is said to be a German invention.[161] Customs unions are international economic organizations in which the free movement of all goods within the customs area is guaranteed; and in order to achieve this aim, all intra-union restrictions are removed while a common external customs tariff is created for goods from outside the customs union.[162] (The original US proposal only contained this single regional exception within Article XXIV, yet the FTA exception was subsequently added.[163]) Within a free trade area, the free movement of goods is only guaranteed for goods produced by Member States of the trade area.[164] For unlike a customs union, no common external tariff

[160] Article XXIV(4) and (5)(a). Subparagraph (b) continues: 'with respect to a free-trade area, or an interim agreement leading to the formation of a free trade area, the duties and other regulations of commerce maintained in each of the constituent territories and applicable at the formation of such free-trade area or the adoption of such interim agreement to the trade of [Members] not included in such area or not parties to such agreement shall not be higher or more restrictive than the corresponding duties and other regulations of commerce existing in the same constituent territories prior to the formation of the free-trade area, or interim agreement as the case may be'.

[161] B. Nolde, 'Droit et technique des traités de commerce', 440. For the great study of the nineteenth-century German Customs Union, see: W. O. Henderson, *The Zollverein*.

[162] For GATT purposes, the European Union constitutes a customs union; and another example here is the Southern African Customs Union (SACU), which unites Botswana, Lesotho, Namibia, South Africa, and Swaziland.

[163] For an excellent summary, see: C. Wilcox, *A Charter for World Trade*, 70–2.

[164] A famous free trade area is that established by the North American Free Trade Agreement (NAFTA), which has brought together Canada, Mexico, and the United States

vis-à-vis third countries exists—an absence that allows each Member State to maintain its own 'national' tariff arrangements with the outside world. Going beyond these two basic forms of closer (regional) international economic coordination are 'common markets' and (full) 'economic unions'. Both—wider—forms are not expressly mentioned by Article XXIV GATT but are implicitly covered by the provision. Common markets are markets in which not only the free movement of goods is established, but in which the free movement of persons, services, and capital is equally guaranteed. Economic unions, finally, go even beyond that by providing for the full economic and monetary integration of the contracting States. The three scales of economic integration can be seen in Figure 2.

What is the rationale behind Article XXIV? The regional exception(s) offered by the provision flew into the face of one of the central purposes of the GATT: the eradication of trading preferences, and in particular the British Commonwealth preferences. Yet when the GATT was drafted, customs unions in particular were seen as beneficial towards the gradual and general liberalization of international trade.[165] For no one could imagine 'that post-World War II commercial policy would be dominated by the rise of a multitude of regional arrangements which would challenge the draftsmen's universalist principles in the most fundamental manner'.[166]

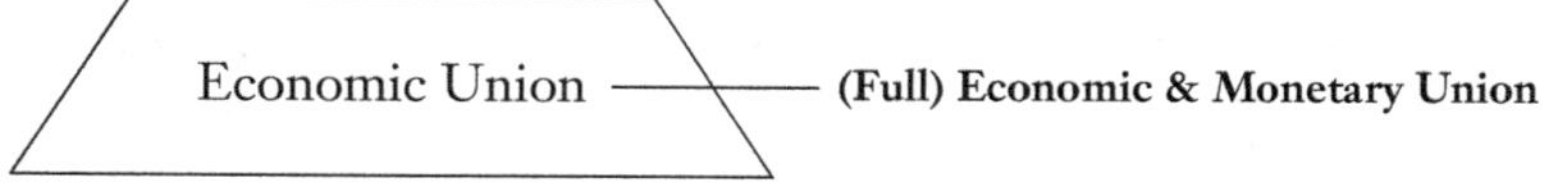

Figure 2. International scales of economic cooperation

into one economic area. Within 'Europe', the 'European Free Trade Association' (EFTA), which brings together Iceland, Liechtenstein, Norway, and Switzerland, is a second good example.

165 This 'romantic' view changed somewhat after 1950 with the publication of J. Viner's *The Customs Union Issue*.

166 K. W. Dam, *The GATT: Law and International Economic Organization*, 274.

Article XXIV had however not been conceived as a carte blanche. It was indeed one of the most concrete and precise provisions within the GATT. Yet this textual precision soon turned out to be 'deceptive',[167] and subsequent GATT practice has not taken it too seriously. The exception embodied in Article XXIV gradually became the rule;[168] and the most famous example of this legal tolerance towards 'regional' economic integration is probably the European Union.[169] The establishment of the European 'common market' has thus replaced, as between the EU Member States, the general GATT rules with the European Union's own special trade rules. They will be discussed in the Special Part of this book.

Conclusion

Commerce had become a 'reason of state' in the eighteenth century.[170] The mercantilist State competed with all other States; and in its attempt to control its national market and its international trade balance it developed a range of trade instruments that structure international economic law until today. The advantages of economic cooperation and trade, on the other hand, were however not unknown to eighteenth-century philosophers: 'The natural effect of commerce is to lead to peace. Two nations that trade with each other become reciprocally dependent; if one has an interest in buying, the other has an interest in selling, and all unions are founded on mutual needs.'[171] And with the publication of Smith's *Wealth of Nations*, the idea that free international trade was also economically beneficial gradually gained prominence. The long nineteenth century saw timid—bilateral—attempts to implement the new politico-economic philosophy. Yet the two World Wars and the Great Depression in the twentieth century destroyed almost all

[167] Ibid.

[168] For a more recent analysis, see: A. D. Mitchell and N. J. S. Lockhart, 'Legal Implications for PTAs under the WTO'.

[169] The 1957 European Economic Community Treaty did qualify as a customs union under Article XXIV. For an analysis of the problems involved here, see: P. Hay, 'The European Common Market and the Most-Favored-Nation Clause'; as well as: D. Vignes, 'La Clause de la nation la plus favorisée et la pratique contemporaine. Problèmes posés par la Communauté économique européenne'.

[170] This is the famous pronouncement by D. Hume, see: I. Nakhimovsky, *The Closed Commercial State*, 80.

[171] C. de Montesquieu, *Spirit of the Laws*, 338.

trade liberalization achieved, and the neo-mercantilist policies of the 1920s and 1930s indeed seemed to turn the wheels of commerce backwards!

The Second World War had nonetheless strengthened the belief that a peaceful world order could only be founded on a stable international economic order; and in the aftermath of the Second World War, a number of institutional attempts to liberalize—and harness—the world economy were made.[172] The most famous attempt here is the (failed) International Trade Organization. It was subsequently replaced by the much narrower General Agreement on Tariffs and Trade. The 1947 GATT thereby enshrined three liberal principles that have structured international trade in goods ever since. First, the sole legitimate category of trade barriers is tariff barriers but States are asked to continuously negotiate their reduction and must apply the MFN principle. Secondly, quantitative restrictions are generally banned. And thirdly, States are not allowed to discriminate between imported and domestic goods either by fiscal or regulatory means.

Unlike the 'classic' model of international economic law, States are today invited to 'open' up under international law. The move from the 'closed' commercial State to the 'open' commercial State here parallels the changing structure of international law from a law of (economic) co-existence to a law of (economic) cooperation.[173] It goes nonetheless too far to identify this transition with 'international federalism'.[174] For although States here commit themselves to binding international rules that limit their *external* sovereignty, even the modern international model respects the *internal* sovereignty of those States over their own market. When this changes, and only then, has a federal (or national) market model arrived. This happened in the establishment and evolution of the American market, which will be discussed in the next chapter.

[172] For classic post-war studies on economic integration generally, see: B. Balassa, *The Theory of Economic Integration*; J. Tinbergen, *International Economic Integration*; J. Viner, *Studies in the Theory of International Trade*; and F. Machlup, *A History of Thought on Economic Integration*.

[173] W. G. Friedmann, *The Changing Structure of International Law*.

[174] J. H. Jackson, *World Trade and the Law of GATT*, 772 speaks of 'international federalism', that is: 'the problem of determining to what degree the international regulatory measures should impinge upon domestic social and political decisions'. And see already W. Röpke, *International Order and Economic Integration*, 46: 'international federalism'.

2

American Law and Market Integration

Introduction

What is the structure of the 'American' market; and how was the latter 'established'? Having claimed their independence from Great Britain, the American colonies-turned-States had swiftly entered 'into a firm league of friendship with each other, for their common defense, the security of their liberties, and their mutual and general welfare'.[1] The 1777 'Confederacy' of the 'United States of America' was primarily a defence league, which only marginally dealt with commercial matters.[2] This lack of a 'united' power over commerce was quickly seen as a constitutional defect, for the commercial rivalry between the States increasingly divided them. Indeed, '[t]he interfering and unneighborly regulations of some States contrary to the true spirit of the Union, have in different instances given just cause of umbrage and complaint to others'.[3] When the Philadelphia Convention debated the 1787 Constitution, there was therefore little argument that the (new) Union needed the power to regulate commerce.[4] The Federalist Papers presented the advantages of such an economic union very well:

> The importance of the Union, in a commercial light, is one of those points about which there is least room to entertain a difference of opinion, and which has in fact commanded the most general assent of men, who have any acquaintance with the subject. This applies as well to our intercourse with foreign countries, as with each other ... An unrestrained intercourse between the States themselves will advance the trade of each, by an interchange of their respective productions, not only for the supply of reciprocal wants at home, but for exportation to foreign markets.

[1] 1777 US Articles of Confederation, Article III.

[2] According to Article IV, Clause 1 of the 1777 Articles of Confederation, each citizen of the various States 'shall enjoy therein all the privileges of trade and commerce, subject to the same duties, impositions, and restrictions as the inhabitants thereof respectively'; and according to Article IX, the United States had the power to conclude international treaties but only 'provided that no treaty of commerce shall be made whereby the legislative power of the respective States shall be restrained from imposing such imposts and duties on foreigners, as their own people are subjected to, or from prohibiting the exportation or importation of any species of goods or commodities whatsoever'.

[3] A. Hamilton, J. Madison, and J. Jay, *The Federalist*, 99.

[4] A. Abel, 'The Commerce Clause in the Constitutional Convention and in Contemporary Comment', 443–4: 'Among the first things that strikes one on going through the mass of materials dealing with the formation and adoption of the Constitution is the nearly universal agreement that the federal government should be given the power of regulating commerce ... In the convention itself, that part of the report from the committee of detail which gave power to regulate commerce "with foreign nations, and among the several States" was agreed to without dissent[.]'

The veins of commerce in every part will be replenished, and will acquire additional motion and vigor from a free circulation of the commodities of every part. Commercial enterprise will have much greater scope, from the diversity in the productions of different States.[5]

The 1787 Constitution consequently delegated the power to adopt uniform customs duties as well as the power '[t]o regulate Commerce with foreign Nations, and among the several States' to the Union,[6] and it expressly prohibited the States unilaterally to 'lay any Imposts or Duties on Imports or Exports'.[7] The ensemble of all these provisions together here 'reflect[ed] a central concern of the Framers that was an immediate reason for calling the Constitutional Convention: the conviction that in order to succeed, the new Union would have to avoid the tendencies toward economic Balkanization that had plagued relations among the Colonies and later among the States under the Articles of Confederation'.[8]

The economic object of the new Constitution however seemed primarily *foreign* commerce. The power over *interstate* commerce, by contrast, 'while coordinate in expression' was seen as 'distinctly secondary in scope and intended operation'.[9] And yet, it was this 'supplemental provision', [10] which rose to become the founding stone of the American common market. By the middle of the twentieth century, the Supreme Court could thus hold:

Our system, *fostered by the Commerce Clause*, is that every farmer and every craftsman shall be encouraged to produce by the certainty that he will have free access to every market in the Nation, that no home embargoes will withhold his export, and no foreign State will by customs duties or regulations exclude them. Likewise, every consumer may look to the free competition from every producing area in

[5] A. Hamilton, J. Madison, and J. Jay, *The Federalist*, 46–7 and 51.

[6] 1787 US Constitution, Article I, Section 8: Clause 1 and 3. This federal power was limited by Section 9, Clause 5: 'No Tax or Duty shall be laid on Articles exported from any State'; as well as Clause 6: 'No Preference shall be given by any Regulation of Commerce or Revenue to the Ports of one State over those of another: nor shall Vessels bound to, or from, one State, be obliged to enter, clear, or pay Duties in another.'

[7] Article I, Section 10, Clause 2.

[8] *Oklahoma Tax Comm'n v Jefferson Lines*, 514 US 175 (1995), 180.

[9] A. Abel, 'The Commerce Clause in the Constitutional Convention', 469.

[10] A. Hamilton, J. Madison, and J. Jay, *The Federalist*, 205: 'The defect of power in the existing confederacy, to regulate the commerce between its several members, is in the number of those which have been clearly pointed out by experience. To the proofs and remarks which former papers [Nos. 11 and 22] have brought into view on this subject, it may be added, that without this supplemental provision, the great and essential power of regulating foreign commerce would have been incompleat, and ineffectual.'

the Nation to protect him from exploitation by any. Such was the vision of the Founders; such has been the doctrine of this Court which has given it reality.[11]

This chapter analyses the constitutional principles that governed the building (and evolution) of the US 'common market'. Would interstate barriers to trade be 'regulated' away by the federal legislature; or would the Commerce Clause operate as a directly effective judicial norm? Was the centralizing will that built the American market a legislative or a judicial one? And more importantly, what type of common market had the US Constitution wished to establish? Section I explores these questions in the context of the liberalization of regulatory restrictions to the free movement of goods. Section II extends the analysis to fiscal barriers, which have traditionally been subject to distinct constitutional principles.

I. Creating a Common Market: Regulatory Barriers to Trade

The 1787 Constitution had provided *Congress* with the power 'to *regulate* Commerce with foreign Nations, and among the several States';[12] and this legislative competence soon proved to be the broadest power of the American Union.[13] Yet from the very beginning, the Commerce Clause was not only a positive grant of legislative power to the Union. 'Instead, it was uniformly mentioned as a device for preventing the obstructive or partial regulations by the States.'[14] This 'negative side' of the Commerce

[11] *Hood v Du Mond*, 336 US 525 (1949), 539 (emphasis added).

[12] US Constitution, Article I, Section 8, Clause 3 (emphasis added).

[13] The provision is often supported by the 'Necessary & Proper' Clause. This is the last clause in Article I, Section 8, and provides Congress with the power '[t]o make all Laws which shall be necessary and proper for carrying into Execution the foregoing Powers, and all other Powers vested by this Constitution in the Government of the United States'. In American constitutional practice, the clause can only be used in combination with one of the 'foregoing powers'. The 'sweeping clause' is thus 'not a self-contained power' as it 'must always be tied to the exercise of some other identifiable constitutional power of the national government' (G. Lawson and P. B. Granger, 'The "Proper" Scope of Federal Power: A Jurisdictional Interpretation of the Sweeping Clause', 274–5).

[14] A. Abel, 'The Commerce Clause in the Constitutional Convention', 471–5 and 488: 'There is thus not a single occasion in the proceedings of the convention itself where the grant of power over commerce between the States was advanced as the basis for independent affirmative regulation by the federal government. Instead, it was uniformly mentioned as a device for preventing the obstructive or partial regulations by the States ... All the extent contemporary

Clause was swiftly to become 'the' constitutional instrument for the creation of the American 'common market'.

Let us look at the general scope and rationale of the negative Commerce Clause before exploring some of its special aspects.

1. *The Commerce Clause: General Aspects*

a. *From Exclusive to Concurrent Competence*

What was the liberalizing potential of the 'Commerce Clause'; and what was its doctrinal rationale? These questions have received different answers in the constitutional history of the United States. In a first period, the Commerce Clause was viewed as an exclusive competence that prevented the States—*eo ipso*—from regulating interstate commerce.

The *textual* foundations for an exclusive competence were thereby not so strong. For unlike the 1777 Articles of Confederation that had expressly referred to the exclusive powers of the Union, this technique had been less explicit in the 1787 Constitution. The idea that the Union and the States were operating in mutually exclusive spheres of competences nonetheless emerged as the dominant 'context' in the long nineteenth century: 'The United States are sovereign as to all the powers of Government actually surrendered: Each State in the Union is sovereign as to all the powers reserved.'[15] This philosophy of 'dual federalism' particularly influenced the 'Commerce Clause'. The Union power to regulate commerce was consequently not simply a delegation of legislative power; it was originally conceived as automatically preventing the States from restricting trade within the emerging 'national' market.[16]

This original view found—wavering—support in the Supreme Court. In *Gibbons v Ogden*,[17] Chief Justice Marshall still found 'great force' in the

evidence thus tends to confirm ... that the power as to commerce between the States was in the main a "negative and preventive" provision. It is a shield against State exactions and no two-edged sword for positive federal attack ... [I]t is submitted, that the delegates were thinking in terms of grants of jurisdiction to the federal government which would exclude State power on the same subjects.'

[15] *Chisholm v State of Georgia*, 2 US 419 (1793), 435.

[16] A. Abel, 'The Commerce Clause in the Constitutional Convention'; as well as D. H. Regan, 'The Supreme Court and State Protectionism: Making Sense of the Dormant Commerce Clause', 1125: 'There is much evidence that the main point of this grant (unlike the grant of power over foreign commerce) was not to empower Congress, but rather to disable the States from regulating commerce among themselves.'

[17] *Gibbons v Ogden*, 22 US 1 (1824).

argument that the Commerce Clause 'implies in its nature full power over the thing to be regulated' and therefore concluded that the competence '*excludes necessarily the action of all others that would perform the same operation on the same thing*'.[18] The power to regulate interstate commerce was thus an exclusive federal power. The States did not enjoy a 'concurrent' power over interstate commerce; they could only act upon the acknowledged residual 'power of a State to regulate its police, its domestic trade, and to govern its own citizens'.[19] But importantly, as soon as a State law interfered with interstate commerce, it was no longer an emanation of a State's—legitimate—police power,[20] but an—illegitimate—arrogation of the (federal) commerce power.

The distinction between (external) interstate commerce and (internal) police powers here mapped onto the international law distinction between external and internal sovereignty; and while the States had 'lost' the former by joining the Union, they had retained the latter as a core aspect of their State sovereignty. The determinative key to arbitrate between the (federal) commerce and the (State) police sphere was thereby the character of the legislative act according to its object or purpose.[21] The Court delineated the two spheres of federal and State powers according to whether a law primarily concerned 'commerce'—that is: interstate trade—or 'internal affairs' like intrastate production. Under this category approach, the States could regulate manufacture or public health; but as soon as a statute entered into the sphere of interstate commerce, it would be excluded.

This exclusivity reading of the Commerce Clause, predominant until the early twentieth century, nonetheless received a severe blow with *Cooley v Board of Wardens of the Port of Philadelphia*.[22] A State statute here touched upon the Commerce Clause; yet, the Supreme Court was not prepared to declare it *ipso facto* void. Instead the Court proposed an intellectual compromise between the exclusivity camp and the partisans of a concurrent

[18] Ibid., 209 (emphasis added). [19] Ibid., 208.

[20] *Mayor, Aldermen and Commonality of City of New York v Miln*, 36 US 102 (1837), 131–2: '[W]e are of the opinion that the act is not a regulation of commerce, but of police; and that being thus considered, it was passed in the exercise of a power which rightfully belonged to the States.'

[21] H. W. Biklé, 'The Silence of Congress', 216.

[22] *Cooley v Board of Wardens of Port of Philadelphia*, 53 US 299 (1851). The decision was a pragmatic compromise between the 'exclusive theory' proponents and the State-rightists on the Court.

power approach.[23] The result was the idea of 'partial exclusivity'. In a well-known passage, the Court explained this constitutional compromise as follows:

> The grant of commercial power to Congress does not contain any terms which expressly exclude the States from exercising an authority over its subject-matter. If they are excluded it must be because the nature of the power, thus granted to Congress, requires that a similar authority should not exist in the States ... Either absolutely to affirm, or deny that the nature of this power requires exclusive legislation by Congress, is to lose sight of the nature of the subjects of this power, and to assert concerning all of them, what is really *applicable but to a part*. Whatever *subjects* of this power are *in their nature national*, or admit only of one uniform system, or plan of regulation, may justifiably be said to be of such a nature as to require exclusive legislation by Congress.[24]

The *Cooley* Court thus introduced 'the new doctrine of selective exclusiveness'.[25] This was done by analytically separating the Commerce Clause 'power' from the 'subject-matters' over which it operated. While the Supreme Court—paradoxically—continued to play with the idea that the entire Commerce Power was exclusive,[26] the *Cooley* Court nonetheless posited that only subjects that were 'national' in character would require a uniform federal regime. However, 'local' subjects would here *not* be exclusively reserved to the States. Congress could act within them,[27] yet '[i]naction by Congress upon these subjects of a local nature, unlike its inaction upon matters affecting all the States and requiring uniformity of

[23] An outspoken advocate of the concurrent power thesis was Marshall's successor as Chief Justice: R. B. Taney. See in particular his separate opinion in the *License Cases*, 46 US 504 (1847).

[24] *Cooley v Board of Wardens of Port of Philadelphia* (see n. 22), 319 (emphasis added).

[25] F. Frankfurter, 'Taney and the Commerce Clause', 1292.

[26] In subsequent jurisprudence, the Supreme Court would confirm that the *entire* Commerce Clause was exclusive; see: *Southern Railway Co. v King*, 217 US 524 (1910), 531: 'It has been frequently decided in this Court that the right to regulate interstate commerce is, by virtue of the Federal Constitution, exclusively vested in the Congress of the United States. The States cannot pass any law directly regulating such commerce.'

[27] In *James Clark Distilling Co. v Western Maryland R. Co.*, 242 US 311 (1917), the Supreme Court expressed this in the following words (ibid., 327–8): 'It is settled, says the argument, that Interstate commerce is divided into two great classes, one embracing subjects which do not exact uniformity and which, although subject to the regulation of Congress, are in the absence of such regulation subject to the control of the several States (*Cooley v Board of Wardens*, 12 How. 299), and the other embracing subjects which do require uniformity and which in the absence of regulation by Congress remain free from all State control[.]'

regulation is not to be taken as a declaration that nothing should be done with respect to them, but is rather to be deemed a declaration that, for the time being and until it sees fit to act, they may be regulated by State authority'.[28]

With *Cooley*, the Supreme Court introduced a constitutional distinction between a positive and a negative dimension of the Commerce Clause. (For while Congress's legislative power over interstate commerce could reach local subjects, the 'negative' dimension of the Commerce Clause was confined to 'national' subjects.[29]) This was a constitutional compromise that seemed acceptable to both the Union and the States. Indeed, the divorce of the positive from the negative side of the Commerce Clause would ingeniously allow an expansive interpretation of the Union's legislative competence without simultaneously creating a regulatory vacuum in the absence of congressional legislation.[30]

This constitutional split would be finalized in the first part of the twentieth century, when the Court completely abandoned the exclusive power rationale after the 'New Deal'.[31] Henceforth, the Supreme Court cultivated the idea that the Commerce Clause was throughout an almost plenary 'concurrent' power;[32] and with the exclusive competence theory in ruins, a new doctrine rose to prominence: the *dormant* Commerce Clause doctrine.

[28] *Parkersburg & Ohio River Transportation Co. v Parkersburg*, 107 US 691(1883), 703–4.

[29] *Bowman v Chicago &c. Railway Co.*, 125 US 465 (1888), 507: '[W]here the subject is national in its character, and admits and requires uniformity of regulation, affecting alike all the States, such as transportation between the States, including the importation of goods from one State into another, Congress can alone act upon it, and provide the needed regulations. The absence of any law of Congress on the subject is equivalent to its declaration that commerce in that matter shall be free.'

[30] B. Cushman, 'Formalism and Realism in Commerce Clause Jurisprudence'.

[31] In particular, F. H. Cooke, 'The Pseudo-Doctrine of the Exclusiveness of the Power of Congress to Regulate Commerce', 298. The idea of an exclusive Commerce Clause power was branded as 'an empty form of words, a pseudo-doctrine, a myth, an illusion, an unreality, a superstition, if you please', since 'from the standpoint of sound constitutional construction, the contrary view, that Congress and the States have general concurrent power in this respect is the true one'.

[32] The Court has developed a modern effect-centred test for establishing a legislative competence of the Union, which cuts across all categories of dual federalism and potentially penetrates all spheres of social life. For a discussion of this point, see: R. Schütze, *From Dual to Cooperative Federalism: The Changing Structure of European Law*, Chapter 2, Section I.

b. The Rise of the 'Dormant Commerce Clause' Doctrine

Should States be allowed to frustrate interstate commerce in 'local' matters until Congress removed the dangers of economic protectionism through federal legislation? With the decline of dual federalism, the Supreme Court increasingly solved this problem by means of a novel constitutional weapon: the *dormant* Commerce Clause.[33] The Commerce Clause is here constructed to have an *independent* negative side that operates even where Congress's legislative powers have remained 'dormant'. Unlike the exclusive competence rationale, the theory of the dormant Commerce Clause provides an *independent constitutional rationale*.[34] But what was the rationale and ambit of the negative dimension behind the 'new' Commerce Clause? The answer to this question has changed over time.

aa. From the Direct/Indirect Test to the Excessive Burden Test

Struggling to overcome the heritage of dual federalism, the Supreme Court developed at first a variety of constitutional rationales to prohibit State measures restricting interstate trade. In parallel to an emerging 'anti-discrimination principle', the most prominent test here asked whether a State law directly or indirectly affected interstate commerce.[35] State measures that were held to directly affect interstate commerce were prohibited, while State laws that would only indirectly burden trade were allowed.[36]

[33] Following *Cooley*, the Court did however also develop a second tool to check State laws: the (substantive) due process clause under the Fourteenth Amendment; and according to some, it was this parallel instrument that allowed the Court not (!) to develop a coherent theory for the dormant Commerce Clause for a long time. Cf. M. Tushnet, 'Rethinking the Dormant Commerce Clause'.

[34] This is the reason why some constitutional law scholars and Supreme Court judges have come to doubt the legitimacy of the dormant Commerce Clause. For once the exclusive nature of the Commerce Clause is denied, there are no textual pointers to root the dormant Commerce Clause in Article I, Section 8, Clause 3.

[35] Cf. *Smith v Alabama*, 124 US 465 (1888); as well as *Crenshaw v Arkansas*, 227 US 389 (1913), esp. 395: 'This law is attacked, and the conviction of Crenshaw and Gannaway alleged to be unlawful, because, among other reasons, the law imposes a direct burden upon interstate commerce, exclusively within federal control, and therefore beyond the power of the State to regulate.'

[36] For some, the anti-discrimination principle emerges as an independent principle with *Welton v Missouri*, 91 US 275 (1875), see: R. A. Sedler, 'The Negative Commerce Clause as a Restriction on State Regulation and Taxation: An Analysis in terms of

The problem with this test was that it proved soon 'too mechanical, too uncertain in its application, and too remote from actualities, to be of value'.[37] In search for a new constitutional rationale, the Supreme Court therefore introduced a second test in *Southern Pacific Co. v Arizona*.[38] The case concerned the Arizona Train Limit Law (1912) that made it unlawful to operate trains with more than fourteen passengers or seventy freight cars. This *non*-discriminatory law operated in the interest of public safety; yet the appellant claimed that it directly affected the Commerce Clause. Having paid tribute to past precedents,[39] the Court nonetheless introduced a novel 'excessive burden' test to examine whether a State law violated the Commerce Clause:

> [T]he matters for ultimate determination here are the nature and extent of the burden which the State regulation of interstate trains, adopted as a safety measure, imposes on interstate commerce, and whether the relative weights of the State and national interests involved are such as to make inapplicable the rule, generally observed, that the free flow of interstate commerce and its freedom from local restraints in matters requiring uniformity of regulation are interests safeguarded by the Commerce Clause from State interference...

Constitutional Structure', 933–4. Nonetheless, the emergence of the discrimination rationale within the dormant Commerce Clause has retained a degree of mystery, cf. B. P. Denning, 'Reconstructing the Dormant Commerce Clause Doctrine', 441: '[B]oth its emergence and its constitutional pedigree remain something of a mystery.' Be that as it may, we can see a discrimination principle already fully at work in *Robbins v Shelby County Taxing District*, 120 US 489 (1887) as well as *South Carolina State Highway Dept. v Barnwell*, 303 US 177(1938). In the latter case, the Supreme Court found (ibid., 185–6): 'The Commerce Clause by its own force, prohibits discrimination against interstate commerce, whatever its form or method, and the decisions of this Court have recognized that there is scope for its like operation when State legislation nominally of local concern is in point of fact aimed at interstate commerce, or by its necessary operation is a means of gaining a local benefit by throwing the attendant burdens on those without the State.' For a general discussion of the origins of the non-discrimination principle here, see: D. S. Day, 'Revisiting Pike: The Origins of Nondiscrimination Tier of the Dormant Commerce Clause Doctrine'.

[37] In the famous—dissenting—words of Justice Stone in *Di Santo v Pennsylvania*, 273 US 34 (1927) at 44: '[T]he traditional test of the limit of State action by inquiring whether the interference with commerce is direct or indirect seems to me too mechanical, too uncertain in its application, and too remote from actualities, to be of value. In thus making use of the expressions, "direct" and "indirect interference" with commerce, we are doing little more than using labels to describe a result rather than any trustworthy formula by which it is reached.'

[38] *Southern Pacific Co. v Arizona*, 325 US 761 (1945).

[39] Ibid., 766.

> If one State may regulate train lengths, so may all the others, and they need not prescribe the same maximum limitation. The practical effect of such regulation is to control train operations beyond the boundaries of the State exacting it because of the necessity of breaking up and reassembling long trains at the nearest terminal points before entering and after leaving the regulating State. The serious impediment to the free flow of commerce by the local regulation of train lengths and the practical necessity that such regulation, if any, must be prescribed by a single body having a nation-wide authority are apparent ... *The decisive question is whether in the circumstances the total effect of the law as a safety measure in reducing accidents and casualties is so slight or problematical as not to outweigh the national interest in keeping interstate commerce free from interferences which seriously impede it and subject it to local regulation which does not have a uniform effect on the interstate train journey which it interrupts.*[40]

The Court found that the State law afforded 'at most slight and dubious advantage, if any, over unregulated train lengths', while interstate commerce was substantially affected.[41] And rejecting the idea that States could breach the dormant Commerce Clause by 'simply invoking the convenient apologetics of the police power',[42] the Court held that the State had gone 'too far'.[43] This 'excessive burden' test was the—rhetorical—heart of the case.[44] The new balancing rationale thereby expressly pitted the interest of the Union in creating a national market against the interest of a State in regulating the health and safety of its citizens. This 'national' test would allow the Supreme Court to test every State measure that somehow hindered trade against a single Union standard.

This excessive burden test was however not the only test under the Commerce Clause. For the Supreme Court subsequently clarified that there was no need to engage in a complex balancing exercise, where a State had engaged in economic protectionism by discriminating against out-of-State goods. This constitutional shortcut was made in *Pike v Bruce Church*.[45]

[40] Ibid., 770–6 (emphasis added). [41] Ibid., 779. [42] Ibid., 780.

[43] Ibid., 781.

[44] For an argument that the case should be understood in light of an economic protectionism rationale, see: D. H. Regan, 'The Supreme Court and State Protectionism'.

[45] *Pike v Bruce Church*, 397 US 137 (1970).

bb. Pike *and the Two-Pronged Commerce Clause Test*

Dealing with—another—Arizona law, the question in *Pike* was whether the 'Fruit and Vegetable Standardization Act' (1929) violated the Commerce Clause because it prohibited unpacked melons from being exported outside the State. The Court quickly found that the State law burdened interstate commerce and the only question was therefore whether it did so excessively. But what was an 'excessive burden'; and would it need to be shown for every State measure that affected interstate commerce? The answer of the Court was this:

> Although the criteria for determining the validity of State statutes affecting interstate commerce have been variously stated, the general rule that emerges can be phrased as follows: *Where the statute regulates evenhandedly to effectuate a legitimate local public interest, and its effects on interstate commerce are only incidental, it will be upheld unless the burden imposed on such commerce is clearly excessive in relation to the putative local benefits.* If a legitimate local purpose is found, then the question becomes one of degree. And the extent of the burden that will be tolerated will of course depend on the nature of the local interest involved, and on whether it could be promoted as well with a lesser impact on interstate activities.[46]

This famous '*Pike* formula' clarified two things. First, the balancing test was confined to State laws that regulated 'evenhandedly'; that is, State laws that did not discriminate against imports (or exports). Second, where the State pursued a 'legitimate local public interest', the Court would only invalidate the State measure where the burden imposed on interstate commerce was 'clearly excessive'.[47]

For discriminatory measures, on the other hand, the Court would develop a 'virtual per se rule'. This was clarified a few years later in *Philadelphia v New Jersey*.[48] The case involved a New Jersey import ban on solid waste from other States. Without engaging in a balancing approach,

[46] Ibid., 142 (emphasis added).

[47] In the present case, the Court held (ibid., 145): 'Although it is not easy to see why the other growers of Arizona are entitled to benefit at the company's expense from the fact that it produces superior crops, we may assume that the asserted State interest is a legitimate one. But the State's tenuous interest in having the company's cantaloupes identified as originating in Arizona cannot constitutionally justify the requirement that the company build and operate an unneeded $200,000 packing plant in the State. The nature of that burden is, constitutionally, more significant than its extent. For the Court has viewed with particular suspicion State statutes requiring business operations to be performed in the home State that could more efficiently be performed elsewhere. Even where the State is pursuing a clearly legitimate local interest, this particular burden on commerce has been declared to be virtually per se illegal.'

[48] *City of Philadelphia v New Jersey*, 437 US 617 (1978).

the Court here found that 'whatever New Jersey's ultimate purpose, *it may not be accomplished by discriminating* against articles of commerce coming from outside the State unless there is some reason, apart from their origin, to treat them differently'.[49] The State law at issue discriminated '[b]oth on its face and in its plain effects',[50] and therefore fell foul of '*a virtually per se rule of invalidity*'.[51] Importantly, this *virtual* per se rule is not an *actual* per se rule. The Court has thus accepted that discriminatory measures can be justified—though they must pass the 'strictest scrutiny'.[52] 'When a State statute clearly discriminates against interstate commerce, it will be struck down, unless the discrimination is demonstrably justified by a valid factor unrelated to economic protectionism.'[53]

In the past, the anti-discrimination test has become the Supreme Court's primary test.[54] The discrimination prong is thereby easily applied, where the State law 'facially discriminates' against out-of State goods.[55] The Supreme Court has however equally outlawed State measures that discriminate in fact.[56] And the boundary between discrimination and non-discrimination may here be very slim. In *Bibb*,[57] the Supreme Court held a State (product) requirement that obliged trucks and trailers to be equipped with a specific type of mudguard to be non-discriminatory.[58] By contrast,

[49] Ibid., 627 (emphasis added). [50] Ibid. [51] Ibid., 624 (emphasis added).

[52] *Oregon Waste Systems, Inc. v Department of Environmental Quality of Oregon*, 511 US 93 (1994), 101.

[53] *Wyoming v Oklahoma*, 502 US 437 (1992), 454.

[54] D. H. Regan, 'The Supreme Court and State Protectionism: Making Sense of the Dormant Commerce Clause', 1092: 'For almost fifty years, scholars have urged the Court to "balance" in dormant Commerce Clause cases; and the scholars have imagined that the Court was following their advice. The Court has indeed claimed to balance, winning scholarly approval. But the Court knows better than the scholars. Despite what the Court has said, it has not been balancing. It has been following a simpler and better-justified course. In the central area of dormant Commerce Clause jurisprudence, comprising what I shall call "movement-of-goods" cases (*Pike v. Bruce Church, Inc.* may be taken as paradigmatic), the Court has been concerned exclusively with preventing States from engaging in purposeful economic protectionism. Not only is this what the Court has been doing, it is just what the Court should do. This and no more.' For a re-confirmation of this position, see: B. P. Denning, 'Reconstructing the Dormant Commerce Clause Doctrine'.

[55] *City of Philadelphia v New Jersey*, 437 US 617 (1978).

[56] Cf. *Dean Milk Co. v City of Madison, Wisconsin*, 340 US 349 (1951); *Hunt v Washington State Apple Advertising Comm'n*, 432 US 333 (1977).

[57] *Bibb v Navajo Freight Lines, Inc.*, 359 US 520 (1959).

[58] The Court nonetheless outlawed the State law as an excessive burden on interstate trade (ibid., 529–30): 'This is one of those cases—few in number—where local safety measures that are nondiscriminatory place an unconstitutional burden on interstate commerce. This conclusion is especially underlined by the deleterious effect which the Illinois law will have on the

when dealing with a State law that prohibited the use of any State product-grading scheme for apples, the Court found discrimination.[59] The Court's unclear definition of discrimination indeed deserves much criticism.[60] For even if non-discriminatory measures may—if an excessive burden on interstate trade is found—violate the balancing prong of the *Pike* test, the distinction between discriminatory and even-handed measures remains very important in light of the respective standards of review that the Court has cultivated for each type of State measure.

But to conclude: the modern US jurisprudence governing the dormant Commerce Clause is based on a number of analytic elements. First, any State (or local) measure that directly or indirectly affects interstate commerce will fall within the jurisdictional scope of the negative Commerce Clause.[61] Secondly, wherever a State law so restricts interstate commerce, States will need to point to a legitimate public policy ground. The list of

"interline" operation of interstate motor carriers. The conflict between the Arkansas regulation and the Illinois regulation also suggests that this regulation of mudguards is not one of those matters "admitting of diversity of treatment, according to the special requirements of local conditions," to use the words of Chief Justice Hughes in *Sproles v. Binford*, supra, at 390. A State which insists on a design out of line with the requirements of almost all the other States may sometimes place a great burden of delay and inconvenience on those interstate motor carriers entering or crossing its territory. Such a new safety device—out of line with the requirements of the other States—may be so compelling that the innovating State need not be the one to give way. But the present showing—balanced against the clear burden on commerce—is far too inconclusive to make this mudguard meet that test.'

[59] *Hunt v Washington Apple Advertising Company* (see n. 56), 350–1: '[T]he challenged statute has the practical effect of not only burdening interstate sales of Washington apples, but also discriminating against them. This discrimination takes various forms. The first, and most obvious, is the statute's consequence of raising the costs of doing business in the North Carolina market for Washington apple growers and dealers, while leaving those of their North Carolina counterparts unaffected. As previously noted, this disparate effect results from the fact that North Carolina apple producers, unlike their Washington competitors, were not forced to alter their marketing practices in order to comply with the statute. They were still free to market their wares under the [federal] grade or none at all as they had done prior to the statute's enactment. Obviously, the increased costs imposed by the statute would tend to shield the local apple industry from the competition of Washington apple growers and dealers who are already at a competitive disadvantage because of their great distance from the North Carolina market.'

[60] Cf. L. Tribe, *American Constitutional Law*, 1078; as well as B. P. Denning, 'Reconstructing the Dormant Commerce Clause', esp. 494.

[61] The Supreme Court has, in a long line of jurisprudence, clarified that 'local' restrictions imposed by cities or counties will fall within the scope of the dormant Commerce Clause; see especially: *City of Philadelphia v New Jersey* (see n. 55); as well as *Dean Milk Co. v City of Madison, Wisconsin* (see n. 56).

public policy grounds is thereby open-ended—regardless of whether the State measure discriminates or not. Thirdly, the nature of the measure—whether discriminatory or not—determines the degree of judicial scrutiny applied. Discriminatory measures will be subject to strict scrutiny, while non-discriminatory measures will only violate the Commerce Clause if the burden on interstate commerce is 'clearly excessive' in relation to the legitimate State interest. Virtual per se illegality for discriminatory measures here contrasts with a margin of regulatory discretion for non-discriminatory State policies.[62]

2. *The Commerce Clause: Special Aspects*

Textually, the Commerce Clause contains no reference to the fact that State restrictions on interstate trade may be justified on public policy grounds. Yet as the previous section has shown, the Court has constructed the dormant aspect of the Commerce Clause in a way that State police powers can be invoked. Discriminatory or non-discriminatory measures can here be 'justified' by reference to an open-ended list of public policy exceptions. Yet quite apart from this general justification route, US jurisprudence has also produced a number of 'special' justificatory alleys for commerce restrictions.

Two of these special regimes shall be discussed in this section.[63]

[62] In the words of the Supreme Court: 'A nondiscriminatory regulation serving substantial State purposes is not invalid simply because it causes some business to shift from a predominantly out-of-State industry to a predominantly in-State industry. Only if the burden on interstate commerce clearly outweighs the State's legitimate purposes does such a regulation violate the Commerce Clause.' See: *Minnesota v Clover Leaf Creamery* (1981) 449 US 456 at 474.

[63] There is one very important third special regime that needs to be mentioned here: the 'market participant principle'. For the Supreme Court has traditionally considered the Commerce Clause to cover solely generally applicable *regulatory* (or fiscal) measures—to the exclusion of direct subsidies (cf. D. T. Coenen, 'Business Subsidies and the Dormant Commerce Clause'). In the words of the Supreme Court in *Hughes v Alexandria Scrap Corp.*, 426 US 794 (1976) at 810: 'Nothing in the purposes animating the Commerce Clause prohibits a State, in the absence of congressional action, from participating in the market and exercising the right to favor its own citizens over others.' This momentous decision was upheld in *Reeves, Inc. v Stake*, 447 US 429 (1980), where the Court confirmed the distinction between 'States as market participants and States as regulators', and—quoting L. Tribe—that 'the Commerce Clause was directed, as an historical matter, only at regulatory and taxing actions taken by States in their sovereign capacity' (ibid., 437). The justification behind this special exception for financial subsidies is the argument that a State can sovereignly decide how to spend its own money—even if that de facto disadvantages out-of-State companies. The distinction between a direct subsidy (outside the Commerce Clause) and a discriminatory tax (inside the Commerce Clause) has thus been fundamental (cf. *West Lynn Creamery, Inc. v Healy*, 512 US 186 (1994)).

a. Congressional Consent and the Dormant Commerce Clause

The Commerce Clause was originally conceived as a legislative competence. It primarily gives Congress the power to *regulate* commerce; and this competence entitles Congress—if it so wishes—to *delegate* the power to regulate commerce back to the States. This followed from the (partially) exclusive competence theory and indeed reflected early constitutional practice.[64] Yet with the rise of the dormant Commerce Clause theory, this understanding was put onto a less secure constitutional footing. For if the negative side of the Commerce Clause is seen to be independent of its positive side and inherent in the Constitution, could Congress delegate the power to regulate and interfere with the 'common market' to a State? Surprisingly, the Court has answered this question affirmatively. Thus, even where a State law violates the dormant Commerce Clause, the Court has found that the ultimate touchstone under the Commerce Clause is congressional consent; and the latter could therefore *condone* a State restriction to interstate trade.

But in the absence of express constitutional language,[65] where did this idea come from? Its source has been aptly summed up as follows:

> The idea that Congress possessed such a power arose toward the end of the nineteenth century, when the exclusivity theory lost its influence. After the Civil War, although the Court did not repudiate the exclusivity theory, it offered an alternative explanation for the Dormant Commerce Clause. According to the Court,

Recently, the Supreme Court appears to have even extended this 'market participant' exception to general regulatory and fiscal measures that discriminated in favour of public State entities (cf. *United Haulers Assn., Inc. v Oneida-Herkimer Solid Waste Management Authority*, 550 US 330 (2007) and *Department of Revenue of Kentucky v Davis*, 553 US 328 (2008)). According to Williams and Denning, this has created a new form of protectionism, see: N. R. Williams and B. P. Denning, 'The "New Protectionism" and the American Common Market', 250: 'In our view, these decisions create a new exception to the dormant Commerce Clause, one for protectionist State and local taxes and regulations that favour public rather than private entities. Under the Court's new approach, which we call the "New Protectionism", State and local governments may not favour private business as such, but they may adopt taxes and regulations that protect State or local government operations from out-of-State competition, whether public or private.'

[64] For a famous early example, see the 1789 Act that was invoked in *Gibbons v Ogden* (see n. 17).

[65] For such express language, see for example Article I, Section 10, Clause 2: 'No State shall, *without the consent of the Congress*, lay any imposts or duties on imports or exports' (emphasis added). And see also Clause 3: 'No State shall, *without the consent of Congress*, lay any duty of tonnage' (emphasis added).

the fact that Congress failed to regulate a particular facet of interstate commerce itself demonstrated Congress's intent that such commerce be left free from State regulation. So conceived, the Dormant Commerce Clause was not a constitutional limitation on State authority but merely a species of statutory preemption—albeit a strange form of such preemption, resting as it did upon the absence rather than presence of a federal statute.[66]

A good illustration of this judicial deference to Congress can be found in the case law on alcoholic beverages.

Could the importation or sale of intoxicating sprits be prohibited by individual States? In a series of cases decided at the end of the nineteenth century,[67] the Supreme Court had set strict limits upon the States' regulatory powers; yet it had also pointed to the fact that congressional consent could overturn that result. In *Leisy v Hardin*,[68] the Supreme Court thus held: 'The conclusion follows that as the grant of the power to regulate commerce among the States, so far as one system is required, is exclusive, the States cannot exercise that power *without the assent of Congress*, and, in the absence of legislation, it is left for the courts to determine when State action does or does not amount to such exercise—or, in other words, what is or is not a regulation of such commerce.'[69] This judicial invitation to be overruled by Congress was almost immediately taken up. The 'Wilson Act' (1890) thus allowed each State to subject all imported liquors 'to the operation and effect of the law of such State or territory enacted in the exercise of its police powers, to the same extent and in the same manner as though such liquids or liquors had been produced in such State or Territory'.[70] State laws restricting interstate commerce could consequently be specifically 'exempted' by Congress from the negative aspect of the Commerce Clause.

The idea that it was Congress—not the Court—that ultimately determined the federal balance under the Commerce Clause became triumphant after the New Deal. Having found strong academic support,[71]

[66] N. R. Williams, 'Why Congress May not "Overrule" the Dormant Commerce Clause', 178.

[67] See: *Mugler v Kansas*, 123 US 623 (1887); as well as: *Bowman v Chicago*, 125 US 465 (1888).

[68] *Leisy v Hardin*, 135 US 100 (1890).

[69] Ibid., 119 (emphasis added).

[70] (1890) Wilson Act, Chapter 728 (codified at 27 USC § 121). The constitutionality of the act was challenged in *In re Rahrer*, 140 US 545 (1891).

[71] The theory that 'congressional will' is the touchstone within the (dormant) Commerce Clause was popularized by N. T. Dowling, 'Interstate Commerce and State Power', 20: 'It is, that in the absence of affirmative consent a Congressional negative will be presumed in the courts against State action which in its effect upon interstate commerce constitutes an

the Supreme Court now expressly found: '*Congress has undoubted power to redefine the distribution of power over interstate commerce*'; and it can thus 'permit the States to regulate the commerce *in a manner which would otherwise not be permissible*'.[72] In a doctrinal development that seemed to contradict the Court's earliest jurisprudence,[73] Congress even felt entitled to sanction *discriminatory* State laws that hindered interstate commerce.[74] This legislative 'supremacy' in the interpretation of the Commerce Clause has been academically defended.[75] The Supreme Court has offered the following constitutional rationale to explain its judicial deference towards congressional ad hoc exemptions:

> Unrepresented interests will often bear the brunt of regulations imposed by one State having a significant effect on persons or operations in other States ... On the other hand, when Congress acts, all segments of the country are represented, and there is significantly less danger that one State will be in a position to exploit others. Furthermore, if a State is in such a position, the decision to allow it is a collective one. A rule requiring a clear expression of approval by Congress ensures that there is, in fact, such a collective decision and reduces significantly the risk that unrepresented interests will be adversely affected by restraints on commerce.[76]

unreasonable interference with national interests, the presumption being rebuttable at the pleasure of Congress.'

[72] *Southern Pacific Co. v Arizona*, 325 US 761 (1945), 769 (emphasis added).

[73] In *Cooley v Board of Wardens* (see n. 22), the Court held at 318: 'If the States were divested of the power to legislate on this subject by the grant of the commercial power to Congress, it is plain this act could not confer upon them power thus to legislate. If the Constitution excluded the States from making any law regulating commerce, certainly Congress cannot re-grant, or in any manner re-convey to the States that power.'

[74] *Prudential Insurance Co. v Benjamin*, 328 US 408 (1946).

[75] For Tribe, the power to overrule the Court derives from the positive grant of power in the Commerce Clause (see n. 60), 1041: 'It is important to understand that, in this explanation of the dormant Commerce Clause, Congress does not transmute the constitutional valence of the State law at issue from negative to positive, in apparent violation of *Marbury v. Madison*. No such constitutional alchemy need be posited. Rather, the congressional enactment into which the State law fits should be understood to transform the State law itself—changing not what its words say, of course, but what it means and how it operates once it has been transplanted from a context in which its very existence threatens to provoke retaliation by other States and to fragment the Union, to a context in which its threatening sting has been removed by the congressionally established grid into which it fits. In essence, the entry of Congress onto the legal landscape serves to tame, in a sense to domesticate, a State law that, before Congress entered the picture, represented a paradigmatic instance of what the Commerce Clause was designed to prevent.'

[76] *South-Central Timber Development v Wunnicke*, 467 US 82 (1984), 92.

This 'representation' enforcing argument will be discussed later;[77] yet in the second part of this section, we need to explore a second special exemption under the Commerce Clause: the Twenty-First Amendment.

b. Alcoholic Drinks and the Twenty-First Amendment

The 'Prohibition Period' seems today a peculiarly illiberal fit of 'moralism'. But between 1920 and 1933, the United States had imposed a constitutional ban on the importation, manufacture, and sale of intoxicating liquors. This constitutional ban was embodied in the Eighteenth Amendment.[78] The Amendment decreased the consumption of alcohol, yet it equally increased organized crime; and after this sobering realization, public opinion tipped, and in 1933, the Twenty-First Amendment duly repealed the Eighteenth Amendment.[79] But while the new amendment did repeal the nationwide 'prohibition' of alcoholic drinks, it expressly allowed States to continue *State-wide* prohibitions. Section 2 of the Twenty-First Amendment here stated:

> The transportation or importation into any State, Territory, or possession of the United States for delivery or use therein of intoxicating liquors, *in violation of the laws thereof*, is hereby prohibited.[80]

Was this a constitutional carte blanche for the States when it came to interstate restrictions for alcoholic drinks? Early jurisprudence indeed seemed to grant the States an unlimited justification. In *State Board of Equalization v Young's Market Co.*,[81] the Court had to deal with a Californian law that required an import licence and a licence fee of $500 for the privilege of importing beer into that State. The plaintiffs challenged the State law on the ground that it was discriminatory; yet the Court held as follows:

> Prior to the Twenty-First Amendment, it would obviously have been unconstitutional to have imposed any fee for that privilege ... The amendment which

[77] For an extensive discussion of the relationship between markets and democracy, see the *Epilogue* in this volume.

[78] Section 1 of the Eighteenth Amendment states: 'After one year from the ratification of this article the manufacture, sale, or transportation of intoxicating liquors within, the importation thereof into, or the exportation thereof from the United States and all the territory subject to the jurisdiction thereof for beverage purposes is hereby prohibited.'

[79] Section 1 of the Twenty-First Amendment states: 'The eighteenth article of amendment to the Constitution of the United States is hereby repealed.'

[80] Emphasis added.

[81] *State Board of Equalization v Young's Market Co.*, 299 US 59 (1936).

'prohibited' the 'transportation or importation' of intoxicating liquors into any State 'in violation of the laws thereof' abrogated the right to import free, so far as concerns intoxicating liquors. The words used are apt to confer upon the State the power to forbid all importations which do not comply with the conditions which it prescribes. The plaintiffs ask us to limit this broad command. They request us to construe the amendment as saying, in effect: the State may prohibit the importation of intoxicating liquors provided it prohibits the manufacture and sale within its borders, but if it permits such manufacture and sale, it must let imported liquors compete with the domestic on equal terms. To say that would involve not a construction of the amendment, but a rewriting of it.[82]

This broad reading of the Twenty-First Amendment appeared to suggest that 'a State is totally unconfined by traditional Commerce Clause limitations when it restricts the importation of intoxicants destined for use, distribution, or consumption within its borders'.[83] (Indeed, the *Young's Market* Court expressly held that the ability to prohibit importation included the ability to discriminate against out-of-State goods!) Yet the Court subsequently clarified that an equilibrium between the Commerce Clause and the Amendment needed to be found.[84] This was particularly so where foreign spirits were concerned; but with regard to interstate restrictions, the Court still held that 'the Twenty-first Amendment demands wide latitude for regulation by the State'.[85]

This wide latitude would nonetheless gradually encounter some constitutional limits.[86] And in what must be seen as a major U-turn, the

[82] Ibid., 62.

[83] *Hostetter v Idlewild Bon Voyage Liquor Corp.*, 377 US 324 (1964), 330.

[84] Ibid. 331–2: 'To draw a conclusion from this line of decisions that the Twenty-first Amendment has somehow operated to "repeal" the Commerce Clause wherever regulation of intoxicating liquors is concerned would, however, be an absurd oversimplification. If the Commerce Clause had been *pro tanto* "repealed," then Congress would be left with no regulatory power over interstate or foreign commerce in intoxicating liquor. Such a conclusion would be patently bizarre, and is demonstrably incorrect.'

[85] *Seagram & Sons v Hostetter*, 384 US 35 (1966), 42.

[86] *Brown-Forman v N.Y. State Liq. Auth.*, 476 US 573 (1986), 584–5: 'It is well settled that the Twenty-first Amendment did not entirely remove State regulation of alcohol from the reach of the Commerce Clause ... Section 2 of the Twenty-first Amendment, however, speaks only to State regulation of the "transportation or importation into any State ... for delivery or use therein" of alcoholic beverages. That Amendment, therefore, gives New York only the authority to control sales of liquor in New York, and confers no authority to control sales in other States. The Commerce Clause operates with full force whenever one State attempts to regulate the transportation and sale of alcoholic beverages destined for distribution and consumption in a foreign country, *Idlewild Bon Voyage Liquor Corp.*, *supra*, or another State.'

Supreme Court ultimately held that the Twenty-First Amendment did *not* justify economic protectionism in the form of discriminatory State measures. Having first established this key limitation in the context of fiscal measures,[87] the Court subsequently extended it to regulatory measures in *Granholm v Head*.[88] The case involved two State laws that regulated the sale of wine from out-of-State wineries to consumers. Michigan and New York had both adopted a three-tier distribution system, according to which (licensed) producers would have to sell to (licensed) wholesalers, who would have to distribute the wine to (licensed) retailers. This distribution arrangement generally prevented the direct sale of wine from producers to consumers; yet both States permitted exceptions for in-State wineries. These laws clearly discriminated against out-of-State wineries; and the question arose whether they could nonetheless be justified under the Twenty-First Amendment. In clearly overruling *State Board of Equalization v Young's Market*, the Court now held as follows:

The aim of the Twenty-first Amendment was to allow States to maintain an effective and uniform system for controlling liquor by regulating its transportation, importation, and use. *The Amendment did not give States the authority to pass nonuniform laws in order to discriminate against out-of-State goods, a privilege they had not enjoyed at any earlier time* ... A State which chooses to ban the sale and consumption of alcohol altogether could bar its importation; and, as our history shows, it would have to do so to make its laws effective. States may also assume direct control of liquor distribution through State-run outlets or funnel sales through the three-tier system ... State policies are protected under the Twenty-first Amendment when they treat liquor produced out of State the same as its domestic equivalent. The instant cases, in contrast, involve straightforward attempts to discriminate in favor of local producers. *The discrimination is contrary to the Commerce Clause and is not saved by the Twenty-first Amendment.*[89]

[87] The famous case here is *Bacchus Imports, Ltd v Dias*, 468 US 263 (1984), which dealt with a discriminatory tax measure. The Court held (ibid., 276): 'Approaching the case in this light, we are convinced that Hawaii's discriminatory tax cannot stand. Doubts about the scope of the Amendment's authorization notwithstanding, one thing is certain: the central purpose of the provision was not to empower States to favor local liquor industries by erecting barriers to competition. It is also beyond doubt that the Commerce Clause itself furthers strong federal interests in preventing economic Balkanization. State laws that constitute mere economic protectionism are therefore not entitled to the same deference as laws enacted to combat the perceived evils of an unrestricted traffic in liquor. Here, the State does not seek to justify its tax on the ground that it was designed to promote temperance or to carry out any other purpose of the Twenty-first Amendment, but instead acknowledges that the purpose was "to promote a local industry."'

[88] *Granholm v Heald*, 544 US 460 (2005).

[89] Ibid., 480–4 (emphasis added).

The ruling has been likened to a textual awakening of the Commerce Clause;[90] but the better view holds that the Twenty-First Amendment was never intended to save discriminatory State measures that amounted to clear economic protectionism. However: non-discriminatory 'even-handed' measures will, on the other hand, always be justified under the Amendment—even if they unduly burden interstate trade. For alcoholic drinks, US constitutionalism thus accepts a special justificatory ground. State measures regulating liqueurs will only violate the Constitution, where they discriminate against imported out-of-State goods.

II. Fiscal Barriers: A Fiscal Affairs 'Exception'?

'[T]he Court has long subjected taxation to other limits and has long treated taxation differently from other kinds of regulation.'[91] The reasons for this exceptional treatment partly stemmed from the text of the US Constitution itself. For unlike regulatory measures, the Constitution not only specifically mentioned the Union power 'to lay and collect taxes, duties, imposts and excises';[92] it also contained two express limitations on the fiscal powers of the States. According to the 'Import–Export Clause', States were generally prohibited to 'lay any Imposts or Duties on Imports or Exports'; and this general prohibition was complemented by a second special clause that outlawed 'any Duty of Tonnage' imposed by the States.[93] Besides these two

[90] R. G. Ballard, '"Dormant" No More: The Supreme Court Awakens the Dormant Commerce Clause in *Granholm v Heald*'.

[91] L. Tribe, *American Constitutional Law*, 1105.

[92] Article I, Section 8, Clause 1: 'The Congress shall have power to lay and collect taxes, duties, imposts and excises, to pay the debts and provide for the common defense and general welfare of the United States; but all duties, imposts and excises shall be uniform throughout the United States[.]' This power is limited in Section 9, Clause 5: 'No tax or duty shall be laid on articles exported from any State.'

[93] Article I, Section 10 Clause 3 ('Tonnage Clause'): 'No State shall, without the Consent of Congress, lay any Duty of Tonnage, keep Troops, or Ships of War in time of Peace, enter into any Agreement or Compact with another State, or with a foreign Power, or engage in War, unless actually invaded, or in such imminent Danger as will not admit of delay.' The 'Tonnage Clause', while not discussed in detail here, specifically targeted port dues, and was designed to disallow maritime States to burden commerce through this old-fashioned fiscal instrument. On this point, see: B. P. Denning, 'Confederation-Era Discrimination against Interstate Commerce and the Legitimacy of the Dormant Commerce Clause Doctrine', 87–8: 'This clause was added at the Philadelphia Convention to settle an interpretative dispute that had arisen concerning whether the Commerce clause, by itself, forbade the States from levying tonnage duties to

specific limitations on State fiscal powers, the US Constitution was however said to have left the individual States with 'an independent and uncontrollable authority to raise their own revenues ... in the most absolute and unqualified sense'.[94]

This picture has dramatically changed over time. Today, the Union has adopted a constitutional regime that significantly controls the fiscal powers of the States. Yet ironically, these significant limitations on the States' fiscal powers did not evolve from the two express limitations within the 1787 Constitution. For even if the Import–Export Clause had been intended as the 'principal remedy proposed by the Philadelphia Convention to remedy the commercial strife that characterized the relations among the States under the Articles of Confederation',[95] with the passage of time, it was to be the (dormant) Commerce Clause that assumed this constitutional role.[96]

This section explores the special constitutional regime for fiscal barriers to interstate trade. We shall start with the decline of the Import–Export Clause and then analyse the rise of the dormant Commerce Clause.

1. *Customs Duties: The Decline of the Import–Export Clause*

The Import–Export Clause states:

> No State shall, without the Consent of the Congress, lay any *Imposts or Duties on Imports or Exports*, except what may be absolutely necessary for executing it's

offset, for example, the cost of erecting lighthouses along the coast ... The Tonnage Clause was a sensible supplement to the Import–Export Clause. Without it, States could have evaded the Import–Export Clause by levying duties on ships from out of State, or from foreign countries.'

[94] A. Hamilton, J. Madison, and J. Jay, *The Federalist*, 145.

[95] B. I. Bittker and B. P. Denning, 'The Import–Export Clause'. On this point, see also Chief Justice Marshall in *Brown v Maryland*, 25 US 419 (1827), 438–9: 'From the vast inequality between the different States of the confederacy as to commercial advantages, few subjects were viewed with deeper interest or excited more irritation than the manner in which the several States exercised, or seemed disposed to exercise, the power of laying duties on imports. From motives which were deemed sufficient by the statesmen of that day, the general power of taxation, indispensably necessary as it was and jealous as the States were of any encroachment on it, was so far abridged as to forbid them to touch imports or exports, with the single exception which has been noticed.'

[96] B. I. Bittker and B. P. Denning, 'The Import–Export Clause', 525: '[T]he Commerce Clause was a handkerchief thrown over something already covered by a blanket. With the passage of time, of course, the Commerce Clause became vastly more important than the Import–Export Clause ... By the end of the twentieth century, therefore, the Commerce Clause became the blanket, and the Import–Export Clause a handkerchief, covering only the few discriminatory State taxes that escape the Commerce Clause's coverage.'

inspection Laws: and the net Produce of all Duties and Imposts, laid by any State on Imports or Exports, shall be for the Use of the Treasury of the United States; and all such Laws shall be subject to the Revision and Controul of the Congress.[97]

The text of the prohibition is confined to 'imposts' and 'duties', and as such covers only fiscal measures. Where these fiscal measures relate to 'imports' or 'exports', they will be prohibited—unless they are 'absolutely necessary' to pay for the application of the 'inspection laws'. (Congress is admittedly entitled to permit State customs duties; yet in such an event, the net produce will have to be transferred to the federal treasury.) This much seemed clear; but two central issues with regard to the clause's scope remained controversial. First, to what extent would the Import–Export Clause protect imported goods, and when would the sovereign State power over internal taxation begin? And secondly, would the clause apply to all import and export duties imposed by the States; or would it only apply to customs duties imposed on *foreign* goods?

Let us explore both questions in turn.

a. *The Rise and Fall of the Original Packaging Doctrine*

What were 'Imposts or Duties on Imports or Exports'? A wide definition was offered in *Brown v Maryland*.[98] The case centred around the question whether Maryland could impose a licence requirement, for which a fee of $50 had to be paid, upon all importers of certain foreign goods. Brown had refused to pay the fee and, as an importing merchant without a licence, was indicted before a State court. The case went up to the Supreme Court, where the latter was asked to decide whether the State licence fee was a duty prohibited under the Import–Export Clause. Maryland argued that the prohibition only related to 'laws imposing duties *on the act of importation or exportation*'.[99] But this narrow view was rejected by Chief Justice Marshall, who found that a 'duty on imports' was 'not merely a duty on the act of importation, but is a duty on the thing imported'. 'It is not, taken in its literal sense, confined to a duty levied while the article is entering the country, but extends to a duty levied after it has entered the country.'[100] Moreover, it made no difference

[97] Article I, Section 10, Clause 2 (emphasis added).

[98] *Brown v Maryland*, 25 US 419 (1827).

[99] Ibid., 437 (emphasis added).

[100] Ibid., 437–8.

whether the charge was levied on the import or the importer, since both led to the same substantive result.[101]

This wide definition raised an important question: when would the prohibition on import duties end and the sovereign power of the States over internal taxation begin? For the Court, the internal power over taxation only started once goods had ceased to be 'imports'. The Import–Export Clause thus clearly covered charges imposed at the moment of entering the country; yet it also reached inside the country and would only end 'when the importer has so acted upon the thing imported that it has become incorporated and mixed up with the mass of property in the country'. Only then would imports lose their '*distinctive character as an import*' and become subject to the taxing power of the States. '[B]ut while remaining the property of the importer in his warehouse *in the original form or package* in which it was imported, a tax upon it is too plainly a duty on imports to escape the prohibition in the Constitution.'[102]

This became famous as the 'original packaging' doctrine. It states, in essence, that States are prohibited from imposing any duties on imported goods as long as they have remained in their original packaging. The doctrine created a constitutional transit corridor in which no State could tax an imported good until it was sold or used.[103]

[101] Ibid., 444: 'So a tax on the occupation of an importer is in like manner a tax on importation.'

[102] Ibid., 441–2 (emphasis added).

[103] See *License Cases*, 46 US 504 (1847), 575–6: 'The immense amount of foreign products used and consumed in this country are imported, landed, and offered for sale in a few commercial cities, and a very small portion of them are intended or expected to be used in the State in which they are imported. A great (perhaps the greater) part imported, in some of the cities, is not owned or brought in by citizens of the State, but by citizens of other States, or foreigners. And while they are in the hands of the importer for sale, in the form and shape in which they were introduced, and in which they are intended to be sold, they may be regarded as merely in transitu, and on their way to the distant cities, villages, and country for which they are destined, and where they are expected to be used and consumed, and for the supply of which they were in truth imported. And a tax upon them while in this condition, for State purposes, whether by direct assessment, or indirectly, by requiring a license to sell, would be hardly more justifiable in principle than a transit duty upon the merchandise when passing through a State. A tax in any shape upon imports is a tax on the consumer, by enhancing the price of the commodity. And if a State is permitted to levy it in any form, it will put it in the power of a maritime importing State to raise a revenue for the support of its own government from citizens of other States, as certainly and effectually

A good illustration of the doctrine can be found in *Low v Austin*.[104] Could California impose a (non-discriminatory) *ad valorem* property tax on bottles of French champagne, duly imported into the United States, when stored in their original cases in a warehouse in San Francisco? The plaintiff refused to do so, and the case went up to the Californian Supreme Court. The latter held the Import–Export Clause to be inapplicable 'because the tax levied is not directly upon imports as such, and consequently the goods imported are not subjected to any burden as a class, but only are included as part of the whole property of its citizens which is subjected equally to an *ad valorem* tax'.[105] However, the US Supreme Court rejected this view by insisting that '*the goods imported do not lose their character as imports and become incorporated into the mass of property of the State until they have passed from the control of the importer or been broken up by him from their original cases*'.[106] Thus: as long as the bottles retained their status as 'imports', '[t]he question is not as to the extent of the tax or its equality with respect to taxes on other property, but as to the power of the State to levy any tax'.[107]

The result of *Low v Austin* was consequently this: as long as goods remained in their original packaging, no State was entitled to lay *any* taxes on imports—even if these taxes indistinctly applied to home State goods.[108] (This constitutional immunity was, mutatis mutandis, extended to exports.[109])

This expansive version of the Import–Export Clause cut deep into the internal taxing powers of the States. But after a hundred years and heavy criticism,[110] the Court adjusted its doctrine in

as if the tax was laid openly and without disguise as a duty on imports. Such a power in a State would defeat one of the principal objects of forming and adopting the Constitution. It cannot be done directly, in the shape of a duty on imports, for that is expressly prohibited. And as it cannot be done directly, it could hardly be a just and sound construction of the Constitution which would enable a State to accomplish precisely the same thing under another name, and in a different form.'

[104] *Low v Austin*, 80 US 29 (1871). [105] Ibid., 34. [106] Ibid. (emphasis added).

[107] Ibid.

[108] Ibid., 35: 'Imports, therefore, whilst retaining their distinctive character as such, must be treated as being without the jurisdiction of the taxing power of the State.'

[109] *Coe v Errol*, 116 US 517 (1886); as well as *Richfield Oil Corp. v State Bd. of Equalization*, 329 US 69 (1946).

[110] T. R. Powell, 'Notes: State Taxation of Imports: When Does an Import Cease to Be an Import?'; A. R. Early and R. G. Weitzman, 'A Century of Dissent: The Immunity of Goods Imported for Resale From Nondiscriminatory State Personal Property Taxes'.

Michelin.[111] While not a total abandonment of the original packaging doctrine, the Court nevertheless clarified that a State tax that *indistinctly* applied to imported as well as domestic goods did not fall under the Import–Export Clause. Georgia had here imposed an *ad valorem* property tax on imported French tyres that had remained in a warehouse in that State. Yet despite the clear parallel to *Low v Austin*, the Court now found:

> Commentators have uniformly agreed that *Low v. Austin* misread this dictum in holding that the Court in *Brown* included nondiscriminatory *ad valorem* property taxes among prohibited 'imposts' or 'duties,' for the contrary conclusion is plainly to be inferred from consideration of the specific abuses which led the Framers to include the Import-Export Clause in the Constitution ... Our independent study persuades us that a nondiscriminatory *ad valorem* property tax is not the type of State exaction which the Framers of the Constitution or the Court in *Brown* had in mind as being an 'impost' or 'duty,' and that *Low v. Austin's* reliance upon the *Brown* dictum to reach the contrary conclusion was misplaced.[112]

Reminding itself of the very purpose of the prohibition, the Court here dramatically restricted the Import–Export Clause.[113] Instead of focusing on whether the taxed goods were 'imports', 'it analyzed the nature of the tax to determine whether it was an "Impost or Duty"'.[114] This new approach meant that only charges or taxes that *distinctly* applied to imports (or exports[115]) would be caught by the provision. Indistinctly

[111] *Michelin Tire Corp. v Wages*, 423 US 276 (1976). For an extensive discussion of the case, see: F. M. Keesling, '*Michelin Tire Corporation v Wages*: The Demise of the Original Packaging Doctrine'.

[112] *Michelin Tire* (above), 282–3.

[113] For an analysis of this point, see: W. Hellerstein, 'State Taxation and the Supreme Court: Towards a More Unified Approach to Constitutional Adjudication'.

[114] *Department of Revenue v Stevedoring Assn.*, 435 US 734 (1978), 752. In *Michelin* (see n. 111, 290–1), the Supreme Court referred to the work of Professor Crosskey, *Politics and the Constitution in the History of the United States*, Volume 1, 296–7: 'Indeed, Professor Crosskey makes a persuasive demonstration that the words "imposts" and "duties" as used in 1787 had meanings well understood to be exactions upon imported goods as imports. "Impost," were like customs duties, that is, charges levied on imports at the time and place of importation. "Duties" was a broader term embracing excises as well as customs duties, and probably only capitation, land, and general property exactions were known by the term "tax", rather than the term "duty."'

[115] *Department of Revenue v Stevedoring Assn.*, 435 US 734 (1978).

applicable charges were thus not 'import' duties. Such internal taxes could not be controlled by the Import–Export Clause.

b. Teleological Reductions: From Interstate Commerce to International Commerce

Would the Import–Export Clause apply only to customs duties (and equivalent charges) on *foreign* goods; or would it also outlaw duties on goods from sister States?

On its textual face, the broader—general—interpretation appears intended. And this reading received *some* support from the (early) Supreme Court. In *Brown v Maryland*, the Supreme Court thus suggested that the Import–Export Clause would extend to interstate commerce.[116] This also appeared to be the assumption behind *Almy v California*.[117] The Supreme Court here dealt with a California stamp duty on the export of gold dust destined for New York, and it simply held the charge violated the Import–Export Clause.[118]

Nonetheless, despite its textual openness and early judicial ambivalences, the Supreme Court has come to clearly reject the application of the Import–Export Clause to *interstate* trade. This momentous constitutional choice was made in *Woodruff v Parham*.[119] The case involved a sales tax imposed for auctions, which was challenged by traders of out-of-State goods. Cleverly distinguishing its previous jurisprudence, the Court revisited the language and history of the Import–Export Clause and found that 'the words imports and imposts were used with exclusive reference to articles imported from *foreign countries*'.[120] The Court consequently concluded 'that no intention existed to prohibit, by this clause, the right of one State to tax articles brought into it from another'.[121]

[116] *Brown v Maryland* (see n. 98), 449: 'It may be proper to add that we suppose the principles laid down in this case to apply equally to importations from a sister State. We do not mean to give any opinion on a tax discriminating between foreign and domestic articles.'

[117] *Almy v California*, 65 US 169 (1860).

[118] Ibid., 173–4: 'If the tax was laid on the gold or silver exported, everyone would see that it was repugnant to the Constitution of the United States, which in express terms declares that "No State shall, without the consent of Congress, lay any imposts or duties on imports or exports, except what may be absolutely necessary for executing its inspection laws."'

[119] *Woodruff v Parham*, 75 US 123 (1868).

[120] Ibid., 133 (emphasis added).

[121] Ibid., 136.

This enormous judgment—arguably not in line with the original meaning intended by the 1787 Constitution[122]—completely emasculated the Import–Export Clause for charges or taxes imposed on interstate commerce. The sole provision that was henceforth available to control the fiscal powers of the States in interstate trade was the Commerce Clause. And today, the Supreme Court indeed considers that '[t]he paradigmatic example of a law discriminating against interstate commerce is *the protective tariff or customs duty*, which taxes goods imported from other States, but does not tax similar products produced in State'.[123] Tariffs and all customs charges would thus have to be analysed—like all other restrictions—under the (dormant) Commerce Clause.

2. *Fiscal Restrictions: The Rise of the (Dormant) Commerce Clause*

Would the power to 'regulate' commerce embrace a power over fiscal measures; and in particular, would the dormant Commerce Clause cover fiscal restrictions?

In *Brown v Maryland*,[124] Chief Justice Marshall had favoured a broad interpretation. The taxing powers of the States 'cannot interfere with any regulation of commerce'. Thus, '[a]ny charge on the introduction and incorporation of the articles into and with the mass of property in the country must be hostile to the power given to Congress to regulate commerce'.[125] The Commerce Clause would consequently cover both *regulatory* as well as *fiscal* measures, and with regard to the latter it would not only capture indirect taxes on goods: 'The distinction between a tax on the thing imported and on the person of the importer can have no influence on this part of the subject. It is too obvious for controversy that they interfere equally with the power to regulate commerce.'[126] The Commerce Clause would consequently cover *indirect* as well as *direct* taxes.

But what were the constitutional principles governing fiscal restrictions? Would they follow the ordinary doctrinal rules established for regulatory measures? The answer to this question has again changed over time.

[122] W. W. Crosskey, *Politics and the Constitution in the History of the United States*, Volume I, Chapter X: 'The True Meaning of the Imports and Export Clause: Herein of "Interstate Trade Barriers" in 1787'.

[123] *West Lynn Creamery, Inc. v Healy*, 512 US 186 (1994) at 193 (emphasis added).

[124] *Brown v Maryland* (see n. 98). [125] Ibid., 448. [126] Ibid.

a. Classic Doctrine: Interstate Commerce as a Tax-Free Zone

Classic Commerce Clause doctrine considered the power to regulate commerce (partially) exclusive;[127] and this meant that all State laws falling within its scope would be void. This dual federal vision strictly distinguished between 'interstate commerce' and 'internal commerce'; and while the States had the 'sovereign' power to tax the latter, they were constitutionally prohibited from taxing the former.

This vision is clearly presented in the *State Freight Tax Case*.[128] The legislature of Pennsylvania had imposed a tax for the use of the State's transportation system. This tax was not discriminatory, as it was imposed regardless of whether the transportation occurred exclusively within the State or crossed State lines. The Court was nonetheless quick in its condemnation. The transportation of goods was commerce; and it was 'of national importance that over that subject there should be but one regulating power, for if one State can directly tax persons or property passing through it or tax them indirectly by levying a tax upon their transportation, every other may, and thus commercial intercourse between States remote from each other may be destroyed'.[129] The tax on freight was thus a regulation of commerce, and as such violated the Commerce Clause.[130] And while the Court recognized 'fully the power of each State to tax at its discretion its own *internal* commerce', interstate commerce 'must remain free'.[131]

The doctrine that interstate commerce had to be tax-free was confirmed in *Robbins v Shelby County Taxing District*.[132] The case involved a tax on wandering salesmen without a licensed business premise in the county in which they sold their goods. Robbins, a dealer of paper and stationery

[127] See Section I(1/a) of this chapter.

[128] *Case of the State Freight Tax*, 82 US 232 (1872).

[129] Ibid., 280.

[130] Ibid., 279: 'If, then, this is a tax upon freight carried between States and a tax because of its transportation, and if such a tax is in effect a regulation of interstate commerce, the conclusion seems to be inevitable that it is in conflict with the Constitution of the United States.' And earlier (ibid., 276): 'It would hardly be maintained, we think, that had the State established custom houses on her borders wherever a railroad or canal comes to the State line and demanded at these houses a duty for allowing merchandise to enter or to leave the State upon one of those railroads or canals, such an imposition would not have been a regulation of commerce with her sister States. Yet it is difficult to see any substantial difference between the supposed case and the one we have in hand.'

[131] Ibid., 282 (emphasis added).

[132] *Robbins v Shelby County Taxing District*, 120 US 489 (1887).

articles, had taken neither a licence nor paid the tax and was consequently sentenced to pay a fine. When the case came up to the US Supreme Court, the Court—having dutifully paid homage to the philosophical principles underlying dual federalism—held: '[N]o regulations can be made directly affecting interstate commerce. Any taxation or regulation of the latter character would be an unauthorized interference with the power given to Congress over the subject.'[133] It thus did not matter that the tax was not discriminatory. For *'[i]nterstate commerce cannot be taxed at all, even though the same amount of tax should be laid on domestic commerce or that which is carried on solely within the State'*.[134]

The constitutional principle that 'interstate commerce cannot be taxed at all' would however gradually give way to a very different rule.[135]

b. Modern Doctrine: Interstate Commerce Must Pay Its Fair Share

The transition from the classic doctrine to a modern one parallels the decline of dual federalism and the rise of a different rationale for the Commerce Clause.

In *Western Live Stock v Bureau of Revenue*,[136] the Supreme Court expressly rejected the idea of a tax-free zone for interstate commerce and replaced it with the rule that '[e]ven interstate business must pay its way'.[137] Interstate commerce could consequently be taxed by the States; yet the Court warned against multiple State taxation and insisted that State taxes must be 'fairly apportioned'.[138] Indeed, under the modern doctrine, the primary task of the Commerce Clause was henceforth to protect interstate commerce against '*cumulative burdens* not imposed on local commerce'.[139] For once States were allowed to tax interstate commerce, the danger existed that '[t]he multiplication of State taxes ... would spell the destruction of interstate commerce and renew the barriers to interstate trade which it was the object of the Commerce Clause to remove'.[140]

[133] Ibid., 494.

[134] Ibid., 497 (emphasis added); and the Court continued (ibid., 498): 'A New Orleans merchant cannot be taxed there for ordering goods from London or New York, because, in the one case, it is an act of foreign, and, in the other, of interstate, commerce, both of which are subject to regulation by Congress alone.'

[135] For an excellent account of this transition, see: W. Hellerstein, 'State Taxation of Interstate Business: Perspectives on Two Centuries of Constitutional Adjudication'.

[136] *Western Live Stock v Bureau of Revenue*, 303 US 250 (1938). [137] Ibid., 254.

[138] Ibid., 255. [139] Ibid., 256 (emphasis added). [140] Ibid.

aa. The Complete Auto *Test within the Commerce Clause*

How did the Court deal with the multiple tax-burden problem? The modern doctrine, and its constituent principles, had erratically wandered into various directions for over forty years until the Supreme Court gave them an authoritative expression in *Complete Auto Transit v Brady*.[141] The case has—perhaps somewhat surprisingly—come to represents the crown jewel of the modern doctrine. The Supreme Court here summed up its modern jurisprudence by reference to the following four basic principles: a State tax could only survive a Commerce Clause challenge 'when the tax is applied to an activity with a substantial nexus with the taxing State, is fairly apportioned, does not discriminate against interstate commerce, and is fairly related to the services provided by the State'.[142]

This four-part test has become well-established jurisprudence. According to the first criterion, a State tax must have a 'substantial nexus' with the taxable activity. In the past, the Court has interpreted this 'jurisdictional' criterion in such a way that even minimal connections to a taxable event would suffice.[143] This minimalism has also been applied to the fourth criterion: the fair relation between a State's jurisdiction and its 'service' for interstate commerce. For not only is this criterion very closely related to the first one; in the course of time, the Court has emasculated it to such an extent that it has lost much of its independent meaning.[144] Criterion two and three, on the other hand, have proven to be the very heart of the *Complete Auto* test. Once a State is regarded as having a legitimate jurisdictional competence—and a State will normally do if there is some commercial 'presence' within it, these two substantive criteria insist

[141] *Complete Auto Transit, Inc. v Brady*, 430 US 274 (1977).

[142] Ibid., 279.

[143] See especially: *Exxon Corp. v Wisconsin Dept. of Revenue*, 447 US 207 (1980), 219: '"minimal connection" or "nexus" between the interstate activities and the taxing State'. For a general analysis of the case law, see: W. Hellerstein, 'State Taxation of Interstate Business', 56.

[144] *Exxon Corp. v Wisconsin Dept. of Revenue* (above), 220: 'a rational relationship between the income attributed to the State and the intrastate values of the enterprise'. The Court has interpreted this criterion in *Commonwealth Edison Co. v Montana*, 453 US 609 (1981), where it held that this criterion is closely related to the nexus requirement but that 'the fourth prong of the *Complete Auto Transit* test imposes the additional limitation that the measure of the tax must be reasonably related to the extent of the contact' (ibid., 626). According to Tribe, *American Constitutional Law*, 1125–6 'the Court has transformed this prong of *Complete Auto Transit* into the fairly trivial requirement that a State provide *some* services to all who are its taxpayers'; the fourth *Complete Auto* prong has therefore 'little independent significance as a restraint on State tax power'.

that a State must not discriminate against out-of-State commerce;[145] and even when it adopts a non-discriminatory tax, the latter must be 'fairly apportioned'.

This—second—*Complete Auto* criterion is thereby the most interesting one.

bb. Fair Apportionment as a Non-Excessive Burden Test?

Is the 'fair apportionment' criterion the fiscal equivalent to *Pike's* excessive burden test; or, has the Court developed a different doctrinal test?

The Court's jurisprudence has clarified that 'fair apportionment' did not imply that double taxation by different States was constitutionally prohibited. In *Moorman*,[146] the Court dealt with a challenge to Iowa's single-factor sales formula that had been adopted by the State to determine income tax on interstate business. The appellant argued that the formula was unconstitutional because most of the other States used a three-factor formula; and, consequently, 'Iowa's longstanding single factor formula must be held responsible for the alleged [income tax] duplication'.[147] Yet the Court rejected this view. Insisting that the duplication was not the result of Iowa's law but followed from the *disparity* in State laws on the issue,[148] it held:

> If the Constitution were read to mandate such precision in interstate taxation, the consequences would extend far beyond this particular case. For some risk of duplicative taxation exists whenever the States in which a corporation does business do not follow identical rules for the division of income. Accepting appellant's view of the Constitution, therefore, would require extensive judicial lawmaking. Its logic is not limited to a prohibition on use of a single factor apportionment formula. The asserted constitutional flaw in that formula is that it is different from that presently employed by a majority of States, and that difference creates a risk of duplicative taxation …
>
> The prevention of duplicative taxation, therefore, would require national uniform rules for the division of income. Although the adoption of a uniform code would undeniably advance the policies that underlie the Commerce Clause, it would require a policy decision based on political and economic considerations that vary from State to State. The Constitution, however, is neutral with respect to the content of any uniform rule … It is clear that the legislative power granted

[145] *Bacchus Imports, Ltd v Dias*, 468 US 263 (1984).

[146] *Moorman Mfg. Co. v Bair*, 437 US 267 (1978).

[147] Ibid., 276.

[148] Ibid., 277.

to Congress by the Commerce Clause of the Constitution would amply justify the enactment of legislation requiring all States to adhere to uniform rules for the division of income. It is to that body, and not this Court, that the Constitution has committed such policy decisions.[149]

The complete removal of fiscal barriers created by the diversity of State legislation was thus not the task of the Court—but that of the Union legislature. Until Congress had acted, States were not constitutionally prohibited from levying an even-handed tax—as long as the latter did not produce arbitrary results.

This last qualification was elaborated in *Container Corporation*.[150] The Court here held that the fair apportionment criterion would only be violated, where there was 'no rational relationship' between the tax and the interstate value; that is, where a State tax was '*out of all appropriate proportion* to the business transacted by the appellant in that State'.[151] This was an extremely deferential review standard. Yet the Court subsequently also restricted its tolerance towards even-handed fiscal measures; and it did so by introducing a new sub-test under the fair apportionment criterion: a dual consistency test. This doctrinal substructure is best expressed in *Jefferson Lines*.[152] Could Oklahoma impose a sales tax on the full price of a bus ticket from Oklahoma to another State? The Court explored the multiple-taxation problem in the following manner:

The difficult question in this case is whether the tax is properly apportioned within the meaning of the second prong of *Complete Auto's* test, 'the central purpose [of which] is to ensure that each State taxes only its fair share of an interstate transaction.' ... For over a decade now, we have assessed any threat of mal-apportionment by asking whether the tax is 'internally consistent' and, if so, whether it is 'externally consistent' as well.

Internal consistency is preserved when the imposition of a tax identical to the one in question by every other State would add no burden to interstate commerce that intrastate commerce would not also bear ... A failure of internal consistency shows as a matter of law that a State is attempting to take more than its fair share of taxes from the interstate transaction, since allowing such a tax in one State would place interstate commerce at the mercy of those remaining

149 Ibid., 278–80.

150 *Container Corp. v Franchise Tax Bd.*, 463 US 159 (1983).

151 Ibid., 180–1 (emphasis added).

152 *Oklahoma Tax Comm'n v Jefferson Lines*, 514 US 175 (1995).

> States that might impose an identical tax ... External consistency, on the other hand, looks not to the logical consequences of cloning, but to the economic justification for the State's claim upon the value taxed, to discover whether a State's tax reaches beyond that portion of value that is fairly attributable to economic activity within the taxing State. Here, the threat of real multiple taxation (though not by literally identical statutes) may indicate a State's impermissible overreaching.[153]

Finding the Oklahoma law internally consistent,[154] the Court spent much of its time on the external consistency principle; yet it ultimately confirmed its low review standard with regard to particular (State) apportionment formulas. A non-discriminatory State tax would consequently only violate the (dormant) Commerce Clause, where 'the income attributed to the State is in fact *out of all appropriate proportions* to the business transacted ... in that State, or has led to a *grossly distorted result*'.[155] This test resembles the excessive burden test developed for regulatory measures in *Pike*; [156] yet, as we shall in the Conclusion below, the better view sees the fair-apportionment test as part of a federal market model.

Conclusion

The central constitutional instrument for the creation of the American—federal—market has been the Commerce Clause; and the latter is 'perhaps most famous for what it does not say'.[157] The 'negative' side of the Commerce Clause was from the very beginning perceived to automatically outlaw State laws that interfered with interstate commerce. Yet the constitutional rationale underlying the negative force of the Commerce Clause has changed over time. While the Supreme Court originally

[153] Ibid., 184–5.

[154] Ibid., 185: 'If every State were to impose a tax identical to Oklahoma's, that is, a tax on ticket sales within the State for travel originating there, no sale would be subject to more than one State's tax.' For a critical analysis of the internal consistency rule, see: W. Hellerstein, 'Is "Internal Consistency" Foolish?: Reflections on an Emerging Commerce Clause Restraint on State Taxation'.

[155] *Jefferson Lines* (see n. 152), 195.

[156] *American Trucking Association v Michigan Public Service Commission*, 545 US 429 (2005).

[157] L. Heinzerling, 'The Commercial Constitution', 218.

seemed to locate the exclusion of State laws in the idea that interstate commerce constituted an exclusive competence of the Union, subsequent developments split the positive from the negative dimension of the clause and created an independent constitutional prohibition known as the 'dormant' Commerce Clause. Under the *Pike* test, this 'dormant' clause outlaws both discriminatory State measures as well as State laws that excessively burden interstate commerce; and the excessive burden test here follows a *national* market philosophy. Importantly, under either prong of the test, States can justify their trade-restricting measures by reference to an open-ended number of legitimate policy grounds; yet, for discriminatory measures, the Court has developed a presumption of virtual per se illegality, whereas for non-discriminatory measures a margin of discretion is conceded to the States.

This *Pike* test has been primarily developed for regulatory barriers to trade. Fiscal measures, by contrast, were subject to a distinct doctrinal evolution that has found expression in the *Complete Auto* test. Fiscal barriers to trade will here escape the Commerce Clause if they fulfil four conditions: two jurisdictional and two substantive in nature. First, a State must justify its 'jurisdictional' nexus with the tax imposed and, second, it must be able to point to a (nominal) benefit that the taxpayer receives in exchange. Once these two criteria are fulfilled, a State tax is then subjected to two substantive conditions. For a State tax must not discriminate against out-of-State goods (or persons), and non-discriminatory taxes must be fairly apportioned. The fair-apportionment criterion here operates, to some extent, as the functional equivalent of the second prong of the *Pike* test for regulatory measures. Yet unlike the *Pike* excessive burden test, the fair apportionment criterion has a 'federal' aspect. For the excessive burden is not so much seen as a consequence of the (unilateral) State law. It is rather considered as the result of multiple States imposing their parallel fiscal 'sovereignty'. Importantly, then, the Supreme Court does not seem to apply a 'national' test that prohibits all double taxation. But on the contrary, in the past, it has granted the States a degree of freedom in choosing their own apportionment formulas—as long as the State tax 'reasonably reflects the in-State component of the activity being taxed'.[158]

[158] *Goldberg v Sweet*, 488 US 252 (1989), 262.

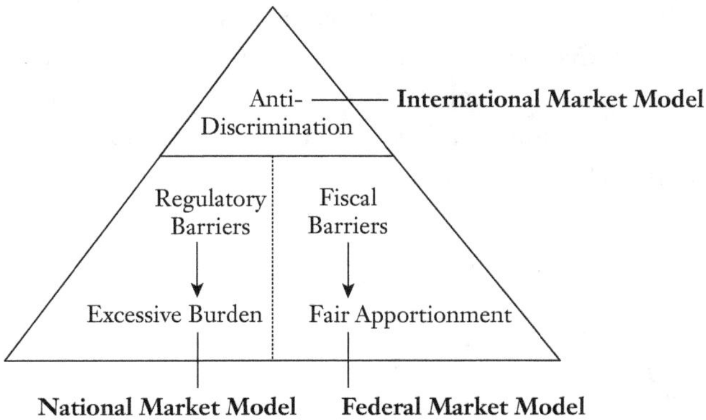

Figure 3. Market models under the Commerce Clause

National fiscal harmonization is thus a constitutional task reserved for the Union legislature.

How best, then, to characterize the structure of the US American 'common market'? Is it a 'national' common market,[159] which is based on the philosophy that 'our economic unit is the Nation';[160] or is it better seen as a 'federal free trade unit',[161] because the 'very purpose of the Commerce Clause was to create an area of free trade among the several States'?[162] As we saw above, the jurisprudence of the Supreme Court has confirmed a number of different tests: a discrimination test informed by an *international* market model is joined by a an excessive burden test that is based on a *national* market philosophy, while the fair-apportionment criterion for fiscal measures, finally, contains elements of a *federal* market model (see Figure 3). Nonetheless: in light of the general nature of the excessive burden test for all regulatory measures, the

[159] In *Hunt v Washington State Apple Advertising Comm'n* (see n. 56), 350, the US Supreme Court speaks of 'the Commerce Clause's overriding requirement of a national "common market"'.

[160] *H. P. Hood & Sons, Inc. v Du Mond*, 336 US 525 (1949), 537–8: 'This principle that our economic unit is the Nation, which alone has the gamut of powers necessary to control of the economy, including the vital power of erecting customs barriers against foreign competition, has as its corollary that the States are not separable economic units.'

[161] In this sense also: ibid., 538: 'federal free trade unit'.

[162] *Boston Stock Exchange v State Tax Comm'n*, 429 US 318 (1977), 328.

overall structure of the American market is best characterized as that of a 'unitary national market'.[163] States can regulate and burden interstate commerce—but not too much;[164] and the 'how much' is ultimately determined by a single Union standard, whether determined by the judiciary or the legislature.[165]

[163] *West Lynn Creamery v Healy* (see n. 123), 193.

[164] In the famous joke by Thomas Powell: if there was to be a Restatement of constitutional law on the Commerce Clause it would state: 'Congress may regulate interstate commerce ... The States may also regulate interstate commerce, but not too much ... How much is too much is beyond the scope of this restatement.' See: P. A. Freund, Foreword to T. R. Powell, *Vagaries and Varieties in Constitutional Interpretation*, ix.

[165] Despite this 'national' reading of the Commerce Clause, the latter has—importantly—always been perceived as a structural limit on State powers and not as an individual right. See especially: J. N. Eule, 'Laying the Dormant Commerce Clause to Rest', 443: 'The Framers unquestionably rejected free trade as a constitutionally protected value. Invalidation of State commercial legislation can only, therefore, be done on some basis other than its interference with the "right" of an individual or corporation to engage in interstate trade unhindered by government restriction.' The Commerce Clause here contrasts to other provisions within the Constitution, and especially the due process provisions under the Fourteenth Amendment. The Fourteenth Amendment (1868), Section 1 states: 'All persons born or naturalized in the United States, and subject to the jurisdiction thereof, are citizens of the United States and of the State wherein they reside. No State shall make or enforce any law which shall abridge the privileges or immunities of citizens of the United States; nor shall any State deprive any person of life, liberty, or property, without due process of law; nor deny to any person within its jurisdiction the equal protection of the laws.' Prior to the New Deal, the Supreme Court had here steered a controversial course of 'economic due process'—the most famous manifestation of which is *Lochner v New York*, 198 US 45 (1905). In this case, an employer had violated a New York State statute limiting the maximum number of working hours for bakers; and he challenged the State law under the Fourteenth Amendment as an undue interference with his (economic) freedom to contract. Infamously, the Court accepted a substantive due process rationale according to which economic (federal) rights could be enforced as against the States. The judgment received a sever critique in a dissent by Justice Holmes, who famously quipped that '[t]he Fourteenth Amendment does not enact Mr. Herbert Spencer's Social Statistics'. The idea of economic due process however eventually declined (cf. *West Coast Hotel v Parrish*, 300 US 379 (1937)), and today *Lochner* has become a veritable 'pariah' (D. A. Strauss, 'Why was *Lochner* Wrong?', 3744) with the (then) Supreme Court being seen as superimposing its laissez-faire philosophy on the democratic will of the State legislatures. The reaction against the Supreme Court was indeed so strong that the counter-majoritarian difficulty became the cornerstone of American constitutional thinking about judicial review. For a more general discussion of the relationship between democracy and judicial review in the creation of common markets, see the *Epilogue* in this volume.

SPECIAL PART

The Changing Structure of European Law

3

The Decline of the International Model

Introduction

The various expressions of European cooperation after the Second World War formed part of a general transition within international law from a law of *coexistence* to a law of *cooperation*.[1] Within Europe's economic sphere, this development began with the 1948 Organisation for European Economic Cooperation (OEEC). The latter had brought together sixteen European States to administer the post-Second-World-War aid offered by the United States for European reconstruction.[2] European economic *integration* however started somewhere else, namely: the 1951 Treaty of Paris establishing the European Coal and Steel Community (ECSC).[3] The idea to integrate the coal and steel industries had—after a strong American suggestion—come from France.[4] The French Foreign Minister, Robert Schuman, explained 'his' plan to build the European Community for Coal and Steel on 9 May 1950 as follows:

> Europe will not be made all at once, nor according to a single, general plan. It will be formed by taking measures which work primarily to bring about real solidarity. The gathering of the European nations requires the elimination of the age-old opposition of France and Germany. The action to be taken must first of all concern these two countries. With this aim in view, the French Government proposes to take immediate action on one limited but decisive point. The French Government proposes that Franco-German production of coal and steel be placed under a common [Commission], within an organisation open to the participation of the other

[1] W. G. Friedmann, *The Changing Structure of International Law*.

[2] The 'European Recovery Programme', also known as the 'Marshall Plan', was named after the (then) Secretary of State of the United States, George C. Marshall. Article 1 of the OEEC Treaty stated: 'The Contracting Parties agree to work in close cooperation in their economic relations with one another. As their immediate task, they will undertake the elaboration and execution of a joint recovery programme.'

[3] For a detailed discussion of the negotiations leading up to the signature of the ECSC Treaty, see: H. Mosler, 'Der Vertrag über die Europäische Gemeinschaft für Kohle und Stahl'.

[4] This is how the (then) US Secretary of State, Dean Acheson, wrote to the French Foreign Minister, Robert Schuman: 'Whether Germany will in the future be a benefit or a curse to the free world will be determined, not only by Germany, but by the occupying powers. No country has a greater stake than France in the answer. Our own stake and responsibility is also great. Now is the time for French initiative and leadership of the type required to integrate the German Federal Republic promptly and decisively into Western Europe ... We here in America, with all the will in the world to help and support, cannot give the lead. That, if we are to succeed in this joint endeavour, must come from France.' (US Department of State, Foreign Relations of the United States (Government Printing Office, 1974), vol. III (1949), 623 and 625.)

European nations. *The pooling of coal and steel production will immediately ensure the establishment of common bases for economic development as a first step in the federation of Europe*[.][5]

The resulting European Coal and Steel Community would have six founding Member States: Belgium, France, Germany, Italy, Luxembourg, and the Netherlands. It was designed to *integrate* a critical industrial sector and to thereby 'remove the main obstacle to an economic partnership'.[6] The pooling of the war industries was however only a first step; and a plan to extend the integration project to the economy as whole was soon made. Economic integration *writ large* was consequently discussed in 1955 at a conference in Messina—a conference that charged Paul-Henry Spaak to produce a report on the advantages of a European 'common market'. The 'Spaak Report' described these advantages as follows:

By establishing a common market we shall construct an enormous economic space in which the conditions for a common economic policy will be created. The latter will—built by the unity of powerful forces of production—aim at a continuous expansion, an increase in stability, an accelerated raising of the standard of living and the development of harmonious relations between the States. These aims can be achieved through a unification of diverse markets; and a better division of labour will here not only prevent a misuse of production forces but the greater security in the production of goods will also allow us to close production processes that are run without regard to their costs ... *And even if we much desire a far-reaching liberalisation of world trade, for the reason set out above, a true common market can only be created by a limited group of States—although their number should be as big as the creation of such a common market would allow.*[7]

European economic growth and efficiency are here presented as direct consequences of a better division of labour between European nations, which could—mutually—exploit comparative advantages.[8] Yet interestingly, the establishment of a 'true common market' was presented as

[5] Schuman Declaration (Paris, 9 May 1950), reproduced in A. G. Harryvan and J. van der Harst (eds.), *Documents on European Union*, 61 (emphasis added).

[6] J. Gillingham, *Coal, Steel, and the Rebirth of Europe, 1945–1955: The Germans and French from Ruhr Conflict to Economic Community*, 298.

[7] Bericht der Delegationsleiter ('Spaak Report'), in R. Schulze and T. Hoeren (eds.), *Dokumente zum Europäischen Recht*, Volume 1: *Gründungsverträge*, 752 at 755–6 (my translation, emphasis added).

[8] For the two classic studies on the advantages of an international division of labour, see: A. Smith, *Wealth of Nations*; and D. Ricardo, *The Principles of Political Economy and Taxation*. For a discussion of both masterpieces, see: Chapter 1, Section I(2) of this volume.

requiring a limited number of States so as to allow for the—simultaneous—establishment of a common economic *policy*.

Based on these Messina recommendations, the 1957 Treaty establishing the European Economic Community (EEC) embraced the idea of a comprehensive 'common market'. The central task(s) of the new Community was thus defined as follows:

> The Community shall have as its task, *by establishing a common market and progressively approximating the economic policies of Member States*, to promote throughout the Community a harmonious development of economic activities, a continuous and balanced expansion, an increase in stability, an accelerated raising of the standard of living and closer relations between the States belonging to it.[9]

The centrality of the 'common market' idea for the young EEC simply cannot be exaggerated.[10] It would thereby go well beyond the idea of a 'Free Trade Area' and a 'Customs Union',[11] because the EEC was from the start committed to 'the abolition, as between Member States, of obstacles to freedom of movement for persons, services and capital'.[12] The European common market would indeed aim at the establishment of all four fundamental freedoms, which—once established—would transform the national markets into 'an enormous economic space in which the conditions for a common economic policy will be created'.

But what was the structure of this European common market? Did the 1957 EEC Treaty here follow the international structures established by the 1947 General Agreement on Tariffs and Trade (GATT); or did it wish to gradually establish a 'national' market like in the United States? The Special Part of this book explores these questions in four chapters. The aim of this particular chapter is to present a first overview of the divers textual tools offered to the (old) EEC—and today, the European Union—to integrate the diverse markets of the Member States into a common European market. And concentrating on Europe's 'dormant Commerce Clause', it will claim that the EEC initially followed an international

9 Ex-Article 2 EEC (emphasis added).

10 The association between the young European Economic Community and 'The Common Market' was so strong that the latter provided for a long time a handy shortcut for the EEC writ large. The best illustrations here continue to be two academic journals that have shaped the discipline, namely: the '*Common Market* Law Review', and the 'Journal of *Common Market* Studies'.

11 For a brief discussion of these concepts, see: Chapter 1, Section II(2/d/bb) of this volume.

12 Ex-Article 3(c) EEC.

market model, whose philosophy was closely inspired by the solutions offered by the GATT. This only changed with the judicial invention of a federal model in *Cassis de Dijon*.[13] The rise of this federal model will be discussed in Chapters 4 and 5 for regulatory measures, while Chapter 6 argues that the EU has—like the US—also come to establish special regimes for fiscal barriers to trade.

I. Creating the European Market: A Constitutional Overview

How would the European Economic Community create a 'common' market out of 'diverse' national markets?[14] To create a 'European' market, the EEC Treaty had adopted a dual strategy: negative and positive integration.[15] The Community was—first—tasked to 'free' its (future) common market from national barriers to trade in goods, persons, services, and capital. This strategy of negative integration was complemented by a—second—strategy: positive integration. The Community was thus to positively pursue common 'policies' to establish and regulate its common market. Such market regulation would principally take place through harmonization; and for that purpose, the EEC Treaty enumerated a number of 'legislative' competences that allowed the Community to adopt secondary law.

What were the provisions governing the free movement of goods within the EEC Treaty? While reserving a special title to agricultural goods,[16] the Treaty drafters had decided to split the legal regime for industrial goods over two sites, as can be seen in Table 1.

[13] Case 120/78, *Rewe-Zentral AG v Bundesmonopolverwaltung für Branntwein ('Cassis de Dijon')*.

[14] In light of the historical exploration that is the aim of this first section, I shall primarily describe the legal structures of the 1957 Rome Treaty that created the 'European Economic Community'. Most of the original Treaty provisions on the common market have, apart from their number, changed little in terms of substance but I will of course point to relevant textual changes as well as the post-Lisbon article number.

[15] J. Pinder, 'Positive and Negative Integration: Some Problems of Economic Union in the EEC'.

[16] Part II, Title II: 'Agriculture'. For early discussions of the Common Agricultural Policy, see: P. Baumann, 'Common Organizations of the Market and National Law'; J. Usher, 'The Effects of Common Organisations and Policies on the Powers of a Member State'; G. Berardis, 'The Common Organization of Agricultural Markets and National Price Regulations'.

Table 1. Goods: structure of the 1957 EEC Treaty

Part II—Title I. Free Movement of Goods	Part III—Title I. Common Rules
Chapter 1: The Customs Union	**Chapter 1: Rules on Competition**
Section 1. Elimination of Customs Duties	Section 1. Rules applying to Undertakings
Section 2. Common Customs Tariff	Section 2. Dumping
Chapter 2: Quantitative Restrictions	Section 3. Aids granted by States
	Chapter 2: Tax Provisions
	Chapter 3: Approximation of Laws

The constitutional system governing goods within the EEC Treaty thereby made a number of systemic choices from the beginning. The most important GATT-consistent choice related to the structure of the Treaty chapter dedicated to the 'customs union'. For instead of placing the provisions on the 'Common Customs Tariff' into Part III of the Treaty,[17] the 'negative' and the 'positive' aspect of the customs union were placed—together—into one chapter within Part II. The EEC Treaty here strictly followed the structure suggested by Article XXIV GATT, which distinguished between an 'internal' and an 'external' aspect of a customs union.[18] And to qualify under the regional exception offered by the GATT provision, the Community committed itself to the abolition of all internal customs duties, while a common external tariff was to be created.

Secondly, the EEC Treaty also contained a chapter on quantitative restrictions that was modelled on Article XI GATT.[19] The chapter within the Treaty Title on the Free Movement of Goods thereby dealt with regulatory—not fiscal—matters and here distinguished between import

[17] Title II ('Economic Policy') of Part III here contained a third chapter specifically dedicated to the establishment of a 'Commercial Policy'.

[18] For the (partial) text of Article XXIV GATT, see: Chapter 1, Section II(2/d/bb) of this volume.

[19] For this point, see: H. von der Groeben et al. (eds.), *Kommentar zum EWG-Vertrag*, 134: 'Die dieser Zollunion im Sinne des Kapitels 1 noch mangelnde GATT-Konformität (Art. XXIV des GATT) wird durch Kapitel 2 hergestellt, das parallel zum Binnenzollabbau die Beseitigung der mengenmäßigen Beschränkungen und anderer Handelsschranken zwischen den Mitgliedstaaten regelt[.]'

restrictions and export restrictions, while also offering a justificatory clause specifically reserved for both forms of quantitative restrictions.

Yet surprisingly, and unlike the GATT solution, the Treaty Title on goods did not contain a general prohibition demanding—like Article III GATT—the equal treatment of imported goods. The reason for this absence may have been the presence of a general non-discrimination clause covering all four freedoms and placed at the very beginning of the EEC Treaty.[20] But there may also have existed a second reason. For in line with the idea of a customs union, the particular Treaty Title on goods had chosen to assimilate third-country goods in 'free circulation',[21] and the absence of a national treatment clause here might have signalled a wish *not* to extend all the benefits of the common market to goods from outside. Instead, the Treaty drafters placed a good-specific national treatment principle into Part III of the Treaty;[22] yet this provision was confined to *fiscal* measures, and it therefore seemed that no equivalent of Article III GATT existed with regard to *regulatory* measures.

[20] Ex-Article 7 EEC stated: 'Within the scope of application of this Treaty, and without prejudice to any special provisions contained therein; any discrimination on grounds of nationality shall be prohibited. The Council may, on a proposal from the Commission and after consulting the Assembly, adopt, by a qualified majority, rules designed to prohibit such discrimination.'

[21] According to ex-Article 9(2) EEC, the assimilation of third-country goods only applied to (parts) of Chapter 1 and Chapter 2 of Part II of the EEC Treaty; and the assimilation principle would therefore—a priori—not reach outside these provisions.

[22] According to its wording, ex-Article 95 EEC clearly did not apply to third-country goods in free circulation, as it was expressly confined to 'products of other Member States'—a formulation that excluded goods from third States even if in free circulation. However, twenty years later, in Case 193/85, *Cooperativa Co-Frutta Srl v Amministrazione delle finanze dello Stato*, the Court would align ex-Article 95 EEC with the free-movement-of-goods part of the Treaty, see: paras. 28–9: 'It follows that any interpretation of [ex-] Article 95 which precluded it from applying to products in free circulation would lead to a result which would be contrary both to the spirit of the Treaty expressed in [ex-]Articles 9 and 10 and to the system of the Treaty. Commercial policy with regard to non-member countries falls within the exclusive competence of the Community, subject to the requisite protective measures which may be taken under the conditions laid down in [ex-]Article 115 of the Treaty. Consequently, Member States cannot remain free to charge discriminatory taxation on products which originated in non-member countries but are in free circulation in the Community. The fourth question must therefore be answered in the following terms: [ex-]Article 95 of the EEC Treaty covers all products coming from Member States, including products originating in non-member countries which are in free circulation in the Member States.'

Fourthly, the most important divergence from the GATT arrangement however related to the existence of a Treaty chapter dedicated to the approximation of national laws so as to positively integrate the European common market. The central provision here entitled the Community to adopt measures 'for the approximation of such laws, regulations or administrative provisions of the Member States *as directly affect the establishment or functioning of the common market*'.[23] This competence covered regulatory as well as fiscal measures; and it seemed—on its face—to be partly inspired by the US American 'Commerce Clause'.[24] Would this in turn inspire the European Court of Justice to develop a 'dormant'—negative—side to this positive competence, which would outlaw discriminatory national measures?

Let us look at this question, as well as many others, by exploring in greater detail the four constitutional choices made by the 1957 Rome Treaty. In line with the structure of that Treaty, we shall start with fiscal barriers to trade and only subsequently explore the provisions on regulatory barriers in the European common market.

1. *Fiscal Barriers to Trade: (External) Customs and (Internal) Taxes*

a. *Customs Duties and the Common Market*

Customs duties are the classic commercial weapon of the mercantilist State. They are designed to 'protect' domestic goods and to financially support the importing State.[25] Customs duties are, as we saw above, not per se prohibited under (cooperative) international law.[26] The European Economic Community, by contrast, was to be 'based upon a customs union' that was founded on 'the *prohibition* between Member States of customs duties on imports and exports and of all charges having equivalent effect'.[27] The *elimination* of all customs barriers for goods originating in the Member States was to be complemented by the establishment of a common customs tariff for goods coming from third States. These goods, coming from outside the common market, would also enjoy the benefits of free movement once 'the import formalities ha[d] been complied with

[23] Ex-Article 100 EEC (emphasis added).

[24] For a discussion of the US American 'Commerce Clause', see: Chapter 2 of this volume.

[25] On this point, see: Chapter 1, Section I(1) of this volume.

[26] On this point, see: Chapter 1, Section II(2) of this volume.

[27] Ex-Article 9(1) EEC (emphasis added).

and any customs duties or charges having equivalent effect which are payable ha[d] been levied'.[28] Such third-country goods were considered to be 'in free circulation' within the common market under ex-Article 9(2) EEC.

The EEC Treaty had set out detailed rules with regard to the internal and external aspects of the customs union. While the elimination of customs duties between Member States was dealt with in ex-Articles 12–17 EEC, the setting up of the common customs tariff was to be achieved on the basis of ex-Articles 18–29 EEC. The most important provisions with regard to the internal aspect of the customs union were here the prohibition against introducing new customs duties on imports and exports in ex-Article 12 EEC, as well as the obligation to abolish all such customs barriers by 1970 for imports (ex-Article 13) and exports (ex-Article 16). The task of eliminating such barriers was originally seen as a 'political' one,[29] yet with the rise and expansion of the constitutional doctrine of direct effect,[30] the sphere of negative integration soon became the province of the Community judiciary.

The choice of enforcing the customs union through the courts was memorably made in *Van Gend en Loos*.[31] The Court here dealt with ex-Article 12 EEC. The provision simply demanded: 'Member States shall refrain from introducing between themselves any new customs duties on imports or exports or any charges having equivalent effect, and from

[28] Ex-Article 10 (1) EEC. The provision stated in full: 'Products coming from a third country shall be considered to be in free circulation in a Member State if the import formalities have been complied with and any customs duties or charges having equivalent effect which are payable have been levied in that Member State, and if they have not benefited from a total or partial drawback of such duties or charges.'

[29] During the transitional period from 1958 to 1970, the speed and direction of the customs union was to be set by the Community's political organs. Ex-Article 13(2) EEC here stated: 'The Commission shall determine by means of directives the timetable for such abolition. It shall be guided by the rules contained in [ex-]Article 14(2) and (3) and by the directives issued by the Council pursuant to [ex-]Article 14(2).' The Council declared the customs union to be completed, ahead of schedule, by 1 July 1968 (see: Council Decision 66/532 relative à la suppression des droits de douane et à l'interdiction des restrictions quantitatives entre les Etats membres et à la mise en application des droits du tarif douanier commun pour les produits autres que ceux énuméré à l'annexe II du traité ('Accelleration Decision') (1966) OJ 2971/66; as well as: Council Regulation 950/68 on the common customs tariff (1968) OJ L172/1).

[30] On the nature and expansion of the doctrine of direct effect, see: R. Schütze, *European Constitutional Law*, Chapter 3.

[31] Case 26/62, *Van Gend en Loos*.

increasing those which they already apply in their trade with each other.'[32] The Netherlands appeared to have violated this stand-still provision and Van Gend & Loos—a Dutch importing company—brought proceedings in a Dutch court against the National Inland Revenue. Could a private party thus enforce an *international* treaty in a *national* court? The Court famously held that some provisions within the EEC Treaty would indeed have direct effect[33] and, having briefly presented the general scheme of the Treaty in relation to customs duties,[34] the Court focused on the wording of ex-Article 12 EEC and found:

> The wording of [ex-]Article 12 [EEC] contains a *clear and unconditional prohibition* which is not a positive but a *negative obligation*. This obligation, moreover, is *not qualified by any reservation on the part of the States, which would make its implementation conditional upon a positive legislative measure enacted under national law*. The very nature of this prohibition makes it ideally adapted to produce direct effects in the legal relationship between Member States and their subjects. The implementation of [ex-]Article 12 [EEC] does not require any legislative intervention on the part of the States. The fact that under this Article it is the Member States who are made the subject of the negative obligation does not imply that their nationals cannot benefit from this obligation.[35]

While somewhat repetitive, the test for direct effect was clearly presented: wherever the Treaties contained a 'prohibition' that was 'clear' and 'unconditional', that prohibition would have direct effect. To be an unconditional prohibition thereby required two things. First, the provision had to be an *automatic* prohibition—that is, it should not depend on subsequent positive legislation. And secondly, the prohibition should ideally be *absolute*—that is, 'not

[32] The provision has been repealed. Strictly speaking, it is therefore not correct to identify Article 30 TFEU as the successor provision, for the latter is based on ex-Articles 13 and 16 EEC. The normative content of ex-Article 12 EEC solely concerned the introduction of *new* customs duties; and therefore did not cover the abolition of existing tariff restrictions.

[33] Case 26/62, *Van Gend en Loos*, 12 (emphasis added): 'The objective of the EEC Treaty, which is to establish a common market, the functioning of which is of direct concern to interested parties in the Community, implies that this Treaty is *more than an agreement which merely creates mutual obligations between the contracting States* ... The conclusion to be drawn from this is that the Community constitutes a *new legal order of international law* for the benefit of which the States have limited their sovereign rights, albeit within limited fields, and the subjects of which comprise not only Member States but also their nationals. *Independently of the legislation of Member States*, [European] law therefore not only imposes obligations on individuals but is also intended to confer upon them rights which become part of their legal heritage.'

[34] The Court considered ex-Article 12 EEC as an 'essential provision' in the general scheme of the Treaty as it related to customs duties (ibid., 12).

[35] Ibid., 13 (emphasis added).

qualified by any reservation on the part of the States'. This was a—very—strict test; yet ex-Article 12 EEC was 'ideally adapted' to satisfy it. It was a clear prohibition and unconditional in the double sense outlined above.

And yet: if the Court had insisted on a strict application of these three criteria, very few provisions—including the ones in the customs union chapter—would have had direct effect. In its subsequent jurisprudence the Court therefore loosened the test considerably, and—eventually—found that it also covered 'the' central provision governing the customs union. After numerous Treaty amendments, it can today be found in Article 30 of the Treaty on the Functioning of the European Union (TFEU) and states: 'Customs duties on imports and exports and charges having equivalent effect shall be prohibited between Member States. This prohibition shall also apply to customs duties of a fiscal nature.' Within the European Union, all customs duties are consequently—unlike the GATT solution—prohibited; and Article 30 TFEU therefore shares a strong family resemblance to the (original) 'Import–Export Clause' within the US Constitution—discussed earlier in this book.[36]

b. Discriminatory Taxation and the Common Market

Within the EEC Treaty Title on 'Common Rules' and following a first chapter on competition, a second chapter contained a collection of tax provisions. This was no accident. Indeed, the purpose of these provisions was primarily to ensure equal competition within the Common Market.[37]

The Treaty's tax chapter was thereby confined to taxes on *goods*.[38] It was 'formulated in the most limiting kind of language', and it therefore depended greatly on what the Community institutions would make of its bare textual bones.[39] The central provisions within that chapter were ex-Articles 95 and 96 EEC. The former prohibited all discriminatory taxation of goods *imported* from other Member States, while the latter provided that tax refunds for *exported* goods should not exceed the internal taxation imposed on them.[40] (This seemed to leave exports in a much weaker position. But the Court subsequently extended the scope of ex-Article 95

[36] For the text of the 'Import–Export Clause', see: Chapter 2, Section II(1) of this volume.

[37] Advocate General Grand in Case 31/67, *Firma August Stier v Hauptzollamt Hamburg-Ericus*, 165.

[38] Case 20/76, *Schöttle & Söhne OHG v Finanzamt Freudenstadt.*

[39] W. Hallstein, *Europe in the Making*, 157.

[40] This prohibition of export subsidies in ex-Article 96 EEC was complemented by the Treaty's anti-dumping provision in ex-Article 91 EEC. Ex-Article 96 EEC was not seen to impose a general obligation to reimburse internal taxes and charges when goods were imported.

to cover the discriminatory tax treatment of *exports*.[41]) Finally, ex-Articles 97–99 EEC specifically dealt with turnover taxes and other forms of indirect taxation and here particularly encouraged their harmonization.[42]

The key prohibition on discriminatory taxation, originally within ex-Article 95 EEC, can today be found in Article 110 TFEU and states:

> No Member State shall impose, directly or indirectly, on the products of other Member States any internal taxation of any kind in excess of that imposed directly or indirectly on similar domestic products. Furthermore, no Member State shall impose on the products of other Member States any internal taxation of such a nature as to afford indirect protection to other products.[43]

See: Case 27/74, *Demag AG v Finanzamt Duisburg-Süd*, para. 7: 'This difference is confirmed by [ex-]Article 96 [EEC] which provides that where products are exported to the territory of any Member State, any repayment of internal taxation shall not exceed the internal taxation imposed on them, whether directly or indirectly and thus leaves open the question whether Member States have the power to reduce the amount of the repayment, a measure which could, however, affect Community trade.'

[41] Case 142/77, *Statens Kontrol med ædle Metaller v Preben Larsen; Flemming Kjerulff v Statens Kontrol med ædle Metaller*, paras. 21–6: 'The wording of [ex-]Article 95 refers only to the discriminatory application of systems of internal taxation to products imported from other Member States. The application of the same systems of taxation to exports is referred to in [ex-]Articles 96 to 98 from the point of view of the repayment of excessive taxation which may distort conditions of trade within the common market. It follows from a comparison of those provisions that the aim of the Treaty in this field is to guarantee generally the neutrality of systems of internal taxation with regard to intra-Community trade whenever an economic transaction going beyond the frontiers of a Member State at the same time constitutes the chargeable event giving rise to a fiscal charge within the context of such a system. It therefore seems necessary to interpret [ex-]Article 95 as meaning that the rule against discrimination which forms the basis of that provision also applies when the export of a product constitutes, within the context of a system of internal taxation, the chargeable event giving rise to a fiscal charge. It would in fact be incompatible with the system of the tax provisions laid down in the Treaty to acknowledge that Member States, in the absence of an express prohibition laid down in the Treaty, are free to apply in a discriminatory manner a system of internal taxation to products intended for export to other Member States. Although it is true that as a general rule the States have no interest in curbing their exports by measures of that kind, it is however impossible to rule out the possibility of such discrimination in cases such as the export of rare products which are particularly valuable or especially sought after.'

[42] Ex-Article 99 EEC stated: 'The Commission shall consider how the legislation of the various Member States concerning turnover taxes, excise duties and other forms of indirect taxation, including countervailing measures applicable to trade between Member States, can be harmonised in the interest of the common market. The Commission shall submit proposals to the Council, which shall act unanimously without prejudice to the provisions of [ex-]Articles 100 and 101.'

[43] The provision was held to be directly effective in Case 57/65, *Lütticke GmbH v Hauptzollamt Sarrelouis*, 210: 'This prohibition is therefore complete, legally perfect and consequently

Like its GATT counterpart, the provision was designed to outlaw discriminatory and protectionist taxation systems; yet, unlike the GATT regime,[44] the European Treaty contained no express justifications for such illegal taxes. Its principal function was to complement the provision(s) on the customs union: while the latter were confined to the review of national measures imposing a charge on goods when crossing an *external* State frontier, Article 110 would apply to (discriminatory) *internal* State taxation. The two constitutional regimes were therefore—from the very start—seen as mutually exclusive.[45] The customs union regime was designed to outlaw measures that were *distinctly* applicable to imports, whereas Article 110 was designed to apply to *indistinctly* applicable measures—that is, measures that equally applied to foreign and domestic goods.[46]

2. *Regulatory Barriers to Trade: (External) Restrictions and (Internal) Harmonization*

a. Quantitative Restrictions and the Common Market

The second chapter within the Treaty Title on the 'Free Movement of Goods' dealt with the 'Elimination of Quantitative Restrictions between Member States'. Designed to patrol regulatory barriers to trade, the chapter comprised seven provisions. Ex-Articles 30 and 34 EEC contained the two general prohibitions that outlawed—respectively—quantitative restrictions on imports and exports, while ex-Article 36 contained a general justification clause for national measures pursuing a legitimate policy objective. These provisions were complemented by ex-Articles 31–33 and 35, which set out more specific obligations as well as a timetable for the removal of

capable of producing direct effects on the legal relationships between the Member States and persons within their jurisdiction. The fact that this Article describes the Member States as being subject to the obligation of non-discrimination does not imply that individuals cannot benefit from it.' This was confirmed in Case 27/67, *Firma Fink-Frucht GmbH v Hauptzollamt München-Landsbergerstrasse*.

[44] Article XX GATT covers also discriminatory tax measures. For the text of the provision, see: Chapter 1, Section II(2/d/aa) of this volume.

[45] Case 57/65, *Lütticke GmbH v Hauptzollamt Sarrelouis*. For an elaboration of this point, see: Chapter 6 of this volume.

[46] The dividing line may however be hard to draw, especially with regard to formally discriminatory internal taxes. See, for example, Case 29/72, *Marimex v Italian Finance Administration*. For an elaboration of this point, see: Chapter 6 of this volume.

quantitative restrictions; and ex-Article 37 finally concerned the progressive adjustment of State monopolies of a commercial character.

Despite some editorial changes following various Treaty amendments, the central prohibitions on quantitative restrictions have remained remarkably stable. They can today be found in Articles 34 and 35 TFEU and state as follows:

> Quantitative restrictions on *imports* and all measures having equivalent effect shall be prohibited between Member States.
>
> Quantitative restrictions on *exports*, and all measures having equivalent effect, shall be prohibited between Member States.[47]

Following the GATT solution, Articles 34 and 35 TFEU were designed to apply exclusively to regulatory measures.[48] But what types of regulatory measures were to be caught? The provisions were clearly designed to cover quotas as well as import and export bans;[49] yet interpretive uncertainty arose with regard to the concept of 'measures having equivalent effect' to quantitative restrictions (MEEQR). The concept appeared intended to parallel the customs concept of 'charges having an equivalent effect' to customs duties; and it could therefore be argued that, in line with Article XI GATT, it was confined to 'border measures'. Indeed, in the absence of any reference to discrimination in Articles 34 and 35 TFEU,[50] it seemed that

[47] Emphasis added. The Court originally denied the direct effect of Articles 34 and 35 during the transitional period in Case 20/64, *Albatros v Société des pétroles et des combustibles liquides (Sopéco)*, 35: 'The Treaty thus does not imply the immediate abrogation of all the measures for controlling imports existing when it entered into force, but does on the other hand involve the prohibition of any new restriction or discrimination, the obligation progressively to abolish existing restrictions and discriminations and the necessity that they should disappear totally at the latest by the end of the transitional period.' The direct effect of both provisions was however subsequently confirmed in Case 8/74, *Procureur du Roi v Benoît and Gustave Dassonville*; and Case 83/78, *Pigs Marketing Board v Raymond Redmond.*

[48] This principal exclusion of fiscal measures was confirmed in Case 7/68, *Commission v Italy*, 430: 'The prohibitions and restrictions in question are by nature clearly distinguished from customs duties and assimilated charges whereby the economic conditions of importation or exportation are affected without restricting the freedom of decision of those involved in commercial transactions.'

[49] In the words of the Court, the provisions covered 'State intervention in intra-[Union] trade by measures in the nature of prohibitions, total or partial, on import, export or transit, according to the circumstances' (ibid., 430).

[50] Discrimination was however expressly mentioned in some specific contexts such as ex-Article 33(1) EEC with regard to the conversion of bilateral into global quotas; and ex-Article 37 EEC applied the idea to the public procurement rules for State monopolies of a commercial character.

'internal measures' that restricted the free movement of goods were meant to be covered by other provisions within the European Treaties.

Be that as it may, the two prohibitions in Articles 34 and 35 were complemented by a general justification clause in Article 36. The latter expressly acknowledged the fact that *regulatory* barriers to trade would often pursue a legitimate *regulatory* interest. These legitimate interests were set out as follows:

> The provisions of Articles 34 and 35 shall not preclude prohibitions or restrictions on imports, exports or goods in transit justified on grounds of public morality, public policy or public security; the protection of health and life of humans, animals or plants; the protection of national treasures possessing artistic, historic or archaeological value; or the protection of industrial and commercial property. Such prohibitions or restrictions shall not, however, constitute a means of arbitrary discrimination or a disguised restriction on trade between Member States.

The provision was clearly modelled on Article XX GATT but, unlike the latter, the European provision seemed much stricter. It expressly covered only those national laws that restricted the free movement of goods on six—exhaustive—grounds, while the last sentence of Article 36 further stipulated that any restrictions must not 'constitute a means of arbitrary discrimination or a disguised restriction on trade between Member States'. This replicated the 'chapeaux' in Article XX GATT (almost) verbatim—and revealed the intellectual proximity of both provisions.[51]

b. Legislative Approximation and the Common Market

Unlike the international regime governing the 1947 GATT, the founding fathers of the 1957 Rome Treaty had originally envisaged that the creation of the European common market was to be achieved by *two* complementary means. The EEC Treaty would itself—directly or indirectly—'negate' particularly restrictive national barriers to interstate trade,[52] while other obstacles within the common market would fall into the 'positive' integration sphere. The latter was based on the belief that the Community's political organs should gradually adopt positive harmonization measures that would approximate those national laws within the Member States that hindered free movement. To that effect, the Rome Treaty contained a special

[51] According to a most authoritative source, the formulation within the second sentence of ex-Article 36 EEC 'ist ohne besonderen Grund dem Art. XX des GATT entnommen worden' (H. von der Groeben et al. (eds.), *Kommentar zum EWG- Vertrag*, 293).

[52] Ex-Article 3(a)–(c) of the original EEC Treaty.

chapter dedicated to the 'approximation of laws' immediately following the 'Tax Provisions' within the Treaty.[53] Its central provision stated:

> The Council shall, acting unanimously on a proposal from the Commission, issue directives for the approximation of such provisions laid down by law, regulation or administrative action in Member States *as directly affect the establishment or functioning of the common market*.[54]

The article offered the Community a legislative competence that shared a family resemblance with the US 'Commerce Clause'. Yet unlike the latter, the textual potential for a 'dormant' aspect that could—directly—eliminate obstacles to trade was much lower. For in expressly linking the 'establishment or functioning of the common market' to positive action by the Council, it seemed unlikely that the Court would give the provision direct effect—despite an early suggestion that ex-Article 100 EEC offered an exclusive competence to the Community.[55] And since the provision would apply to fiscal as well as regulatory measures, it seemed furthermore unlikely—also in light of ex-Article 95 EEC—that the Community would develop a general non-discrimination principle on the basis of this provision. The principal task behind ex-Article 100 was consequently soon seen to remove obstacles to interstate trade that arose from the *un*-harmonized coexistence of national laws. It was—like ex-Article 101 EEC[56]—designed

[53] For early literature on the harmonization competence of the Community, see: M. Seidel, 'Aktuelle Probleme der Rechtsangleichung gemäß Art.100 EWG-Vertrag'; T. W. Vogelaar, 'The Approximation of the Laws of Member States under the Treaty of Rome'; F. Marx, *Funktion und Grenzen der Rechtsangleichung nach Art.100 EWG-Vertrag*; G. Close, 'Harmonisation of Laws: Use or Abuse of the Powers under the EEC Treaty'; R. Starkowski, *Die Angleichung technischer Rechtsvorschriften und industrieller Normen in der Europäischen Wirtschaftsgemeinschaft*; and W. Schmeder, *Die Rechtsangleichung als Integrationsmittel der Europäischen Gemeinschaft*.

[54] Ex-Article 100 EEC (emphasis added).

[55] C.F. Ophüls, 'Die Geltungsnormen des Europäischen Gemeinschaftsrechts', 22 (my translation): 'The answer to the question how the Community legal order and the national legal orders relate is simple: the Member States and the European Community stand, their respective jurisdiction delimited by policy areas, side by side ... The Community is sovereign over those areas that have been transferred to it; the Member States are sovereign over those areas that they have retained ... Legislative power can either exclusively belong to the States (as part of their original sovereignty) or exclusively belong to the Community (when transferred).' And see already: Case 30/59, *De Gezamenlijke Steenkolenmijnen in Limburg v High Authority of the European Coal and Steel Community*, 22: 'In the Community field, namely in respect of everything that pertains to the pursuit of the common objectives within the Common Market, the institutions of the Community have been endowed with exclusive authority.'

[56] The provision stated: 'Where the Commission finds that a difference between the provisions laid down by law, regulation or administrative action in Member States is distorting the conditions of competition in the common market and that the resultant distortion needs to be

to attack legislative 'disparities' that directly affected the establishment or functioning of the common market.

II. Europe's 'Dormant Commerce Clause': Article 34 TFEU

How would the young Union remove barriers to the free movement of goods beyond 'border measures'? For fiscal measures, Article 110 TFEU had clearly answered this question: *internal* State taxes would violate the European common market if they discriminated against foreign goods; yet what about *regulatory* measures that applied *indistinctly* to imported as well as domestic goods? Would the anti-discrimination principle apply to them too and, if so, on what textual basis? Or would, in the absence of a goods-specific national treatment clause à la Article III:4 GATT, these internal regulatory barriers have to be harmonized away?

The central purpose of this second section is to show that—in the absence of any better textual candidate—Article 34 TFEU came to combine the scope of Article XI GATT with that of Article III:4 GATT. But not only that: Article 34 soon became 'the' fundamental provision governing the rhythm and structure of the European common market. Yet unlike the—absolutely—dominant view in the literature holds, this did not happen through the '*Dassonville* revolution'.[57] The gradual transition from the 'international' (GATT) solution to a 'federal' market solution only started with *Cassis de Dijon*.[58] For only then did the Court challenge the foundation of the international model—namely, the idea that due to its internal sovereignty, each State retains substantively unrestricted control

eliminated, it shall consult the Member States concerned. If such consultation does not result in an agreement eliminating the distortion in question, the Council shall, on a proposal from the Commission, acting unanimously during the first stage and by qualified majority thereafter, issue the necessary directives. The Commission and the Council may take any other appropriate measures provided for in this Treaty.'

[57] Case 8/74, *Procureur du Roi v Benoît and Gustave Dassonville*. (Almost) every single EU law textbook that I have seen espouses this—wrong—view. This unhistorical interpretation has received its 'canonical' expression in J. H. H. Weiler, 'Epilogue: Towards a Common Law of International Trade', 201. For an extended criticism of that 'theory', see: R. Schütze, *Framing Dassonville: Text and Context in European Law.*

[58] Case 120/78, *Rewe-Zentral AG v Bundesmonopolverwaltung für Branntwein.*

over its own 'internal' market. In order to explore this attack on the intellectual basis of the international model by the '*Cassis* revolution', we shall try to re-establish the academic and institutional context to Article 34 first and then, subsequently, engage with the early judgments of the European Court until *Cassis de Dijon*.

1. *Early Academic and Institutional Views on Article 34*

With the notion of 'quantitative restrictions' having a (relatively) well-defined international meaning, the breadth of Article 34 ultimately hinged on the (relatively) new concept of 'measures having equivalent effect' (MEE).[59] Would that concept, because of its 'equivalence' to quantitative restrictions, be confined to 'border measures' that *distinctly* applied to imports; or would it also cover 'internal measures' that *indistinctly* applied to domestic goods? This question was hotly debated in the early European law literature. Three positions can be distinguished.

A first group of academic scholars saw a clear parallel between the prohibition on customs duties and the prohibition on quantitative restrictions. The notion of MEE within Article 34 was here identified with the equivalent notion of CEE in Article 30—that is, with national laws that *distinctly* applied to imports.[60] (This parallel between the absolute prohibition with regard to customs charges and import restrictions was indeed anchored in the text of the Treaties.[61]) And since Article 34 would only capture measures

[59] R. C. Béraud, 'Les Mesures d'effet équivalent au sens des articles 30 et suivants du Traité de Rome', 266. The ECSC Treaty did not contain the notion of 'MEEQR'. Its Article 4 simply read: 'The following are recognised as incompatible with the common market for coal and steel and shall accordingly be abolished and prohibited within the Community, as provided in this Treaty: (a) import and export duties, or charges having equivalent effect, and quantitative restrictions on the free movement of products … ' The ECSC thus recognized the notion of charge(s) having an equivalent effect to customs duties (CEECD) but it did not expressly acknowledge MEEQRs. However, it is important to remember that Article XI GATT positively refers to 'other measures', in addition to quantitative restrictions, and this can indeed be seen as textually recognizing a prohibition similar to that covered by MEEQR.

[60] For the respective scope of Article 30, see Section I(1/a), as well as Chapter 6, Section I of this volume.

[61] Ex-Article 3(a) EEC indicated that the concept of a 'measure of equivalent effect' was identical for customs duties as well as for quantitative restrictions, for the provision stated that the activities of the Community would include 'the elimination, as between Member States, of customs duties and of quantitative restrictions on the import and exports of goods, *and of all other measures having equivalent effect*'. This combined use of the notion of MEE suggested that the founding fathers had intended the two regimes to run alongside each other;

that *specifically* applied to imports, a comprehensive and absolute definition of MEEQR was suggested. The most important German textbook of that period thus comments:

Because European [Union] law focuses on *restrictions* on the free movement of goods that are created by *measures having equivalent effect* to quantitative restrictions, the jurisprudence of the Court with regard to *measures having equivalent effect* to customs duties can be used to determine their scope. Irrespective of their designation, their way of introduction and their content, the sole criterion here is whether the movement of goods, which constitutes a fundamental objective of the Treaty ([ex-]Articles 3a, 7, 30 EEC), is restricted, hindered or circumvented; and that this would not be the case without these measures. The definition of measures of equivalent effect must be *a comprehensive teleological one*. It is therefore already sufficient to focus on the *potential* effect of a measure without any need to concretely establish its actual effect in each individual case. A potential hindrance of intra-[Union] trade is thus enough.[62]

A second group of scholars, by contrast, insisted on reading Article 34 in light of a discrimination rationale. Looking at the other three fundamental freedoms, and especially the free movement of workers, these authors claimed that Article 34 had to be seen as a specific expression of the general principle of non-discrimination on which the Union was built.[63] Textually, this argument was nonetheless hard to defend. For not only did Article 34 *not* mention discrimination; other provisions within the chapter on quantitative restrictions expressly used the concept,[64] and this strongly pointed away from a discrimination rationale underlying

and if there was any doubt left that the free movement of goods would be thematically closer to the customs union than to the other three fundamental freedoms, why would the 'establishment of a common customs tariff and of a common commercial policy towards third countries' be interspersed in subpara. 3(b), while ex-Article 3(c) only subsequently dealt with 'the abolition, as between Member States, of obstacles to freedom of movement of persons, services and capital'?

[62] H. P. Ipsen, *Europäisches Gemeinschaftsrecht*, 589 (emphasis added, my translation).

[63] M. Seidel, 'Der EWG-rechtliche Begriff der "Maßnahmen gleicher Wirkung wie eine mengenmäßige Beschränkung"', 2086: 'Maßnahmen gleicher Wirkung sind alle nationalen Rechts- und Verwaltungsvorschriften, Verwaltungsübungen und staatliche Einzelanordnungen, die bewirken, daß das Einfuhr—oder Ausfuhrvolumen niedriger gehalten wird, als es ohne sie der Fall wäre, sofern durch sie eingeführte oder zur Ausfuhr bestimmte Waren gegenüber der inländischen Produktion bzw. den zum inländischen Absatz bestimmten Waren diskriminiert werden.' See also: M. Graf, *Der Begriff 'Maßnahmen gleicher Wirkung wie mengenmäßige Einfuhrbeschränkungen' in dem EWG-Vertrag*, 125: 'MglW. sind Diskriminierungen ausländischer Ware.'

[64] On this point, see n. 50 and text.

Article 34. Moreover, unlike some of the other freedoms, Article 34 was not centred on a comparison between imported and domestic goods. Its focus was exclusively on imports and the hindering effect of a national measure on these imports.

A third academic position combined these two alternative readings into a sophisticated synthesis.[65] This 'synthetic' pragmatism rejected—like the first school—the belief that the concept of MEEQR necessitated a discriminatory treatment of imports: 'Articles [34] *et seq.*—like Article[] [30]—prohibit in a general manner between the Member States quantitative restrictions and customs charges without exempting those that do not have an actual effect on imports or those that are not discriminatory.'[66] The prohibition of MEEQR was thus—like the equivalent prohibition on customs duties—an absolute prohibition; yet it was an absolute prohibition that only covered *distinctly* applicable measures.[67] Indistinctly applicable measures, and especially national product requirements, would therefore not constitute MEEQR.[68] The third view however pragmatically recognized an exception to this rule: where a Member State had 'abused' its sovereign right to internally regulate its national market, such arbitrary and unnecessary restrictions on imports would constitute violations of Article 34.

It was this third academic view that came closest to that of the European Commission. Entitled by ex-Article 33(7) EEC to 'issue directives establishing the procedure and timetable' for the abolition of MEEQR, the Commission had adopted its official position in the form of Directive 70/

[65] R. C. Béraud, 'Les Mesures d'effet équivalent'; as well as: P. Ulmer, 'Zum Verbot mittelbarer Einfuhrbeschränkungen im EWG Vertrag'.

[66] R. C. Béraud, 'Les Mesures d'effet equivalent', 286 (my translation).

[67] Ibid., 288.

[68] Ibid., 289. Béraud here expressly rejected the counter-thesis offered by P. VerLoren Van Themaat's 'Bevat Artikel 30 van het EEG-Verdrag slechts een non-discriminatie-beginsel ten aaanzien van invoerbeperkingen'. In his words: 'Ainsi les Etats membres devraient-ils renoncer à des mesures telles qu'un blocage général des prix ou à l'obligation de fermeture des magasins le dimanche puisque de telle mesures peuvent faire obstacle aux importations. Comme il serait pour le moins irréaliste de condamner de telles réglementations, force serait d'interpréter très largement les raisons mentionnées à l'article 36 telles que l'ordre public ou la sécurité publiques et si ces notions sont interprétées d'une manière extensive pour de telles mesures, elles devront nécessairement l'être aussi à l'égard de celles qui frappent les seules importations.' For a contemporary British view, see only: A. Parry and S. Hardy, *EEC Law*, 177: 'There is some doubt, however, as to whether measures applying equally to nationally produced and to imported goods would be caught by Article [34] et seq. The better view would seem to be that they are not so caught.'

50 'on the abolition of measures which have an effect equivalent to quantitative restrictions on imports'.[69] The Directive thereby distinguished between two types of measures. Article 2 dealt with measures that were *not* equally applicable to domestic and imported products and 'which hinder[ed] imports which could otherwise take place'. These were measures that specifically and distinctly affected imports. (And while the Commission here formally endorsed the idea that Article 34 only captured measures that *distinctly* applied to imports; it ingeniously 'smuggled' into that concept a material dimension that came close to a *discrimination* criterion;[70] and in this way it could potentially combine the two opposing views within the academic literature.) However, national marketing measures that were 'applicable equally' to imported and domestic goods were generally not seen as falling into the scope of Article 34. These measures were not MEEQR,[71] *unless* they were shown to be 'abuses' of the internal sovereignty of a State. Article 3 of the Directive here exceptionally extended the concept of MEEQR to 'internal measures' that equally applied to imported and domestic products:

> This Directive also covers measures governing the *marketing of products* which deal, in particular, with shape, size, weight, composition, presentation, identification or putting up and which are equally applicable to domestic and imported products, *where the restrictive effect of such measures on the free movement of goods exceeds the effects intrinsic to trade rules.*
>
> This is the case, in particular, where:
>
> - the restrictive effects on the free movement of goods are out of proportion to their purpose;
> - the same objective can be attained by other means which are less of a hindrance to trade.[72]

[69] (Commission) Directive 70/50/EEC on the abolition of measures which have an effect equivalent to quantitative restrictions on imports and are not covered by other provisions adopted in pursuance of the EEC Treaty (1969) OJ L 13/29. The Directive was based on ex-Article 33 (7) EEC that stated: 'The Commission shall issue directives establishing the procedure and timetable in accordance with which Member States shall abolish, as between themselves, any measures in existence when this Treaty enters into force which have an effect equivalent to quotas.' Interestingly, the Directive clarified that it applied 'to products originating in third countries and put into free circulation in the other Member States' (Directive 70/50, recital 14).

[70] See only: Directive 70/50, Article 2(2): 'Equally, it covers, in particular, measures which favour domestic products or grant them a preference, other than aid, to which conditions may or may not be attached.'

[71] Ibid., recital 8.

[72] Ibid., Article 3 (emphasis added).

Unlike Article XI GATT (and its predecessor),[73] this subjected equally applicable 'internal' measures to the discipline of Article 34. This was however only the case where the restrictive effects of these measures 'exceed[ed] the effects intrinsic to [international] trade rules'. But apart from this—theoretically very exceptional—situation, Directive 70/50 thoroughly followed international law philosophy. For the Directive was principally confined to cover import-related measures, while internal (marketing) measures were generally not considered to fall within the scope of Article 34. The reason for this exclusion derived from the fundamental background premise of the international market model: indistinctly applicable (*internal*) measures do principally not qualify as (*international*) trade rules, as any burden on interstate trade is here seen as '*inherent in the disparities* between rules applied by Member States';[74] and these legislative disparities had to be removed through positive harmonization. Article 34 would, by contrast, only target national measures that *themselves* restricted intra-Union trade; and with regard to equally applicable measures, this would only *exceptionally* be the case, where they had 'a restrictive effect on the free movement of goods *over and above that which is intrinsic to such rules*'.[75]

2. *Early Jurisprudence I: From* International Fruit *to* Dassonville

What would the European Court make of Article 34? Leaving aside the Court's earliest—passing—comments about the free-movement provisions,[76] the first case that directly dealt with Article 34 was *International*

[73] For the text of Article XI GATT and Article 4 of the 1927 Convention on the Abolition of Import and Export prohibitions and Restrictions, see: Chapter 1, Section II of this volume.

[74] Directive 70/50, recital 8 (emphasis added). And to remember: Article 4(7) of the 1927 Convention expressly stated that those prohibitions and restrictions were not (!) prohibited that were simply 'designed to extend to foreign products the regime established within the country in respect of the production of, trade in, and transport and consumption of native products of the same kind'.

[75] Directive 70/50, recital 9. For an application of this idea to indications of origin, see: Written Question 197/69 (M. Deringer) (1969) OJ C151/2: 'De même, une disposition prescrivant l'obligation d'indiquer l'origine aussi bien pour les produits nationaux qu'importés est également susceptible de constituer une mesure d'effet équivalent à des restrictions quantitatives au sens des articles [34] et suivants du traité lorsque ses effets restrictifs sur la libre circulation des marchandises dépassent le cadre des effets propres d'une réglementation en la matière.'

[76] The early cases here are: Case 7/61, *Commission v Italy*; Joined Cases 56–8/64, *Établissements Consten S.à.R.L. and Grundig-Verkaufs-GmbH v Commission*; Case 24/67, *Parke, Davis and Co. v Probel, Reese, Beintema-Interpharm and Centrafarm*; Case 27/67, *Firma Fink-Frucht GmbH v*

Fruit.[77] In this preliminary ruling, the Court was asked whether Articles 34 and 35 would apply to national rules prohibiting the importation of goods without a licence even if the national rules 'in fact are not applied because exemptions are granted from the prohibition and, where this is not so, because the licence is always issued on request'.[78] The Court, in its answer, interestingly distinguished between the intra-Union system for quantitative restrictions and restrictions with regard to third countries and held:

> Under Articles [34 and 35] of the Treaty quantitative restrictions and measures having equivalent effect are prohibited between Member States both with regard to imports and exports. Consequently, apart from the exceptions for which provision is made by [Union] law itself those provisions preclude the application to intra-[Union] trade of a national provision which requires, *even purely as a formality*, import or export licences or any other similar procedure.
>
> *On the other hand in trade with third countries* the application of quantitative restrictions and of measures having equivalent effect forms part of the common commercial policy under Article [207] of the Treaty and the provisions on the common agricultural policy, in particular Article 40[2], which provides for the establishment of 'common machinery for stabilizing imports or exports'.[79]

This judgment was important in two ways. First, the Court clarified that the application of Article 34 depended on whether trade with Member States or trade with non-Member States was involved; and second, it held, with regard to intra-Union trade, that import formalities—even if they had no actual effect on imports—would fall within the scope of Article 34.[80] This was a very important signal: Article 34 would, as a result, not require an actual effect on imports but a potential effect on interstate trade was enough. And while not expressly contradicting Directive 70/50,[81] the Court

Hauptzollamt München-Landsbergerstrasse; Case 13/68, *Salgoil v Italian Ministry of Foreign Trade*; Case 40/70, *Sirena S.r.l. v Eda S.r.l. and others.*

[77] Joined Cases 51–4/71, *International Fruit Company NV and others v Produktschap voor groenten en fruit.*

[78] Ibid., para. 5.

[79] Ibid., paras. 7–10 (emphasis added).

[80] In its written observations, the Dutch government had insisted that only the 'actual application' of the measure could be contrary to Article 34 (ibid., 1112), while the Commission expressly argued that a potential effect on intra-Union trade was enough (ibid., 1113).

[81] Directive 70/50 had suggested in its Article 2(2) that import formalities would, as a rule, not be covered; yet recital 3 also envisaged exceptions to this rule: '[w]hereas the formalities to which imports are subject do not as a general rule have an effect equivalent to that of quantitative restrictions and, consequently, are not covered by this Directive'.

here nonetheless showed its willingness to establish its own—judicial—definition of MEEQR.[82]

In *Geddo v Ente Nazionale Risi*,[83] the Court subsequently tried its hand at a general definition of MEEQR and held:

> The prohibition on quantitative restrictions covers measures which amount to a total or partial restraint of, according to the circumstances, imports, exports or goods in transit. *Measures having equivalent effect not only take the form of restraint described; whatever the description or technique employed, they can also consist of encumbrances having the same effect.*[84]

This suggested that Article 34 covered all 'encumbrances' or hindrances that amounted to even any 'partial restraint' of imports; and this very comprehensive definition was soon joined by a—famous—second one. In *Dassonville*,[85] a family of wholesalers with establishments in France and Belgium had imported eighty-four bottles of Scottish whisky from France to Belgium. The bottles had been purchased on the French market, as French (direct) imports from the United Kingdom were significantly cheaper than Belgian imports coming directly from that (then) third State.[86] The British imports into France had been properly cleared, and a French excise bond duly accompanied the whisky bottles. However, according to Belgian law, all *foreign* spirits bearing a *foreign* designation of origin were required to have that designation officially

[82] The importance of Directive 70/50 as an intellectual pointer for the Court was nonetheless subsequently confirmed in Case 155/73, *Sacchi*. The Court here expressly referred to Article 3 in the context of a national rule that granted a monopoly of commercial advertising to a single national audio-visual body (ibid., para. 8: 'In the same way, the fact that an undertaking of a Member State has an exclusive right to transmit advertisements by television is not as such incompatible with the free movement of products, the marketing of which such advertisements are intended to promote. It would however be different if the exclusive right were used to favour, within the [Union], particular trade channels or particular commercial operators in relation to others. As is stressed by Article 3 of the Commission Directive of 22 December 1969 on the abolition of measures having an effect equivalent to quantitative restrictions on imports and are not covered by other provisions adopted in pursuance of the EEC Treaty, measures governing the marketing of products where the restrictive effect exceeds the effects intrinsic to trade rules are capable of constituting measures having an effect equivalent to quantitative restrictions. Such is the case, in particular, where the restrictive effects are out of proportion to their purpose, in the present case the organization, according to the law of a Member State, of television as a service in the public interest').

[83] Case 2/73, *Geddo v Ente Nazionale Risi*.

[84] Ibid., para. 7 (emphasis added).

[85] Case 8/74, *Procureur du Roi v Benoît and Gustave Dassonville*.

[86] While the case was decided in 1974—that is, after the accession of the United Kingdom—the facts of the case occurred in 1970, when the Kingdom was still a third country.

recognized by the Belgian government. (And since 1934, a Royal Decree even prohibited the importation or sale of any product with a designation of origin—even an accredited one—unless it was accompanied by an official certificate confirming the right to bear the designation.) The Dassonvilles had sold their Scottish whisky bottles without such a certificate, and a Belgian royal prosecutor consequently brought proceedings against them. The Dassonvilles defended themselves by invoking a violation of Article 34 TFEU; and the Court indeed found that this was the case. In the course of a very short judgment, the Court here famously offered an extremely broad definition of measures having an equivalent effect to quantitative restrictions. This *Dassonville* formula stated:

> All trading rules enacted by Member States which are capable of hindering, directly or indirectly, actually or potentially, intra-[Union] trade are to be considered as measures having an effect equivalent to quantitative restrictions.[87]

What did this mean? Did the reference to 'trading rules' deliberately limit the scope of the formula to measures that were, in principle, *distinctly* applicable to imports or exports? (After all, the Belgian law in *Dassonville distinctly* applied to imports!) The meaning of the *Dassonville* formula has, for a long time, been shrouded in mystery; and while this cannot be the place to discuss the context and significance of *Dassonville* in any detail,[88] suffice to say here that the formula was designed to allow the Court to capture quantitative as well as *qualitative* restrictions on imports. Yet as the subsequent section will show, the post-*Dassonville* jurisprudence continued to place Article 34 into a classic international law frame that respected the GATT rules on 'border' and 'internal' measures.

3. *Early Jurisprudence II: From* Dassonville *to* Cassis de Dijon

Was the *Dassonville* formula the radical neo-liberal statement that some want us to believe?[89] Early interpreters of the case hardly thought so;[90] and

[87] *Dassonville* (see n. 85), para. 5.

[88] For an extensive historical discussion, see: R. Schütze, *Framing Dassonville: Text and Context in European Law*.

[89] For the classic (mis)reading, see: J. H. H. Weiler, 'Epilogue: Towards a Common Law of International Trade'.

[90] For early analyses of the judgment, see: R. Joliet, 'EEC Law and Appellations of Origin: The Scotch Whisky Case'; as well as W. Wellinghausen, 'Anmwerkung zu EuGH, Slg. 1974,

while the *Dassonville* definition did rise to become a 'formula',[91] this nevertheless did not mean that the Court applied it as a substantive decision rule for all measures falling within Article 34. On the contrary, a closer analysis of the post-*Dassonville* jurisprudence reveals that the Court used the 'formula' as a general *jurisdictional* rule, which—in parallel to a strategy developed in European competition law[92]—was to allow it to claim that Article 34 was formally 'concerned', while subsequently applying different *substantive* criteria to different categories of rules. And the principal distinction that the Court cultivated in its early jurisprudence was the GATT distinction between 'border measures' and 'internal measures'. [93] In line with the GATT solution, the former would be subject to an absolute test whereas the latter would be subject to a discrimination test.

a. *'Border Measures': Article 34 as an Absolute Prohibition*

A first group of cases immediately following *Dassonville* concern—in GATT terminology—'border measures'. In *Rewe*,[94] for example, the Court dealt with phytosanitary inspections conducted at the national border; and these border inspections were easy prey for the Court. And importantly,

837 ("Dassonville")'; and see also Commission, Eighth General Report of the Activities of the European Communities (1974) (Brussels, 1975), para. 105 ('Measures having equivalent effect'): 'The Commission has been concerned to define the concept "measure having an effect equivalent to quantitative restrictions", notably in the directives adopted in December 1969 on the basis of Article [ex-]33(7) of the EEC Treaty. The Court of Justice confirmed the Commission's interpretation in a judgment given on 11 July in Case 8/74, in which it declared that "every commercial regulation of Member States which is capable of creating, whether directly or indirectly, presently or potentially, barriers to inter-state trade, is to be considered as a measure of equivalent effect to a quantitative restriction". Such confirmation can only be of assistance to the Commission in the numerous cases it is dealing with.'

[91] R. Schütze, *Framing Dassonville: Text and Context in European Law*, esp. Chapter 5.

[92] A central issue within EU competition law in the 1960s (and early 1970s) was the problem of 'parallel imports'; and the question here was whether such qualitative (!) restrictions of competition would be covered by the EU competition law provisions even when they did not—quantitatively—diminish competition. The Court answered this question positively in Joined Cases 56 and 58–64, *Établissements Consten and Grundig-Verkaufs-GmbH v Commission.* The Court here famously held (ibid., 341) that any agreement that was 'capable of constituting a threat, either direct or indirect, actual or potential, to freedom of trade between Member States in a manner which might harm the attainment of the objectives of the single market between States' would—jurisdictionally fall within the scope of European competition law. It is this case—in my view—that constitutes the true source of inspiration behind *Dassonville.*

[93] For an extensive analysis, see: R. Schütze, *Framing Dassonville: Text and Context in European Law*, Chapter 4.

[94] Case 4/75, *Rewe-Zentralfinanz eGmbH v Landwirtschaftskammer.*

the Court did not come to its conclusion on the basis of the *Dassonville* formula alone;[95] it grounded its substantive reasoning in Article 2(2) of Directive 70/50 and held:

> It is clear from the questions put that the phytosanitary inspections in question *only concern importations* of plant products and that similar domestic products, such as apples, are not subject to comparable compulsory examinations for the purpose of distribution. *These inspections thus amount to a condition which is required in respect of imported products only, within the meaning of Article 2(2) of the abovementioned Directive* ... It follows that phytosanitary inspections at the frontier which plant products, such as apples, coming from another Member State are required to undergo, constitute measures having an effect equivalent to quantitative restrictions within the meaning of Article [34] of the Treaty, and are prohibited under that provision subject to the exceptions laid down by [Union] law.[96]

This clear rule against *frontier* inspections was elaborated in *Simmenthal*.[97] The Court here categorically held: 'inspections *at the frontier*—whether carried out systematically or not—on the occasion of the importation ... constitute measures having an effect equivalent to quantitative restrictions within the meaning of Article [34] of the Treaty'.[98] This absolute rule thereby also extended to exports. Thus in line with the absolute prohibition of import formalities established in *International Fruit*, the Court subsequently held: 'Indeed the imposition of any special export formality constitutes an obstacle to trade by the delay which it involves and the dissuasive effect that is has upon exporters.'[99]

Would this absolute rule apply to all goods—including third-country goods in free circulation within the Union? In *Donckerwolke*,[100] Belgian traders had imported Lebanese and Syrian textile products from Belgium into France. The importation of these goods had violated French customs legislation, which required third-country goods to be accompanied by a certificate or origin. Were these customs certificates still allowed in the European customs union? According to Article 28(2) TFEU, they were clearly not;[101] yet the Court made this *theoretical* solution imposed by

[95] The Court cites the formula in para. 3 of the judgment. [96] Ibid., paras. 3–5.

[97] Case 35/76, *Simmenthal SpA v Ministero delle Finanze italiano*.

[98] Ibid., para. 8 (emphasis added). [99] Case 68/76, *Commission v France*, para. 16.

[100] Case 41/76, *Suzanne Criel, née Donckerwolcke and Henri Schou v Procureur de la République au tribunal de grande instance de Lille and Director General of Customs*.

[101] Ibid., paras. 14–23. The main elements of the Court's reasoning here were, in addition to Article 28(2), the *Dassonville* formula (ibid., para. 19), and the more specific judgment in *International Fruit* (ibid., para. 20).

Article 34 'conditional upon the establishment of a common commercial policy'.[102] And the Court thus held:

> *The assimilation to products originating within the Member States of goods in 'free circulation' may only take full effect if these goods are subject to the same conditions of importation both with regard to customs and commercial considerations, irrespective of the State in which they were put in free circulation.* Under Article [207] of the Treaty this unification should have been achieved by the expiry of the transitional period and supplanted by the establishment of a common commercial policy based on uniform principles. The fact that at the expiry of the transitional period the [Union] commercial policy was not fully achieved is one of a number of circumstances calculated to maintain in being between the Member States differences in commercial policy capable of bringing about deflections of trade or of causing economic difficulties in certain Member States.[103]

In essence: since the third-country goods in question did not yet come within a (unified) Common Commercial Policy (CCP),[104] the Member States were '*not* prevented from requiring from an importer a declaration concerning the actual origin of the goods in question even in the case of goods put into free circulation in another Member State'.[105] This general permission was nonetheless—like in *Dassonville* itself—subject to a Union rule of reason.[106] While the certificate of origin would thus '*not in itself* constitute a measure equivalent to a quantitative restriction',[107] it would violate Article 34 if it was excessive in the means to achieve its given end.[108] The Court here confirmed that the scope of Article 34 was—in the absence of a completed CCP—narrower in the context of third-country goods. The scope of Article 34 would consequently depend on whether Member State or third-country goods were involved.[109]

[102] Ibid., para. 24. [103] Ibid., paras. 25–7 (emphasis added). [104] Ibid., para. 6.

[105] Ibid., para. 33.

[106] Ibid., para. 35: 'Nevertheless the Member States may not require from the importer more in this respect than an indication of the origin of the products in so far as he knows it or may reasonably be expected to know it.'

[107] Ibid., para. 41.

[108] Ibid., para. 42. See also; Case 52/77, *Leonce Cayrol v Giovanni Rivoira & Figli*.

[109] The Court had already indicated this solution in Case 86/75, *EMI Records Limited v CBS Grammofon A/S* in the context of intellectual property rights. In this case, the Court confined the assimilating effects of Articles 28 and 29 TFEU to customs matters (ibid., paras. 14–16): 'According to Article [29] of the Treaty products coming from a third country shall be considered to be in free circulation in a Member State if the import formalities

b. 'Internal Measures': Article 34 as a Relative Prohibition

aa. In Particular I: Discriminatory Price-Fixing Measures

The regulation of prices was—from the very beginning—a core problem for Article 34. It was therefore hardly surprising that Directive 70/50 listed a whole range of possible price regulations that could constitute MEEQRs. When dealing with national measures *not* equally applicable to domestic and imported goods, Article 2 of Directive 70/50 thus stated:

> The measures referred to must be taken to include those measures which:
>
> (a) lay down, *for imported products only*, minimum or maximum prices below or above which imports are prohibited, reduced or made subject to conditions liable to hinder importation;
> (b) lay down *less favourable prices for imported products* than for domestic products;
> (c) fix profit margins or any other price components *for imported products only* or fix these differently for domestic products and for imported products, to the detriment of the latter;
> (d) preclude any increase in the price *of the imported product* corresponding to the supplementary costs and charges inherent in importation;
> (e) fix the prices of products *solely on the basis of the cost price or the quality of domestic products* at such a level as to create a hindrance to importation[.][110]

These categories of price measures were perceived as *distinctly* applicable to imports; and the question therefore remained how the Court would eventually deal with *indistinctly* applicable price measures.[111] One such

have been complied with and any customs duties or charges having equivalent effect which are payable have been levied in the importing Member State. According to Article [28(2)] of the Treaty the provisions of Chapter [3 of this Title] shall apply to products coming from third countries which are in free circulation in Member States. Since those provisions only refer to the effects of compliance with customs formalities and paying customs duties and charges having equivalent effect, they cannot be interpreted as meaning that it would be sufficient for products bearing a mark applied in a third country and imported into the [Union] to comply with the customs formalities in the first Member State where they were imported in order to be able then to be marketed in the common market as a whole in contravention of the rules relating to the protection of the mark.' For an extensive discussion of the status of third-country goods in the common market, see: Chapter 5, Section I(1) of this volume.

[110] Directive, 70/50, Article 2 (a)–(e) (emphasis added).

[111] For a brilliant early academic discussion of this question, see: D. Waelbroeck, *Les Réglementations nationales de prix et le droit communautaire*, esp. 40 et seq. See also: K. Winkel, 'Die Vereinbarkeit staatlicher Preislenkungsmaßnahmen mit dem EWG-Vertrag'.

case was *GB Inno.*[112] It concerned a Belgian measure that imposed a fixed consumer price for tobacco products; and in the absence of (agricultural) Union legislation,[113] the Court here began its Article 34 analysis with a reference to the *Dassonville* formula,[114] then pointed to Directive 70/50,[115] but finally settled on the following solution:

> *Although a maximum price applicable without distinction to domestic and imported products does not in itself constitute a measure having an effect equivalent to a quantitative restriction*, it may have such an effect, however, when it is fixed at a level such that the sale of imported products becomes, *if not impossible*, *more difficult than that of domestic products.* On the other hand a system whereby the prices are freely chosen by the manufacturer or the importer as the case may be and imposed on the consumer by a national legislative measure, and whereby no distinction is made between domestic products and imported products, *generally has exclusively internal effects.* However, the possibility cannot be excluded that in certain cases such a system may be capable of affecting intra-[Union] trade.[116]

In essence, indistinctly applicable price measures will not—in themselves—be regarded as MEEQRs, because they generally have exclusively *internal* effects. However, even if formally applicable to imported and domestic goods, these measures will fall within the scope of Article 34 where they (materially) *discriminate* against imports.

This solution was subsequently confirmed in *Van Tiggerle.*[117] A Dutch victualler was accused of selling gin at a price below the minimum price set by a Dutch distillers agency. In the course of the national action against him, he argued that Article 34 was violated; and when asked about this, the

[112] Case 13/77, *G.B.-INNO-B.M. v Association des détaillants en tabac (ATAB).*

[113] For an analysis of this special jurisprudential line, see: R. Schütze, *Framing Dassonville: Text and Context in European Law*, Chapter 4.

[114] Case 13/77, *G.B.-INNO-B.M. v Association des détaillants en tabac (ATAB)*, paras. 46–7: 'Article [34] of the Treaty prohibits in trade between Member States all measures having an effect equivalent to quantitative restrictions. For the purpose of this prohibition it is sufficient that the measures in question are likely to hinder, directly or indirectly, actually or potentially, imports between Member States.'

[115] Ibid., para. 48: 'It should be pointed out that, as stated in Commission Directive No 70/50 of 22 December 1969, "measures, other than those applicable equally to domestic or imported products, which hinder imports which could otherwise take place, including measures which make importation more difficult or costly than the disposal of domestic production" are measures which have an effect equivalent to a quantitative restriction on imports.'

[116] Ibid., paras. 52–4 (emphasis added).

[117] Case 82/77, *Openbaar Ministerie (Public Prosecutor) v Jacobus Philippus van Tiggele.*

European Court again emphatically underlined that the marketing rule in question applied to domestic and imported products alike and therefore 'cannot produce effects detrimental to the marketing of *imported products alone* and *consequently* cannot constitute a measure having an effect equivalent to a quantitative restriction on imports'.[118] Only where a specific form of discrimination against imports could be shown would the national measure violate Article 34.[119]

bb. In Particular II: Discriminatory Quality-Ensuring Measures

This discrimination criterion was subsequently developed in a group of cases that predominantly concern quality-ensuring measures.

In *Commission v Germany (Sekt & Weinbrand)*,[120] the Court had been asked to review a German law that reserved the appellations 'Sekt' (sparkling wine) and 'Weinbrand' (brandy) to wines produced in Germany or from a fixed amount of German grapes. The solution suggested by Directive 70/50 was here clear: national laws that 'confine names which are not indicative of origin or source to domestic products only' were *distinctly* applicable measures that would constitute measures having an equivalent effect to quantitative restrictions.[121] And rejecting the German argument that the appellations were true geographic indications of origins,[122] the Court had no scruples in finding that the German law was 'calculated to favour the disposal of the domestic products on the German market to the detriment of the products of other Member States'.[123] Without even citing *Dassonville*, the Court exclusively based its analysis on the presence of formal discrimination.

This solution was confirmed in *Eggers*,[124] where the Court substantially dealt with the same questions.[125] This time, however, the bone of contention was the German condition that *home* produced brandies could only use the designation 'Weinbrand' if 85 per cent of the alcoholic content would be derived from wine distillate whose distillation had taken place inside

[118] Ibid., para. 16 (emphasis added). [119] Ibid., para. 18.

[120] Case 12/74, *Commission v Germany (Sekt & Weinbrand)*.

[121] Directive 70/50, Article 2(3)(s).

[122] Case 12/74, *Commission v Germany*, para. 7; and see also: para. 12: 'It results from the foregoing considerations that the appellations 'Sekt' and 'Weinbrand' do not constitute indications or origin.'

[123] Ibid., para. 14. [124] Case 13/78, *Eggers Sohn & Co. v Freie Hansestadt Bremen*.

[125] Interestingly, the Court now refers to the *Dassonville* formula in para. 23; yet immediately reverts to Directive 70/50 and in particular its Article 2(3)(s). The subsequent analysis then reproduces extensively the ruling in Case 12/74, *Commission v Germany*.

the national territory. This element was new, since the German rule was confined to the designation of *German* products. Yet the Court followed its previous reasoning and insisted that while the Member States were 'empowered to lay down quality standards for products marketed on their territory and may make use of designations of quality subject to compliance with such standards', this was 'dependent solely on the existence of the intrinsic objective characteristics which give the product the quality required by law'.[126] To thus insist that part of a production process had to take place within Germany was to formally (!) discriminate against production processes in other Member States and therefore clearly constituted a MEEQR.[127] The 'internal' measure here violated Article 34 because it *discriminated* against foreign goods.

4. *The* Cassis *Revolution: The Decline of the International Model*

In the first decade following the end of the transitional period, the Court had found an interesting compromise within Article 34: the provision would—like Article XI GATT—contain an absolute prohibition for border measures;[128] while with regard to internal measures, the provision would—like Article III:4 GATT—outlaw discriminations against imports. Article 34 TFEU thus combined two GATT provisions; yet in combining—and not altering—them, it had remained loyal to the international market model.

This international law loyalty was originally premised on the promises of positive integration. For positive and negative integration were, as discussed earlier, seen as complementary parts within the creation of the European common market. Negative integration was designed to eliminate the traditional 'international' obstacles to interstate trade, while the task of positive integration was to go beyond this by also removing obstacles to trade that arose from legislative disparities between national laws that would 'directly affect the establishment or functioning of the common market'.[129] And with regard to such regulatory barriers to trade, the primary objective for the young Union was the removal of 'technical' barriers to trade. Technical barriers are 'obstacles to international trade *resulting*

[126] Case 13/78, *Eggers*, para. 25. [127] Ibid., para. 26.

[128] For the exception to this absolute rule with regard to third-country goods, see: Chapter 5, Section I of this volume.

[129] Ex-Article 100 EEC.

from differences between national legislative and administrative provisions concerning the marketing or the use of products, which necessitates the adoption of export products during the production process'.[130]

The original harmonization programme of the Union with regard to these technical barriers was here 'epic'. To remove these barriers, the Council had adopted a 'General Programme for the Elimination of technical barriers to trade which result from disparities between the provisions laid down by law, regulation or administrative action in Member States'.[131] The Programme was adopted in 1969,[132] but, being far too ambitious, a supplementary Programme followed in 1973,[133] which was once again adjusted in 1977.[134] The reason for this slow progress in the second half of the 1970s was the revival of neo-protectionism in the Member States during a world recession. An ever wider number of national measures were adopted to 'isolate' national markets; and the most prevalent of these new obstacles to intra-Union trade were technical barriers to trade. By 1978, the Commission was exasperated. For instead of reacting against the rising tide of restrictive measures, the Union was 'adopting fewer and fewer directives each year'.[135] 'A large number of Commission proposals still outstanding in the Council ha[d] been studied from the technical point of view and their adoption now require[d] only political agreement.'[136] But without agreement in the Council, it seemed that

[130] P. J. Slot, *Technical and Administrative Obstacles to Trade*, 4 (emphasis added). But see already, F. Bonn, 'Les Entraves techniques aux échanges communautaires', 369–87.

[131] General Programme of 28 May 1969 for the Elimination of Technical Barriers to Trade which result from disparities between the provisions laid down by law, regulation or administrative action in Member States (1969) OJ C 76/1.

[132] Council Resolution of 28 May 1969 drawing up a Programme for the Elimination of Technical Barriers to Trade (1969) OJ C76/1.

[133] Resolution of the Council of 21 May 1973 concerning the Elimination of Technical Obstacles to Trade in Industrial Products (1973) OJ C38/1.

[134] For an academic assessment of the slowness of the harmonization progress at the time, see: A. Dashwood, 'Hastening Slowly: The Communities' Path Towards Harmonization'; and more recently: M. Egan, *Constructing a European Market: Standards, Regulation and Governance*, esp. Chapter 4.

[135] Commission, Twelfth General Report on the Activities of the European Communities (1978), para. 104.

[136] Ibid. One of these measures on the purgatory shelf within the Council was a proposal for a common organization of the market in ethyl alcohol and products containing ethyl alcohol, see: Amended Proposal for a Council Regulation on the Common Organization of the market in ethyl alcohol of agricultural origin and laying down additional provisions for certain products containing ethyl alcohol OJ C 309/2. The (draft) Regulation will of course play an important (silent) role in *Cassis de Dijon*.

technical barriers to trade were—in the absence of Union harmonization—there to stay.

This pitiful state of affairs changed in 1979. For after a decade of patiently accepting the decisional blockage within the Council, the Court famously came to rescue the 'deficient [Union] legislator'.[137] This famous shift from positive to negative integration within the common market came with *Cassis de Dijon*.[138] The case involved a German company, Rewe, which specialized in the importation of goods from other Member States. It had requested an import authorization for 'Cassis de Dijon' from the (German) Spirits Monopoly Administration; and while this *import* authorization was waived, the national authority nevertheless informed Rewe that the French liqueur could not be *marketed* in Germany because of a national law regulating fortified wines. The law fixed the minimum alcohol content for fruit liqueurs to 25 per cent; and since Cassis de Dijon only had an alcohol content below 20 per cent, the French liqueur could consequently not be sold as a 'liqueur' within Germany. Rewe brought proceedings against the decision, for even if the goods could be imported, the marketing rule severely restricted its ability to sell the French goods to German consumers.

But did the German marketing measure violate Article 34? Was this a measure equivalent to a quantitative restriction; and was there discrimination? In their submissions to the European Court of Justice, all parties invoked Article 3 of Directive 70/50.[139] It will be recalled that the latter dealt with indistinctly applicable measures that could—exceptionally—fall within the scope of Article 34 on the condition that they '*exceed[] the effects intrinsic to trade rules*'.[140] Was this the case here? Rewe insisted that the German product requirement was excessive in its restrictive effect on the free movement of goods, while the German government relied on the presumption of innocence benefiting marketing measures equally applicable to domestic and imported products.[141] And expressly rejecting the idea

[137] P. Pescatore, 'La Carence du législateur communautaire et le devoir du juge', 559.

[138] Case 120/78, *Rewe-Zentral AG v Bundesmonopolverwaltung für Branntwein*. The shift from positive to negative integration also triggered a shift from decisional intergovernmentalism (in the Council) to decisional supranationalism (in the Court).

[139] Ibid., 653.

[140] Directive 70/50 (see n. 69), recital 9.

[141] Case 120/78, *Rewe-Zentral AG v Bundesmonopolverwaltung für Branntwein*, 655.

that the marketing law exceeded the effects intrinsic to trade rules,[142] the German line of argument was thereby as follows:

> The mere fact that German law contains stricter minimum requirements, which, when viewed objectively, give no advantage to national producers, cannot constitute a material discrimination within the meaning of Article [34] of the Treaty … In view of the fundamental importance to an assessment of the technical specifications of all other sectors of production of the line of argument adopted by the plaintiff in the main action, *it should be noted that its consequence would be that the minimum alcohol content of a given product in the Federal Republic of Germany would no longer be governed by German law but by French law*; in consequence, the lower minimum alcohol content fixed by French law should also be extended to the whole of German national production. In the final analysis, the rules of the least exigent Member State would be authoritative in all the others[.][143]

For Germany, this result was simply unacceptable: Article 34 had to be seen from 'the general framework of the national legislative system';[144] and according to the latter, each Member State had retained *full internal sovereignty over its national market*. The sole way to attack barriers to international trade resulting from legislative diversities caused by the—sovereign—parallelism of multiple State legislation was to harmonize national laws under ex-Article 100 EEC.[145]

This international law reasoning was heavily attacked by the Advocate General,[146] and in its judgment, the Court famously abandoned

[142] Ibid., 657: 'The restrictive effect on trade of such provisions does not exceed the normal limits of the "effects intrinsic to mere trade rules." The principle of proportionality is not threatened: a mere requirement as to labelling cannot replace the fixing of a minimum alcohol content; the fact that manufacturers must adapt their products intended for export to the specifications of the importing country pending harmonization is merely of the necessary consequence of the differences between national specifications.'

[143] Ibid., 656 (emphasis added).

[144] Ibid., 657: 'In accordance with the case-law of the Court concerning the interpretation of Article [110] of the [FEU] Treaty it must be accepted that the general framework of the national legislative system must remain the determining factor, even as regards products which do not normally exist within the importing country, in those fields requiring harmonization which still come under the control of the Member States.'

[145] Ibid., 668–70. And since ex-Article 100 EEC required unanimity, the 'internal' sovereignty of Germany was of course also preserved.

[146] See Opinion of Advocate General Capotorti in Case 120/78, *Cassis de Dijon*. Tracing the view that Member States retained legislative sovereignty over equally applicable internal measures to Directive 70/50, the learned Advocate General took it upon himself to discredit the Commission act as well as he could.

the international presumption of internal sovereignty and ruled as follows:

> *In the absence of common rules relating to the production and marketing of alcohol—a proposal for a regulation submitted to the Council by the Commission on 7 December 1976 not yet having received the Council's approval*—it is for the Member States to regulate all matters relating to the production and marketing of alcohol and alcoholic beverages on their own territory. Obstacles to movement within the [Union] resulting from disparities between the national laws relating to the marketing of the products in question must be accepted in so far as those provisions *may be recognized as being necessary in order to satisfy mandatory requirements* relating in particular to the effectiveness of fiscal supervision, the protection of public health, the fairness of commercial transactions and the defence of the consumer.[147]

What was happening here and, in particular, what were the Court's jurisprudential coordinates in this passage from nowhere? With no reference to *Dassonville*, nor Directive 70/50, the Court mentioned the absence of European secondary law; and then strangely posits that, in the absence of such common rules, obstacles to trade arising—not from a single national law—but resulting 'from *disparities* between the national laws' must be accepted yet only in so far as they satisfy 'mandatory requirements' protecting public interests.

Did the German law satisfy such mandatory requirements? Germany had invoked public health—a justification that the Court quickly brushed aside.[148] As regards the public interest in protecting the consumer against unfair practices—an interest not mentioned in Article 36—the Court was more sympathetic; yet it soon found that even 'this line of argument cannot be taken so far as to regard the mandatory fixing of minimum alcohol contents as being an essential guarantee of the fairness of commercial transactions, since it is a simple matter to ensure that suitable information is conveyed to the purchaser by requiring the display of an indication of origin and of the alcohol content on the packaging of products'.[149]

The Court thus concluded that 'the rule[] of a Member State of a minimum alcohol content for the purposes of the sale of alcoholic beverages

[147] Ibid., para. 8 (emphasis added). The Council Regulation mentioned is the one discussed in n. 136.

[148] Ibid., para. 11: 'Such considerations are not decisive since the consumer can obtain on the market an extremely wide range of weakly or moderately alcoholic products and furthermore a large proportion of alcoholic beverages with a high alcohol content freely sold on the German market is generally consumed in a diluted form.'

[149] Ibid., para. 13.

constitutes an obstacle to trade which is incompatible with the provisions of Article [34] of the Treaty'.[150] And following this concrete conclusion came a fundamental judicial afterthought:

> There is therefore no valid reason why, provided that they have been lawfully produced and marketed in one of the Member States, alcoholic beverages should not be introduced into any other Member State; the sale of such products may not be subject to a legal prohibition on the marketing of beverages with an alcohol content lower than the limit set by the national rules.[151]

This famous coda, subsequently integrated into the formal ground(s) of judgment,[152] was to become known as the principle of mutual recognition. And it is this principle that was soon to become the cornerstone for a new—federal—structure of the European common market.[153]

Conclusion

The creation of a common market was (and is) a central task of the European Economic Community and today the European Union. The 1957 EEC Treaty thereby offered a variety of legal instruments to unite the different national markets into a 'common' European market. Originally, it closely followed the GATT suggestions in Article XXIV and outlawed customs duties (and equivalent measures), while it equally prohibited quantitative restrictions (and equivalent measures). The EEC Treaty also contained a non-discrimination provision for imported goods, yet the latter was textually confined to fiscal measures; and the question therefore arose how the 1957 Rome Treaty would regard State regulatory measures that discriminated against out-of-State goods. Early academic views were divided as to whether Article 34 TFEU was modelled on Article XI GATT or whether

[150] Ibid., para. 14, third indent. [151] Ibid., para. 14, fourth indent.

[152] The formal judgment reads: 'The concept of "measures having an effect equivalent to quantitative restrictions on imports" contained in Article [34 TFEU] is to be understood to mean that the fixing of a minimum alcohol content for alcoholic beverages intended for human consumption by the legislation of a Member State also falls within the prohibition laid down in that provision where the importation of alcoholic beverages lawfully produced and marketed in another Member State is concerned.'

[153] As one early commentator presciently stated (cf. E. Millarg, 'Anmerkung zum Urteil in der Rs. 120/78', 423): 'Bedeutung und Tragweite des Urteils ergeben sich nicht aus der Auslegungsformel, sondern nur aus den Entscheidungsgründen.'

it would (also) prohibit discriminatory measures à la Article III:4 GATT. Importantly however, and unlike the GATT, the EEC Treaty did additionally envisage positive integration; and one possible solution to the elimination of regulatory barriers to trade could therefore have been to use the Union's (exclusive) legislative competence over its common market.

How did the European Court develop the textual possibilities offered by the 1957 Rome Treaty? The judicial solution developed in the early jurisprudence ingeniously combined Article XI and Article III:4 GATT under the common roof of Article 34 TFEU. For border measures, the Court thus adopts an absolute test, while for internal measures it borrows the discrimination test from Article III:4 GATT. Fundamentally, this discrimination test is in line with the international law model. For in reviewing whether a State refuses to apply its 'ordinary' domestic rules to imports, a discrimination rationale never formally challenges the internal sovereignty of a State with regard to its own (internal) market.

Neither was this international model challenged by the presence of a 'Commerce Clause'-like provision in ex-Article 100 EEC that allowed the Community/Union to harmonize national laws that 'directly affect the establishment or functioning of the common market'.[154] For even if the provision entitled the Union to remove *non*-discriminatory 'internal' measures from the very beginning, decision-making within the Council required unanimity and could thus be vetoed by every single Member State. This reliance on (positive) integration through the political process was however completely discredited by the end of the 1970s. And with *Cassis de Dijon*, the Court signalled its willingness to replace positive integration with negative integration by 'integrating' non-discriminatory measures into the scope of Article 34.

Cassis thereby constitutes a *contextual* revolution. For the text of Article 3 of Directive 70/50 had already envisaged that certain indistinctly applicable measures could fall within the scope of Article 34, yet prior to *Cassis*, the Court generally interpreted the provision to only cover *discriminatory* 'internal' measures; and in any event, there was a general—contextual—presumption that indistinctly applicable measures would not constitute MEEQRs. The *Cassis* Court—radically—overturned this international presumption. Finding that obstacles to free movement created by a legislative disparity between national laws may well fall within the scope of

[154] Ex-Article 100 EEC.

Article 34, the Court here 'breaks' with the international law model. The *Cassis* Court changed the Union's philosophical perspective: through the very act of recognizing 'cumulative' burdens, the Court stepped outside the international frame offered by the GATT. After all, only a federal perspective can perceive such 'double' burdens! The growth and evolution of this—new—federal perspective into an independent 'model' will be the subject of the next chapter.

4

The Rise of the Federal Model I

Introduction

What is the nature of a 'federal' common market? A 'federal' market is based on the principle that States not only lose a part of their 'external sovereignty'; they will also have to give up a part of their 'internal sovereignty' over their internal markets. This happened in the United States when the (dormant) Commerce Clause expanded to cover *intra*-State commerce and, consequently, measures that—even if not distinctly applicable to imports—were nevertheless seen as 'excessively burdening' interstate commerce.[1]

Within the European Union, such a federal moment arrived with the emergence of the principle of mutual recognition.[2] According to the latter, goods are principally entitled to move freely within the European market once they comply with the law of their *home* State; and the *host* State is principally no longer allowed to exercise its (internal) sovereignty over the 'marketing' of imported goods. Within Article 34, the federal model is thus not concerned with the question of whether or not the host State rules themselves discriminate against imports; it examines whether the *extension of host State laws to imports* imposes a 'restriction' or 'obstacle' to intra-Union trade. Through the 'federal' prism, a restriction or obstacle is here seen to arise because a good is subject to two—or worse, twenty-eight—different national standards that simultaneously demand application in the common market.

Cassis de Dijon had introduced this federal perspective into Article 34; yet what were the constitutional principles governing this federal model? And what was its scope? While invented for one specific category of measures—technical barriers through product requirements—would the Court expand the idea of mutual recognition to other categories of State laws? In the post-*Cassis* period, the Court struggled with these questions; and, as we shall see in Section I, it developed a number of diverse doctrinal approaches for what came to be known as 'selling arrangements'. A radical redefinition of the doctrinal framework subsequently occurred with *Keck*.[3] The judgment seemingly suggested that—for selling arrangements—the international model should after all apply, because the Court here held that Article 34 was confined to outlawing *discriminatory* selling arrangements.

[1] For a discussion of the US American market, see: Chapter 2 of this volume.

[2] For an overview of the principle, see: K. Armstrong, 'Mutual Recognition'.

[3] Joined Cases C-267–8/91, *Criminal proceedings against Bernard Keck and Daniel Mithouard*.

But was this really what the Court was doing? And what about other classes of 'internal' State laws? Section II analyses these questions, and we shall see there that—after *Keck*—the doctrinal framework governing Article 34 expressly recognizes various distinct jurisprudential lines. Have these distinct lines been reconverging into an overarching general framework governing Article 34? And if so, what type of overall market model best characterizes Article 34 today?

Let us explore these questions one by one.

I. Doctrinal Divergences: From *Cassis* to *Keck*

The *Cassis* judgment provoked an enormous reaction.[4] For the German government, the *Cassis* solution was, as a general rule, simply unacceptable.[5] The Commission, on the other hand, energetically propagated a generalization of the judgment.[6] In a Communication concerning the consequences of *Cassis*, it thus argued:

> In its judgment of 20 February 1979 the Court indicates the scope of Article [34] as it applies to technical and *commercial rules. Any product lawfully produced and marketed in one Member State must, in principle, be admitted to the market of any other*

[4] For early academic commentaries, see: E. Millarg, 'Anmerkung zum Urteil in der Rs. 120/78'; A. Mattera, 'L'Arrêt "Cassis de Dijon". Une nouvelle approche pour la réalisation et le bon fonctionnement du marché intérieur'; J. C. Masclet, 'Les Articles 30, 36 et 100 du traité C.E.E. à la lumière de l'arrêt "Cassis de Dijon"'; D. Wyatt, 'Quantitative Restrictions and Measures Having Equivalent Effect'.

[5] In the words of the German government: 'Die Bundesregierung hat bereits in ihrer Stellungnahme gegenüber dem Gerichtshof die Auffassung vertreten, daß Handelshemmnisse, die sich aus unterschiedlichen Rechtsvorschriften ergeben, grundsätzlich nur durch Maßnahmen der Rechtangleichung, nicht dagegen durch die wechselseitige Anerkennung der jeweiligen nationalen Regelungen beseitigt werden können. Sie betrachtet die Regelungen über den Mindestalkoholgehalt von Spirituosen insoweit als einen Ausnahmefall und würde sich einer Verallgemeinerung des im Urteil vom 20. Februar 1979 enthaltenen Grundsatzes widersetzen.' (Quoted in: U. Loewenheim, *Die Beseitigung Nichttarifärer Handelsschranken im Innergemeinschaftlichen Handel unter besonderer Berücksichtigung der gewerblichen Schutzrechte und des Urheberrechts: Deutscher Landesbericht, FIDE 1982*, Volume II: *The Elimination of Non-Tariff Barriers with Particular Reference to Industrial Property Rights Including Copyright*, 4.1 at 4.9.)

[6] Communication from the Commission concerning the Consequences of the Judgment given by the Court of Justice on 20 February 1979 in Case 120/78 ('Cassis de Dijon'), (1980) OJ C 256/2. For an early analysis of the Communication, see: L. Gormley, 'Quantitative Restrictions and Measures Having Equivalent Effect', 454 et seq.

Member State. Technical and commercial rules, even those equally applicable to national and imported products, may create barriers to trade only where those are necessary to satisfy mandatory requirements and to serve a purpose which is in the general interest and for which they are an essential guarantee.[7]

This was a clear attempt to 'export' the *Cassis* solution, and the principle of mutual recognition, beyond technical rules. Federal principles should thus in principle apply to all 'commercial' rules. But what did the phrase 'lawfully produced and marketed in one Member State' here imply? And what were the constitutional principles governing the federal European common market? Let us analyse the constitutional principles governing the federal model with regard to product requirements first. Thereafter, we shall explore the tumultuous relationship between Article 34 and selling arrangements. The Court here tried its hand with all three market models but ultimately returned to the international model in *Keck*.

1. *Product Requirements: Consolidating the Federal Model*

What were the (new) constitutional principles for the (new) federal philosophy within Article 34? After *Cassis*, the Court developed a veritable—independent—jurisprudential line for product requirements that was subject to its own constitutional principles.

These principles were first clarified in *Gilli & Andres*.[8] Criminal proceedings had been brought against two traders from Bolzano that had sold apple vinegar made in Germany. The vinegar contained acetic acid not derived from the fermentation of wine and thereby violated a 1965 Italian decree that prohibited the marketing of such products. The case fitted the *Cassis* pattern perfectly; and the judicial analysis was consequently quick. Repeating its '*Cassis* formula',[9] the Court confirmed that indistinctly applicable product requirements would violate Article 34 when extended to imports—unless they were justified by mandatory requirements.[10] In the present case, the Italian rules, while found to be non-discriminatory, could nevertheless not be justified on consumer protection grounds because, in

[7] Commission Communication on 'Cassis de Dijon' (see above), 2 (emphasis added).

[8] Case 788/79, *Criminal proceedings against Gilli and Andres*.

[9] Ibid., para. 5.

[10] And importantly, the Court here also clarified that the new *Cassis* justifications would only be available to 'national rules, which apply *without discrimination* to both domestic and imported products' (ibid., para. 6 (emphasis added)). This point will be extensively discussed in Chapter 5, Section II(2) of this volume.

the eyes of the Court, the German vinegar was 'provided with a sufficiently clear label indicating that it is in fact apple vinegar, thus avoiding any possibility of the consumer's confusing it with wine vinegar'.[11] Arbitrating between the—higher—Italian and the—lower—German consumer standard, the Court here implicitly held that Italy had engaged in illicit economic protectionism.[12]

This federal approach was subsequently generalized.[13] And a good illustration of the rising '*Cassis* formula' is *Kelderman*.[14] Dealing with criminal proceedings against an importer of French 'brioches' that did not fulfil the Dutch product requirements for bread, the Court held:

> [I]n the absence of common or harmonized rules on the making and marketing of bread it is for Member States to regulate all matters relating to the composition, making and marketing of that foodstuff on their own territory. As the Court stated in its judgments of 20 February 1979 in Case 120/78 *REWE* and of 26 June 1980 in Case 788/79 *Gilli*, obstacles to intra-[Union] trade resulting from disparities between the national laws relating to the marketing of the products in question must be accepted in so far as those provisions may be recognized as being necessary in order to satisfy imperative requirements relating in particular to the protection of public health, fair trading and consumer protection.
>
> *The extension to imported products* of a requirement that they contain a specific amount of dry matter may prevent bread originating in other Member States from being marketed in the State concerned. It may make it necessary to vary the method of manufacture according to the place where the bread is to be sold

[11] Case 788/79, *Criminal proceedings against Gilli and Andres*, para. 7.

[12] Ibid., paras. 9–10: 'From that it follows that the provisions relating to the prohibition on the marketing of products containing acetic acid other than that derived from wine as set out in Article 51 of Decree No 162 do not serve a purpose which is in the general interest and such as to take precedence over the requirements of the free movement of goods, which constitutes one of the fundamental rules of the [Union]. In practice, the principal effect of provisions of this nature is to protect domestic production by prohibiting the putting on to the market of products from other Member States which do not answer the descriptions laid down by the national rules.'

[13] For the extensive jurisprudence in the first post-*Cassis* decade, see only: Case 27/80, *Criminal proceedings against Anton Adriaan Fietje*; Case 113/80, *Commission v Ireland (Irish Souvenirs)*; Case 130/80, *Criminal proceedings against Fabriek voor Hoogwaardige Voedingsprodukten Kelderman BV*; Case 193/80, *Commission v Italy (Vinigar)*; Case 220/81, *Criminal proceedings against Timothy Frederick Robertson and others*; Case 261/81, *Rau Lebensmittelwerke v De Smedt*; Case 94/82, *Criminal proceedings against De Kikvorsch Groothandel-Import-Export BV*; Case 16/83, *Criminal proceedings against Karl Prantl*; Case 188/84, *Commission v France (Woodworking Machines)*; Case 178/84, *Commission v Germany (Beer Purity)*; Case 407/85, 3 *Glocken GmbH and Gertraud Kritzinger v USL Centro-Sud and Provincia autonoma di Bolzano*.

[14] Case 130/80, *Kelderman* (see above).

and thus impede the movement of bread lawfully produced in the Member State of origin if identical manufacturing standards are not prescribed in that State. In view of the existence of an obstacle which may impede trade between Member States it is necessary to consider whether that obstacle may be justified in the public interest[.][15]

Without referring to *Dassonville*,[16] the judgment directly drew on the '*Cassis* formula'; and it here clarified that Article 34 would not prohibit national product requirements *as such*. It was—crucially—only their 'extension to imported products' that fell foul of the federal common market. Products lawfully produced in their 'home' State should thus, in principle, not be prohibited on the ground that they did not conform to the production or marketing standards of the 'host' State; yet, all Member States would of course continue to be entitled to apply *their* standards to *their* own goods. This constitutional solution would however give rise to the phenomenon of reverse discrimination.

a. Federal Principles I: Reverse Discrimination against Domestic Goods

Part and parcel of the federal model is the possibility of 'reverse discrimination'.[17] It arises when a Member State is prevented from imposing *its* national rules to imported goods within its domestic market but nonetheless applies *its* stricter standards to *its* domestic goods. The discrimination is here 'reversed' because—unlike a typical protectionist State—the application of national legislation leads to an economically disadvantageous

[15] Ibid., paras. 5–8 (emphasis added).

[16] There indeed was no direct or indirect reference to *Dassonville* or the *Dassonville* formula; yet in a great number of post-*Cassis* cases, the Court would apply a two-part test in which *Dassonville* functioned as a general jurisdictional definition which was followed by the concrete substantive criterion laid down in *Cassis*. For examples where the Court did refer to *Dassonville* implicitly or explicitly, see only: Case 16/83, *Prant*, para. 20 as well as Case 178/84, *Commission v Germany (Beer Purity)*, para. 27.

[17] On the idea of reverse discrimination generally see: S. D. Kon, 'Aspects of Reverse Discrimination in Community Law'; D. M. W. Pickup, 'Reverse Discrimination and Freedom of Movement for Workers'; H. U. J. d'Oliveira, 'Is Reverse Discrimination Still Possible under the Single European Act?'; as well as: E. Cannizzaro, 'Producing "Reverse Discrimination" through the Exercise of EC Competences'; H. Weyer, 'Freier Warenverkehr, rein innerstaatliche Sachverhalte und umgekehrte Diskriminierung'; M. Poiares Maduro, 'The Scope of European Remedies: The Case of Purely Internal Situations and Reverse Discrimination'; C. Ritter, 'Purely Internal Situations, Reverse Discrimination, *Guimont*, *Dzodzi* and Article 234'; D. Hanf, '"Reverse Discrimination" in EU Law: Constitutional Aberration, Constitutional Necessity, or Judicial Choice?' (which includes extensive bibliographical references at 58–61).

situation for domestic goods. *Cassis de Dijon* itself offered a good illustration of such reverse discrimination. For if the minimum alcohol requirement applied to German liqueurs only, imported—French—liqueurs could enjoy a competitive advantage over the more expensive German goods.

How has the European Court dealt with reverse discrimination? In order to protect the legislative competences of each State with regard to its own goods, the Court has clarified that Article 34 cannot be used to challenge reverse discrimination. Dealing with a Belgian law that required—solely—Belgian butter to indicate the name and address of the producer, the Court thus held in *Mathot*: 'With regard to Article [34], it must be emphasized that the purpose of that provision is to eliminate obstacles to the importation of goods *and not to ensure that goods of national origin always enjoy the same treatment as imported goods*.'[18] And 'even if there is discrimination against domestically-produced butter, such a difference of treatment can in no circumstances restrict the importation of butter or prejudice the marketing of imported butter'.[19] Article 34 could consequently not apply.

But even if reverse discrimination could not violate Article 34, what about the Union's general prohibition of all discrimination on grounds of nationality? The latter is expressly found in Article 18 TFEU and states: 'Within the scope of application of the Treaties, and without prejudice to any special provisions contained therein, *any discrimination on grounds of nationality shall be prohibited*.'[20] Could that prohibition perhaps be used to eradicate reverse discrimination? Early on, the Court however clarified that the provision would be of no avail when it came to the free movement of goods. In *Stichting*,[21] the Court thus invoked a categorical difference between 'distinction[s] drawn by national legislation between goods according to their origin' and 'distinction[s] between

[18] Case 98/86, *Criminal proceedings against Arthur Mathot*, para. 7 (emphasis added).

[19] Ibid., para. 8. See also Case 355/85, *Commissioner of Police, Thouars, carrying out the duties of Public Prosecutor v Michel Cognet*, esp. para. 10: 'It should be added that Article [34] of the [TFEU] does not forbid such a difference of treatment. The purpose of that provision is to eliminate obstacles to the importation of goods and not to ensure that goods of national origin always enjoy the same treatment as imported or reimported goods. The absence of restrictions as regards the selling price of reimported books does not prejudice the sale of such books. A difference in treatment between goods which is not capable of restricting imports or of prejudicing the marketing of imported or reimported goods does not fall within the prohibition contained in Article [34].'

[20] Emphasis added.

[21] Joined Cases 80 and 159/85, *Nederlandse Bakkerij Stichting and others v Edah BV*.

traders according to their nationality or according to the place where they are established';[22] and insisted that only the latter would fall within the scope of Article 18 TFEU. National legislation regulating goods would consequently fall outside the prohibition because there would be 'no "discrimination *on grounds of nationality*", even disguised or indirect, within the meaning of Article [18 TFEU]'.[23]

The Court has equally discarded a—third—challenge to the constitutionality of reverse discrimination. This challenge stemmed from the (unwritten) general principle of non-discrimination; yet in *Cogniet*, the Court resolutely held that '[a]s regards the *general principle of non-discrimination*, it must be observed that [Union] law does not apply to treatment which works to the detriment of national products as compared with imported products'.[24] Thus, even the broadest constitutional principle protecting equal treatment could not be marshalled against reverse discrimination.

Is the constitutional immunity of reverse discrimination within the federal model defensible? The existence of reverse discrimination has received much academic criticism;[25] and various remedies have been suggested to cure it. Some authors have argued that reverse discrimination should disappear through (exhaustive) Union harmonization.[26] Others have pointed

[22] Ibid., para. 22. [23] Case 355/85, *Cognet*, para. 9 (emphasis added).

[24] Ibid., para. 11 (emphasis added).

[25] See only: A. Tryfonidou, *Reverse Discrimination in EC Law*, 215: 'The clear conclusion at which we can arrive following the analysis in this chapter, is that reverse discrimination is no longer acceptable in the European internal market. At a time when the main (and only) aim of the [Union] was the construction of the internal market, reverse discrimination was considered a necessary evil of the system adopted for the attainment of that aim. Nevertheless, following the completion of the internal market and the increasing importance attached to the aim of ensuring that the market is one that functions properly, reverse discrimination suffered in cases where traders involved in cross-border trade and traders that are in a purely internal situation are similarly situated, is a form of differential treatment that comes into conflict with the broader aims of the [Union] in the context of its policy on the internal market. If unjustified, it is a form of discrimination which comes into conflict with the main aim of maintaining a properly functioning market since it gives rise to a distortion of the conditions of competition.'

[26] Ibid. In this sense see also: Advocate General Mischo in Joined Case 80 and 159/85, *Nederlandse Bakkerij Stichting and others v Edah BV*, at 3375: 'Reverse discrimination is clearly impossible in the long run within a true common market, which must of necessity be based on the principle of equal treatment. Such discrimination must be eliminated by means of the harmonization of legislation.' Yet the problem with this solution is that reverse discrimination will only disappear if the Union adopts exhaustive harmonization that field pre-empts the Member States. For under minimum harmonization, the phenomenon of reverse discrimination persists. On this point, see: R. Schütze, *From Dual to Cooperative Federalism: The Changing Structure of European Law*, 212 et seq.

their fingers to the national level;[27] and the European Court of Justice has traditionally favoured this second solution:

> Any discrimination which nationals of a Member State may suffer under the law of that State fall within the scope of that law and must therefore be dealt with within the framework of the internal legal system of that State.[28]

A Member State may thereby deal with reverse discrimination through legislative adjustment and 'spontaneous harmonization';[29] or, its national judiciary might find that reverse discrimination violates the national constitution.[30] It should however be remembered—also at the national level—that reverse discrimination is a constitutional reflex that directly follows from a federal philosophy recognizing an autonomous space for national regulatory autonomy.[31] When measured against the ideal of (individual) equality, reverse discrimination may therefore appear as an 'evil'; yet, within a federal model it is a necessary evil that directly flows from a conception of the common market that accepts collective differences stemming from distinct political communities: the Member States.

[27] M. Maduro, 'The Scope of European Remedies', 137: 'The evidence so far presented clearly demonstrates that reverse discrimination is an EU issue. But should we automatically assume that it requires an EU-level remedy? … I do not believe that it should be an EU institution which decides whether nationals of a particular State should or should not be subjected to stricter rules imposed by that State. Since this judgment implies a balancing of different national interests, national institutions are usually (though not always) better suited to make that decision.' For an extensive analysis of the German legal order in this respect, see: A. Epiney, *Umgekehrte Diskriminierungen: Zulässigkeit und Grenzen der discrimination à rebours nach europäischem Gemeinschaftsrecht und nationalem Verfassungsrecht*, Part III.

[28] Joined Cases C-64–5/96, *Land Nordrhein-Westfalen v Kari Uecker and Vera Jacquet v Land Nordrhein-Westfalen*, para. 23.

[29] Cf. C. Dautricourt and S. Thomas, 'Reverse Discrimination and Free Movement of Persons under Community Law: All for Ulysses, Nothing for Penelope?', 437. The authors offer the example of the Belgian law on immigration which, for the purposes of family reunifications, gives Belgian nationals the same rights as all EU citizens.

[30] In this sense: Case C-132/93, *Steen v Deutsche Bundespost*, paras. 10–11: 'It is for the national court, faced with a question of national law, to determine whether there is any discrimination under that law and whether that discrimination must be eliminated and, if so, how. Consequently, the reply to be given to the question put by the national court is that [Union] law does not preclude a national court from examining the compatibility with its constitution of a national rule which, in a situation unconnected with any of the situations contemplated by [Union] law, treats national workers less favourably than nationals from other Member States.'

[31] R. E. Papadopoulou, *Situations purement internes et droit communautaire: un instrument jurisprudentiel à double fonction ou une arme à double tranchant?*, 125.

b. Federal Principles II: 'Produced and Marketed within one of the Member States'

The normative crux of the federal model is the principle of mutual recognition; and the central question after *Cassis de Dijon* here was what was meant by the phrase 'produced *and* marketed in one of the Member States'. Would *Cassis* only cover 'traditional' goods of a Member State—that is, products that were historically produced and sold in, say, Italy or France—or, would the principle also protect goods that were exclusively produced for export markets? And what about goods produced in third States yet legally marketed in a Member State of the Union?

A partial answer to the first question was offered in *Schutzverband gegen Unwesen in der Wirtschaft*.[32] In 1971, Germany had adopted legislation that made the marketing of foreign wine-based beverages in Germany dependent on whether they were also marketed in their country of origin. (This was designed to prevent exports specifically targeting the German market.) In this case, the importer of Italian vermouth with an alcoholic content of less than 16 per cent had been charged with a violation of the German law because—even if there was no German minimum alcohol requirement for vermouth—an *Italian* law required such a minimum alcohol content. The question before the European Court was therefore not whether Germany could impose its German standard on Italian products; on the contrary, it was whether a *German* law could require goods produced in *Italy* to conform to the 'traditional' *Italian* marketing standard. Put differently, the question was: could a host State insist that imported goods, if they wished to benefit from the principle of mutual recognition, had to be 'good enough' for their home State market? Or, in legal terms: did products need to be 'produced *and* marketed' within their home State before they could benefit from mutual recognition; or was lawful production sufficient?

In its judgment, the Court found a breach of Article 34; yet, importantly, the Court did not base its decision on the *Cassis* line but—brilliantly—identified the issue as one of (formal) discrimination. For in the absence of a minimum alcohol content for German vermouths, the German law's insistence on a minimum alcohol content for all *imported* goods (where this was required in their home country) was directly discriminatory;[33] and the

[32] Case 59/82, *Schutzverband gegen Unwesen in der Wirtschaft v Weinvertriebs-GmbH*.

[33] Ibid., paras. 7–8: 'It is apparent from the argument before the Court, which has not been challenged in that respect by the plaintiff in the main action, that a provision of the importing Member State fixing a minimum degree of alcohol only for imported vermouth

German law thus fell outside the *Cassis* jurisprudential line. Nonetheless, the ruling pointed to a non-cumulative reading of the 'lawfully produced and marketed' phrase in which it would *not* seem to matter that a product was legally *produced* in one State (Italy) and legally *marketed* in another (Germany).

This tendency has been confirmed in the context of third-country goods. In the past, the question here emerged whether the principle of mutual recognition would also apply to goods that, while not produced within a Member State, were nonetheless legally marketed there. Would these third-country goods be entitled to freely circulate within the EU common market; or was the principle of mutual recognition confined to products produced within the Union? This—complex—issue deserves a complex answer, and that answer will be fully given in Chapter 4, Section I(1) of this volume. Suffice to say here, however, that the Court indeed seems not (!) to insist that goods be lawfully 'produced *and* marketed' in a Member State. Third-country products lawfully marketed within one Member State may thus benefit from the *Cassis* presumption and are consequently integrated into the federal market model.

In sum: the principle of mutual recognition appears to apply where one of the—alternative—conditions is satisfied. The cumulative 'and' within the phrase 'produced *and* marketed' within one of the Member States has been judicially transformed into an alternative 'produced *or* marketed' within the Union.

2. *Selling Arrangements I: Split Philosophical Rationales*

Having clarified the constitutional principles governing the federal model, the second central question in the post-*Cassis* jurisprudence concerned the scope of the new federal paradigm. Had the Court suspended the discrimination test solely for product requirements;[34] or, did the judgment

prevents the marketing of a product lawfully made in the exporting Member State, whereas it imposes no condition in relation to the minimum content of alcohol for the marketing of similar domestic products. Since such a provision affects only imported products, it is of a discriminatory nature.'

[34] In its early cases, the Court struggled with the classification of product requirements as discriminatory or non-discriminatory measures. For a discrimination rationale, see: Case 119/78, *SA des grandes distilleries Peureux v Directeur des Services fiscaux de la Haute-Saône et du territoire de Belfort*, para. 23; and much later: Case 16/83, *Prantl*, esp. para. 21; yet the Court would subsequently clearly—and rightly—embrace the idea that these measures were non-discriminatory.

signal a more general wish to drop the discrimination test for all internal measures?

The Court appeared at first to adopt the narrow view. With the exception of border measures,[35] it thus continued to insist on a discrimination test for all internal measures, except product requirements.[36] And the continued validity of the 'old' international law model could clearly be seen with regard to 'selling arrangements', such as advertising restrictions. For example: in *Commission v France*,[37] the Union challenged a French law regulating the advertising of alcoholic drinks that had divided these drinks into five groups each of which was subject to specific advertisement restrictions. The Commission claimed that the law discriminated against imported beverages—especially whisky—by systematically placing them at a disadvantage;[38] and the Court followed this view:

As a preliminary point it should be observed that there is no dispute between the parties on whether a restriction on freedom of advertising for certain products may constitute a measure having an effect equivalent to a quantitative restriction within the meaning of Article [34] of the Treaty. Although such a restriction does not directly affect imports it is however capable of restricting their volume owing to the fact that it affects the marketing prospects for the imported products. *The issue in point is therefore whether the prohibitions and restrictions on advertising laid*

[35] For post-Cassis border measures, see only: Case 153/78, *Commission v Germany*; Case 251/78, *Denkavit Futtermittel GmbH v Minister für Ernähung, Landwirtschaft und Forsten des Landes Nordrhein-Westfalen*; as well as Case 34/79, *Regina v Maurice Donald Henn and John Frederick Ernest Darby*.

[36] For post-*Cassis* price-fixing measures, see only: Case 5/79, *Procureur général v Hans Buys, Han Pesch and Yves Dullieux and Denkavit France SARL*, para. 26: 'Although price-freeze rules applicable without distinction to domestic and imported products do not in themselves constitute a measure having an effect equivalent to a quantitative restriction, they may have such an effect, however, when prices are fixed at a level such that the sale of imported products becomes either impossible or more difficult than that of domestic products'; as well as Case 229/83, *Association des Centres distributeurs Édouard Leclerc and others v SARL 'Au blé vert' and others*, para. 25: 'Contrary to the French Government's contention, such a provision does not merely assimilate the rules applying to imported books to those applying to domestic books but creates separate rules for imported books which are liable to impede trade between Member States. Such a provision must therefore be viewed as a measure equivalent in effect to a quantitative restriction on imports, contrary to Article [34 TFEU].'

[37] Case 152/78, *Commission v France*. According to Advocate General Reichl (ibid., 2320), this was the first time that the Court had to decide 'whether a national restriction on advertising in respect of certain alcoholic drinks, which does not relate to the fact of importation, can, in any event, be a measure having an effect equivalent to a quantitative restriction on imports within the meaning of Article [34 TFEU]'.

[38] Ibid., paras. 7 and 9.

down by the French legislation place a handicap on the importation of alcoholic products from other Member States ... Even though it is true that the system adopted by the Code has the effect of subjecting some national products to prohibitions or restrictions on advertising, including widely-consumed products, *nevertheless the fact remains that it still has undeniably discriminatory features.*[39]

This discrimination rationale for selling arrangements however gradually waned.[40] And wishing to move away from the international market model, but unsure in which direction to go, the Court soon developed two—parallel—lines of reasoning for selling arrangements. One jurisprudential line thereby borrowed from the federal philosophy behind *Cassis*; the other line slowly developed a national market philosophy.

a. *Selling Arrangements and Obstacles from Legislative Disparities*

The marginalization of the discrimination rationale for selling arrangements can clearly be seen in *Oosthoeck*.[41] Dutch legislation restricted the freedom of traders to give free gifts as part of an advertising strategy. The plaintiff complained that the national law 'oblige[d] it to adopt different sales promotion schemes in the various Member States which constitute a single market'.[42] And while the Court, in the absence of discrimination, rejected a challenge to the law on the basis that it constituted an export restriction;[43] with regard to imports and Article 34, it expressly referred to *Cassis*,[44] and held:

Legislation which restricts or prohibits certain forms of advertising and certain means of sales promotion may, although it does not directly affect imports, be such as to restrict their volume because it affects marking opportunities for the imported products. The possibility cannot be ruled out that to compel a producer either to adopt *advertising or sales promotion schemes which differ from one Member State to another or to discontinue a scheme which he considers to be particularly effective may constitute an obstacle to imports even if the legislation in question applies to domestic products and imported products without distinction.*[45]

[39] Ibid., paras. 11–13 (emphasis added).

[40] It goes without saying that the Court, of course, continued to outlaw discrimination wherever it found it in the application of selling arrangements, see only: Case 304/84, *Criminal proceedings against Claude Muller and others.*

[41] Case 286/81, *Criminal proceedings against Oosthoek's Uitgeversmaatschappij BV.*

[42] Ibid., para. 10.

[43] Ibid., para. 13. On the constitutional principles governing Article 35 TFEU, see Chapter 5, Section I(2) in this volume.

[44] Ibid., para. 14.

[45] Ibid., para. 15 (emphasis added).

The judgment carried the *Cassis* logic of trade obstacles arising from disparities between national laws beyond product requirements. And this extension of the logic of mutual recognition was further developed in *Cinéthèque*.[46] The case involved a French law prohibiting the sale of films on video-cassettes for a period between six and eighteen months so as to guarantee an exclusive screening period for cinemas. The temporary sales ban for videos had been breached by Cinéthèque, which defended itself by arguing that the French law constituted an import restriction 'in view of the fact that its application prevents certain products from being made available for sale in the national territory even though they may circulate freely in the territory of other Member States'.[47] The Court, in principle, accepted that view:

> In that connection it must be observed that such a system, if it applies without distinction to both video-cassettes manufactured in the national territory and to imported video-cassettes, does not have the purpose of regulating trade patterns; its effect is not to favour national production as against the production of other Member States, but to encourage cinematographic production as such. Nevertheless, the application of such a system may create barriers to intra-[Union] trade in video-cassettes *because of the disparities between the systems operated in the different Member States and between the conditions for the release of cinematographic works in the cinemas of those States*. In those circumstances a prohibition of exploitation laid down by such a system is not compatible with the principle of the free movement of goods provided for in the Treaty unless any obstacle to intra-[Union] trade thereby created does not exceed that which is necessary in order to ensure the attainment of the objective in view and unless that objective is justified with regard to [Union] law.[48]

The Court ultimately found that the national law could be justified;[49] yet the idea that Article 34 outlawed obstacles to trade resulting from legislative disparities in national selling arrangements emerged strengthened.[50]

[46] Joined Cases 60–1/84, *Cinéthèque SA and others v Fédération nationale des cinémas français*.

[47] Ibid., para. 14.

[48] Ibid., paras. 21–2 (emphasis added).

[49] Ibid., para. 23: 'It must be conceded that a national system which, in order to encourage the creation of cinematographic works irrespective of their origin, gives priority, for a limited initial period, to the distribution of such works through the cinema, is so justified.'

[50] This was further strengthened in Case C-382/87, *Buet and Educational Business Services (EBS) v Ministère public*, where the Court—referring to *Oosthoek*—held that (ibid., para. 7): '[T]o compel a trader either to adopt advertising or sales promotion schemes which differ from one Member State to another or to discontinue a scheme which he considers to be particularly

But did this mean that the Court had come to embrace a federal model for selling arrangements? Our answer must be nuanced. For the Court also developed a second—alternative—strategy to review non-discriminatory selling arrangements during this period; and this strategy concentrated on the 'excessive burden' test also mentioned in *Cinéthèque*.

b. *Selling Arrangements and Excessive Trade Burdens*

The life of law—especially that of a court of law—is not always about logic. And we thus find a second jurisprudential line that the Court develops in parallel during the same period.

We can see this second argumentative frame at work in *Oebel*.[51] The Court was asked to assess the legality of a German law on working hours in bakeries, which prohibited the baking and delivery at night on working days. The national measure was accused of constituting a restriction on exports and imports; and while the Court was quick to dismiss a violation of Article 35,[52] a much more complex answer was given in the context of Article 34. Was the national restriction on the delivery of bakery products—clearly not a product requirement but a selling arrangement—a measure(s) having an equivalent effect to quantitative restriction outlawed under that provision?

In its judgment, the Court reasoned as follows:

> [T]he restrictive effect of the rules controlling the times for the transport and delivery of ordinary and fine baker's wares, in connection with the control of the hours when those products may be manufactured, must be evaluated in the light of their scope. If such rules are confined to transport for delivery to individual consumers and retail outlets only, without affecting transport and delivery to warehouses or intermediaries, they cannot have the effect of restricting imports or exports between Member States. In this case, indeed, trade within the [Union] remains possible at all times, subject to the single exception that delivery to consumers and retailers is restricted to the same extent for all producers, wherever they are established. Under these circumstances, such rules are not contrary to Article[][34] of the Treaty.[53]

effective may constitute an obstacle to imports even if the legislation in question applies to domestic and imported products without distinction.'

[51] Case 155/80, *Summary proceedings agains Sergius Oebel.*

[52] Ibid., paras. 15–16. The export aspect of the judgment will be dealt with in the next chapter.

[53] Ibid., paras. 19–20.

This judicial argumentation did not refer to discrimination; nor did it use an obstacle-through-disparity rationale. Instead, the Court referred to the 'restrictive effect' of the national rule on intra-Union trade (even if that effect was so minimal here that it fell below an invisible substantive threshold that the Court felt Article 34 would have).[54]

This idea was subsequently developed in *Blesgen*.[55] A Belgian rule prohibited the keeping and consuming of strong spirits in public places so as to combat youth alcoholism. There were no apparent obstacles to trade caused by a legislative disparity among the Member States; and the Belgian government equally protested that the national rules were not discriminatory.[56] Yet the Court followed a very different argumentative route. Having referred to its *Dassonville* formula, it suddenly unearthed an old acquaintance to operate as a substantive decision rule:

> Article [34] provides that quantitative restrictions on imports and all measures having equivalent effect shall be prohibited between Member States. It follows that any national measure likely to hinder, directly or indirectly, actually or potentially, intra-[Union] trade is to be regarded as a measure having an effect equivalent to quantitative restrictions ... Moreover, according to Article 3 of Commission Directive 70/50 on the abolition of measures which have an effect equivalent to quantitative restrictions on imports and are not covered by other provisions adopted in pursuance of the [EU Treaties], *the prohibition in Article [34 TFEU] also covers national measures governing the marketing of products even though equally applicable to domestic and imported products, where the restrictive effect of such measures on the free movement of goods exceeds the effects intrinsic to trade rules*. That is not however the case with a legislative provision concerning only the sale of strong spirits for consumption on the premises in all places open to the public and not concerning other forms of marketing the same drinks.[57]

This part of the judgment clearly centred on an analysis of Article 3 of Directive 70/50: any national law that *excessively* burdened the free

[54] In the light of this reading of *Oebel*, Professor Weiler is right to claim that *Oebel* is 'at odds with [the Court's] normal jurisprudence' but he is terribly wrong about the reasons. For the case is in no way 'a sign of subterranean cracks appearing in the *Dassonville* construct' ('Epilogue: Towards a Common Law of International Trade', 225). The very opposite is the case: it is the beginning of a line of cases that would lead to the mechanical application of the *Dassonville* formula. For a discussion of the absurdities of the 'Weiler interpretation' of Article 34 TFEU, see my *Framing Dassonville: Text and Context in European Law*, Chapter 6.

[55] Case 75/81, *Blesgen v Belgian State*.

[56] Ibid., para. 6.

[57] Ibid., paras. 7–9 (emphasis added).

movement of goods would violate Article 34. What was the nature of this test? All here depends on context. For as we saw in Chapter 3,[58] the Commission had originally used Article 3 to identify when an *indistinctly* applicable measure had nonetheless *distinctive* effect on imports; and the Court had subsequently 'translated' this test into a (material) *discrimination* test.[59] The *Blesgen* Court however did *not* place Article 3 of Directive 70/50 into this international context. It held, on the contrary, that *non*-discriminatory measures could fall within the scope of Article 34 if their effects were excessive in relation to trade as such. This transposed the excessiveness test from an international to a national trade context. (For unlike the federal model, the Court's analysis did not explore what other Member States do.) And the central operating argument within this—new—national context was whether the national law did 'concern[] other forms of marketing' apart from the prohibition not to sell strong spirits in public places; and—because the national law did not—the Court could find that it did not substantially impede distribution channels within the *national* market. This contextual shift also triggered a rhetorical shift from restrictions to '*intra-[Union]* trade' to a restriction on 'trade *within the [Union]*'.[60] And this semantic shift announced a national market model.

3. *Selling Arrangements II: The (Short) Triumph of the National Model*

According to the 'national' market model, all trade restrictions that are above a legislative or judicial Union standard must be removed. The constitutional regime governing the European 'internal market' is here completely assimilated to that of a 'national market'. Where a State adopts rules that differ from the Union standard, the national standard will violate the free-movement provisions, even when this standard is also applied to the State's own 'home' production. This third model is consequently not based on a relative test that balances the regulatory claims of the host State against those of the home State; it is, on the contrary, based on an absolute criterion: where a State law reduces the volume of trade within the European

[58] See Chapter 3, Section II(1) of this volume.

[59] See Chapter 3, Section II(3/b) of this volume.

[60] See only: Case 247/84, *Criminal proceedings against Léon Motte*, para. 17. Due to the significantly broadened scope, the Court reintroduces the open-ended 'rule of reason' approach within Article 3 of the Directive so as not to limit the grounds of justification to Article 36. The Court could have used the language of mandatory requirements, but it did not do so as the case did not fall within the *Cassis* line of jurisprudence!

market disproportionately, it will violate the free-movement provisions. Within the national model, the free-movement provisions are therefore no longer concerned with *inter*state trade but with trade *tout court*. They aim 'to encourage the unhindered pursuit of commerce in individual Member States'.[61]

This 'national market' model gained strength in the second half of the 1980s. Its (short) triumph is symbolized by a series of judgments concerning the opening of shops on Sunday.[62] In *Torfaen*,[63] a British Borough Council had invoked the 1950 British Shops Act so as to force B&Q to close its do-it-yourself centres on Sunday. The retailer claimed that the prohibition to trade on Sundays constituted a MEEQR as it reduced, in absolute terms, the sales of imported goods. In its judgments, the Court expressly acknowledged that the national marketing rules did not make the sale of imported products more difficult than that of domestic products,[64] but nonetheless—citing *Cinéthèque*—held:

> [A] prohibition was not compatible with the principle of the free movement of goods provided for in the Treaty unless any obstacle to [Union] trade thereby created did not exceed what was necessary in order to ensure the attainment of the objective in view and unless that objective was justified with regard to [Union] law. In those circumstances it is therefore necessary in a case such as this to consider first of all whether rules such as those at issue pursue an aim which is justified with regard to [Union] law.[65]

[61] Advocate General Tesauro in Case C-292/92, *Hünermund and others v Landesapothekerkammer Baden-Württemberg*, para. 1. The Advocate General warned against this development (ibid., para. 27): 'Article [34] would otherwise come to be relied on and used, not for its proper purposes but in order to enable certain traders to avoid the application of national provisions which, in regulating a given activity, restrict freedom to trade, whether by imposing opening hours on shops, or by requiring prior authorization in order to carry on a given activity (why not, even a simple trading licence), or else by imposing professional requirements (sometimes technical as well) on those intending to sell certain classes of goods. In that context, I cannot refrain from pointing out that such a use of Article [34] would ultimately render nugatory the Treaty provisions on the free movement of goods and on establishment, or in any event devalue them.'

[62] For an analysis of these (in)famous Sunday trading cases, see: A. Arnull, 'What Shall We Do on Sunday?'; P. Diamond, 'Dishonourable Defences: The Use of Injunctions and the EEC Treaty—Case Study of the Shops Acts 1950'; R. Rawlings, 'The Eurolaw Game: Some Deductions from a Saga'; C. Barnard, 'Sunday Trading: A Drama in Five Acts'.

[63] Case C-145/88, *Torfaen Borough Council v B&Q plc*.

[64] Ibid., para. 11.

[65] Ibid., paras. 12–13. (As we saw above, the judgment in *Cinéthèque* had arguably not been based on this ground but on the—federal—argument that obstacles to trade resulting from disparities between the national laws were created.)

And without any reference to either Article 36 or any mandatory requirements,[66] the Court found that the national law at issue reflected 'political and economic choices' that accorded 'with national or regional socio-cultural characteristics, and that, in the present state of [Union] law, [was] a matter for the Member States'.[67] The question was thus one of proportionality, and there the Court returned to an old friend:

> [I]t is necessary to ascertain whether the effects of such national rules exceed what is necessary to achieve the aim in view. As is indicated in Article 3 of Commission Directive 70/50/EEC of 22 December 1969, the prohibition laid down in Article [34] covers national measures governing the marketing of products where the restrictive effect of such measures on the free movement of goods exceeds the effects intrinsic to trade rules. The question whether the effects of specific national rules do in fact remain within that limit is a question of fact to be determined by the national court.[68]

The Court here, once more, insisted that selling arrangements could be subject to an absolute trade-restrictiveness test. For it was not the intra-Union *disparities* between national opening times that created an obstacle to trade but the very *existence* of the national measure that restricted trade. (The judicial reasoning thus marginalized not only the discrimination rationale within the international model; it equally disqualified the federal rationale of eliminating obstacles to trade resulting from disparities in national laws.) And realizing that this could potentially unleash the full forces of unbound market liberalization, the Court (almost) instantaneously tried to erect a substantial 'remoteness' criterion.[69] In

[66] On the question of Article 36 TFEU and mandatory requirements, see Chapter 5, Section II(2) of this volume.

[67] Case C-145/88, *Torfaen*, para. 14. The Court here—somewhat mischievously—refers to *Oebel* as precedent; yet, the statement there was made to exclude a national law from the scope of Article 35 by showing that the national law was not intended to regulate exports.

[68] Case C-145/88, *Torfaen*, paras. 15–16.

[69] See only: Case C-69/88, *Krantz GmbH & Co. v Ontvanger der Directe Belastingen and Netherlands State*, paras. 9–11: 'As the Court has consistently held, initially in the judgment of 11 July 1974 in Case 8/74 *Procureur du Roi v Dassonville* (1974) ECR 837, all measures capable of hindering, directly or indirectly, actually or potentially, intra-[Union] trade are to be regarded as measures having an effect equivalent to quantitative restrictions. It must, however, be observed that the national provision referred to by the national court applies without distinction to both domestic and imported goods, and does not seek to control trade with other Member States. Furthermore, the possibility that nationals of other Member States would hesitate to sell goods on instalment terms to purchasers in the Member State concerned because such goods would be liable to seizure by the collector of taxes if the purchasers failed

Quietlynn,[70] dealing with a British law prohibiting the sale of sex articles in unlicensed sex establishments, the Court thus held:

> First, it must be noted that national legislation prohibiting the sale of sex articles from unlicensed sex establishments applies without distinction to imported and domestic products. It thus does not constitute an absolute prohibition on the sale of the products in question, but merely a rule regarding their distribution, regulating the outlets through which the products may be marketed ... It must also be pointed out that the provisions prohibiting the sale of sex articles from unlicensed sex establishments have in fact no connection with intra-[Union] trade, since the products covered by the Act may be marketed through licensed sex establishments and other channels, that is to say through shops in which sex articles account for *only an insignificant proportion of sales and which are therefore not required to be licensed, or by mail order*.[71]

This represented an attempt to limit the 'national' interpretation of Article 34 by introducing a substantive remoteness threshold—an attempt that however ultimately failed. With this failure, an unapologetic liberal genie had slipped out of the bottle, and over-eager traders soon started to relentlessly challenge any national legislation that they felt restricted their commercial freedom.[72]

Leaving the various post-*Torfaen* Sunday trading cases aside,[73] a good illustration of the (short) reign of the national model is *Monteil and*

to discharge their Netherlands tax debts is too uncertain and indirect to warrant the conclusion that a national provision authorizing such seizure is liable to hinder trade between Member States.'

Importantly, at an earlier time, the Court had expressly rejected the idea of a (quantitative) *de minimis* rule, see: Joined Cases 177–8/82, *Criminal proceedings against Jan van de Haar and Kaveka de Meern BV*, para. 13: 'It must be emphasized in that connection that Article [34] of the Treaty does not distinguish between measures having an effect equivalent to quantitative restrictions according to the degree to which trade between Member States is affected. If a national measure is capable of hindering imports it must be regarded as a measure having an effect equivalent to a quantitative restriction, even though the hindrance is slight and even though it is possible for imported products to be marketed in other ways.'

[70] Case C-23/89, *Quietlynn Limited and Brian James Richards v Southend Borough Council*.

[71] Ibid., paras. 9 and 11 (emphasis added).

[72] Advocate General Van Gerven had predicted that this would happen in *Torfaen*. If the Court were to find—he warned—the Sunday trading ban to (potentially) violate Article 34, then 'the Court will inevitably have to decide in an increasing number of cases on the reasonableness of policy decisions of Member States taken in the innumerable spheres where there is no question of direct or indirect, factual or legal discrimination against, or detriment to, imported products' (Case C-145/88, *Torfaen*, para. 26).

[73] See only: Case C-332/89, *Criminal proceedings against André Marchandise, Jean-Marie Chapuis and SA Trafitex*; Case C-312/89, *Union départementale des syndicats CGT de l'Aisne v SIDEF Conforama, Société Arts et Meubles and Société Jima*; as well as Case C-169/91, *Council of the City of Stoke-on-Trent and Norwich City Council v B&Q plc.*

Samanni.[74] The case involved a commercial monopoly granted to pharmacists in respect of the marketing of medicinal products. Did this indistinctly applicable measure violate Article 34? The Court positively found that 'in so far as it restricts sales to certain channels', the national law indeed 'affect[ed] the possibilities of marketing imported products and may accordingly constitute a measure having an effect equivalent to a quantitative restriction on imports within the meaning of Article [34] of the Treaty'.[75] But did the national law really affect the sale of *imported* products more that the sale of domestic products? The concept of 'trade channels', invoked by the Court, here no longer had its original 'international law' meaning. Instead of channels giving access *into* the host State's market, the concept of 'trade channels' here suddenly referred to distribution channels *within* a national market.

4. *Selling Arrangements III: The* Keck *Revolution*

The imminent danger of a 'national' interpretation of Article 34 was that its scope would become uncontrollable. Outside its international or federal context(s), the provision could potentially become an 'economic due process' clause that would allow individual traders to challenge all *national* laws regulating trade.[76] This judicial development indeed attracted heavy academic criticisms.[77] But what was the Court to do? Where was it to draw the line between illegitimate and legitimate interferences into 'Union trade'? The most important academic suggestion here came from the pen of a member of the Legal Service of the Commission (writing in his personal capacity).[78] Published in 1989, his prophetic analysis argued as follows:

[74] Case C-60/89, *Criminal proceedings against Jean Monteil and Daniel Samanni*.

[75] Ibid., para. 38; and see also: Case C-1/90, *Aragonesa*, where the Court found that 'national legislation such as that at issue in the main proceedings, which prohibits the advertising in certain places of beverages having an alcoholic strength of more than 23 degrees may constitute a hindrance to imports from other Member States and, therefore must in principle be regarded as a measure having equivalent effect within the meaning of Article [34]' (ibid., para. 11).

[76] On the US American concept of 'economic due process' under the Fourteenth Amendment, see: Chapter 2, 'Conclusion' in this volume.

[77] See only: E. L. White, 'In Search of the Limits to Article 30 of the EEC Treaty'; K. Mortelmans, 'Article 30 of the EEC Treaty and Legislation Relating to Market Circumstances: Time to Consider a New Direction?'; J. Steiner, 'Drawing the Line: Uses and Abuses of Article 30 EEC'. But for the opposite view, see only: L. Gormley, 'Actually or Potentially, Directly or Indirectly? Obstacles to the Free Movement of Goods'.

[78] E. L. White, 'In Search of the Limits to Article 30 of the EEC Treaty'.

The different legal and economic environment of the Member State of origin finds its expression in the different *characteristics* of an imported product compared with the national product. Consequently, as the judgment of the Court in *Cassis de Dijon* clearly shows, Member States are not entitled to require that imported products have the same *characteristics* as are required of, or are traditional in, domestic products unless this is strictly necessary for the protection of some legitimate interest. There is not, however, the same need to require the rules relating to the *circumstances* in which certain goods may be sold or used in the importing Member State to be overridden for this purpose as long as imported products enjoy *equal access* to the market of the importing Member State compared with national products.[79]

And exactly four years and a day following *Torfaen*, the Court took heed. In a remarkably 'realist' spirit, the Court now admitted that something had gone badly wrong with its 'national' interpretation of Article 34:

In view of the increasing tendency of traders to invoke Article [34] of the Treaty as a means of challenging any rules whose effect is to limit their commercial freedom even where such rules are not aimed at products from other Member States, the Court considers it necessary to re-examine and clarify its case-law on this matter.[80]

This famous admission that the liberal philosophy behind Article 34 had got out of hand was made in *Keck*.[81] The case marked a dramatic turnaround—a revolution (in the original sense of the term). For the Court here abandoned the idea that Article 34 was to liberalize *all* trade within the Union and returned to the older idea that the provision was intended to liberalize *intra-Union* trade.

Keck concerned criminal proceedings against two supermarket managers who had violated a French law prohibiting the selling of goods at a loss. This was a sales restriction designed to prevent unfair competition and which indistinctly applied to all goods—whether domestic or imported.

[79] Ibid., 246. For a severe criticism of this proposal, see: L. W. Gormley, 'Actually or Potentially, Directly or Indirectly?'.

[80] Joined Cases C-267–8/91, *Criminal proceedings against Bernard Keck and Daniel Mithouard*, paras. 14 and 16.

[81] For the vast literature on the *Keck* judgment, see only: D. Chalmers, 'Repackaging the Internal Market: The Ramifications of the *Keck* Judgment'; L. Gormley, 'Reasoning Renounced? The Remarkable Judgment in *Keck* and *Mithouard*'; A. Mattera, 'De l'arrêt "Dassonville" à l'arrêt "Keck". L'obscure clarté d'une jurisprudence riche en principes novateurs et en contradictions'; R. Joliet, 'Der freie Warenverkehr: Das Urteil *Keck und Mithouard* und die Neuorientierung der Rechtsprechung'; S. Weatherill, 'After *Keck*: Some Thoughts on How to Clarify the Clarification'.

And against the express wishes of Advocate General van Gerven,[82] the Court now refused to apply the national market rationale from *Torfaen*. Having quoted the *Dassonville* formula, the Court now found it essential that the national rule was 'not designed to regulate trade in goods between Member States'.[83] And while admitting that the national legislation potentially restricted—in absolute terms—the volume of sales of imported goods,[84] the Court nonetheless considered that 'the question remain[ed] whether such a possibility is *sufficient* to characterize the legislation in question as a measure having equivalent effect to a quantitative restriction on imports'.[85] Confirming its *Cassis* answer to this question with regard to 'rules that lay down requirements to be met by such goods', the Court famously continued:

By contrast, contrary to what has previously been decided, the application to products from other Member States of national provisions restricting or prohibiting certain

[82] The French government had defended itself by pointing to the non-discriminatory nature of the law and had quoted *Van Tiggerle*, yet this argument was 'neutralized' by the Advocate General by means of a reference to *Oosthoek* (Joined Cases C-267–8/91, *Criminal proceedings against Bernard Keck and Daniel Mithouard*, para. 4): 'The judgment in *van Tiggele* most surely cannot be invoked against that case-law, since that judgment antedated the Court's judgments in *Cassis de Dijon* and *Oosthoek*, which greatly reduces, or even negates, its value as a precedent.' How times had changed! Instead, van Gerven expressly pleaded to apply the *Cassis* logic (ibid., para. 6): 'Since it is to be assumed that the rules in question are in principle covered by Article [34], the question which must now be examined is whether the obstacles (actual or potential) to intra-[Union] trade which they entail must nevertheless be accepted upon application of the "Cassis de Dijon" test: for the practice of sale at a loss is not regulated by the [Union] and is regulated differently in the Member States; furthermore, the French legislation applies without distinction to national products and foreign products.' And applying a simple necessity test, the Advocate General found (ibid., para. 10): 'Consequently, my conclusion is that a general prohibition of resale at a loss does not satisfy the necessity test and that a less restrictive alternative is available, which is to define the prohibition in such a way that it better accords with the aforementioned mandatory requirements accepted in [Union] law.' Van Gerven was subsequently asked to provide a second option, because the case had been referred from the Second Chamber to the Full Court; and in light of the new information that the French law only applied at the retail stage and in the present cases only concerned French products, the learned Advocate General now felt that he was dealing with a case that had a 'purely hypothetical effect on trade between Member States' (ibid., para. 13). In light of this weak and wavering opinion, it is hard to understand Professor Weiler's claim that van Gerven was 'the prophet' and 'intellectual hero of a new phase in the writing and rewriting of the economic constitution of Europe' (J. H. H. Weiler, 'Epilogue: Towards a Common Law of International Trade', 225). Admittedly, van Gerven had argued in favour of a discrimination test in *Torfaen*; yet a few years later, he had become less of a prophet and more of a follower. The 'true' judicial hero was of course someone else, namely: Advocate General Slynn.

[83] *Keck*, para. 12. [84] Ibid., para. 13. [85] Ibid. (emphasis added).

> selling arrangements is not such as to hinder directly or indirectly, actually or potentially, trade between Member States within the meaning of the *Dassonville* judgment, *so long as those provisions apply to all relevant traders operating within the national territory and so long as they affect in the same manner, in law and in fact, the marketing of domestic products and of those from other Member States.* Provided that those conditions are fulfilled, the application of such rules to the sale of products from another Member State meeting the requirements laid down by that State is not by nature such as to prevent their access to the market or to impede access any more than it impedes the access of domestic products. Such rules therefore fall outside the scope of Article [34] of the Treaty.[86]

The Court here clearly abandoned the national market model for measures that it formally described as 'selling arrangements'. The latter, even where they prohibited certain distribution channels or certain marketing methods, would not violate Article 34 if two conditions were fulfilled. First, the national measures would need to apply to all traders within the national territory—that is, they must be *indistinctly* applicable; and, secondly, the selling arrangements would have to 'affect in the same manner, in law and in fact' the marketing of domestic and imported goods. Whenever these two conditions were fulfilled, according to the *Keck* Court, a national measure would not 'prevent [imported goods'] access to the market or to impede access any more than it impedes the access of domestic products'. This formulation suggested that the new rationale behind Article 34 was to protect market access; yet, importantly, the Court insisted on a *difference* in market access for imported and domestic products;[87] and by reintroducing a discrimination test, the *Keck* Court therefore seemed to subject selling arrangements to an international market philosophy.

What was the constitutional importance of *Keck*? With *Keck* the Court acknowledges—for the first time in an *express* manner—that different categories of national rules were subject to different tests.[88] And while not saying much about 'rules designed to regulate trade

[86] Ibid., paras. 16–17 (emphasis added).

[87] Somewhat awkwardly, the Court suggested that the *Dassonville* formula was here not fulfilled, as non-discriminatory selling arrangements would not hinder 'directly or indirectly, actually or potentially' trade between Member States. The 'better' view however is that the *Dassonville* formula is fulfilled but complemented by a substantive discrimination test. In this sense also: L. Gormley, 'Reasoning Renounced? The Remarkable Judgment in *Keck and Mithouard*'.

[88] The Court had of course done this—in an implicit manner—since the very beginning. On this point, see Chapter 3, Section II(3) of this volume.

in goods between Member States',[89] the second and third categories were, respectively, 'product requirements' and 'selling arrangements'. This differential approach has been criticized,[90] but for the wrong reasons.[91] For in light of the—previously established—failure of the substantive threshold route, the introduction of a formal rule limiting the scope of Article 34 was a pragmatic, even if second best, solution. This solution nonetheless raised two new questions. First, what exactly were 'selling arrangements'? And secondly, would selling arrangements only violate Article 34, when they *themselves* discriminated against imports; or would the Court here eventually confirm

[89] *Keck*, para. 12. With this formulation, the Court had—perhaps—'border' measures in mind.

[90] Advocate General Jacobs in Case C-412/93, *Société d'Importation Edouard Leclerc-Siplec v TF1 Publicité SA and M6 Publicité SA*, paras. 38–9: 'In my view the Court's reasoning—although not the result—in *Keck* is unsatisfactory for two reasons. First, it is inappropriate to make rigid distinctions between different categories of rules, and to apply different tests depending on the category to which particular rules belong. The severity of the restriction imposed by different rules is merely one of degree. Measures affecting selling arrangements may create extremely serious obstacles to imports. For example, a rule permitting certain products to be sold only in a handful of small shops in a Member State would be almost as restrictive as an outright ban on importation and marketing ... Secondly, the exclusion from the scope of Article [34] of measures which "affect in the same manner, in law and in fact, the marketing of domestic products and those from other Member States" amounts to introducing, in relation to restrictions on selling arrangements, a test of discrimination. That test, however, seems inappropriate. The central concern of the Treaty provisions on the free movement of goods is to prevent unjustified obstacles to trade between Member States. If an obstacle to inter-State trade exists, it cannot cease to exist simply because an identical obstacle affects domestic trade.'

With all due respect, the learned Advocate General here seemed to err with regard to both points. Not only had the Court already developed a number of tests for different categories of national measures, the idea that Article 34 could be used to attack obstacles to domestic trade had been relatively new. Interestingly, Jacobs here proposed an alternative—general—test for all measures, namely (ibid., para. 42): 'If the principle is that all undertakings should have unfettered access to the whole of the [Union] market, then the appropriate test in my view is whether there is a substantial restriction on that access. That would of course amount to introducing a *de minimis* test into Article [34].' And yet, somewhat contradictorily, he subsequently adds that 'it would not be appropriate to apply a *de minimis* test to measures which overtly discriminate against goods from other Member States' (ibid., para. 43), as these would be per se prohibited.

[91] For me, the main reason for criticizing *Keck* is that it gave rise to the idea that there are only two categories of national measures: product requirements and selling arrangements. For not only does the *Keck* Court itself—as many a commentator overlooks—recognize a third category of measures ('rules that are intended to regulate trade in goods between Member States'); there was potentially a whole range of subcategories of measures—such as price regulations—where the Court had developed a distinctive doctrinal approach.

the existence of federal elements and outlaw national legislation that prevented a 'European' wide advertisement campaign? Both of these questions would be dealt with all too soon; and as Section II will show, the promise of legal certainty via a post-*Keck* 'renaissance of formalism' would not be redeemed.[92]

II. Types and Tests: The Post-*Keck* Doctrinal Framework

How would the post-*Keck* Court deal with the distinct jurisprudential lines that had emerged within Article 34; and could they—eventually—be brought within an overarching doctrinal framework? Unsurprisingly, the period immediately following *Keck* was a period in which the Court tried to clarify its 'clarification'.[93] Having confirmed the constitutional function of Article 34 to lie in the liberalization of *intra-Union* trade—and not trade as such—the Court first needed to define the parameters of its new 'selling arrangements' rule. But in its post-*Keck* jurisprudence, the Court also consolidated its *Cassis* line; and during this period, the Court even developed a third jurisprudential line on consumer use restrictions. This last line appears to have prompted—two decades after *Keck*—a return to a national market philosophy. The central question today has however been this: how do the various jurisprudential lines relate to each other? Does the Court see them as mutually exclusive—parallel—lines or rather as specific elements of a broader doctrinal framework? Let us attend to these questions in turn.

[92] Prophetically, though too pessimistically: N. Reich, 'The "November Revolution" of the European Court of Justice: *Keck*, *Meng* and *Audi* Revisited', 470: 'A return to a formal, narrow interpretation might be welcomed as a panacea for the dangers of supra-national law encroaching on traditional rules, habits and uses of Member State law. Analysing [*Keck*] more closely, we submit that the finely-knit distinctions and definitions by the Court will not bring about legal certainty, quite the contrary.' And later on (ibid., 486): 'As far as state rules restricting certain "selling arrangements" are concerned, standards must be developed to distinguish them from regulations relating to product presentations. There is no clear-cut distinction between them. Selling arrangements refer to regulations having an incidence on the pace of doing business and therefore have a more *static* element, while rules on product presentations concern the *dynamic* elements of marketing products.'

[93] S. Weatherill, 'After *Keck*: Some Thoughts on How to Clarify the Clarification'.

1. *The* Keck *Jurisprudential Line: Clarifying the Clarification*

The *Keck* Court had unambiguously insisted on a change of direction. But how far would it wish to go; and what types of measures were included within the 'selling arrangements' line?

An opportunity to determine the parameters of the *Keck* jurisprudential line swiftly presented itself in *Hünermund*.[94] The case dealt with a prohibition against pharmacists advertising, outside their premises, quasi-pharmaceutical products. This rule was neither designed 'to regulate trade in goods between Member States',[95] nor was it a product requirement; and the Court therefore classified it as a selling arrangement. Subjecting the national law to the *Keck* test, the Court found that the rule was indistinctly applicable and did 'not affect the marketing of goods from other Member States differently from that of domestic products'.[96] The selling arrangement was thus outside the scope of Article 34; and this result was confirmed, almost verbatim, in numerous similar cases.[97]

Yet when did the category of 'selling arrangements' begin and the category of 'product requirements' end? The best judicial treatment of the distinction was given in *Familiapress*.[98] The case pitched an Austrian newspaper publisher against a German competitor that had used prize-winning crossword puzzles in its publications. This sales technique was prohibited in Austria and when the German newspapers were sold there, Familiapress brought proceedings against Bauer. The latter counterclaimed that the Austrian measure constituted a MEEQR and the question arose whether it constituted a selling arrangement in the meaning of the *Keck* judgment. Before the Court of Justice, the Austrian government had relied on this idea but the Court did not think so:

> The Austrian Government maintains that the prohibition at issue falls outside Article [34] of the Treaty. In its view, the possibility of offering readers of

[94] Case C-292/92, *Hünermund and others v Landesapothekerkammer Baden-Württemberg*.

[95] Ibid., para. 19. [96] Ibid., para. 23.

[97] See only: Joined Cases C-401–2/92, *Criminal proceedings against Tankstation 't Heukske vof and J. B. E. Boermans*; Joined Cases C-69 and 258/93, *Punto Casa SpA v Sindaco del Comune di Capena and Comune di Capena and Promozioni Polivalenti Venete Soc. coop. arl (PPV) v Sindaco del Comune di Torri di Quartesolo and Comune di Torri di Quartesolo*; Case C-412/93, *Société d'Importation Edouard Leclerc-Siplec v TF1 Publicité SA and M6 Publicité SA*; Case C-418/93, *Semeraro Casa Uno Srl v Sindaco del Comune di Erbusco*.

[98] Case C-368/95, *Vereinigte Familiapress Zeitungsverlags- und vertriebs GmbH v Heinrich Bauer Verlag*.

a periodical the chance to take part in prize competitions is merely a method of promoting sales and hence a selling arrangement within the meaning of the judgment in *Keck and Mithouard*. The Court finds that, even though the relevant national legislation is directed against a method of sales promotion, *in this case it bears on the actual content of the products, in so far as the competitions in question form an integral part of the magazine in which they appear*. As a result, the national legislation in question as applied to the facts of the case is not concerned with a selling arrangement within the meaning of the judgment in *Keck and Mithouard*.[99]

This located the distinction between selling arrangements and product requirements in the 'physical integrity' of the imported good: any national rule that would 'bear[] on the actual content of the product[]' would thus *not* constitute a selling arrangement under the *Keck* jurisprudential line.[100] Nonetheless, the classification of whether or not a measure is a selling arrangement (or not) has never been perfect.[101]

[99] *Familapress*, paras. 10–11 (emphasis added).

[100] See already: Case C-470/93, *Verein gegen Unwesen in Handel und Gewerbe Köln e.V. v Mars GmbH*, where the Court implicitly held that a rule that would 'compel the importer to adjust the presentation of his products according to the place where they are to be marketed' would not be a selling arrangement (ibid., paras. 13–14). And see also: Case C-416/00, *Tommaso Morellato v Comune di Padova*, where the Court added the following qualification (ibid., paras. 33–6): 'The fact that a product must, to a certain extent, be transformed after importation does not in itself preclude a requirement relating to its marketing from falling within the scope of application of Article [34] of the Treaty. It is possible that, as in the main proceedings, the imported product is not simply a component or ingredient of another product but in reality constitutes the product that is intended for marketing as soon as a simple transformation process has been carried out. In such a situation, the relevant question is whether the requirement for prior packaging laid down in the legislation of the Member State of import makes it necessary to alter the product in order to comply with that requirement. In the present case, nothing in the file indicates that it was necessary for the pre-baked bread, as imported into Italy, to be altered in order to comply with that requirement. In those circumstances, the requirement for prior packaging, since it relates only to the marketing of the bread which results from the final baking of pre-baked bread, is in principle such as to fall outside the scope of Article [34] of the Treaty, provided that it does not in reality constitute discrimination against imported products.'

And see also Case C-309/02, *Radlberger Getränkegesellschaft mbH & Co. and S. Spitz KG v Land Baden-Württemberg*; as well as Case C-366/04, *Georg Schwarz v Bürgermeister der Landeshauptstadt Salzburg*, para. 29: 'It follows from this that importers wishing to put those goods up for sale in Austria have to package them, which makes their importation into that Member State more expensive. It is also apparent from the file that vending machines designed for non-packaged goods cannot be used for packaged goods. It follows from this that, in principle, the aforementioned national provision constitutes a measure having equivalent effect to quantitative restrictions within the meaning of Article [34 TFEU].'

[101] See only: Case C-244/06, *Dynamic Medien Vertriebs GmbH v Avides Media AG*, esp. paras. 32–3: 'In the present case, the rules at issue in the main proceedings do not

Be that as it may, once a measure is classified as a selling arrangement, the question arises whether the two *Keck* conditions are fulfilled. Thus: is the measure indistinctly applicable and, if so, would it '*affect in the same manner, in law and in fact, the marketing of domestic products and of those from other Member States*'?[102] While the first question is a simple matter of law,[103] the latter may be a complex matter of fact, and the Court here applies intense judicial scrutiny.

In *De Agostini*,[104] a Swedish company had advertised, on Swedish television, a children's magazine on dinosaurs. (The magazine was printed in Italy and published in a number of language versions all across Europe.) In Sweden, the advertising campaign ran counter to an advertising ban for children under 12 years of age and the question arose, whether the ban constituted a measure of equivalent effect prohibited under Article 34. Having classified the measure as a selling arrangement that was indistinctly applicable, the Court explored the discriminatory nature of the ban and thereby admitted that it could not be 'excluded that an outright ban, applying in one Member State, of a type of promotion for a product which is lawfully sold there might have a greater impact on products from other Member States'.[105] This line of enquiry was picked up in *Gourmet*.[106] The Court here again dealt with the Swedish advertising prohibition, which was designed to reduce the sale of alcoholic drinks. Would the latter be

constitute a selling arrangement within the meaning of the case-law resulting from *Keck and Mithouard*. Those rules do not prohibit sale by mail order of image storage media. They provide that, in order to be marketed in that way, image storage media must be subject to a national examination and classification procedure for the purpose of protecting young persons, regardless of whether a similar procedure has already been followed in the Member State from which those image storage media were exported. Furthermore, those rules lay down a condition with which image storage media must comply, namely that with regard to their labelling.'

102 *Keck*, para. 16 (emphasis added).

103 For a distinctly applicable selling arrangement that the Court outlawed, see only: Case C-531/07, *Fachverband der Buch- und Medienwirtschaft v LIBRO Handelsgesellschaft mbH*.

104 Joined Cases C-34–6/95, *Konsumentombudsmannen (KO) v De Agostini (Svenska) Förlag AB and TV-Shop i Sverige AB*. For an analysis of the case law on advertising restrictions generally, see: R. Greaves, 'Advertising Restrictions and the Free Movement of Goods and Services'; as well as: D. Doukas, 'Untying the Market Access Knot: Advertising Restrictions and the Free Movement of Goods and Services'.

105 *De Agostini*, para. 42.

106 Case C-405/98, *Konsumentombudsmannen (KO) v Gourmet International Products AB (GIP)*.

regarded as a non-discriminatory selling arrangement that fell outside the scope of Article 34? The Court denied this and held:

It is apparent that a prohibition on advertising such as that at issue in the main proceedings not only prohibits a form of marketing a product but in reality prohibits producers and importers from directing any advertising messages at consumers, with a few insignificant exceptions ... [I]n the case of products like alcoholic beverages, the consumption of which is linked to traditional social practices and to local habits and customs, *a prohibition of all advertising directed at consumers in the form of advertisements in the press, on the radio and on television, the direct mailing of unsolicited material or the placing of posters on the public highway is liable to impede access to the market by products from other Member States more than it impedes access by domestic products*, with which consumers are instantly more familiar ... A prohibition on advertising such as that at issue in the main proceedings must therefore be regarded as affecting the marketing of products from other Member States more heavily than the marketing of domestic products and as therefore constituting an obstacle to trade between Member States caught by Article [34] of the Treaty.[107]

Let us quickly pause here. What is the judicial argumentation in the above passage, and in what ways does it diverge from *Keck*? On a formal level, the Court appears to have inverted its *Keck* reasoning. For instead of examining whether the national measure discriminated in fact and *therefore* impeded market access,[108] it now employed a market-access test to determine whether the national law discriminated or not! This formal inversion elevated the market-access test to centre stage.[109]

Selling arrangements could henceforth be seen discriminatory as soon as—factual not legal—access to the host market was harder for foreign than for domestic goods.[110] Yet the problem with this approach is that

[107] Ibid., paras. 20–1 and 25 (emphasis added).

[108] This had still been the case in Case C-254/98, *Schutzverband gegen unlauteren Wettbewerb v TK-Heimdienst Sass GmbH.*

[109] A. Kaczorowska, '*Gourmet* Can Have His *Keck* and Eat It!', 486.

[110] See expressly: Case C-322/01, *Deutscher Apothekerverband eV v 0800 DocMorris NV and Jacques Waterval*, paras. 74–5: 'A prohibition such as that at issue in the main proceedings is more of an obstacle to pharmacies outside Germany than to those within it. Although there is little doubt that as a result of the prohibition, pharmacies in Germany cannot use the extra or alternative method of gaining access to the German market consisting of end consumers of medicinal products, they are still able to sell the products in their dispensaries. However, for pharmacies not established in Germany, the internet provides a more significant way to gain direct access to the German market. A prohibition which has a greater impact on pharmacies established outside German territory could impede access to the market for products from other Member States more than it impedes access for domestic products. Accordingly, the

a prohibition or limitation on any advertising format will *always* benefit domestic goods 'the consumption of which is linked to traditional social practices and to local habits and customs'.[111] Indeed, *any* reduction of marketing possibilities of foreign products—even if indistinctly applicable—will here automatically lead to material discrimination; and in order to escape this inevitable conclusion, the Court has tried to cultivate a fine line between (absolute) prohibitions and (relative) limitations on the marketing of goods.[112] But regardless of its substantive merit, this judicial qualification

prohibition does not affect the sale of domestic medicines in the same way as it affects the sale of those coming from other Member States.'

[111] *Gourmet*, para. 21.

[112] The Court appears to have adopted a softer position where the national advertising law does only restrict—and not prohibit—advertising or marketing, see: Case C-412/93, *Leclerc-Siplec*, as well as Case C-71/02, *Karner Industrie-Auktionen GmbH v Troostwijk GmbH*, para. 42: 'As regards the second condition, Paragraph 30(1) of the UWG, contrary to the national provisions which gave rise to Joined Cases C-34/95 to C-36/95 *De Agostini and TV-Shop* and to Case C-405/98 *Gourmet International Products*, does not lay down a total prohibition on all forms of advertising in a Member State for a product which is lawfully sold there. It merely prohibits any reference, when a large number of people are targeted, to the fact that goods originate from an insolvent estate if those goods no longer constituted part of the insolvent estate, on grounds of consumer protection. Although such a prohibition is, in principle, likely to limit the total volume of sales in that Member State and, consequently, also to reduce the volume of sales of goods from other Member States, it nevertheless does not affect the marketing of products originating from other Member States more than it affects the marketing of products from the Member State in question. In any event, there is no evidence in the file forwarded to the Court by the national court to permit a finding that the prohibition has had such an effect.'

However, in Case C-441/04, *A-Punkt Schmuckhandels GmbH v Claudia Schmidt*, the Court seems to have qualified this qualification (ibid., paras. 22–5): 'Admittedly, as observed by the Commission of the European [Union], the sale in private homes of jewellery of low value might seem to be more appropriate and efficient than sale in a fixed commercial structure. In fact, for traders specialising in jewellery of that value, sale in a fixed commercial structure is liable to give rise to costs that are proportionately very high. Nevertheless, the fact that a marketing method is apparently more efficient and profitable is not a sufficient reason to assert that the national provision prohibiting it is caught by the prohibition laid down in Article [34 TFEU]. Such a provision constitutes a measure having equivalent effect only if the exclusion of the relevant marketing method affects products from other Member States more than it affects domestic products. In this respect, it is common ground that the prohibition at issue in the main proceedings does not concern all the ways of marketing the goods in question, but only one of them, and therefore does not exclude the possibility of selling those goods in Austria by other methods. However, the information available to the Court does not allow it to ascertain beyond doubt whether the prohibition on selling in private homes laid down in Paragraph 57 of the GewO affects the marketing of products from Member States other than Austria to a greater degree than it affects the marketing of products from that Member State. In such circumstances, it is therefore for the national court to determine whether that condition is met and to do so, in particular, in the light of the considerations developed in paragraphs 20 to 24 of this judgment.'

ironically undermines the 'formalist' philosophy on which the *Keck* revolution was built. For by introducing a substantive standard, the Court has come to destabilize the formal discrimination 'rule' that *Keck* had wished to establish for selling arrangements.[113]

2. *The* Cassis *Jurisprudential Line: Beyond Product Requirements*

What is the material scope of the *Cassis* jurisprudential line? Apart from product requirements *prohibiting* the marketing of a product in a host State, would it also capture national laws that merely *impeded* the sale of a foreign good? The post-*Keck* Court has indeed had to deal with an increasing number of situations in which Member States no longer prescribed mandatory—and fixed—national product requirements but 'only' subjected the sale or marketing of a product to a national authorization procedure.[114] This second-generation *Cassis* jurisprudence thereby goes beyond the first generation in a number of ways.

A good illustration of this development is offered by *Commission v Italy (Ships Equipment)*.[115] Italian legislation here required that all equipment on ships had to have a certificate of conformity issued by the Italian Ships Registry and that such a certificate could only be issued if successful tests had been conducted by the Italian authorities.[116] A Danish producer of marine equipment complained to the Commission, and the Commission brought proceedings in which it argued that the absence of an *Italian* mutual recognition mechanism for conformity certificates violated Article 34.[117] The Court indeed found that such a violation of Article 34

[113] For a positive view of this development, see however: P. Koutrakos, 'On Groceries, Alcohol and Olive Oil: More on Free Movement of Goods after *Keck*'.

[114] This development had become necessary after the new approach to harmonization. On the emergence and rise of the new approach generally, see: R. Schütze, *From Dual to Cooperative Federalism: The Changing Structure of European Law*, 205 et seq. In the wake of the new approach, the Court was thus increasingly asked to assess the validity of 'product authorization procedures'—that is, rules that do not prohibit the marketing of imported products as such but make the marketing of imports dependent on a national authorization. The Court rightly decided to treat this problem as a—procedural version—of its *Cassis* jurisprudence, see only: Case C-388/00, *Radiosistemi Srl v Prefetto di Genova*; Case C-455/01, *Commission v Italy*; Case C-270/02, *Commission v Italy*; Case C-443/02, *Schreiber*; Case C-297/05, *Commission v Netherlands*; Case C-244/06, *Dynamic Medien Vertriebs GmbH v Avides Media AG*; Case C-333/08, *Commission v France*. During this period, the Court is of course also dealing with 'classic' product requirement cases, see only: Case C-184/96, *Commission v France (Froi Gras)*.

[115] Case C-455/01, *Commission v Italy (Ships Equipment)*.

[116] Ibid., para. 11.

[117] Ibid., para. 12.

had taken place. A mere impediment to the principle of mutual recognition by a national authorization procedure was consequently enough to hinder the free movement of goods.[118]

A similar solution was adopted in *Dynamic Medien v Avides Media*.[119] The case concerned a German law for the protection of young persons that made the sale of image-storage media dependent on having received an age-limit label by the relevant German authorities. Avides Media maintained an electronic trading platform from which it had sold Japanese cartoon DVDs that were imported from the United Kingdom into Germany. A competitor brought proceedings against Avides by claiming that the movies had not received a *German* age-limit examination. This was true; yet the cartoons had already been examined by the *British* Board of Film Classification, which had classified them in the category 'suitable only for 15 years and over'.[120] Would the insistence on an independent German examination be seen as an illegal duplication that violated Article 34? Having referred to its *Cassis* jurisprudential line, the Court considered that it 'has also treated as measures having equivalent effect, prohibited by Article [34], national provisions making a product lawfully manufactured and marketed in another Member State subject to additional controls'.[121] And since the German law made the importation of DVDs 'more difficult and more expensive', it was indeed seen as a MEEQR falling within the scope of Article 34.[122]

3. *A 'New' Jurisprudential Line: Consumer Restrictions*

'Product requirements' and 'selling arrangements' are of course but two categories of internal measures that potentially constitute MEEQRs. But what about national rules that ban drinking—not selling—in public spaces; and what about a law prohibiting smoking in restaurants? For a very long time it seemed that Article 34 could solely cover national rules that somehow interfered with the *commercial* chain beginning with the *production* of a good to its *trading* and subsequent *selling*.

[118] Ibid., para. 22: 'The abovementioned national provisions are thus capable of hindering intra-[Union] trade and therefore constitute a measure having an effect equivalent to a quantitative restriction prohibited by Article [34].' For a similar result and reasoning, see: Case C-171/11, *Fra.bo*; as well as Case C-484/10, *Ascafor*, where the Court however now uses a market-access rationale.

[119] Case C-244/06, *Dynamic Medien Vertriebs GmbH v Avides Media AG*.

[120] Ibid., para. 12. [121] Ibid., para. 28. [122] Ibid., para. 24.

The status of national laws regulating the 'consumer use' of a good therefore seemed (relatively) safe; [123] but this has gradually changed in the last decade.[124] The Court here started its—modern—approach in *Commission v Portugal*.[125] The case involved a Portuguese prohibition against affixing tinted film to the windows of motor vehicles, and the Court held that the ban constituted a MEEQR since 'potential customers, traders or individuals have practically no interest in buying them in the knowledge that affixing such film to the windscreen and windows alongside passenger seats in motor vehicles is prohibited'.[126] Article 34 could consequently cover 'usage bans', because the latter came indeed close to an import or marketing ban.

But what about national rules that did not (absolutely) prohibit but merely restricted the use of a product? In its subsequent jurisprudence, the Court clearly confirmed that these rules could also fall within the scope of Article 34. In *Italian Trailers*,[127] an Italian highway law prohibited the use of trailers on motorcycles and mopeds on highways. The Commission thought the provision constituted an MEEQR and brought proceedings against Italy. Italy ably defended itself by insisting that 'a rule concerning use is covered by Article [34 TFEU] *only if it prohibits all uses of a product or its only use, if the product only has one*', whereas 'if there is a discretion as to the possible uses of the product, the situation no longer falls under Article [34]'.[128]

After considerable disagreement among various Advocates General,[129] the Court tried to play it safe. Differentiating between trailers

[123] For an early approach to these questions, see: Case 75/81, *Blesgen v Belgium*; as well as Case 148/85, *Direction générale des impôts and procureur de la République v Marie-Louise Forest, née Sangoy, and Minoterie Forest SA*, where the Court dealt with a limitation on the use of flower for milling and expressly pointed out that 'the system in question does not affect the possibility of importing flour intended for human consumption from other Member States' (ibid., para. 17). Similarly, Case C-473/98, *Kemikalieinspektionen v Toolex Alpha AB*, was confined to the 'industrial use' of a product (ibid., para. 34).

[124] For general academic analyses of the 'consumer-use restriction' cases, see: E. Spaventa, 'Leaving "Keck" Behind?: The Free Movement of Goods after the Rulings in "Commission v Italy" and "Mickelsson and Roos"'; S. Enchelmaier, '"Moped Trailers", "Mickelsson & Roos", "Gysbrechts": The ECJ's Case Law on Goods Keeps on Moving'; P. Oliver, 'Of Trailers and Jet Skis: Is the Case Law on Article 34 TFEU Hurtling in a New Direction?'; L. Gormley, 'Free Movement of Goods and Their Use: What Is the Use of It?'; P. Wennerås and K. Bøe Moen, 'Selling Arrangements, Keeping *Keck*'.

[125] Case C-265/06, *Commission v Portugal*.

[126] Ibid., para. 33. [127] Case C-110/05, *Commission v Italy (Italian Trailers)*.

[128] Ibid., para. 19 (emphasis added).

[129] This case had been originally allocated to Advocate General Léger, who delivered his opinion on 5 October 2006. His relatively simple view was this (ibid., paras. 40–1): 'Although that prohibition relates only to mopeds, it seems to me that the coupling of a trailer to a

for general use and trailers specifically designed for motorcycles,[130] the Court dismissed the Commission's action with regard to the former (as it had not been shown that the national measure hindered market access);[131]

vehicle of that kind constitutes a normal and frequently used means of transport, particularly in rural areas. However, those rules, although not prohibiting imports of trailers and their marketing in Italy, have the effect of limiting their use throughout Italian territory. I am therefore of the opinion that such a prohibition is liable to limit opportunities for trade between the Italian Republic and the other Member States and to hamper imports and the marketing in Italy of trailers from those States, even though they are lawfully manufactured and marketed there. In those circumstances, it seems to me that the national rules at issue constitute a measure having an effect equivalent to a quantitative restriction, in principle prohibited by Article [34].'

Interestingly, this view was not to be shared by Advocate General Kokott in a related case. In Case C-142/05, *Åklagaren v Percy Mickelsson and Joakim Roos*, she considered that limitations on the use of goods should be assimilated, by analogy, to selling arrangements (ibid., paras. 47 and 55): 'I suggest excluding arrangements for use in principle from the scope of Article [34], in the same way as selling arrangements, where the requirement set out by the Court in *Keck and Mithouard* is met ... Against this background, it therefore appears logical to extend the Court's *Keck* case-law to arrangements for use and thus to exclude such arrangements from the scope of Article [34].' Yet when applying the *Keck* conditions, she ultimately also found that 'a national measure restricting or prohibiting an arrangement for use is not excluded from the scope of Article [34] if it prevents access to the market for the product in question'; and that '[i]n this respect it is not only rules which result in complete exclusion, such as a general prohibition on using a certain product, that are to be regarded as preventing access to the market' (ibid., paras. 66–7).

In light of these conflicting signals, the Court consciously reallocated the case from a five-judge chamber to the Grand Chamber, reopened the oral procedure, and invited all the Member States to give their views on whether, and to what extent, Article [34] should cover usage restrictions. A second opinion, this time by Advocate General Bot, was delivered on 8 July 2008. The latter now argued 'that national measures governing conditions for the use of goods should not [!] be examined in the light of the criteria laid down by the Court in *Keck and Mithouard*' (ibid., para. 11). The principal reason for Bot thereby was this (ibid., para. 91): 'Finally, I think that to exclude from the scope of Article [34 TFEU] national rules governing not only selling arrangements for goods but also arrangements for their use is contrary to the Treaty's objectives, namely the creation of a single and integrated market. In my view, such a solution would undermine the useful effect of Article [34 TFEU], since it would once more make it possible for Member States to legislate in areas which, on the contrary, the legislature wished to "communitarise". That is not the course that European construction and the creation of a single European market should follow. A product must be able to move, unhindered, within the common market, and national measures which, in whatever way, create an obstacle to intra-[Union] trade must be ones that the Member States can justify.' And criticizing the idea of distinct tests for distinct categories of measures, the Advocate General here suggested that all judicial review be based on a market access test (ibid., paras. 108 et seq.): 'The criterion I propose would therefore be a general criterion, based on the effect of the measure on access to the market rather than on the object of the rules in question. That criterion would therefore apply to all types of rules, be they requirements relating to the characteristics of a product, selling arrangements or arrangements for use.'

130 *Italian Trailers*, paras. 51 et seq.

131 Ibid., paras. 52–3.

yet for trailers specifically designed for motorcycles, the Court held as follows:

It should be noted in that regard that a prohibition on the use of a product in the territory of a Member State has a considerable influence on the behaviour of consumers, which, in its turn, affects the access of that product to the market of that Member State. Consumers, knowing that they are not permitted to use their motorcycle with a trailer specially designed for it, have practically no interest in buying such a trailer. *Thus, Article 56 of the Highway Code prevents a demand from existing in the market at issue for such trailers and therefore hinders their importation.* It follows that the prohibition laid down in Article 56 of the Highway Code, to the extent that its effect is to hinder access to the Italian market for trailers which are specially designed for motorcycles and are lawfully produced and marketed in Member States other than the Italian Republic, constitutes a measure having equivalent effect to quantitative restrictions on imports within the meaning of Article [34 TFEU], unless it can be justified objectively.[132]

This judicial reasoning stepped outside the dichotomy of *Cassis*-related 'product requirements' and *Keck*-defined 'selling arrangements'. The Italian measure was in fact neither; and faced with this new category of measure, the Court consequently promoted its market-access test to a third and independent test. (The Court had indeed carefully prepared this constitutional promotion in its 'preliminary observations'.[133])

The extension of Article 34 to national measures that reduce consumer demand was confirmed in *Mickelsson & Roos*.[134] The case involved a Swedish restriction on the use of personal watercraft (jet skis). The skis could only be used on either generally navigable waters or on specifically designated waterways. This restriction had been violated by the defendants; and in the course of criminal proceedings, they pleaded that the Swedish legislation constituted a violation of Article 34 TFEU. In its reply to the preliminary question, the Court confirmed its market access test for consumer use restriction as follows:

Even if the national regulations at issue do not have the aim or effect of treating goods coming from other Member States less favourably, which is for the national court to ascertain, the restriction which they impose on the use of a

[132] Ibid., paras. 56–8 (emphasis added).

[133] For this important point, see Section II(4) of this chapter.

[134] Case C-142/05, *Åklagaren v Mickelsson and Roos*. And see also: Case C-142/09, *Criminal proceedings against Vincent Willy Lahousse and Lavichy BVBA*.

product in the territory of a Member State may, depending on its scope, *have a considerable influence on the behaviour of consumers, which may, in turn, affect the access of that product to the market of that Member State. Consumers, knowing that the use permitted by such regulations is very limited, have only a limited interest in buying that product.*

In that regard, where the national regulations for the designation of navigable waters and waterways *have the effect of preventing users of personal watercraft from using them for the specific and inherent purposes for which they were intended or of greatly restricting their use*, which is for the national court to ascertain, such regulations have the effect of hindering the access to the domestic market in question for those goods and therefore constitute, save where there is a justification pursuant to Article [36] or there are overriding public interest requirements, measures having equivalent effect to quantitative restrictions on imports prohibited by Article [34].[135]

The Court here confirmed that there was no need to show discrimination; nor was there any reference to the principle of mutual recognition. The market-access test simply focused on whether the rules totally or 'greatly' prevented consumers from using products that were lawfully produced in the European Union. This market-access test was clearly informed by a *national* market philosophy, albeit one that was qualified by a substantial threshold.[136] In the immediate post-*Trailer* jurisprudence, this market-access test appeared to become the dominant rationale underlying Article 34—even in areas in which alternative jurisprudential lines provided relatively safe identical solutions.[137] But be that as it may, on a formal level, Article 34 henceforth contained three (plus one) independent jurisprudential lines, which can be seen in Figure 4.

135 *Mickelsson & Roos*, paras. 26–8 (emphasis added).

136 In this sense: P. Wennerås and K. Bøe Moen, 'Selling Arrangements, Keeping *Keck*', 395: 'Judging from the norms set out and applied in *Italian Trailers* and *Mickelsson and Roos* it appears that the threshold inherent in the market hindrance test is high, and that it is significantly more qualified than the 'substantial' market-access test first proposed by Advocate General Jacobs in *Leclerc-Siplec* and nurtured by Advocates General and academics ever since.'

137 See only: Case C-108/09, *Ker-Optika bt v ÀNTSZ Dél-dunántúli Regionális Intézete*; Case C-443/10, *Bonnarde v Agence de Services et de Paiement*; as well as Case C-484/10, *Asociación para la Calidad de los Forjados (Ascafor) and Asociación de Importadores y Distribuidores de Acero para la Construcción (Asidac) v Administración del Estado and others*, esp. para. 56: '[T]he requirements at issue are capable of restricting access to the Spanish market for reinforcing steel manufactured and certified in a Member State other than the Kingdom of Spain, in so far as they may not necessarily be fulfilled by the certifying body of the producing State.'

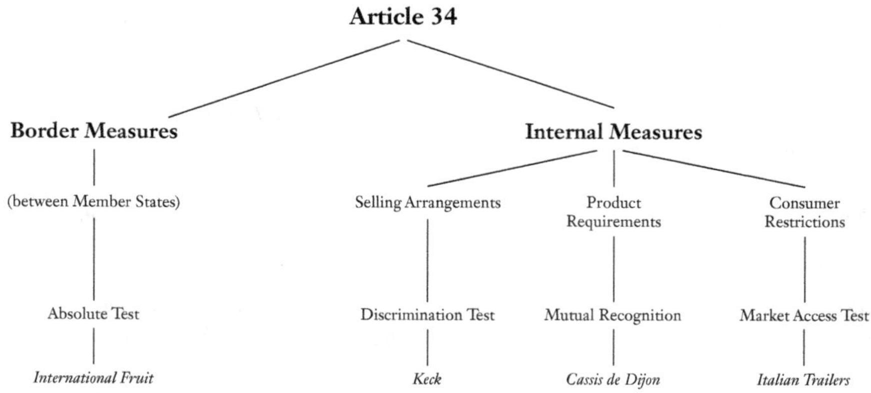

Figure 4. Article 34: four different jurisprudential lines

4. *Converging Lines: Towards a Single Doctrinal Framework?*

One of the central questions raised within academic circles after *Italian Trailers* was whether the Court had abandoned its *Keck* jurisprudence.[138] Some doubts as to the demise of *Keck* surfaced quickly;[139] yet while reports about *Keck's* death may turn out to be greatly exaggerated, the much more important question was always this: what is the relationship between the three tests developed in the three jurisprudential lines for internal measures post-*Keck*? In its preliminary observations in *Italian Trailers*, the Court—following an earlier suggestion[140]—represented its existing case law as follows:

> It should be recalled that, according to settled case-law, all trading rules enacted by Member States which are capable of hindering, directly or indirectly, actually or potentially, intra-[Union] trade are to be considered as measures having an effect equivalent to quantitative restrictions and are, on that basis, prohibited by Article [34].

[138] E. Spaventa, 'Leaving "Keck" Behind?', 915 and 929: '[F]or sure, the Court did not openly overrule *Keck*, and yet the market access formula might suggest, in fact if not in law, the end of the *Keck* dichotomy ... the *Keck* distinction based on the type of rules is no longer relevant; what matters is the effect of the rules on market access.'

[139] See only Case C-531/07, *Fachverband der Buch- und Medienwirtschaft v LIBRO*; as well as Case C-108/09, *Ker-Optika bt v ÀNTSZ Dél-dunántúli Regionális Intézete*. For an argument that *Keck* survived, see also: P. Wennerås and K. Bøe Moen, 'Selling Arrangements, Keeping *Keck*'; as well as P. Oliver, 'Of Trailers and Jet Skis: Is the Case Law on Article 34 TFEU Hurtling in a New Direction?'.

[140] Opinion of Advocate General Maduro in Case C-158/04, *Alfa Vita Vassilopoulos AE*, esp. paras. 43–6.

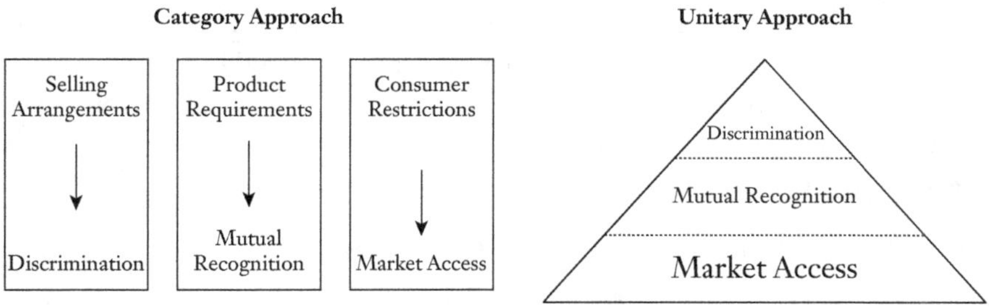

Figure 5. Two modern approaches to Article 34

> It is also apparent from settled case-law that Article [34] reflects the obligation to respect the principles of non-discrimination and of mutual recognition of products lawfully manufactured and marketed in other Member States, as well as the principle of ensuring free access of [European] products to national markets.[141]

The scope of Article 34, as jurisdictionally defined by the *Dassonville* formula, is here broken down into three substantive principles: the *international* principle of non-discrimination, the *federal* principle of mutual recognition, and the *national* principle of free market access. But how did these three principles relate to each other? Two possibilities here exist (see Figure 5). According to the traditional *category approach*, each of the three principles correlates with a specific category of measure. National rules affecting selling arrangements would thus be—exclusively—tested against the discrimination principle, product requirements would be subject to the principle of mutual recognition, and consumer restrictions fall—exclusively—under the market-access test. (Under this approach, the market-access test will consequently only apply to measures that are neither subject to the *Keck* nor *Cassis* line; and non-discriminatory selling arrangements or product requirements would therefore not fall foul of Article 34 via the market-access test.) By contrast, according to a *unitary approach*, the Court could regard the three principles as generally applicable principles, which each concretize the abstract *Dassonville* definition for all categories of measures. Any national measure that hindered trade would thus have to be tested against each of the three principles—vertically ranging from the international discrimination test to the national market-access test.

[141] Case C-110/05, *Italian Trailers*, paras. 33–4 (references to *Dassonville*, *Sandoz*, *Cassis*, and *Keck*). See also Case C-142/05, *Mickelsson & Roos*, para. 24.

Which of the two approaches has the Court favoured in its post-*Trailers* jurisprudence? Would it continue with the status quo and follow a category approach; or would it take up the (US American) idea that various tests could simultaneously apply to all types of measures? Let us explore this question in more detail.

a. The Rise of a Unitary Approach: Ker-Optika *and Beyond*

Has the rise of the market-access test led to a single doctrinal framework in which all three tests could be combined? A first strong signal in favour of such a unitary approach may be seen in *Ker-Optika*.[142] The case involved a Hungarian limited partnership that had sold contact lenses via its Internet site. This sales technique was prohibited by Hungarian legislation, which required that contact lenses be sold in specialized optical goods shops. The applicant challenged this 'selling arrangement' on the ground that it constituted a violation of Article 34. Which test would the Court apply? The analysis of the Court sat on the fence between the (old) category approach and the (new) unitary approach. The Court thereby started out with the latter. Expressly referring to *Dassonville* and *Trailer*, it summed up the normative principles governing Article 34 in the following way:

> According to settled case-law, all trading rules enacted by Member States which are capable of hindering, directly or indirectly, actually or potentially, trade within the European Union are to be considered as measures having an effect equivalent to quantitative restrictions and are, on that basis, prohibited by Article 34 TFEU. It is also apparent from settled case-law that Article 34 TFEU reflects the obligation to comply with the *principles of non-discrimination and of mutual recognition of products lawfully manufactured and marketed in other Member States, as well as the principle of ensuring free access of EU products to national markets*. Accordingly, measures adopted by a Member State the object or effect of which is to treat products coming from other Member States less favourably are to be regarded as measures having an effect equivalent to quantitative restrictions, as are rules that lay down requirements to be met by such goods, even if those rules apply to all products alike. *Any other measure which hinders access of products originating in other Member States to the market of a Member State is also covered by that concept*.[143]

What can we read out of the judgment, and what should we read into it? The Court here defined the scope of Article 34 abstractly by reference to the *Dassonville* formula as well as our three substantive principles. These

[142] Case C-108/09, *Ker-Optika bt v ÀNTSZ Dél-dunántúli Regionális Intézete*.
[143] Ibid., paras. 47–50 (emphasis added).

three principles are presented as exhaustive. For when the Court states that '[a]ny other measure' will be governed by the third principle, it not only appears to rule out the existence of a fourth substantive test within Article 34; it equally seems to disallow the direct application of the *Dassonville* formula. This part of the judgment therefore suggests that the abstract (jurisdictional) definition of Article 34 in *Dassonville* must always be matched and mediated by—at least—one of the three substantive principles listed by the Court.

But what is the relationship between these three principles? On the textual surface, the above passage favours a unitary approach. For the Court did *not* expressly correlate the three principles with specific categories of national laws and instead used the generic 'measures' and 'rules' for each of the three principles. The non-discrimination principle would consequently outlaw *all* national measures that discriminate against imports;[144] while the (federal) principle of mutual recognition will apply to *all* national laws doubly burdening goods produced in other Member States. Finally, the market-access test would apply to '[a]ny other measure', which only clarified that the Court would—practically—only come to test a national measure against the third principle when it had not already been caught by the other two substantive principles.

Had the Court consistently followed this line of argument it would have clearly turned its back on the classic category approach; yet hesitant to de-revolutionize the *Keck*-revolution, a second part of the judgment preferred the more conformist status quo reasoning. For the Court here—directly or indirectly, actually or potentially—returned to *Keck*.[145] National rules

[144] In this sense also, see: P. Wennerås and K. Bøe Moen, 'Selling Arrangements, Keeping *Keck*', 388: 'The latter judgments indicate that non-discrimination is the primary criterion determining whether any measures, not only selling arrangements, fall within Article 34.' And again at 393: 'The distinction between selling arrangements and other measures appears consequently no longer relevant under Article 34—all being subject to an assessment of discrimination in law or in fact—while product requirements remain a distinct category by virtue of their inherent discriminatory effects.' Non-discrimination thus operates 'as the primary' test and market hindrance as a 'subsidiary and thus supplementary test'.

[145] Case C-108/09, *Ker-Optika*, paras. 51–4 read: '[T]he application to products from other Member States of national provisions restricting or prohibiting certain selling arrangements is such as to hinder directly or indirectly, actually or potentially, trade between Member States for the purposes of the case-law flowing from *Dassonville*, unless those provisions apply to all relevant traders operating within the national territory and affect in the same manner, in law and in fact, the selling of domestic products and of those from other Member States ... It is clear that the prohibition on selling contact lenses by mail order deprives traders from other

governing selling arrangements were thus subjected to a discrimination test, although the latter was (again) defined as an *unequal* market-access test. This normative ambivalence stemmed from the Court's wish—to re-employ a delightful *bonmot*—to have its *Keck* and eat it.[146] The result was an 'easy' case making 'bad' law.[147]

Nonetheless, the attempt to systematize and structure the doctrinal framework within Article 34 resurfaced in *ANETT*.[148] The case involved a Spanish import prohibition for tobacco retailers, who were required to purchase their goods from authorized wholesalers. The Spanish legislation thus prohibited parallel imports by retailers and instead of referring to a 'classic' jurisprudential line here,[149] the Court repeated its new doctrinal triptych,[150] and held:

> In the main proceedings, nothing indicates that the national legislation at issue has the object or effect of treating tobacco coming from other Member States *less favourably*. Nor does it concern the *requirements that those products must meet*. However, it is still necessary to examine whether this legislation hinders the *access of tobacco products coming from other Member States* to the Spanish market ... [T]he tobacco retailers are prevented from procuring supplies in other Member States, even if the manufacturers and wholesalers located there could offer more advantageous procurement conditions, particularly in border areas, either because of their geographic proximity or because of the specific delivery methods they offer. All of these elements are capable of having a negative effect on the choice of products

Member States of a particularly effective means of selling those products and thus significantly impedes access of those traders to the market of the Member State concerned. In those circumstances, that legislation does not affect in the same manner the selling of contact lenses by Hungarian traders and such selling as carried out by traders from other Member States.'

[146] This brilliant pun was first used by A. Kaczorowska, '*Gourmet* Can Have His *Keck* and Eat It!'.

[147] P. Caro De Sousa, 'Through Contact Lenses, Darkly: Is Identifying Restrictions to Free Movement Harder than Meets the Eye? Comment on *Ker-Optika*', 81: 'apparently straightforward case is strangely convoluted'.

[148] Case C-456/10, *ANETT v Administración del Estado.*

[149] In Case C-189/95, *Criminal proceedings against Harry Franzén*, for example, when dealing with a Swedish system of production or wholesale licences for alcoholic beverages, the Court—having given its *Dassonville* formula as a definition of the concept of MEEQR—simply held that '[t]he licensing system constitutes an obstacle to the importation of alcoholic beverages from other Member States in that it imposes an additional cost on such beverages' (ibid., para. 71). This was indeed an easy case as the national rule was distinctly applicable to imports. But see also: Case C-54/05, *Commission v Finland*, para. 31: 'In addition, the Court of Justice has already ruled that Article [34] precludes the application in intra-[Union] trade of national provisions which require, even as a pure formality, import licences or any other similar procedure.'

[150] *ANETT*, para. 33.

that the tobacco retailers include in their range of products and, ultimately, on the access of various products coming from other Member States to the Spanish market.[151]

In the above passage, the Court tested the Spanish measure against all three principles: in the absence of discrimination or an application of domestic product requirements to imports, it found that it was 'still' (!) necessary to subject the Spanish measure to a market-access test. This formulation suggested two things. First, the Court—again speaking through its Third Chamber—here appeared to favour a unitary approach to the three substantive principles underlying Article 34; and, secondly, it seemed to indirectly confirm that a breach of at least one of its three substantive principles was required before a violation of Article 34 could be found. This reading was subsequently confirmed, albeit indirectly, in *Elenca*;[152] as well as in *Commission v Poland*.[153]

b. Rhetoric and Reality: Uncertainties in the Latest Jurisprudence

Every constitutional court will wish to appear consistent over time; and yet, every *good* constitutional court will recognize that constitutional change through the judiciary is a necessary undemocratic 'evil', where the social reality underpinning a constitutional order is itself changing.[154] Problems however arise, where judicial inconsistencies are not the result of changes over time but emerge—simultaneously—from dogmatic fragmentation *within* a 'contemporary' court. Sadly, it is this internal inconsistency that has characterized the European Court's latest jurisprudence on Article 34.

[151] Ibid., paras. 36–42 (emphasis added).

[152] Case C-385/10, *Elenca Srl v Ministero dell'Interno*, esp. para. 23.

[153] In Case C-639/11, *Commission v Poland*, the Court dealt with a Polish requirement to reposition the steering wheel of British cars to the left-hand side before they could be registered in Poland. (The facts therefore placed the case in between the *Cassis* and the *Trailer* line, since the vehicles could be sold but not used.) In its reasoning, the Court however did not specifically refer to the principle of mutual recognition but instead generally stated that 'the contested legislation constitutes a measure having equivalent effect to quantitative restrictions on imports within the meaning of Article 34 TFEU, in so far as its effect is to hinder access to the Polish market for vehicles with steering equipment on the right, which are lawfully constructed and registered in Member States other than the Republic of Poland' (ibid., para. 52). This suggested that the Court did not see the mutual recognition principle and the market-access principle as mutually exclusive. Instead, it appeared to view the latter as a—vertically—broader substantive test; and if that perspective is also brought to selling arrangements, then the *Keck* formula could take its doctrinal retirement.

[154] In the famous words of John Marshall: '[W]e must never forget that it is a *Constitution* we are expounding' (*McCulloch v Maryland*, 17 US 316 (1819), 407).

For despite a strong 'rhetorical' push towards a unitary approach, discussed earlier, recent jurisprudence has revealed that the various chambers of the Court do not share the same understanding of Article 34; and this has created two discomforting uncertainties. First, what is the nature of the *Dassonville* formula and its relation to the three substantive principles described above; and, secondly, has the unitary approach really replaced the classic category approach, and with it *Keck*?[155]

Let us explore these problems in the final section of this chapter.

aa. Doctrinal Uncertainties I: Three Tests and the Dassonville *Formula*

The *Ker-Optika* formula suggested that for Article 34 to be breached at least one of the three substantive principles had to be violated; and yet in *Åland*, the Grand Chamber of the Court curiously put this again into question.[156] The case concerned a Swedish law that aimed at assisting the production of green electricity. Sweden had created a system of electricity certificates and the award of these certificates was linked to electricity production installations in Sweden; and when the applicant company sought permission for a wind farm in Finland, the certification was rejected on the ground that the green electricity installation was outside Sweden. This was a (materially) discriminatory measure,[157] yet the Grand Chamber reasoned, without any express reference to any of the three *Ker-Optika* principles, as follows:

> The free movement of goods between Member States is a fundamental principle of the Treaty which finds its expression in the prohibition set out in Article 34 TFEU. It is settled case-law that, in prohibiting between Member States measures

[155] In this sense: S. Dietz and T. Streinz, 'Das Marktzugangskriterium in der Dogmatik der Grundfreiheiten', 69: 'Bei sorgfältiger Prüfung des Drei-Stufen-Tests hat die *Keck*-Formel ausgedient.' And see also: I. Lianos, 'In Memoriam *Keck*: The Reformation of the EU Law on the Free Movement of Goods'.

[156] Case C-573/12, *Ålands vindkraft AB v Energimyndigheten*. For an extensive discussion of the case, see: M. Szydło, 'How to Reconcile National Support for Renewable Energy with Internal Market Obligations? The Task for the EU Legislature after *Ålands vindkraft* and *Essent*'.

[157] In this sense also: Advocate General Bot, Case C-573/12, *Ålands vindkraft AB v Energimyndigheten*, para. 76: 'Although the Swedish green certificate scheme does not prohibit the importation of electricity, it indisputably confers an economic advantage which may favour producers of green electricity located in Sweden as compared with producers located in other Member States, since, whereas the former benefit from additional income from the sale of green certificates, which is in effect a production premium, the income of the latter is derived solely from the sale of green electricity.'

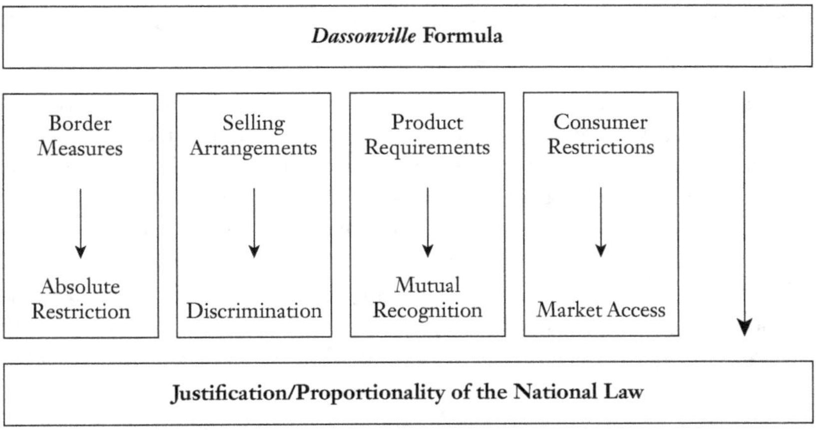

Figure 6. Direct application of *Dassonville* as a substantive rule

> having equivalent effect to quantitative restrictions on imports, Article 34 covers *any national measure capable of hindering, directly or indirectly, actually or potentially, intra-[Union] trade*. As it is, it must be noted in that regard that the legislation at issue is capable, in various ways, of hindering—at least indirectly and potentially—imports of electricity, especially green electricity, from other Member States.[158]

The Court here appeared to apply the *Dassonville* formula as if it was a substantive decision rule! For not only was the judgment devoid of any express references to the principles of discrimination, mutual recognition, or market access; rhetorically, the *Dassonville* formula provided the sole major premise under which the Court subsumed the case (see: Figure 6).[159]

Was this omission of the three substantive tests a conscious choice or an unconscious aberration? If the former, then the Court should recall that any *unmediated* application of the *Dassonville* formula will entail the danger of its mechanical—unbounded—application; and that it was the lack of a substantive—controlling—criterion that caused one of the greatest judicial turnarounds in *Keck*. The Court (Second Chamber) seems to have again shown a preference for a mediated reading of *Dassonville* in *Canadian Oil Company*.[160] Dealing with a Swedish registration requirement for chemical substances

[158] Ibid., paras. 65–7 (emphasis added).

[159] Yet, importantly, the *Dassonville* formula was at least translated into the concrete proposition that national measures must be capable of hindering '*imports* from other Member States'. Advocate General Bot even referred to the old-fashioned idea of 'trading rules' in para. 74 of his opinion.

[160] Case C-472/14, *Canadian Oil Company Sweden AB, Anders Rantén applicants v Riksåklagaren*.

that applied to domestically produced or imported goods alike, the Court explained its finding of a violation of Article 34 TFEU as follows:

> [A]ll measures of a Member State which are capable of hindering, directly or indirectly, actually or potentially, trade within the European Union are to be considered as measures having an effect equivalent to quantitative restrictions within the meaning of Article 34 TFEU ... [T]he mandatory nature of the registration of the import of chemical products with the competent national authority constitutes a measure having an effect equivalent to a quantitative restriction within the meaning of Article 34 TFEU, since the fact of imposing formalities for import is capable of hindering trade within the European Union *and impeding access to the market for goods which are lawfully produced and marketed in other Member States*[.][161]

This reasoning appears to confirm, albeit weakly and without express reference to the *Ker-Optika* formula, that any national measure that formally qualifies under the *Dassonville* formula must also violate a substantive market-access test.

bb. Doctrinal Uncertainties II: Keck*—Neither Alive Nor Dead?*

What about the *Keck* solution for selling arrangements? While *Ker-Optika* (and its progeny) seemed to suggest that the market-access test could independently apply to selling arrangements, the Fifth Chamber of the Court appears to have recently re-strengthened the *Keck* category approach in *Visnapuu*.[162] The case concerned the question whether a seller of alcoholic beverages, established in another Member State, would need to hold a Finnish retail sale licence so as to sell drinks within Finland. The Finnish rule constituted a 'selling arrangement' that—while non-discriminatory—clearly hindered market access. How would the Court doctrinally analyse this situation? The Court held as follows:

> [T]he prohibition of measures having an effect equivalent to a quantitative restriction, laid down in Article 34 TFEU, applies to all legislation of the Member States that is capable of hindering, directly or indirectly, actually or potentially, trade between Member States ... *The Court of Justice has indeed held that national provisions restricting or prohibiting certain selling arrangements that, first, apply to all relevant traders operating within the national territory, and, secondly, affect in the same manner, in law and in fact, the marketing of domestic products and those from other Member States are not liable to hinder, directly or indirectly, actually or potentially, trade between*

[161] Ibid., paras. 43–4.

[162] Case C-198/14, *Visnapuu v Kihlakunnansyyttäjä and Suomen valtio—Tullihallitus.*

Member States within the meaning of the case-law initiated by Dassonville. However, the retail sale licence requirement at issue in the main proceedings does not meet the first condition set out by the Court in *Keck and Mithouard*, according to which the national provisions at issue must apply to all relevant traders operating within the national territory ... and therefore it is not necessary to examine whether that requirement affects in the same manner, in law and in fact, the marketing of domestic products and of those from other Member States.[163]

The Court here gave *Keck* another licence to live;[164] yet it did so by—badly—reading *Keck* into *Dassonville*. For instead of seeing *Keck* as introducing a 'formal' rule that insists on discrimination as a 'substantive' test, the Court once more suggested that it is the *Dassonville* formula as such that directly applied to the specific case. And it was—again—the Second Chamber that questioned this very interpretation in *Scotch Whisky Association*.[165] The case assessed the attempt by the Scottish Parliament to reduce alcohol consumption by introducing a set minimum price for alcoholic beverages on the basis of a set price per unit of alcohol—a decision that was challenged by producer associations of alcoholic beverages, including the Scotch Whisky Association. Having surveyed the various past jurisprudential lines, Advocate General Bot gave the following advice to the Court:

According to the *formula* now usually employed in the case-law, Article 34 TFEU reflects the obligation to comply with the principles of non-discrimination and of mutual recognition of products lawfully manufactured and marketed in other Member States, as well as the principle of ensuring free access of EU products to national markets. I infer from that *standard formula* that a national measure may constitute an obstacle not only when, as a selling arrangement, it is discriminatory, in law or in fact, but also when, irrespective of its nature, it impedes access to the market of the Member State concerned ... The rules at issue in the main proceedings, which are acknowledged to apply without distinction to all the operators concerned who carry out their activity on the national territory, must therefore be regarded as a measure having effect equivalent to a quantitative restriction on imports contrary to Article 34 TFEU in that they are capable

[163] Ibid., paras. 98–108 (emphasis added).

[164] It is therefore at least doubtful whether recent developments on Article 34 have 'put into question two major contributions of *Keck*': 'the Court disposed of the factual presumption that selling arrangements do not constitute an obstacle to trade', and the Court also adopted 'a broad definition of the "market access" rule, which looks very close, if not being identical, to the "obstacles to trade" approach that animated the jurisprudence of the Court since *Dassonville/Cassis de Dijon* until its reversal by *Keck*' (I. Lianos, 'In Memoriam *Keck*', 238).

[165] Case C-333/14, *Scotch Whisky Association and others v Lord Advocate and Advocate General for Scotland.*

of constituting an obstacle to access to the market, solely because they prevent the lower cost price of the imported products from being reflected in the selling price to consumers.[166]

The Second Chamber of the Court was, sadly, less explicit about its reasoning. But making express reference to the opinion of the Advocate General, it held:

[A]ll measures of a Member State which are capable of hindering, directly or indirectly, actually or potentially, trade within the European Union are to be considered as measures having an effect equivalent to quantitative restrictions within the meaning of Article 34 TFEU. As the Advocate General stated in points 59 and 60 of his Opinion, the fact that the legislation at issue in the main proceedings prevents the lower cost price of imported products being reflected in the selling price to the consumer means, by itself, that that legislation is capable of hindering the access to the United Kingdom market of alcoholic drinks that are lawfully marketed in Member States other than the United Kingdom of Great Britain and Northern Ireland, and constitutes therefore a measure having an effect equivalent to a quantitative restriction within the meaning of Article 34 TFEU.[167]

If the Court here wished to follow *all* the logical elements excellently espoused in the Advocate General's opinion, then *Scotch Whisky Association* would be a clear signal in favour of the unitary approach and its idea that all national restrictions will be subject to a (residual) market-access test. But again, the internal inconsistencies within the Court leave a serious legal uncertainty at the heart of the European internal market;[168] and it is hoped that the Full Court will sooner rather than later speak an authoritative *Machtwort* to unify the Babylonian polyphony within the Court.

[166] Ibid., Advocate General Bot, paras. 58–60. While thus rejecting the *Keck* category approach on doctrinal grounds, the Advocate General nonetheless examined 'purely in the interest of completeness' (ibid., para. 61), whether the *Keck* test had been fulfilled or not; and he ultimately found that 'from whatever standpoint they are analysed, the rules at issue in the main proceedings appear to be contrary to Article 34 TFEU' (ibid., para. 69).

[167] *Scotch Whisky Association* (see n. 165), paras. 31–2.

[168] For the latest instalment of uncertainty, compare only the respective argumentative structures of Case C-221/15, *Criminal Proceedings against Etablissement Fr. Colruyt NV* (Sixth Chamber) with Case C-148/15, *Deutsche Parkinson Vereinigung eV v Zentrale zur Bekämpfung unlauteren Wettbewerbs eV* (First Chamber). This 'free style' approach towards each doctrinal step, and the relevant judicial authorities behind it, seriously undermine the 'academic' and 'judicial' legitimacy of the highest court in the European Union.

Conclusion

What philosophy generally governs the European common market today? This chapter tried to answer this question by exploring the doctrinal structure of Article 34 since *Cassis de Dijon*; and we saw that after *Cassis*, the legal structure of the European market could no longer be presented as a 'new legal order of international law'. For the principle of mutual recognition 'breaks' the backbone of the international model, as each State loses a part of its *internal* sovereignty over its own (internal) market. This loss of sovereignty was first established for national rules relating to product requirements; and the question whether this federal solution would equally apply to 'selling arrangements' has preoccupied the Court ever since. In a first post-*Cassis* phase, the Court experimented with a number of doctrinal solutions to this problem. Undecided whether to apply a federal or a national philosophy to selling arrangements, it—ultimately—chose a national solution according to which all selling arrangements that potentially hindered trade could fall within Article 34. This national market model is infamously at work in the *Sunday trading* cases. Yet fearful of an uncontrollable ultra-liberal philosophy within Article 34, the Court radically changed track in *Keck*. The judgment represents a 'true' revolution, which—at least for some time—'returned' to a (international) model for selling arrangements.

With *Keck*, the Court expressly acknowledged the existence of different tests for different categories of measures. Apart from the *Keck* line governing selling arrangements, the post-*Keck* Court refines the parameters of the federal model for product requirements (and related measures); and with *Italian Trailers*, it even cultivates a third jurisprudential line on consumer use restrictions. In the context of this third line, the Court thereby elevates the market-access test to centre stage: any national measure that 'greatly restrict[s]' the use of goods is seen as 'hindering the access to the domestic market in question for those goods' and thus constitutes a measure having equivalent effect to quantitative restrictions on imports.[169] This third line has, ironically, rehabilitated the 'national' market model. For Article 34 here captures national measures that apply without distinction to imported and domestic goods, and whose restrictive effect is not caused by a disparity of national legislation.

[169] Case C-142/05, *Mickelsson & Roos*, para. 28.

How do these three jurisprudential lines relate to each other? Two theoretical approaches were discussed. According to the (old) category approach, each jurisprudential line is subject to a different market model that exclusively applies to the national measures it covers. By contrast, the unitary approach advocates a single-market model; and it therefore subjects all national measures to the three principles of non-discrimination, mutual recognition, and free market access. In its recent jurisprudence, the Court has given rhetorical signals in favour of a unitary approach; yet at the same time, internal inconsistencies within the Court have created new uncertainties. The Court has thus not yet conclusively answered the question whether or not the three principles apply to mutually exclusive categories of national measures; nor has it definitely decided whether one of the three substantive principles always needs to be violated before a breach of Article 34 has occurred.

What is the better solution here? With regard to the first problem, the Court should—following US jurisprudence—adopt the unitary approach.[170] Subjecting all national measures to a (residual) market access test, the Court's jurisprudence could, at the same time, gain dogmatic clarity and casuistic flexibility. For the formal disappearance of the category approach will remove the sharp conceptual edges inherent in subjecting different types of measures to different tests, while the unitary approach could still indirectly draw on the advantages of the non-discrimination and mutual recognition tests as specific 'rules' that will invite strict scrutiny.

Importantly: a generalized market access test should *not* mean that the Court unconditionally outlaws all national measures that restrict freedom of trade generally. Any interpretation of Article 34 must always be balanced—whether through a substantive threshold that protects national regulatory spaces within Article 34 or through the development of an 'excessive burden' test at the justificatory level. Economic interests must never become the Court's sole or dominant value in interpreting Article 34. The best warning against an excessively liberal interpretation here comes from the United States, where the de-legitimizing shockwaves of the *Lochner* Supreme Court are still felt a century later.[171] This also

[170] In line with *Pike v Bruce Church, Inc.*, 397 US 137 (1970), the Court could cultivate a single framework with various prongs against which *each* State measure needs to be examined. Discrimination here simply provides an easy—formal—shortcut to finding a violation of Article 34, while a non-discriminatory rule could fall within the scope of the provision if it—materially—impeded market access.

[171] On this point, see: Chapter 2, 'Conclusion' in this volume.

helps us with regard to the second problem. Because the Court should not forget—only two decades after *Keck*—that a mechanical application of the *Dassonville* formula is inherently indeterminate and dangerously unlimited. It should consequently see the *Dassonville* formula as a *jurisdictional* principle that must always be complemented by one—or all—of the *substantive* principles (or tests) developed in its past jurisprudence. Only in this way can the substantive achievements of the *Keck* revolution be preserved, while its formal categories may—like a used-turned-useless ladder—be thrown away.[172]

[172] For the famous ladder metaphor, see: L. Wittgenstein, *Tractatus Logico-Philosophicus*, 89—Proposition 6.54.

5

The Rise of the Federal Model II

Introduction

The evolution of the European market from an *international* to a *federal* market meant that the Member States would, correspondingly, lose a part of their internal sovereignty over their 'internal' markets. They could no longer lay down indistinctly applicable product standards or consumer use restrictions without being subject to a European normative frame.

This federal model is however potentially subject to two 'special' regimes. First, because the jurisprudence on Article 34 primarily concerned goods produced *within* the Union, the question arises whether the same constitutional principles also apply to restrictions imposed on goods coming from outside the Union. Could an importer of American liqueurs invoke *Cassis de Dijon* to challenge a Member State's minimum alcohol content rules? With Article 34 being silent on the issue, all depended on the meaning of Article 28 TFEU—expressly extending the principles governing Articles 34 et seq. to 'products coming from third countries which are in free circulation in Member States'.[1] A second special problem, on the other hand, relates to export restrictions under Article 35 TFEU. Textually, the provision perfectly mirrored that of Article 34. But would this mean that the Union preferred a federal market structure here too? Logic would dictate that result; yet, as we shall see below, the Court (in)famously chose to follow a different kind of logic here.

While Section I will discuss these special regimes, Section II subsequently explores the various exemptions and justifications for national measures considered to hinder intra-Union trade. According to the so-called 'purely internal situation' rule, the Court has traditionally exempted situations from the scope of Articles 34 and 35 that were, as regards their facts, procedurally confined to a single Member State. This 'procedural' exemption was complemented by those substantive justifications expressly mentioned in Article 36. The latter contains a limited number of legitimate policy objectives that could justify national restrictions on imports or exports. These policy objectives originally catered for an international market model; yet, as we shall see below, the *Cassis* revolution had important repercussions at the justificatory level too. For not only did the Court henceforth allow for an (unlimited) number of implied justifications, the *Cassis* revolution also dramatically changed

[1] Article 28(2) TFEU.

the proportionality standard against which national trade barriers would be reviewed.

I. Special Jurisprudential Regimes: Which Market Model?

Can the general doctrinal evolution of Article 34, discussed in Chapter 4, also be detected with regard to goods coming from outside the European Union? Within a customs union, this should be the case; yet to what extent would it also apply beyond customs matters and, in particular, quantitative restrictions? Could a Member State quantitatively restrict American or Chinese imports without breaking Article 34; and if not, were there nonetheless additional qualifications that could be relied on? And what about Member States restricting their export trade vis-à-vis other Member States? Such measures were clearly not 'protectionist' in the mercantilist sense, but would they nevertheless be subject to a similar constitutional regime as that developed under Article 34?

Let us explore these questions in turn.

1. *Third-Country Goods in the EU Internal Market*

With regard to third-country goods, the EU Treaties had chosen a seemingly simple rule. Founded on the idea of a customs union, they decreed that—unlike in a free trade area—third-country goods were simply assimilated to Member State goods once they had lawfully entered the common market.[2] From the very start, Article 28 TFEU thereby stated that the provisions on the elimination of customs duties as well as the prohibition of quantitative restrictions 'shall apply to products originating in Member States *and to products coming from third countries which are in free circulation in Member States*'.[3] The Treaties thereby defined the concept of 'free circulation' in Article 29 as follows:

> Products coming from a third country shall be considered to be in free circulation in a Member State *if the import formalities have been complied with and any*

[2] The following section will not explore the Union rules with regard to third-country goods in transit.

[3] Article 28(2) TFEU.

customs duties or charges having equivalent effect which are payable have been levied in that Member State, and if they have not benefited from a total or partial drawback of such duties or charges.[4]

The idea behind the provision was straightforward: while *direct* exports into the Union would *not* enjoy free-movement rights,[5] once a third-country good had crossed the Union's customs barriers, it was entitled to circulate freely within the internal market. *Indirect* imports of third-country goods from one Member State to another were consequently protected under EU law—in particular: Article 34. But would Article 34 apply in the very same way, and to the same extent, to third-country goods once in free circulation? The following section explores this question. We shall see that the Union legal order has *not* required full assimilation of these goods. It has, in fact, added two qualifications—one relative and one absolute—to the analysis of Article 34.

a. *Relative Qualification: The Existence of a 'Common Commercial Policy'*

That special considerations would apply to goods coming from third countries had been clear ever since *International Fruit*.[6] Yet for third-country goods in free circulation, the leading case is *Donckerwolke*.[7] Belgian traders had exported foreign textile products into France. The textiles originated in Lebanon and Syria but had lawfully entered the Belgian market and, consequently, they were in free circulation within the Union.

[4] Article 29 TFEU (emphasis added).

[5] These goods could however enjoy substantially similar rights, once the Union had so decided by means of legislation (cf. Regulation 260/2009 on the common rules for imports (2009) OJ L 84/1); or on the basis of an international agreement. In the past, the Court has nonetheless emphasized that not all of the 'internal' market jurisprudence would be projected onto these external market provisions. See only: Case 270/80, *Polydor Limited and RSO Records, Inc. v Harlequin Records Shops Limited and Simons Records Limited*, esp. para. 18: 'The considerations which led to that interpretation of Articles [34 and 36] of the Treaty do not apply in the context of the relations between the [Union] and Portugal [then still a third State] as defined by the Agreement. It is apparent from an examination of the Agreement that although it makes provision for the unconditional abolition of certain restrictions on trade between the [Union] and Portugal, such as quantitative restrictions and measures having equivalent effect, it does not have the same purpose as the [FEU] Treaty, inasmuch as the latter, as has been stated above, seeks to create a single market reproducing as closely as possible the conditions of a domestic market.'

[6] Joined Cases 51–4/71, *International Fruit Company NV and others v Produktschap voor groenten en fruit*. For a discussion of the case: see Chapter 3, Section II(2) of this volume.

[7] Case 41/76, *Criel, née Donckerwolcke and Henri Schou v Procureur de la République au tribunal de grande instance de Lille and Director General of Customs*.

However, according to French customs legislation, third-country goods were required to be accompanied by a certificate of origin so as to assist the French customs authorities in the monitoring of trade flows of non-Union goods. Yet when the Belgian traders exported their textiles into France, they had not declared the original origin of the goods; and the French authorities therefore sentenced the traders to a fine equal the value of the imported goods.

Was that possible in light of Article 28 TFEU and the assimilation principle? According to the text of the provision, it was clearly not and the Court thus held as follows:

> According to Article [28] of the Treaty the [Union] shall be based upon a customs union which shall cover all trade in goods between Member States. According to Article [28 (2)] the provisions adopted for the liberalization of intra-[Union] trade apply in identical fashion to products originating in Member States and to products coming from third countries which are in 'free circulation' in the [Union] ... It appears from Article [28] that, as regards free circulation of goods within the [Union], products entitled to 'free circulation' are definitively and wholly assimilated to products originating in Member States. *The result of this assimilation is that the provisions of Article [34] concerning the elimination of quantitative restrictions and all measures having equivalent effect are applicable without distinction to products originating in the [Union] and to those which were put into free circulation in any one of the Member States, irrespective of the actual origin of these products.*[8]

Having dutifully recited the ordinary constitutional principles governing the free movement of goods generally,[9] the Court nonetheless made this—theoretical—solution '*conditional* upon the establishment of a common commercial policy'.[10] In the unmistakably clear words of the Court, the following additional qualification would thus be required:

> The assimilation to products originating within the Member States of goods in 'free circulation' *may only take full effect if these goods are subject to the same conditions of importation both with regard to customs and commercial considerations, irrespective of the State in which they were put in free circulation.* Under Article [207] of the Treaty this unification should have been achieved by the expiry of the transitional

[8] Ibid., paras. 14–18 (emphasis added).

[9] The Court here gave a definition of the scope of Article 34 TFEU, as defined by Case 8/74, *Procureur du Roi v Benoît and Gustave Dassonville* and Joined Cases 51–4/71, *International Fruit*, paras. 19–20); and it then referred to the 'Movement Certificate DD1' that had been established.

[10] Case 41/76, *Donckerwolcke*, para. 24 (emphasis added).

period and supplanted by the establishment of a common commercial policy based on uniform principles. The fact that at the expiry of the transitional period the [Union] commercial policy was not fully achieved is one of a number of circumstances calculated to maintain in being between the Member States differences in commercial policy capable of bringing about deflections of trade or of causing economic difficulties in certain Member States.[11]

The Court here constitutionally linked the free circulation of third-country goods within the European market with the 'unification' of the Union's common commercial policy (CCP); and since the goods in question did not yet come within the CCP,[12] the Member States were '*not* prevented from requiring from an importer a declaration concerning the actual origin of the goods in question even in the case of goods put into free circulation in another Member State'.[13] However, as in *Dassonville*,[14] the Court subjected this freedom to a rule of reason.[15] Or, to put it in *Cassis*-like terms: in the absence of Union 'harmonization' with regard to third-country goods, the Member States remained entitled to adopt 'reasonable' unilateral measures that were necessary to fulfil imperative requirements. The Court thus confirmed that, in the absence of a CCP, there existed a temporary—and thus relative—suspension of the constitutional demand underlying Article 28(2) TFEU.

This relative qualification of Article 28 TFEU was confirmed in *Tezi*.[16] The case concerned textile products from Macao, which were imported into the Union. This time, the Union had adopted a number of commercial policy measures. Not only were the goods covered by a Multi-Fibre Agreement (concluded pursuant to the 1947 General Agreement on Tariffs and Trade), there also existed an internal Union measure that specified quantitative limits to such textile imports.[17] However, upon a special request from the Benelux countries, the Union had granted them special

[11] Ibid., paras. 25–7 (emphasis added).

[12] Ibid., para. 6.

[13] Ibid., para. 33 (emphasis added).

[14] Case 8/74, *Procureur du Roi v Benoît and Gustave Dassonville*. For an extensive discussion of the facts and legal context of the case, see: R. Schütze, *Framing Dassonville: Text and Context in European Law*, Chapter 3.

[15] Case 41/76, *Donckerwolcke*, para. 35: 'Nevertheless the Member States may not require from the importer more in this respect than an indication of the origin of the products in so far as he knows it or may reasonably be expected to know it.'

[16] Case 59/84, *Tezi Textiel BV v Commission*.

[17] Regulation 3589/82 on common rules for imports of certain textile products originating in third countries (1982) OJ L 374/106.

permission to impose a system of import licences.[18] Tezi challenged this national system by arguing that since there was 'a genuine common commercial policy' the national import licences violated Article 34 as the third-country goods were now fully subject to the provision.[19]

The Court found otherwise. Referring to *Donckerwolke*, it instead held 'that under the system of the Treaty the full application of the principle of free movement of goods imported from non-Member countries is *conditional upon the establishment of a common commercial policy*'.[20] And the latter would only come into existence when Union legislation 'led to the creation of *uniform conditions of importation*'; and while the relevant textile regulation was 'undoubtedly a step towards the establishment of a common commercial policy', it had not brought about '*complete uniformity as regards the conditions of importation*'.[21] In essence: solely complete uniformity under the CCP would lead to the complete assimilation of third-country goods under the principles of the internal market, including Article 34.[22]

This was a high—yet relative—qualification. But, as it turned out, it was not the only dent in the assimilation theory for third-country goods. For the Court came to also think that there existed an—absolute—substantive qualification to Article 28(2) TFEU.

[18] These special authorizations could originally be given by means of ex-Article 115 EEC: 'In order to ensure that the execution of measures of commercial policy taken in accordance with this Treaty by any Member State is not obstructed by deflection of trade, or where differences between such measures lead to economic difficulties in one or more of the Member States, the Commission shall recommend the methods for the requisite cooperation between Member States. Failing this, the Commission shall authorise Member States to take the necessary protective measures, the conditions and details of which it shall determine.'

[19] Case 59/84, *Tezi Textiel BV v Commission*, para. 14.

[20] Ibid., para. 30 (emphasis added).

[21] Ibid., paras. 35–7 (emphasis added).

[22] See also: Case C-212/88, *Criminal proceedings against F. Levy*, paras. 8–9 (emphasis added): 'It must be borne in mind that the provisions of Article [34] of the Treaty on the elimination of quantitative restrictions and all measures having equivalent effect are applicable without distinction to products originating in the [Union] and those which have been put into free circulation in any of the Member States, regardless of where those products first originated. Furthermore, Article [28 (2)] of the Treaty prohibits any administrative procedure which is designed to establish different rules concerning the movement of products according to whether they originate in the [Union] or they originate in a non-member country but have been put into free circulation in one of the Member States, since the two categories of products are both included without distinction in the same system of free circulation. *However, under the system established by the Treaty, the application of those principles is conditional on the introduction of a common commercial policy*. In its present incomplete state, differences in commercial policy between the Member States are likely to continue and, in some of those States, may lead to deflections of trade or economic difficulties.'

b. Absolute Qualification: Substantive Limits to Full Assimilation

aa. Article 28 TFEU and Border Measures

The *Donckerwolke* Court had dealt with an easy case: a *customs* formality. But would the assimilation principle for third-country goods, requested by Article 28, apply to all categories of national measures that fell into Article 34? Doubts emerged with *EMI v CBS*.[23] The case involved the question whether the Court's free-movement jurisprudence on intellectual property rights could be projected to goods coming from third countries in free circulation. And the answer of the Court was a clear 'no':

> According to Article [29(1)] of the Treaty products coming from a third country shall be considered to be in free circulation in a Member State if the import formalities have been complied with and any customs duties or charges having equivalent effect which are payable have been levied in the importing Member State. According to Article [28(2)] of the Treaty the provisions of [Article 30 and Chapter 3 of this Treaty Title] shall apply to products coming from third countries which are in free circulation in Member States.
>
> *Since those provisions only refer to the effects of compliance with customs formalities and paying customs duties and charges having equivalent effect, they cannot be interpreted as meaning that it would be sufficient for products bearing a mark applied in a third country and imported into the [Union] to comply with the customs formalities in the first Member State where they were imported in order to be able then to be marketed in the common market as a whole in contravention of the rules relating to the protection of the mark.*[24]

The Court consequently held that the assimilation concept within Article 28 was a 'customs concept': only those national measures that were 'border measures' would be prohibited when they hindered the free movement of third-country goods. And from this—customs—perspective, the judgment in *Commission v Ireland (Potato Licence)* came as no surprise.[25] Ireland had adopted an order according to which any potato import from a country other than a EU Member State was prohibited unless the Minister for Agriculture had granted an import licence.[26] An Irish trader had been refused such a licence for potatoes originating in Cyprus (then not a Member State) but in free circulation within the United Kingdom.[27] The Commission considered this a violation of Articles 28, 29, and 34 of

[23] Case 51/75, *EMI Records Limited v CBS United Kingdom Limited*.

[24] Ibid., paras. 14–16 (emphasis added).

[25] Case 288/83, *Commission v Ireland (Potato Licence)*.

[26] Ibid., para. 2.

[27] Ibid., para. 4.

the Treaty; and the Court followed suit. For not only had the Union concluded an Association Agreement with Cyprus and thereby adopted a common commercial policy towards this third country,[28] the import licence was clearly a border measure. The Court—paying homage to the 'wholly assimilated' theory[29]—had thus little difficulty in finding a breach of Article 34.[30]

bb. Article 28 TFEU and Product Requirements

What about product requirements? Would third-country goods in free circulation also benefit from the *Cassis* presumption that non-discriminatory obstacles to trade arising from legislative disparities between the Member States fall within the scope of Article 34?[31] Would the Court, in other words, extend the—federal—philosophy of mutual recognition to goods not produced by one of the Member States? The wording of the *Cassis* judgment militated against this view. For the Court had textually insisted that mutual recognition was dependent on goods being 'lawfully *produced* and marketed in one of the Member States'.[32] This seemed to exclude third-country goods from the *Cassis* jurisprudential line and, as a consequence, from the free circulation rule.

[28] For a brief overview of the Association Agreement, see: Advocate General Darmon, ibid., para. 1.

[29] Ibid., para. 24: 'In accordance with those principles, laid down in Articles [28, 29, and 34 TFEU], the measures intended to free intra-[Union] trade are applicable, as the Court pointed out in its judgment of 15 December 1976 (*Donckerwolcke*, cited above), without distinction to products originating in the Member States and to those coming from non-member countries which have been put into "free circulation" in the [Union]. Once the latter products have been duly imported into the [Union] in accordance with the provisions in force relating to tariffs and trade, they are, as the Court emphasized, "definitively and wholly assimilated to products originating in Member States" (judgment cited above, paragraph 17).'

[30] Ibid., para. 27. Interestingly, the Association Agreement had established a special tariff and quota system but the Court found this immaterial (ibid., para. 27): 'It is of little importance whether that measure concerns products subject to the general rules laid down in the applicable provisions relating to tariffs and trade or products subject to special rules under an agreement, such as the tariff quota accorded to the Republic of Cyprus. The Irish measure thus constitutes, as such, a quantitative restriction prohibited by Article [34] of the Treaty.'

[31] For a closer analysis of this question, see: L. Ankersmit, 'What if Cassis de Dijon Were Cassis de Quebec?: The Assimilation of Goods of Third Country Origin in the Internal Market'.

[32] Case 120/78, *Rewe-Zentral AG v Bundesmonopolverwaltung für Branntwein (Cassis de Dijon)*, para. 14.

This theoretical result has been powerfully defended by Eric White.[33] Emphasizing that the GATT provisions do not require a customs union to adopt a *Cassis*-style approach towards third countries,[34] he has argued:

> Why, therefore, should Article [34], in conjunction with Article [28(2)], prohibit the application of indistinctly applicable measures of the *Cassis de Dijon* kind to products imported from third countries via another Member State? Such an interpretation would allow third country goods to enter the [Union] via the Member State with the least restrictive rules and then be entitled to be imported into any other Member State without the goods of those Member States being given reciprocal treatment by the third country involved. It is also contrary to the philosophy behind the prohibition of indistinctly applicable measures of the *Cassis de Dijon* kind ... [namely:] that producers should be free to take advantage of the legal and economic environment prevailing in a Member State without the access of their products to the market of another Member State being hindered as a result.[35]

The idea that Article 28(2) TFEU is confined to *distinctly* applicable (border) measures has nonetheless also received severe criticisms. For some academics, the *Cassis* reference to goods 'being lawfully produced *and* marketed in one of the Member States' is simply a 'famous mistake'. What the Court really meant to say was that all goods 'lawfully produced *or* marketed in one of the Member States' would benefit from free circulation via the principle of mutual recognition.[36] According to this view, mutual

[33] E. L. White, 'In Search of the Limits to Article 30 of the EEC Treaty', 259 et seq.

[34] White points in particular to Article XXIV 8(a)(i) GATT, which only insists that a customs union must eliminate duties and other restrictive regulations of commerce 'with respect to substantially all the trade between the constituent territories of the Union or at least with respect to substantially all trade in products originating in such territories'.

[35] E. L. White, 'In Search of the Limits to Article 30 of the EEC Treaty', 263.

[36] P. Eeckhout, *The European Internal Market and International Trade: A Legal Analysis*, 272: 'In the *Cassis de Dijon* example, if the liquor imported into Germany had been American, but previously imported and marketed in France in accordance with French regulations, it would also have benefited from the mutual recognition rule. It is true that the *Cassis de Dijon* judgment speaks of products "lawfully *produced and* marketed in one of the Member States", at first sight excluding products imported from third countries. But in view of the above-mentioned fundamental and unequivocal language on the assimilation—with respect to free movement—of imports to domestic goods, there seem to be no reasons for not also extending the rule of mutual recognition. Submitting the opposite would produce insurmountable difficulties.' See also: L. Gormley, 'Free Movement of Goods and Their Use: What Is the Use of It?', 1611: 'As is well known, this paragraph makes the famous mistake of using the term "lawfully produced and marketed" instead of "lawfully produced *or* marketed" that the scheme of the free movement within the European Union requires.'

recognition 'almost certainly extends to goods produced outside the EU, at least if it is lawful to produce and market them in the Member State where they were first put into free circulation'.[37] Article 34, in combination with Article 28, would consequently cover all third-country goods that are lawfully *marketed* in at least one Member State of the Union.[38]

What has the European Court of Justice said? There are no perfect judicial authorities for the constitutional proposition that a Member State must recognize the products of a third State lawfully marketed in another Member State; yet the Court has come close to it in a (small) number of cases. Leaving aside casual references,[39] the Court seemed to implicitly extend its *Cassis* jurisprudence to third-country goods in *Nijman*.[40] A Dutch trader had been prosecuted on the ground that he had sold a third-country good– called 'Improsol'—without having complied with the Dutch legislation concerning prior product approval. In a preliminary ruling, the Court here simply held:

As to whether the national legislation meets the requirements of Articles [34] to 36 of the Treaty, it must first be borne in mind that those provisions apply without distinction to products originating in the [Union] *and to those admitted into free circulation in any of the Member States, whatever the real origin of such products.* It is therefore subject to those reservations that Articles [34] to 36 of the Treaty apply to the product 'Improsol'. In the present case, the prohibition, enforced by

[37] P. Oliver, 'Free Movement of Goods', 344. Oliver however admits that he found no direct judicial authority to back up his view (ibid., n. 142). For an even more liberal position, see: L. Ankersmit, 'What if Cassis de Dijon Were Cassis de Quebec', who argues that the view that insists on the actual marketing of a product in a Member State would be 'overly formalist' (ibid., 1399); and that the decisive criterion should therefore be that the third-country goods are 'lawfully *marketable* in another Member State' (ibid., 1401 (emphasis added)). In essence (ibid.): 'The advantage here over the "lawfully marketed" standard is that it is less formalist, and does not require the actual offering for sale by a trader or an actual transaction as long as the trader can demonstrate that the product can legally be put on the market in another Member State.' This position may however be much harder to defend after Case C-525/14, *Commission v Czech Republic*—to be discussed below.

[38] This reading received some indirect—legislative—reinforcement by Regulation 764/2008 on the application of technical rules to products lawfully marketed in another Member State ((2008) OJ L 218/21). For the Regulation places exclusive emphasis on the marketing—not the producing—within a Member State of the Union.

[39] Cf. Case 27/80, *Criminal proceedings against Anton Adriaan Fietje*, para. 10 (emphasis added): 'Although the extension to imported products of an obligation to use a certain name on the label does not wholly preclude the importation into the Member State concerned of products originating in other Member States *or in free circulation in those States* it may none the less make their marketing more difficult, especially in the case of parallel imports.'

[40] Case C-125/88, *Criminal proceedings against Nijman*.

penalties in criminal law, of selling, storing or using any plant-protection product not authorized by a national law is capable of affecting imports from other Member States where the same product is admitted wholly or in part and thus of constituting a barrier to intra-[Union] trade. Such rules therefore constitute a measure having an effect equivalent to a quantitative restriction.[41]

The Court here appeared to extend its *Cassis* logic to products produced in non-Member States that were in free circulation within the Union.[42] However, free circulation significantly meant that the product had been lawfully marketed in at least one Member State:

[I]t would seem that there first has to be some degree of marketing in one Member State, before the benefit of mutual recognition in another Member State can be invoked. To give an example, if a German importer of a beer brewed in the United States, which does not conform to the *Reinheitsgebot*, but which does conform to the relevant Belgian regulations, wishes to sell that beer in Germany, he can only invoke the mutual recognition rule in case it has first been marketed in Belgium.[43]

This reading has—very recently—been strengthened in *Commission v Czech Republic (Hallmarks)*.[44] The Commission had brought infringement proceedings against a Czech law on the hallmarking of precious metals because it did not mutually recognize the hallmarks of WaarborgHolland, an independent assay office established in the Netherlands with branches in third countries. Disputing a violation of Article 34, the Czech Republic counterclaimed 'that precious metals *hallmarked in a third country* do not benefit from the free movement of goods guaranteed by Article 34 TFEU'.[45] For even if the third-country goods had been hallmarked in accordance

[41] Ibid., paras. 11–12 (emphasis added).

[42] Similarly, in Case C-216/01, *Budějovický Budvar, národní podnik v Rudolf Ammersin*, while not dealing with a product requirement as such but national legislation restricting the use of a geographical name, the Court held (ibid., paras. 97–8): 'National legislation prohibiting the use of a geographical name for goods originating in a non-member country which are admitted into free circulation in other Member States where they are lawfully marketed does not, it is true, absolutely preclude the importation of those products into the Member State concerned. It is, however, likely to make their marketing more difficult and thus to impede trade between Member States. It is therefore necessary to examine whether that restriction on the free movement of goods can be justified under [Union] law.' This solution seems to have been confirmed in Case C-244/06, *Dynamic Medien Vertriebs GmbH v Avides Media*; and, more recently, Case C-95/14, *Unione Nazionale Industria Conciaria (UNIC) and Unione Nazionale dei Consumatori di Prodotti in Pelle, Materie Concianti, Accessori e Componenti (Uni.co.pel) v FS Retail and others*.

[43] P. Eeckhout, *The European Internal Market and International Trade*, 275.

[44] Case C-525/14, *Commission v Czech Republic*.

[45] Ibid., para. 28 (emphasis added).

with the legislation of a Member State, they had not actually been marketed in that Member State; and for that reason, they could not benefit from the free-circulation principle established by Article 28 TFEU.[46] And, while the Court ultimately ruled against the Czech Republic,[47] it nevertheless confirmed the following constitutional proposition:

> [P]lacing on the market is a stage subsequent to import. Just as a product lawfully manufactured within the EU may not be placed on the market on that ground alone, the lawful import of a product does not mean that it will automatically be allowed onto the market. A product coming from a third country which is in free circulation is thus assimilated to products originating in the Member States as regards the elimination of customs duties and quantitative restrictions between Member States. Where, however, there is no EU legislation harmonising the conditions of marketing of the products concerned, the Member State in which they are put into free circulation may prevent their being placed on the market if they do not satisfy the conditions laid down for that purpose under national law in compliance with EU law ... *[I]t follows from the above that, contrary to the Commission's argument, the principle of mutual recognition established by the case-law ... cannot apply to trade within the EU in goods originating in third countries and in free circulation where they have not, before being exported to a Member State other than that in which they are in free circulation, been lawfully marketed in the territory of a Member State.*[48]

With regard to product requirements, the extension of Article 34 to third-country goods therefore appears to rest on an additional—substantive—qualification that must be read into Article 29. Third-country goods would not only have to comply with the relevant customs rules, they would also have to conform to one set of national marketing rules within the European Union! And by insisting that a product be in compliance with the technical requirements of at least one Member State, the closer social and economic homogeneity within the—closer—regional market of the European Union is thereby protected. For the extension of the principle of mutual recognition to third-country goods generally would severely undermine the 'closer union' of the Member States within a federal market.

[46] Ibid., para. 29.

[47] The Court held that the Czech legislation generically applied to all WaarborgHolland hallmarks, regardless of whether they had been lawfully marketed in the territory of the Netherlands or in that of another Member State or in the territory of a third State (ibid., paras. 43 and 64); and it was this general application that the Czech measure fell victim of.

[48] Ibid., paras. 38–9 (emphasis added).

2. *Export Restrictions under Article 35 TFEU*

The story so far has exclusively focused on the changing structure of European law through the prism of *import* restrictions. Yet the free-movement title also contains a provision with regard to exports: Article 35 TFEU. The wording of Article 35 perfectly mirrors that of Article 34: 'Quantitative restrictions on exports, and all measures having equivalent effect, shall be prohibited between Member States.'

Would it therefore not be 'logical' if the interpretative principles governing quantitative restrictions on exports mirrored those on imports? Originally, the Union legal order indeed held that the scope of Article 35 would run in parallel to that of Article 34. The Court thus expressly clarified that the concept of 'quantitative restriction' was identical for both provisions: 'The prohibition of quantitative restrictions covers measures which amount to a total or partial restraint of, according to the circumstances, imports, *exports* or goods in transit.'[49]

But would this constitutional parallelism also extend to the wider concept of a measure having an equivalent effect to quantitative restrictions (MEEQR)? In the early 'international' period of Article 34, the Court indeed subscribed to the identity of import and export restrictions here too. This can clearly be seen in *Bouhelier*.[50] French legislation required quality controls for all watches destined for export. This could be achieved in one of two ways: exporters could obtain an export licence or, alternatively, they could apply for a quality standard certificate that replaced the export licence.[51] Was this a MEEQR under Article 35? The Court answered this question in the positive; and it did so by simply projecting the 'ordinary' Article 34 principles to Article 35. For not only had it already held that import licences were prohibited as such,[52] the French measure formally

[49] Case 2/73, *Geddo v Ente Nazionale Risi*, para. 7 (emphasis added). See also: Case C-1/96, *The Queen v Minister of Agriculture, Fisheries and Food, ex parte Compassion in World Farming.*

[50] Case 53/76, *Procureur de la République de Besançon v Les Sieurs Bouhelier and others*.

[51] Ibid., para. 5.

[52] Ibid., para. 11. While the Court did not expressly refer to *International Fruit* (see n. 6) in this case, it did do so in another Article 35 case. In Case 68/76, *Commission v France*, the Court held (ibid., paras. 14–16): 'As the Court stated in its judgment of 15 December 1971, in Joined Cases 51 to 54/71 (*International Fruit Company NV and others v Produktschap voor Groenten en Fruit* [1971] ECR 1107), apart from the exceptions for which provision is made by [Union] law itself Articles [34 and 35] preclude the application to intra-[Union] trade of a national provision which requires, even purely as a formality, import or export licences or any other similar procedure. Accordingly, even if in connexion with intra-[Union] trade the FORMA granted

discriminated in that it applied 'in respect of exports alone' and was thus 'capable of constituting a *direct or indirect, actual or potential obstacle* to intra-[Union] trade'.[53] (This reference to the *Dassonville* formula here provided unequivocal evidence that the Court originally perceived Article 34 and Article 35 as Siamese twins;[54] and for border measures, this is still the case today.[55])

Importantly, however, once the scope of the free-movement rules went beyond international trade rules, the parallelism between Articles 34 and 35 was bound to stop. For if the *federal* principle of mutual recognition is to work, the product standards of the home State must be presumed legitimate. After the *Cassis* revolution within Article 34, the Court was thus bound to abandon its unitary concept of MEEQR and to conceptually limit the scope of Article 35 by reference to the scope of Article 34. This logical extension of *Cassis* was made in *Groenveld*—six months after the *Cassis* revolution.[56]

a. *The Patterns of Export Test: Product Requirements (and Beyond)*

In what many academic writers—wrongly—perceive as a curious, unimportant, or self-explanatory anomaly,[57] the *Groenveld* Court interpretively

its endorsement without delay and for all quantities requested, and even if the object of the measure was merely to ascertain the intentions of exporters, it must be held to be a measure having an effect equivalent to a quantitative restriction on exports. Indeed the imposition of any special export formality constitutes an obstacle to trade by the delay which it involves and the dissuasive effect that it has upon exporters.'

[53] Case 53/76, *Bouhelier*, para. 15.

[54] For a closer analysis of this point, see: R. Schütze, *Framing Dassonville: Text and Context in European Law*.

[55] Cf. Case C-5/94, *The Queen v Ministry of Agriculture, Fisheries and Food, ex parte: Hedley Lomas (Ireland)*.

[56] Case 15/79, *Groenveld v Produktschap voor Vee en Vlees*.

[57] Exemplary here is L. Gormley, 'The Definition of Measures Having Equivalent Effect', 202: 'Infamously, the Court declined to apply the *Dassonville* basic principle without more ado in the context of Article [35 TFEU] in relation to measures applicable irrespective of the distinction of the product. This demonstrates the truth of the old adage that hard cases make bad law[.]' However, the early Gormley was slightly more thoughtful and in 'Prohibiting Restrictions on Trade within the European Economic Community: The Theory and Application of Articles 30–36 of the E.E.C. Treaty', he at least tried to provide a reason beyond the (pragmatic) commonplace that export restrictions are less likely to happen than import restrictions because of the economic self-interest of a Member State. The distinguished commentator here opined, though without revealing his source, that the best explanation for the Court's deviation from *Dassonville* and *Cassis* was 'that the Court was influenced by American cases concerning commerce-clause attacks on state legislation which, although of general

confined Article 35 to those national laws that *distinctly* applied to exports. A wholesaler of horsemeat had challenged the legality of a Dutch law prohibiting the (industrial) production of horsemeat sausages. The law was to protect Dutch meat exports in light of the fact that the consumption of horsemeat was not allowed in the foreign markets of some important trading partners. Famously, the Court held that the Dutch measure did *not* constitute a MEEQR on exports, and here reasoned as follows:

> Article [35] concerns national measures which have as *their specific object or effect the restriction of patterns of exports and thereby the establishment of a difference in treatment between the domestic trade of a Member State and its export trade* in such a way as to provide a particular advantage for national production or for the domestic market of the State in question at the expense of the production or of the trade of other Member States.[58]

This passage has become known as the '*Groenveld* formula'.[59] It suggested three criteria for a violation of Article 35. First, a national measure must affect the 'patterns of exports', and—whatever this meant—it seemed to be a jurisdictional criterion à la *Dassonville*. This was followed by two additional substantive criteria. For there had to be, secondly, a 'difference in treatment' that would, thirdly, 'provide a particular advantage for national production'.[60] The Court consequently insisted on the existence

application, adversely affected out-of-state buyers' (ibid., 102). And see also: J. H. H. Weiler, 'Epilogue: Towards a Common Law of International Trade', 217: 'Another anomaly which I shall not elaborate here is the divergence between the Court's *Dassonville* obstacle jurisprudence on imports and its discrimination-based jurisprudence [for] Article [35] on exports. This anomaly was prompted by two factors: a more relaxed attitude by the Court to restrictions on exports which are rarely motivated by protectionist impulses and a clearer vision—antedating *Keck* by a generation—of the constitutional implications of *Dassonville*.' With due respect, nothing could be further from the truth, cf. R. Schütze, *Framing Dassonville: Text and Context in European Law*, Chapter 6.

[58] Case 15/79, *Groenveld v Produktschap voor Vee en Vlees*, para. 7 (emphasis added).

[59] The formula was originally less 'formulaic' with the Court fluctuating between slightly different versions, compare only: Case 155/80, *Oebel*, para. 15 with Case 286/81, *Criminal proceedings against Oosthoek's Uitgeversmaatschappij*, para. 13. For a criticism of the textual instability of the formula, see: P. Oliver et al., *Free Movement of Goods in the European Union*, 136.

[60] On the last criterion, see: Case 80/92, *Commission v Belgium*. The Court here clarified that a difference in treatment would not violate Article 35 where it favours exports, ibid., paras. 24–5: 'It should be borne in mind that, as the Court has consistently held, Article [35] of the Treaty concerns national measures which have as their specific object or effect the restriction of patterns of exports and thereby the establishment of a difference in treatment between the domestic trade of a Member State and its export trade, in such a way as to provide a special advantage for national production or for the domestic market of the State in question. In that

of some—formal—discriminatory treatment; and 'this is not so in the case of a prohibition like that in question which is applied objectively to the production of goods of a certain kind *without drawing a distinction depending on whether such goods are intended for the national market or for export*'.[61] In essence, indistinctly applicable product requirements, which did not formally discriminate against exports would *not* constitute MEEQR.

This insistence on a discrimination test was confirmed in *Kaas*.[62] Traders had challenged Dutch quality rules intended to improve the domestic production of cheese. The national legislation however exclusively applied to *domestic* goods; and the Court was therefore quick to dismiss a challenge on the basis of Article 34.[63] Yet the traders ingeniously argued that 'the impossibility of producing new types of cheeses in the Netherlands *entails the loss of export opportunities in respect of such cheeses*'; and '[a]s regards the cheeses which may still be produced, the [Dutch] provisions have an impact on the cost of Netherlands cheese and therefore in its competitiveness *on foreign markets*'.[64] But the Court, expressly invoking the *Groenveld* formula,[65] rejected this view and clarified 'that Article [35] does not have the effect of exempting producers from any rules which may, by affecting the conditions of production, have an impact on the volume or the cost of domestic production'.[66]

With similar clarity, the Court has also found that non-discriminatory 'production arrangements' and/or 'selling arrangements' would not violate Article 35. When dealing with a German baking prohibition before 4.00 am,[67] the Court thus held with regard to the former:

> Article [35] concerns national measures which have *as their specific object or effect the restriction of patterns of exports and thereby the establishment of a difference in treatment between the domestic trade of a Member State and its export trade, in such a way as to provide a particular advantage for national production or for the domestic market of the State in question*. This is clearly not the case with rules such as those in issue, which are part of

connection, the Belgian legislation relating to transmitters and transceivers applies both to products intended for the Belgian market and to those intended for export, while the latter alone qualify for exemption from certification. That fact cannot, however, be regarded as constituting a difference in treatment between domestic trade and export trade which has as its specific object or effect the restriction of patterns of exports.'

[61] Case 15/79, *Groenveld v Produktschap voor Vee en Vlees*, para. 7 (emphasis added).

[62] Case 237/82, *Kaas BV and others v State of the Netherlands and Stichting Centraal Orgaan Zuivelcontrole*.

[63] Ibid., para. 20.

[64] Ibid., para. 21 (emphasis added).

[65] Ibid., para. 22.

[66] Ibid., para. 23.

[67] Case 155/80, *Oebel*.

economic and social policy and apply by virtue of objective criteria to all the undertakings in a particular industry which are established within the national territory, *without leading to any difference in treatment whatsoever on the ground of the nationality of traders and without distinguishing between the domestic trade of the State in question and the export trade.*[68]

And this requirement of a discriminatory treatment was subsequently extended—even before *Keck*—to 'selling arrangements':

[N]ational legislation prohibiting the employment of workers on Sundays after 12 noon is not incompatible with Article [35] of the Treaty, since it *is not designed to control patterns of trade between Member States and is applied in accordance with objective criteria to all traders in a given sector, without distinguishing between goods which the consumer intends to use where they are bought and those which he wishes to export.*[69]

In light of this *Groenveld* formula, it seemed—for a long time—that Article 35 would only apply to national measures that were *distinctly* applicable to exports.[70] Yet the Court has subsequently clarified that this was not the case.

b. *Indistinctly Applicable Measures that Materially Discriminate*

Could Article 35 apply to equally applicable 'internal measures'—provided they materially discriminated against exports? It took almost thirty years before the Court gave a definite answer to this question.

Gysbrechts involved a Belgian law that prohibited distant-selling contracts from forcing consumers to provide their credit card number before a period of seven working days (within which withdrawal from

[68] Ibid., paras. 15–16 (emphasis added).

[69] Case C-332/89, *Criminal proceedings against André Marchandise, Jean-Marie Chapuis and SA Trafitex*, para. 17 (emphasis added). This pre-*Keck* case illustrates, in the context of selling arrangements, the difference that the Court made between Article 34 and 35 during this period. For while the Court followed its *Torfaen* judgment with regard to Article 34 (ibid., para. 11), it quoted *Groenveld* to say that such national legislation could not fall within Article 35.

[70] See for example: Case C-47/90, *Établissements Delhaize frères and Compagnie Le Lion SA v Promalvin SA and AGE Bodegas Unidas SA*; Case C-388/95, *Belgium v Spain*; as well as: Case C-108/01, *Consorzio del Prosciutto di Parma and Salumificio S. Rita SpA v Asda Stores Ltd and Hygrade Foods Ltd*. However, there were also some cases of doubt. In Case C-209/98, *Sydhavnens Sten & Grus*, the Court thus—enigmatically—found (ibid., para. 40) that '[i]n the absence of an express exemption for exports, a provision such as the 1992 municipal regulation might be construed as containing an implicit prohibition on exports, contrary to Article [35] of the Treaty'; yet in Case C-12/02, *Grilli*, the Court again insisted on the fact that 'Article [35 TFEU] prohibits only national measures which provide for a difference in treatment between products destined for exports and those sold within the Member State concerned' (ibid., para. 42).

the contract was possible).[71] Was this indistinctly applicable consumer law a MEEQR on exports? In light of past academic criticisms,[72] the Advocate General in the case expressly invited the Court to consider whether the *Groenveld* test was 'still appropriate'.[73] And offering a range of arguments in favour of ending the 'heterogeneous definition of measures having equivalent effect in relation to the free movement of goods',[74] Trstenjak proposed that the jurisprudence on Article 35 could be modified in two ways:

The first possibility is for the Court to apply to Article [35] the definitions it has developed in the context of Article [34]. This implies that, in order to define measures having an equivalent effect to quantitative restrictions on exports, it must apply an appropriately adapted formulation drawn from *Dassonville*, that it must accept expressly the justification for those measures on the basis of the mandatory requirements set out in *Cassis de Dijon*, and that selling arrangements must fall outside the definition of those measures, in accordance with the conditions laid down by it in *Keck and Mithouard*. The second possibility is for the Court to make the very definition of 'measures having equivalent effect' narrower than that in *Dassonville*, which may perhaps also justify non-application of the criteria set out in *Keck and Mithouard* to restrictions on exports. Even in the context of the second

[71] Case C-205/07, *Gysbrechts and Santurel Inter*, esp. para. 13. For an analysis of this case, see M. Szydło, 'Export Restrictions within the Structure of Free Movement of Goods: Reconsideration of an Old Paradigm'; as well as: A. Dawes, 'A Freedom Reborn? The New Yet Unclear Scope of Article 29 EC'.

[72] Perhaps the best critique of the *Groenveld* test has come from W.-H. Roth, 'Wettbewerb der Mittgliedstaaten oder Wettbewerb der Hersteller? Plädoyer für eine Neubestimmung des Art. 34 EGV', esp. 90: 'Dieses Recht der Nachfrager, überall im Gemeinsamen Markt den Bedarf zu decken, wird über [Artikel 34 AEUV] nicht nur nach Maßgabe eines Diskriminierungsverbotes geschützt, sondern in Form eines umfassenden Behinderungsverbotes, vorbehaltlich einer Rechtfertigung durch das Allgemeininteresse. Für [Artikel 35 AEUV], der die Freiheit des Exports sicherstellt, kann prinzipiell nichts anderes gelten: Der Exporteur muß das Recht haben, die Waren überall im Gemeinsamen Markt zu Bedingungen des jeweiligen Absatzmarktes anbieten zu können. Mit dieser Sicht ist eine Deutung des [Artikels 35 AEUV] als bloßes Diskriminierungsverbot inkompatibel. Auch [Artikel 35 AEUV] muß, soweit es um produktbezogene Regelungen geht, als ein umfassendes Beschränkungsverbot verstanden werden, vorbehaltlich zwingender Erfordernisse des Allgemeininteresses der Exportstaaten.' Roth has subsequently repeated his criticism in 'Exports of Goods and Services within the Single Market: Reflections on the Scope of Article 29 and 49 EC', 40, where the author found that 'the Court's approach to Article [35 TFEU] is not wholly in tune with the idea of the Single Market'.

[73] Advocate General Trstenjak, in Case C-205/07, *Gysbrechts*, para. 41.

[74] Ibid., para. 46. Trstenjak thereby referred back to Advocate General Capotorti's opinion in Case 155/80, *Oebel*, where the latter had urged the Court to adopt a 'unitary interpretation of the prohibitions contained in Articles [34 and 35]' (ibid., para. 6).

possibility, a national measure may be justified by the imperative requirements set out in *Cassis de Dijon*.[75]

The Advocate General thereby favoured the first option—that is, a complete parallelism between Article 34 and 35.[76] Yet the Court did *not* follow suit. Instead, it confirmed *Groenveld* as judicial authority.[77] But it also went on to say the following:

[T]he prohibition on requiring an advance payment deprives the traders concerned of an efficient tool with which to guard against the risk of non-payment. That is even more the case when the national provision at issue is interpreted as prohibiting suppliers from requesting that consumers provide their payment card number even if they undertake not to use it to collect payment before expiry of the period for withdrawal. As is clear from the order for reference, the consequences of such a prohibition are generally more significant in cross-border sales made directly to consumers, in particular, in sales made by means of the internet, by reason, inter alia, of the obstacles to bringing any legal proceedings in another Member State against consumers who default, especially when the sales involve relatively small sums. Consequently, *even if a prohibition such as that at issue in the main proceedings is applicable to all traders active in the national territory, its actual effect is none the less greater on goods leaving the market of the exporting Member State than on the marketing of goods in the domestic market of that Member State*.[78]

[75] Advocate General Trstenjak, in Case C-205/07, *Gysbrechts*, para. 50.

[76] Ibid., para. 52: 'Consequently, in my view it would be more appropriate for the definitions, restrictions and criteria set out in *Dassonville*, *Cassis de Dijon* and *Keck and Mithouard* to be applied also to the interpretation of Article [35 TFEU]. It would be necessary, however, to adapt that case-law to Article [35 TFEU]. I shall therefore set out below the criteria which the Court should apply when it decides whether a measure has an effect equivalent to a quantitative restriction on exports.' And specifically with regard to *Keck*, she found (ibid., paras. 57–9): 'Next, there is the question of how to apply, in the context of interpreting Article [35 TFEU], the criteria laid down in *Keck and Mithouard* on the basis of which non-discriminatory selling arrangements fall outside the scope of Article [34 TFEU]. In my view, it is true that we can transpose to the context of an assessment on the basis of Article [35 TFEU] the test developed by the Court in *Keck and Mithouard*, but it must be adapted to the characteristics of exports … However, I think we should take into consideration the fact that certain selling arrangements hinder or restrict *exit from the market* even though they do not discriminate either in law or in fact. There are many reasons in favour of such an adaptation of the *Keck and Mithouard* test.' And on the basis of this new test, the Advocate General found that the Belgian measure would violate Article 35 (ibid., para. 75).

[77] Ibid., para. 40. In favour of this reading, A. Defossez, 'L'Histoire d'une divergence et d'une possible reconciliation. L'article 29 CE', 448: 'La Cour se fonde formellement sur la jurisprudence *Groenveld* [.]' See also: P. Oliver et al., *Oliver on Free Movement of Goods in the European Union*, 140: 'While some widening of the scope of Article 35 would be welcome, the Court was correct, it is submitted, to avoid the radical path proposed by the Advocate General in *Gysbrechts*.'

[78] Case C-205/07, *Gysbrechts*, paras. 41–3 (emphasis added).

The Court here expressly accepted that *indistinctly* applicable measures—that is, 'internal' measures that do not specifically concern exports—fall within scope of Article 35 where they materially *discriminate* against exports. It found that the national law in this case did discriminate and therefore needed justification.[79] This elegantly integrated indistinctly applicable measures into the *Groenveld* formula; yet it also unquestionably confirmed that Article 35 was based on a discrimination test.[80]

The move from *Groenveld* to *Gysbrechts* is consequently a move from direct to indirect discrimination—that is, a move *within* the international model. Under Article 35, the Union has thus not yet embraced the federal model.[81] And there are some good reasons for this choice: Article 35 deals with a State's export trade and therefore concerns primarily a State's *external* sovereignty; and here the international model might simply be more suitable. But more importantly: the international philosophy behind Article 35 stems from the constitutional need to coordinate the scopes of Articles 34 and 35. Indeed, the federal model governing Article 34 can only work when the product requirements of the home State are presumed to be legitimate. (For if Article 35 would allow traders to attack indistinctly applicable product requirements that govern their 'home' state, the provision would pull the rug underneath the principle of home State control that informs the principle of mutual recognition

[79] Ibid., para. 44.

[80] For a recent confirmation of this approach, see: Case C-15/15, *New Valmar v Global Pharmacies Partner Health*, esp. para. 43: 'While it is true that such legislation, since it applies indiscriminately [*sic*] to all invoices issued by an undertaking which has its place of establishment within that region, can affect both domestic trade within the Member State concerned and cross-border trade, the fact remains that it is more likely to affect the latter, as the Advocate General observed in points 61 to 68 of his Opinion, given that a purchaser established in a Member State other than the Kingdom of Belgium is less likely to be able to understand Dutch than a purchaser established in the latter Member State, where that language is one of the official languages.'

[81] For an argument that the Court should however move in this direction, see M. Szydło, 'Export Restrictions within the Structure of Free Movement of Goods', 779: 'It is submitted that the concept of measures having equivalent effect to quantitative restrictions on exports must be elaborated in full conformity with an analogous concept in the field of import of goods, as well as in accordance with the concept of export restrictions adopted in the field of other Treaty freedoms. Therefore, apart from all the discriminatory measures constituting direct or indirect discrimination of export trade of goods as compared with production or commercialization of goods for the domestic market only, the category of measures having equivalent effect in the field of export of goods should also encompass the non-discriminatory measures that hinder access to the markets in other Member States, unless their effect is too uncertain or indirect in that respect.'

under Article 34.[82]) The Union legal order therefore legitimately—and logically—adopts two distinct interpretations of MEEQR under Articles 34 and 35. While the former captures non-discriminatory measures, the latter does not.

c. *Excursus: Transit Restrictions—The Exception to the Exception*

With regard to regulatory measures, Article 35 constitutes an international enclave within the federal structure of the European market. Yet—curiously—there is one context in which the Court appears to approve a 'homogeneous' definition of MEEQR for both import and export restrictions. This context concerns transport or transit restrictions; and the case law here has created an independent jurisprudential line.

This special jurisprudential line was opened in *Oebel*.[83] In addition to the German law limiting production times to after 4.00 am,[84] a (secondary) prohibition here restricted the transportation and delivery of baker's wares to consumers or retail shops until after 5.45 am. Potentially restricting imports and exports alike, the Court subjected this non-discriminatory national rule to a joint analysis in light of both Articles 34 and 35 and held:

> If such rules are confined to transport for delivery to individual consumers and retail outlets only, without affecting transport and delivery to ware-houses or intermediaries, they cannot have the effect of restricting imports or exports between Member States. In this case, indeed, trade within the [Union] remains possible at all times, subject to the single exception that delivery to consumers and retailers is restricted to the same extent for all producers, wherever they are established. Under these circumstances, such rules are not contrary to Articles [34 and 35] of the Treaty.[85]

While the Court found that there was no actual violation of either Article 34 or 35, it nevertheless showed its willingness to interpret both provisions in

[82] And there is a third argument to be taken into account: since the Union has assimilated reimports under Article 34, there is a danger that specifically produced export productions may use that provision to force their way back into their 'home' State market. On this point, see: P. Oliver, 'Some Further Reflections on the Scope of Articles 28–30 (Ex 30–36) EC', 803: '[T]here is a danger that goods, which enjoy an exemption from national technical standards on the basis that they are intended for export, might nevertheless find their ways into the market of the Member State concerned. To obviate the risk, it may in some instances be justified for that State to decline to exempt exports from such rules, particularly where public health is at stake.' For a criticism of this view, see however, M. Szydło, 'Export Restrictions within the Structure of Free Movement of Goods', 784.

[83] Case 155/80, *Oebel*.

[84] For a fuller discussion of the case, see Chapter 4, Section I (2/b) of this volume.

[85] Case 155/80, *Oebel*, para. 20.

a parallel manner. This willingness returned in *Monsees*,[86] where the Court assessed an indistinctly applicable Austrian law governing the maximum journey times and distances for the transport of life animals for slaughter. The Austrian law was neither a border measure that directly affected imports or exports nor a product requirement or a selling arrangement. Would it nonetheless fall under Article 34 or 35 and, if so, why? Taciturnly, the Court stated that the transportation measure 'constitute[d] an obstacle to *international* transport as regards both journeys to or from Austria and transit through that country' that was *ipso facto* prohibited by Articles 34 and 35 alike.[87]

This reasoning was confirmed in *Schmidberger*.[88] But the clearest sign of a parallel approach to Articles 34 and 35 for transport restrictions is offered by *Commission v Austria*.[89] The Court here examined a national traffic rule that prohibited lorries above 7.5 tonnes from being driven on a section of an Austrian motorway. This was an indistinctly applicable rule that applied to all lorries driving on that route. Yet positing 'the existence of a *general principle of free transit of goods* within the [Union]' that directly derived from the free-movement provisions,[90] the Court found an obstacle to trade and the existence of alternative routes or other means of transport did 'not negate the existence of an obstacle'.[91] Without any reference to the *Groenveld* formula, the Court thus seemed to directly apply a trade restriction test that operated without any regard to discrimination. This absolute restriction test (albeit with a substantive threshold) came indeed close to a 'national' market philosophy.[92]

[86] Case 350/97, *Monsees v Unabhängiger Verwaltungssenat für Kärnten*.

[87] Ibid., para. 23.

[88] Case C-112/00, *Schmidberger, Internationale Transporte und Planzüge v Republik Österreich*. In para. 64, the Court here applies the *Dassonville* formula mechanically: 'In the light of the foregoing, the fact that the competent authorities of a Member State did not ban a demonstration which resulted in the complete closure of a major transit route such as the Brenner motorway for almost 30 hours on end is capable of restricting intra-[Union] trade in goods and must, therefore, be regarded as constituting a measure of equivalent effect to a quantitative restriction which is, in principle, incompatible with the [Union] law obligations arising from Articles [34 and 35 TFEU] of the Treaty, read together with Article [4(3) TEU], unless that failure to ban can be objectively justified.'

[89] Case C-320/03, *Commission v Austria (A 12 Motorway I)*.

[90] Ibid., para. 65. [91] Ibid., para. 67.

[92] Case C-28/09, *Commission v Austria (A 12 Motorway II)*, paras. 114–17: 'In the present case, the contested regulation prohibits lorries of over 7.5t carrying certain goods which, according to the Austrian authorities, have an "affinity with rail" from using a section of the A 12 motorway. It thus prevents the use of a mode of transport for those goods in that transalpine

II. General Exemptions and Justifications: Form and Substance

From the very beginning, the Union legal order recognized that some *regulatory* measures hindering intra-Union trade could be justified in specific situations. The EU Treaties thus contained a specific set of public policy justifications in Article 36 TFEU, which could be invoked to neutralize violations of Articles 34 and 35 TFEU. These public policy grounds were originally designed for an international market model; yet, as we shall see below, the *Cassis* revolution within Article 34 here also triggered a revolution at the justificatory level. The Court would henceforth allow for an (unlimited) number of implied justifications and, to a great extent, the philosophical frame within which these justifications worked would also be challenged. This section explores these changes in some detail. But before we analyse the substantive justifications offered by the Union legal order, we need to—quickly—discuss a 'procedural' exemption that nominally applies to all fundamental freedoms: the 'purely internal situation' rule.

1. *Purely Internal Situations: A 'Jurisdictional' Exemption*

The free movement of goods provisions should apply when 'imports' or 'exports' are affected; and the jurisdiction of the courts will thereby be triggered wherever a national law affects 'directly or indirectly, actually or potentially' intra-Union trade.[93]

But what about cases where all the facts of the case are purely *internal* to a single Member State? Should the European Court (or the national courts) have jurisdiction here? The Union legal order has traditionally answered

corridor. The Republic of Austria submits that there are alternative routes or other modes of transport capable of carrying the goods in question. However, the existence of such alternative solutions does not negate the existence of a restriction of the free movement of goods. The section of the A 12 motorway is one of the principal land transport routes between southern Germany and northern Italy. By forcing the undertakings concerned to seek viable alternative solutions for the transport of the goods covered by the contested regulation, the sectoral traffic prohibition is liable to have a substantial effect on the transit of goods between northern Europe and northern Italy. In those circumstances, the sectoral traffic prohibition must be regarded as constituting a measure having equivalent effect to quantitative restrictions, which in principle is incompatible with the obligations under Articles [34 and 35 TFEU], unless that measure can be justified.'

[93] Case 8/74, *Procureur du Roi v Benoît and Gustave Dassonville*.

this question negatively; and the judicial doctrine that negated the jurisdiction to apply Articles 34 and 35 in this context has become known as the 'purely internal situation' doctrine.[94] The doctrine states that the free-movement provisions will not apply in situations 'which are *wholly internal to a Member State*, in other words, where there is *no factor connecting them to any of the situations envisaged by [Union] law*'.[95]

But what did this mean? Two approaches—one situational and one normative—may be distinguished.[96] The traditional approach conceived of a purely internal situation in terms of a specific *factual situation*.[97] If a specific situation did not contain any 'interstate' facts, the Court would find the free-movement provisions inapplicable to the specific case. A good illustration of this approach is given in *Oosthoek*.[98] Dealing with a Dutch law that prohibited the offering of free gifts within the framework of a commercial activity, the Court made a clear distinction as to the situations in which Articles 34 and 35 applied:

> [T]he application of the *Netherlands* legislation to the sale in the *Netherlands* of encyclopaedias produced *in that country* is in no way linked to the importation or exportation of goods and does not therefore fall within the scope of Articles [34 and 35] of the [FEU] Treaty. However, the sale in the Netherlands of encyclopaedias produced in Belgium and the sale in other Member States of encyclopaedias produced in the Netherlands are transactions forming part of intra-[Union] trade.[99]

The passage suggested that the jurisdictional scope of Articles 34 and 35 did not solely depend on whether the national law at issue potentially affected intra-Union trade; what also mattered was the presence of a specific factual element in the *actual* legal proceedings: the commercial gifts would thus have to be produced in a different Member State so as to trigger the free-movement provisions *in this specific case*.

[94] For an excellent overview of the doctrine, see: R.-E. Papadopoulou, 'Situations purement internes et droit communautaire: un instrument jurisprudentiel à double fonction ou une arme à double tranchant?'. For a discussion of the purely-internal-situations doctrine in the context of the free movement of persons, see: N. Nic Shuibhne, 'Free Movement of Persons and the Wholly Internal Rule: Time to Move On?'.

[95] Case 175/78, *The Queen v Vera Ann Saunders*, para. 11.

[96] For a similar terminological choice, see H. U. Jessurun d'Oliveira who has drawn on private international law to distinguish between a 'geographical' and a 'juridical' approach in 'Is Reverse Discrimination Still Permissible Under the Single European Act?'.

[97] A. Tryfonidou, *Reverse Discrimination in EC Law*, 56.

[98] Case 286/81, *Criminal proceedings against Oosthoek's Uitgeversmaatschappij.*

[99] Ibid., para. 9 (emphasis added).

This situational approach subsequently gained particular prominence outside the free movement of goods.[100] However, it was also reconfirmed for this fundamental freedom.[101] Indeed, the rise of the federal model after *Cassis de Dijon* had reinforced the belief that European law could not enter into purely internal situations. Yet the federal model's insistence that Article 34 could not capture situations of reverse discrimination, equally triggered a significant shift in the understanding of the 'purely internal situation' doctrine. [102] This shift was a shift away from the specific facts of the case to the normative scope of the national law involved.

A clean break with the situational approach was finally made in *Pistre*.[103] The Court expressly dismissed the French government's claim that the case fell outside the scope of Article 34 as 'the facts in question in the main proceedings [were] confined to *French* territory since the prosecutions in

[100] See here in particular Case 175/78, *Saunders*, and with regard to services, see Case 52/79, *Procureur du Roi v Marc J.V.C. Debauve and others*, para. 9: '[I]t should be observed that the provisions of the Treaty on freedom to provide services cannot apply to activities whose relevant elements are confined within a single Member State'; as well as Case C-41/90, *Höfner and Elser v Macrotron*, paras. 38–40 (emphasis added): 'The facts, as established by the national court in its order for reference, show that in the present case the dispute is between *German* recruitment consultants and a *German* undertaking concerning the recruitment of a *German* national. *Such a situation displays no link with any of the situations envisaged by [Union] law. That finding cannot be invalidated by the fact that a contract concluded between the recruitment consultants and the undertaking concerned includes the theoretical possibility of seeking German candidates resident in other Member States or nationals of other Member States.*'

[101] Joined Cases 314–16/81 and 83/82, *Procureur de la République and Comité national de défense contre l'alcoolisme v Alex Waterkeyn and others; and Procureur de la République v Jean Cayard and others*, para. 11. The case had evolved out of Case 152/78, *Commission v France (Discriminatory Advertising)*, discussed in Chapter 4, Section I(2) of this volume.

[102] See in particular: Case 98/86, *Criminal proceedings against Mathot*, para. 8: 'However, in a case such as the one described in the order for reference, and even if there is discrimination against domestically produced butter, such a difference of treatment can in no circumstances restrict the importation of butter or prejudice the marketing of imported butter. Article [34 TFEU] is not therefore infringed by such rules.' See also: Case 407/85, *3 Glocken GmbH and Gertraud Kritzinger v USL Centro-Sud and Provincia autonoma di Bolzano*, para. 25: 'It should first be stressed that it is the extension of the law on pasta products to imported products which is at issue, and that [Union] law does not require the legislature to repeal the law as far as pasta producers established on Italian territory are concerned.'

[103] Case C-321/94, *Criminal proceedings against Jacques Pistre*. In the words of R.-E. Papadopoulou, 'Situations purement internes et droit communautaire: un instrument jurisprudentiel à double fonction ou une arme à double tranchant?', 108: 'C'est l'affaire *Pistre* qui marque le "saut qualitatif" consistent à abandonner le "terrain" de la situation d'espèce pour se placer su celui de la règle nationale en cause.'

question have been brought against *French* nationals and concern *French* products marketed on *French* territory'.[104] Finding that the contested national measure did *potentially* apply to foreign products, the Court held that Article 34 '*cannot be considered inapplicable simply because all the facts of the specific case before the national court are confined to a single Member State*'.[105] This unquestionably clarified that it was not the facts of the specific case but the nature and scope of the national measure that determined when the free movement of goods provisions would apply.[106] Therefore, whenever a national rule potentially hinders intra-Union trade, the Court will examine it—even if all of the facts of the specific case are confined to a single Member State.[107]

This 'normative' approach aligns the purely-internal-situation doctrine perfectly to the *Dassonville* formula (understood as a jurisdictional

[104] Case C-321/94, *Pistre*, para. 41 (emphasis added).

[105] Ibid., para. 44 (emphasis added). For a confirmation of this rule, see Case C-184/96, *Commission v France (Foie Gras)*; as well as Case C-448/98, *Guimont*.

[106] See A. Tryfonidou, 'The Outer Limits of Article 28 EC: Purely Internal Situations and the Development of the Court's Approach through the Years', 208: 'The innovation of *Pistre* lies in the fact that, although the specific goods to which the contested legislation was applied were not imported products and thus the application of the contested legislation did not impede the inter-state movement of those specific goods, nonetheless, the Court did not consider this factor to be sufficient in itself for qualifying the situation as purely internal. The Court, contrary to its traditional approach, did not interrupt its inquiry as soon as it found that the specific facts of the case did not involve an impediment to the free movement of goods involved.'

[107] The famous example for Article 34 TFEU here is, of course, Joined Cases C-267–8/91, *Criminal proceedings against Bernard Keck and Daniel Mithouard*. With regard to Article 35 TFEU, see only Case C-293/02, *Jersey Produce Marketing Organisation Ltd v States of Jersey and Jersey Potato Export Marketing Board*, esp. paras. 78–80: 'The 2001 Act's effect as an obstacle to exports to the United Kingdom was not, moreover, denied by the States of Jersey which argued merely in that regard that since, first, only such exports were affected by the 2001 Act and, second, trade between Jersey and the United Kingdom had to be treated as a Member State's domestic trade for the purposes of applying Articles [34 and 35 TFEU], those provisions were not applicable to such legislation. In that connection, it is appropriate, however, to observe that such an analysis disregards the fact, already noted in paragraph 65 of this judgment, that, even though the 2001 Act covers, according to its wording, only potatoes despatched to the United Kingdom for consumption there, there is nothing to rule out the possibility that such potatoes, once within the United Kingdom, might then be re-exported to other Member States. It follows that the restrictions introduced by the 2001 Act with regard to Jersey Royal potatoes despatched to the United Kingdom, the main effect of which, as has been pointed out in paragraphs 75 and 76 of this judgment, is to restrict such patterns of export, are, ultimately, also likely to be an obstacle to the export of those goods to other Member States and to have, with regard to the latters' markets, the same negative effect as that observed in respect of the United Kingdom market.'

formula).[108] For since the latter grants jurisdiction to actual as well as *potential* effects on intra-Union trade, it also textually covers those cases whose factual elements do not lead to an actual restriction on imports.[109] This shift from a situational to a normative approach with regard to purely internal situations has eliminated (most) 'arbitrary' jurisdictional exemptions to Articles 34 and 35.[110] Indeed, if a national measure constitutes a restriction on intra-Union trade it should be challengeable—regardless of whether or not the actual facts of the case contain a cross-border dimension. The 'purely internal situation' doctrine should consequently be renamed the 'purely internal measure' doctrine.[111]

2. *Public Policy Justifications: Article 36 TFEU and Beyond*

From the very beginning, the EU Treaties expressly acknowledged that some quantitative restrictions (and measures having equivalent effect) could be justified on specific public policy grounds. This constitutional acknowledgement reflected the idea that *regulatory* barriers to trade often

[108] On this point, see also: A. Tryfonidou, *Reverse Discrimination in EC Law*, 88: '[T]he Court's new approach is a pure reflection of *Dassonville*[.]' Indeed, in my view, the presence of the *Dassonville* formula as a jurisdictional rule might explain the (relative) absence of the 'purely internal situation' doctrine for the free movement of goods.

[109] The Court has nonetheless limited the 'mechanical' jurisdictional *Dassonville* formula by adding a 'remoteness' doctrine. The Court has thus sometimes held that the effects on intra-Union trade were 'too uncertain and indirect' to classify the respective national measure as a restriction on the free movement of goods, cf. Case C-69/88, *Krantz v Ontvanger der Directe Belastingen and Netherlands State*, para. 11. See also Case C-379/92, *Peralta*, para. 24; and Case C- 190/98, *Graf v Filzmoser Maschinenbau*, para. 25. While itself very uncertain and indirect, the remoteness criterion has nonetheless the advantage that it is capable of capturing actual and potential effects on intra-Union trade. This allows the Court to scrutinize national legislation that may have a minimal—or no—effect in the actual case yet that might potentially affect a much broader category of traders in a serious manner. For a systematization of the various judicial tests minimizing the *Dassonville* formula, see: E. Spaventa, 'The Outer Limits of the Treaty Free Movement Provisions: Some Reflections on the Significance of *Keck*, Remoteness and *Deliège*'; as well as M. S. Jansson and H. Kalimo, '*De Minimis* Meets "Market Access": Transformations in the Substance—and the Syntax—of EU Free Movement Law?'.

[110] This is sadly not the case for the other three fundamental freedoms, and especially not in the context of the free movement of persons. For a severe—and just—criticism of the arbitrary case law here, see only: Opinion of Advocate General Sharpston in Case C-34/09, *Zambrano v Office national de l'emploi (ONEm)*.

[111] For this excellent phrase, see: R.-E. Papadopoulou, 'Situations purement internes et droit communautaire', 129.

pursue a legitimate *regulatory* interest. For the Union legal order, these legitimate interests were set out in Article 36. It states:

> The provisions of Articles 34 and 35 shall not preclude prohibitions or restrictions on imports, exports or goods in transit justified on grounds of public morality, public policy or public security; the protection of health and life of humans, animals or plants; the protection of national treasures possessing artistic, historic or archaeological value; or the protection of industrial and commercial property. Such prohibitions or restrictions shall not, however, constitute a means of arbitrary discrimination or a disguised restriction on trade between Member States.

The article expressly exempts national laws that hinder the free movement of goods on six grounds. Member States may invoke 'public morality'—for example—to justify trade restrictions on the importation of pornographic goods.[112] They may have recourse to 'public policy' to protect—for example—the right to mint coinage.[113] A State has been entitled to plead 'public security' to justify restrictions on imports of petroleum products so as to guarantee a degree of national energy independence.[114] Scientific uncertainty about a product's impact on the health of humans (or animals and plants) can justify a national trade restriction.[115] The export of national art treasures can also be blocked.[116] And a State is finally also allowed to limit intra-Union trade to protect national intellectual property rights.[117]

Article 36 had clearly been inspired by the equivalent provision in the GATT.[118] It was indeed a limited version of that international law provision, and the Court has found its list to be exhaustive: Article 36 'cannot be extended to cases other than those specifically laid down'.[119] (The Court has consequently held, for example, that Article 36 could not cover national

[112] See Case 34/79, *Regina v Henn and Darby*.

[113] See Case 7/78, *R v Thompson, Johnson & Woodiwiss*.

[114] See Case 72/83, *Campus Oil and others v Minister for Industry and Energy and others*.

[115] This is the most popular and most important ground of justification for goods, see only: Case 104/75, *De Peijper*, para. 15: 'health and life of humans rank first among the property or interests protected by Article 36'.

[116] According to P. Oliver et al., *Free Movement of Goods in the European Union*, 281 there is no case law on the direct application of this ground. The ground had been invoked in Case 7/68, *Commission v Italy*, in the context of Article 30 TFEU, where the Court however held that Article 36 could not apply to customs duties and charges having an equivalent effect (CEE).

[117] See Case 192/73, *Van Zuylen frères v Hag AG*.

[118] For the text of Article XX GATT, see Chapter 1, Section II(2/d/aa) of this volume.

[119] Case 113/80, *Commission v Ireland (Irish Souvenirs)*, para. 7.

restrictions on the ground of consumer protection.[120]) Furthermore, the Court has also found that since Article 36 'constitutes a derogation from the basic rule that all obstacles to the free movement of goods between Member States shall be eliminated', it 'must be interpreted strictly'.[121] And yet, despite all these demands for restraint, the Court has—ever since *Cassis de Dijon*—allowed for an unlimited (!) number of implied derogations.[122] Why? Let us explore the emergence and nature of these 'mandatory' or 'imperative' requirements in more detail first before a second subsection analyses the principle(s) of proportionality.

a. Legitimate Policy Grounds: The Emergence of (Unlimited) Imperative Requirements

Why would the Court be strict on the *express* policy grounds mentioned in Article 36 yet allow for an unlimited number of *implied* grounds at the same time?

The explanation for this—apparent—paradox is that Article 36 was originally designed against the backdrop of the international market model within which it was to apply to border measures (and *discriminatory* internal measures). And once Article 34 was seen—after *Cassis*—to cover non-discriminatory internal measures, the Court was caught in a dilemma: on the one hand, it wished to recognize that the expansion of the scope of Article 34 had to trigger a—simultaneous—expansion of the potential grounds of justification; yet, on the other hand, this expansion could not

[120] Cf. Case 229/83, *Édouard Leclerc and others v SARL 'Au blé vert' and others*, para. 30: 'Since it derogates from a fundamental rule of the Treaty, Article 36 must be interpreted strictly and cannot be extended to cover objectives not expressly enumerated therein. Neither the safeguarding of consumers' interests nor the protection of creativity and cultural diversity in the realm of publishing is mentioned in Article 36. It follows that the justification put forward by the French Government cannot be accepted.'

This case, as so many others, fundamentally disproves the 'Weiler thesis' that the invention of mandatory requirements was a reflection of the fact that the Court wished to 'update' Article 36 as a provision that had been 'written with the sensibilities of the 1950s' (J. H. H. Weiler, 'Epilogue: Towards a Common Law of International Trade', 218). For if that had really been the intention of the Court, why does it not allow these 'new values' to be invoked against all national measures that restrict the free movement of goods? And by the way, the 'Weiler thesis' does not explain why Article XX GATT allowed—in the 1940s—for measures that are necessary for the 'prevention of deceptive practices' as well as 'the conservation of exhaustible natural resources'; yet, no such values could be found in Article 36.

[121] Case 46/76, *Bauhuis v The Netherlands*, para. 12.

[122] Case 120/78, *Rewe-Zentral AG v Bundesmonopolverwaltung für Branntwein (Cassis de Dijon)*.

take place within Article 36 because that might invite the Member States to use the new grounds also for discriminatory measures and thereby undermine the Court's tough stance here. The way out of this dilemma was daring but ingenious: the Court simply deposited a second justificatory route but only for those measures that fell outside the international market model. With the emergence of the federal model in *Cassis*, the Court thus began to exempt obstacles to the free movement of goods that were 'necessary in order to satisfy *mandatory requirements* relating in particular to the effectiveness of fiscal supervision, the protection of public health, the fairness of commercial transactions and the defence of the consumer'.[123]

These additional justifications were originally called 'mandatory requirements'; yet the Court increasingly refers to them as 'imperative requirements' or 'overriding reason[s] relating to the public interest'.[124] The distinct constitutional principles governing these 'imperative requirements' were spelled out in the immediate post-*Cassis* jurisprudence; yet the more recent jurisprudence has come to suggest that a convergence of Article 36 and imperative requirements is taking place.

aa. Imperative Requirements for Non-Discriminatory Restrictions

What were imperative requirements designed to be? Were they additional justifications; or did their application mean that a national measure never qualified as a violation of Article 34? The Court seems originally to have espoused the second view. Early judgments therefore suggested that once imperative requirements were invoked, the *indistinctly* applicable measure simply fell outside the scope of Article 34 altogether.[125] However, in later jurisprudence, the Court has come to view imperative requirements as 'justifications' that are on the same level as Article 36.

[123] Ibid., para. 8 (emphasis added).

[124] See only: Case C-110/05, *Commission v Italy (Italian Trailers)*, paras. 59–60.

[125] This 'scope reading' of imperative requirements can for example be found in Case 113/80, *Commission v Ireland (Irish Souvenirs)*. Having held Article 36 inapplicable, the Court here moved on to say (ibid., para. 9): 'However, since the Irish Government describes its recourse to these concepts as "the central issue in the case", it is necessary to study this argument in connexion with Article [34] and to consider whether it is possible, in reliance on those concepts, to say that the Irish orders are not measures having an effect equivalent to quantitative restrictions on imports within the meaning of that article, bearing in mind that, according to the established case-law of the Court, such measures include "all trading rules enacted by Member States which are capable of hindering, directly or indirectly, actually or potentially, intra-[Union] trade".' For a similar 'scope' solution, see also: Case 16/83, *Criminal proceedings against Karl Prantl.*

What constitutional principles would apply to imperative requirements? In its classic jurisprudence, the Court insisted from the very start that they might solely justify national laws 'which apply *without discrimination to both domestic and imported products*'.[126] This was confirmed in *Commission v Ireland (Irish Souvenir).*[127] Ireland here required that all imported jewellery was to bear a designation of origin or the word 'foreign'. This was a clearly discriminatory measure that violated Article 34, but Ireland contended that the measure was justified in the interest of consumer protection.[128] In light of the discriminatory nature of the Irish law the Court held otherwise: 'In view of the fact that neither the protection of consumers nor the fairness of commercial transactions is included amongst the exceptions set out in Article 36, those grounds cannot be relied upon as such in connexion with that article.'[129] Discriminatory national measures could therefore only be justified by reference to the express—and exhaustive—list of public policy grounds in Article 36,[130] while imperative requirements were confined to non-discriminatory rules.[131]

This distinction between two different justificatory routes has been criticized;[132] and the Court has sometimes tried to evade it by sharp scholastic means,[133] or by bluntly fudging the issue of the (non-)discriminatory character of a national measure.[134] In more recent jurisprudence, the Court even appears to have come to accept that discriminatory measures may (sometimes) be justified by imperative requirements.

In favour of the scope reading of imperative requirements, see: A. Dashwood, '*Cassis de Dijon*: The Line of Cases Grows'; R. Barents, 'New Developments in Measures Having Equivalent Effect'. For a revival of this view, see: E. Spaventa, 'On Discrimination and the Theory of Mandatory Requirements', 475: 'The only viable solution seems then to go back to the origin and consider the mandatory requirements as something internal to the definition of a measure having equivalent effect, i.e. something the lack of which is necessary in order to trigger Article [34]. This is because the Treaty cannot be construed as having taken away the regulatory competence of the Member States in fields not harmonized by [Union] law.' On this general doctrinal question, see also: M. Fremuth, '"Cassis de Dijon"—Zu der dogmatischen Einordung zwingender Erfordernisse'.

[126] Case 788/79, *Gilli and Andres*, para. 6 (emphasis added).

[127] Case 113/80, *Commission v Ireland.* [128] Ibid., para. 5.

[129] Ibid., para. 8. [130] Ibid., para. 11. [131] Ibid., para. 10.

[132] See Advocate General F. Jacobs in Case C-379/98, *Preussen Elektra v Schleswag*, paras. 227 et seq.

[133] See Case C-2/90, *Commission v Belgium (Walloon Waste).*

[134] Case C-379/98, *Preussen Elektra v Schleswag.* See also: Case C-54/05, *Commission v Finland*; as well as Case C-531/07, *Fachverband der Buch- und Medienwirtschaft v LIBRO Handelsgesellschaft mbH.*

bb. Imperative Requirements for Discriminatory Restrictions?

Could selling arrangements falling within the *Keck* jurisprudential line ever be justified by imperative requirements? Theoretically, this should not be the case if the constitutional logic of the *Keck* revolution is followed. For since only *discriminatory* selling arrangements can ever theoretically constitute MEEQR under Article 34, these restrictions should be justifiable solely on the grounds mentioned in Article 36.[135] However, the Court has occasionally given reason to believe that a softer rule might apply in practice. This was alluded to in *De Agostini*,[136] and the Court has more recently confirmed its willingness to extent imperative requirements to *discriminatory* selling arrangements in *LIBRO*.[137]

A similar development has taken place within Article 35. It will be recalled that the provision (still) only captures *discriminatory* export restrictions, which should—therefore—never be justifiable by means of imperative requirements. And yet, in *Gysbrecht*, the Court accepted that 'consumer protection may constitute a legitimate objective in the public interest capable of justifying a restriction on the free movement of goods'.[138] This

[135] See Case C-405/98, *Konsumentombudsmannen v Gourmet*.

[136] See Case C-34/95, *Konsumentombudsmannen v De Agostini*, paras. 39–45 (emphasis added): '[T]he Court held that legislation which prohibits television advertising in a particular sector concerns selling arrangements for products belonging to that sector in that it prohibits a particular form of promotion of a particular method of marketing products ... Consequently, an outright ban on advertising aimed at children less than 12 years of age and of misleading advertising, as provided for by the Swedish legislation, is not covered by Article [34] of the Treaty, unless it is shown that the ban does not affect in the same way, in fact and in law, the marketing of national products and of products from other Member States. In the latter case, it is for the national court to determine whether the ban is necessary to satisfy *overriding requirements of general public importance* or one of the aims listed in Article 36 of the [FEU] Treaty if it is proportionate to that purpose and if those aims or requirements could not have been attained or fulfilled by measures less restrictive of intra-[Union] trade.'

[137] Case C-531/07, *Fachverband der Buch- und Medienwirtschaft v LIBRO Handelsgesellschaft mbH*, paras. 32–4: 'In that regard, it must be pointed out, first of all, that the objectives raised by the referring court, such as the protection of books as cultural objects, cannot constitute a justification for measures restricting imports within the meaning of Article [36 TFEU]. The protection of cultural diversity in general cannot be considered to come within the "protection of national treasures possessing artistic, historic or archaeological value" within the meaning of Article [36] ... However, the protection of books as cultural objects can be considered as an overriding requirement in the public interest capable of justifying measures restricting the free movement of goods, on condition that those measures are appropriate for achieving the objective fixed and do not go beyond what is necessary to achieve it.'

[138] Case C-205/07, *Gysbrechts*, para. 47 (with reference to *Cassis*).

implicit extension of imperative requirements to Article 35 was subsequently even described as 'established case-law'.[139]

Do these instances signal that imperative requirements can today be invoked for all categories of measures, including discriminatory ones? Modern judicial rhetoric indeed points in this direction. For the Court now often catholically states that '[a]ccording to settled case-law, an obstacle to the free movement of goods may be justified on one of the public interest grounds set out in Article 36 TFEU *or* in order to meet overriding requirements'.[140] If that really means that *all* national measures may be justified *either* by reference to Article 36 or overriding requirements, the Court should be lauded. For not only would this unitary approach perfectly align itself to the unitary approach discussed in Chapter 4,[141] there is also a 'strong normative appeal to a model whereby all types of justification are in principle available, but according to which the presence of discrimination would make the job of the [national] regulator in showing that the chosen scheme is lawful particularly onerous'.[142] According to this—US American—solution, the (non-)discriminatory nature of a measure should have no influence on what public policy grounds can be invoked; yet it, crucially, determines the degree of judicial scrutiny. Differences in the type of national measure will here be analysed through the prism of the principle of proportionality—to which we shall now turn.

b. Proportionality as Necessity: A Question of Standards

Not every national measure that qualifies under one of the legitimate policy grounds in Article 36 (or imperative requirements) will *ipso facto* be

[139] See: Case C-161/09, *Kakavetsos-Fragkopoulos AE Epexergasias kai Emporias Stafidas v Nomarchiaki Aftodioikisi Korinthias*, para. 51: '[I]t is established case-law that a national measure having equivalent effect to a quantitative restriction on exports, which is in principle contrary to Article [35 TFEU], may be justified not only on one of the grounds stated in Article [36 TFEU] but also by overriding requirements of public interest, provided that the measure is proportionate to the legitimate objective pursued (see, inter alia, Case C-205/07 *Gysbrechts and Santurel Inter* [2008] ECR I-9947, paragraph 45).'

[140] Case C-108/09, *Ker-Optika bt v ÀNTSZ Dél-dunántúli Regionális Intézete*, para. 57 (emphasis added). See also: Case C-443/10, *Bonnarde v Agence de Services et de Paiement*, para. 32. In some cases, the Court does not even make a distinction between Article 36 justifications and imperative requirements any longer but simply refers to 'legitimate objectives in the public interest', see: Case C-15/15, *New Valmar*, para. 48.

[141] On the distinction between the 'category approach' and the 'unitary approach' within the post-*Keck* jurisprudence on Article 34, see: Chapter 4, Section II(4) of this volume.

[142] S. Weatherill, 'Free Movement of Goods', 544.

justified. From the very beginning, the last sentence of Article 36 indeed stipulated that any potentially justified measure 'shall not, however, constitute a means of arbitrary discrimination or a disguised restriction on trade between Member States'; and the Court subsequently clarified that this referred to the 'proportionality' of the national measure: '[T]he principle of proportionality which underlies the last sentence of Article 36 of the Treaty requires that the power of the Member States to prohibit imports of the products in question from other Member States should be *restricted to what is necessary to attain the legitimate aim*[.]'[143] This proportionality-as-necessity test has been unconditionally extended to imperative requirements;[144] and the proportionality principle therefore constitutes a general condition for all express or implied justifications.

What is the relationship between proportionality and necessity? The Court sees the latter as part of the former; because in its most elaborate form, the proportionality principle has been defined as requiring proof that a national measure is suitable, necessary, and proportionate (in a strict sense). The Court however often reduces its 'proportionality' analysis to a 'necessity' test that insists that the public interest pursued 'must not be attainable by measures which are less restrictive of such trade'.[145] This least-restrictive-means test constitutes the very core of the European proportionality principle. Within this core however hides an important question: what standard should the least-restrictive-means test be centred on? For example: if the British legislature favours a high level of public morality and bans all pornography, should it matter that other Member States do not prefer to stand on such high moral ground? Or, should Germany be allowed to insist on 'beer purity' as the highest possible standard of consumer protection, while other Member States allow their beer to be brewed with artificial ingredients? The question of necessity is thus intrinsically linked to the question of the permissible standard of protection.[146]

[143] Case 174/82, *Sandoz*, para. 18.

[144] Case 120/78, *Cassis de Dijon*; as well as: Case 261/81, *Rau Lebensmittelwerke v De Smedt*, para. 12: 'It is also necessary for such rules to be proportionate to the aim in view.'

[145] See: Case C-389/96, *Aher-Waggon GmbH v Germany*, para. 20. See already: Case 261/81, *Rau v De Smedt*, para. 12: 'If a Member State has a choice between various measures to attain the same objective it should choose the means which least restricts the free movement of goods.'

[146] The question is slightly more complex once the Union has adopted legislation designed to harmonize the various national standards. Here the Court originally seemed to suggest that any reference to a national standard under Article 36 was pre-empted, cf. Case 148/78,

And this standard differs—depending on which market model the Union adopts.

aa. Three Market Models, Two Proportionality Standards

How will the question of proportionality fit into our three constitutional models? Will each model recognize a distinct permissible standard of protection that corresponds to a distinct standard of judicial review?

Under the *international* model, all national measures falling within a legitimate ground of justification are justified as long as they do not represent an arbitrary discrimination or a disguised restriction on trade. This review standard principally recognizes each (!) importing State's substantive standard of protection as a sovereign choice; yet it roots out formal inconsistencies that are not 'necessary' to achieve *that* national standard. The Union here defers to the internal sovereignty of the host State; yet it formally reviews whether that substantive standard is consistently applied to foreign goods.

We find good illustrations of such an 'international' necessity test in the early jurisprudence of the Court. In *Henn and Darby*,[147] for example, the Court dealt with a British import ban on pornographic films and magazines from Denmark. Could this national restriction be justified on grounds of public morality, or would the 'lower' Danish standard prove that public morality could survive in a society that was more permissive of pornography? The Court calibrated its necessity test on the higher host State standard. It confirmed that it principally was 'for each Member State to determine *in accordance with its own scale of values and in the form* selected by it the requirements of public morality in its territory'.[148] And while the

Criminal Proceedings against Tullio Ratti, para. 36: '[W]hen, pursuant to Article [115] of the Treaty, [Union] directives provide for the harmonization of measures necessary to ensure the protection of the health of humans and animals and establish [Union] procedures to supervise compliance therewith, recourse to Article [36] ceases to be justified.' Subsequent jurisprudence however clarified that not all types of harmonization measures would block Article 36. Only in cases of complete harmonization would the Member States cease to be entitled to justify national measures hindering trade by recourse to that article, see: Case C-39/90 *Denkavit Futtermittel GmbH v Land Baden-Württemberg*. This move from complete to minimum harmonization was part of a changing structure of European legislation, cf. R. Schütze, *From Dual to Cooperative Federalism: The Changing Structure of European Law*, esp. Chapter 4.

[147] Case 34/79, *Regina v Henn and Darby*. For an extensive discussion of the case, see: L. Catchpole and A. Barav, 'The Public Morality Exception and the Free Movement of Goods: Justification of a Dual Standard in National Legislation?'.

[148] Case 34/79, *Regina v Henn and Darby*, para. 15 (emphasis added).

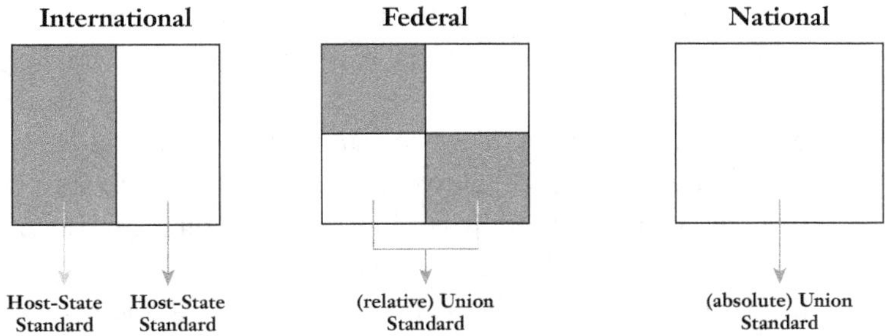

Figure 7. Market models and proportionality standards

Court subsequently clarified that 'a Member State may not rely on grounds of public morality in order to prohibit the importation of goods from other Member States *when its legislation contains no prohibition on the manufacture or marketing of the same goods on its territory*',[149] this qualification did not 'preclude the authorities of the Member State concerned from applying to those goods, once imported, the same restrictions on marketing which are applied to similar products manufactured and marketed within the country'.[150] In these pornography cases, as well as others,[151] the Court thus deferred to the (importing) Member State's own domestic standard and thereby confirmed its 'internal' sovereignty over the matter.

What about the federal and the national model and their—respective—proportionality principles? Within both models, the Union no longer defers to the national standard of the host State but develops its own 'autonomous' standard—yet depending on which market model, the latter is used in a

[149] Case 121/85, *Conegate v HM Customs and Excise*, para. 16 (emphasis added). In this respect *Conegate* overruled *Henn and Darby*.

[150] Case 121/85, *Conegate v HM Customs and Excise*, para. 21.

[151] The 'international' proportionality standard was also used in Case 41/74, *Van Duyn v Home Office*, where the Court held (paras. 19–21): 'It follows from the above that where the competent authorities of a Member State have clearly defined their standpoint as regards the activities of a particular organization and where, considering it to be socially harmful, they have taken administrative measures to counteract these activities, the Member State cannot be required, before it can rely on the concept of public policy, to make such activities unlawful, if recourse to such a measure is not thought appropriate in the circumstances. The question raises finally the problem of whether a Member State is entitled, on grounds of public policy, to prevent a national of another Member State from taking gainful employment within its territory with a body or organization, it being the case that no similar restriction is placed upon its own nationals ... Consequently, the effect of such limitations, when they apply, is that leave to enter the territory of a Member State and the right to reside there may be refused to a national of another Member State.'

different way. Within the federal model, the autonomous Union standard is *indirectly* used to arbitrate between the respective national standards of the host and the home State.[152] While autonomous, the Union standard is thus not used to directly review the two national standards as such. The Union solely examines whether the *extension* of the host State standard to imported products is justified; and the Court will therefore not challenge the legitimacy of the host State standard with regard to its own goods. By contrast, within the national model, this relative Union standard becomes an 'absolute' standard that applies to all traders within the European Union. Under the national model, the Union necessity standard will thus directly apply to both the host as well as the home State measures.

One of the areas in which the Union judicially developed an autonomous 'European' standard is consumer protection. For unlike the deferential approach shown to Article 36 under the international model, the Court has here—from the very beginning—adopted a stricter scrutiny towards 'unnecessarily' high national standards.[153] This stricter proportionality stance vis-à-vis national consumer laws was designed to break open traditional production and marketing rules. The most famous case—certainly for Germans—in this context is *Commission v Germany (Beer Purity)*,[154] where the Court rejected the claim that the traditional German law confining the designation 'beer' to beverages brewed without artificial additives was a proportionate means of consumer protection.[155] The Court here discarded the high German standard, based on the assumption of an uninformed consumer, and—instead—developed its own Union standard of the (reasonably) informed consumer. This Union standard of the 'average

[152] A judicial finding that the national standard of the host State is disproportionately high vis-à-vis the Union standard thus translates into a finding that the national standard of the home State is the appropriate one. And where the host State standard is found proportionate, this essentially means that—within the territory of the host State—the home State standard would be insufficient.

[153] For an analysis of the case law here, see: S. Weatherill, 'Recent Case Law Concerning the Free Movement of Goods: Mapping the Frontiers of Market Deregulation'; and more recently: S. Weatherill, *EU Consumer Law and Policy*, Chapter 2.

[154] Case 178/84, *Commission v Germany* (*Beer Purity*). For Italians, a probably even more famous case is Case 407/85, *3 Glocken* (see n. 102). The passionate opinion of Advocate General Mancini is a delicious meal for any European lawyer!

[155] Case 178/84, *Commission v Germany (Beer Purity)*, para. 53: '[I]n so far as the German rules on additives in beer entail a general ban on additives, their application to beers imported from other Member States is contrary to the requirements of [Union] law as laid down in the case-law of the Court, since that prohibition is contrary to the principle of proportionality.'

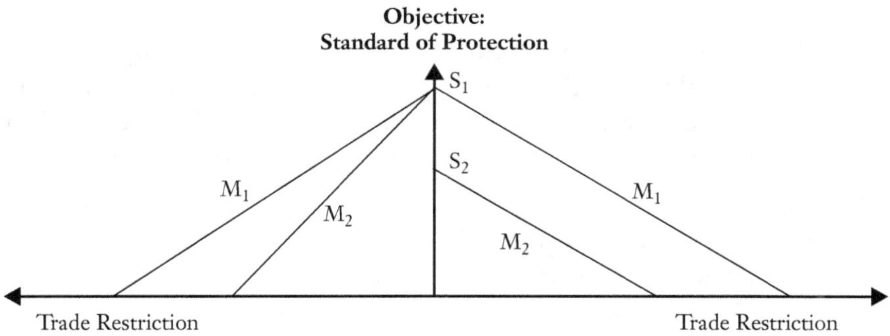

International Proportionality Review	**Federal/National Proportionality Review**
Within the international model, the Court accepts the standard of the host State (S_1) as the legitimate standard against which the necessity of all measures (M_1 and M_2) must be judged. The necessity test is a *least*-restrictive means test that explores whether the *same standard* of protection can be achieved by a means less restrictive to trade (M_2). If that is the case, M_1 constitutes a 'disguised restriction on trade' or an 'arbitrary discrimination' on trade in the sense of Article 36 TFEU.	The Court here compares the original host State standard (S_1) with a second—equivalent—standard of protection (S_2). Under the federal model, that second standard is the standard of the exporting State, whereas it is an absolute Union standard under the national market model. The proportionality test here explores whether the 'equivalent' standard (S_2) can be achieved by a less restrictive means, and the Court thus implicitly engages in a balancing of the costs and benefits of S_1/M_1 and S_2/M_2.

Figure 8. Proportionality standards: contextual differences

consumer who is reasonably well informed and reasonably observant and circumspect' has become a permanent feature of the Court's case law in this context.[156]

bb. Which Standard for Which Public Policy Interest?

When the Union was founded, the international review standard unquestionably prevailed over Article 36. Yet the fundamental shift from the international to the federal market model—following *Cassis*—also took place at the justificatory level. With the emergence of the principle of mutual recognition, the Court thus gradually abandoned the international law

[156] See only: Case C-210/96, *Gut Springenheide v Oberkreisdirektor des Kreises Steinfurt*, para. 31; as well as Case C-220/98, *Estée Lauder Cosmetics*, para. 27.

presumption that the substantive standard governing each State's own—national—market is a question of that State's internal sovereignty. But even within the federal model, the Court regularly pays respect to the idea that Member States have retained *some* freedom as to their desirable level of protection within their territory. In the oft-repeated words of the Court:

> [The] degree of protection may vary from one Member State to the other, Member States must be allowed a margin of appreciation and, consequently, the fact that one Member State imposes less strict rules than another Member State does not mean that the latter's rules are disproportionate.[157]

What does 'margin of appreciation' here mean? Are there judicial criteria to determine when the Court defers to a national standard, and when it will not? Is the Court more deferential in matters affecting public health than, say, environmental protection? And should the Court make a distinction between socio-economic and ethical values?[158] Or, has the Court, as proposed,[159] applied a stricter review standard to discriminatory as opposed to non-discriminatory measures? Sadly, few constitutional criteria appear clearly from the jurisprudence. Some scholars have attempted to tackle the proportionality chaos by doctrinally constructing evaluative guidelines;[160] yet the Court has so far not explained itself

[157] Case C-110/05, *Italian Trailers*, para. 65. And see already: Case C-394/97, *Heinonen*, para. 43: 'It should be pointed out that the Member States, which retain exclusive [*sic*] competence as regards the maintenance of public order and the safeguarding of internal security, enjoy a margin of discretion in determining, according to particular social circumstances and to the importance attached by those States to a legitimate objective under [Union] law, such as the campaign against various forms of criminality linked to the consumption of alcohol, the measures which are likely to achieve concrete results.'

[158] For this point, albeit in the context of the free movement of services, see: J. M. Fernandez and S. O'Leary, 'Judicial Exceptions to the Free Provision of Services', 328–9: 'It appears that moral, political or ethical choices are still to be considered within the scope of Member State competences. The Court is reluctant to interfere in this sphere and to substitute its own judgment for that of the Member States. In contrast, where economically related issues are at stake, the Court is willing to treat them, as a [Union] law matter ... The position of the Court is justifiable in terms of the absence of common ethical or moral standards in the [Union]. Assuming that such a consensus existed in certain areas, there seems to be no effective means at [Union] level, at present, to democratically translate these choices into [Union] policies. In the absence of such consensus, or the means to express whatever consensus does exist, Member States must be accorded a large margin of discretion to give effect to their communities' ethical or political aspirations and choices without the interference of [Union] law.'

[159] S. Weatherill, 'Free Movement of Goods'.

[160] For an early attempt, see: G. de Búrca, 'The Principle of Proportionality and its Application in EC Law'.

sufficiently.[161] Unlike its American counterpart, [162] no clear judicial review principles have ever been announced by the European Court.

The question of which standard should apply, when, and where is particularly urgent in areas in which the Court follows a national market model. For in the absence of Union legislation governing the issue here, the Court's decision as to what is the necessary degree of protecting a particular value will set an absolute standard for all the Member States in the Union. The *Transit Cases*, discussed earlier,[163] provide a good illustration. Because when the Court decides in *Commission v Austria* that the legitimate aim of environmental protection can be achieved by a less restrictive measure than prohibiting lorries of more than 7.5 tonnes from being driven on a motorway, it implicitly makes a cost–benefit analysis that directly translates into a policy statement. And by outlawing all (!) national standards above the Union standard, the Court's proportionality analysis should be as robust and rounded as possible. A clearer indication of what judicial criteria apply would thus be—absolutely—pertinent; and it is hoped that the Court will follow this suggestion in the future.

Conclusion

This chapter has explored a number of special aspects within the general framework of the free movement of goods provisions. Section I tried to explore whether the 'ordinary' constitutional principles that govern Article 34

[161] We can however get a sense of the historical evolution from the excellent study by C. Barnard, 'Derogations, Justifications and the Four Freedoms: Is State Interest Really Protected', 295: 'The cases from 1984, 1994 and 2004 show a remarkable shift by the Court from considerable deference to Member States' regulatory freedom in 1984 (before the 1986 single market programme) to a greater willingness to review Member State justifications in 1994 (two years after the 1992 deadline) and, most recently, a substantial review of the Member States' justifications in 2004, albeit combined with a recognition of a greater number of justifications. The analysis of these cases supports the thesis that while the Court appears increasingly to be "giving" to the Member States through the justifications on the one hand, it is, in fact, taking with the other hand through the onerous requirement that Member States have to prove the justification is made out and through the rigorous application of the principle of proportionality[.]'

[162] For more than sixty years now the Supreme Court has differentiated between a *strict scrutiny test* for discriminatory measures and a *rational basis test* for non-discriminatory measures. On this point, see: Chapter 2, Section I(1/b) of this volume.

[163] See Section I(2/c) of this chapter.

also apply to imports of third-country goods as well as exports of Member State goods. With regard to the former, the text of the EU Treaties seemed to answer this question positively once these goods are in free circulation within the common market. Yet as we saw above, full assimilation has not taken place. For not only did the Court make the assimilation dependent on the existence of a completely 'unified' position under the Common Commercial Policy; it has, in the past, equally insisted on some absolute limits to complete assimilation.

The seemingly greatest divergence from the federal model however appeared to be Article 35. Having remained loyal to an international law reading here, the Union legal order has been forced to acknowledge two heterogeneous definitions of MEEQR for Articles 34 and 35 respectively. How can we explain this? The best answer, in my view, is that the rejection of the federal interpretation of Article 35 is required so as to stabilize the federal interpretation of Article 34; and since the latter is infinitely more important in the fight against State protectionism, the Court sacrificed the development of Article 35 so as to allow Article 34 to grow. Seen in this light, the reductionist interpretation of Article 35 is not an 'aberration' but an integral part of the federal model for regulatory measures restricting the free movement of goods.

Section II, then, moved to the question of exemptions and justifications. According to the so-called 'purely internal situation' rule, the Court originally exempted situations from the scope of Articles 34 and 35 that—while involving national measures potentially limiting intra-Union trade—were factually confined to a single Member State. This jurisdictional exemption has today, at least within the free movement of goods, lost almost all importance. For once the Court moved away from the specifics of the factual situation to a normative analysis of the nature (and scope) of the national measure, the 'purely internal situation' doctrine coincides—jurisdictionally—with the *Dassonville* formula.

With regard to the substantive justifications to trade barriers, we saw above that the Union originally recognized only a (very) limited number of legitimate public policy grounds in Article 36. However, once the Union moved from an international to a federal reading of Article 34, these express grounds were immediately complemented by an unlimited number of imperative requirements. The latter were—at first—confined to non-discriminatory national measures, but the Court seems to be increasingly open towards using imperative requirements also for discriminatory national measures. And indeed, the question of what grounds of justification are available ought to be—as US American jurisprudence shows—of secondary importance.[164] What is fundamental, however, is the judicial review standard against which national measures are judged. The core revolution within the *Cassis* revolution here relates to a change of perspective from which the necessity of a national measure is assessed. Under an international model this is the national standard of the importing (host) State, whereas within a federal (or national) model this will be an independent Union standard. Ever since *Cassis*, the Union has thereby developed its own autonomous standard; yet the precise parameters of (non-)deference have yet to clearly emerge from the jurisprudence of the Court. This should be a matter of priority and the Court should attend to this soon.

[164] We saw in Chapter 2, Section I of this volume that the Supreme Court allows, even for discriminatory measures, for an unlimited range of public policy justifications.

6

Excursus: A Fiscal Affairs Exception?

Introduction

Ever since 1957, the European Treaties made, with regard to goods,[1] a fundamental distinction between *regulatory* and *fiscal* barriers to intra-Union trade.[2] While the former were covered by Article 34 of the Treaty on the Functioning of the European Union (TFEU), fiscal barriers were expressly subject to a different constitutional regime. This constitutional regime was not even uniform and itself distinguished between (external) customs duties and (internal) taxes. Customs duties were seen as 'border measures' that were imposed when goods cross a national frontier; and any limitation on the power of a Member State here related to its *external* sovereignty. (Unlike the General Agreement on Tariffs and Trade,[3] the European Union had thereby gone beyond 'bound' tariffs by committing itself to the total elimination of all tariff barriers within the European common market.) As regards internal taxes, on the other hand, the Treaties decreed—like the GATT—that only *discriminatory* taxes would be outlawed. Overall, the normative structure of the fiscal regime for goods within the common market therefore seemed firmly rooted in an international model that respected the internal sovereignty of the Member States.

Has this changed over the course of the past six decades? Have the Treaty provisions on fiscal barriers been 'federalized'; and if they have, are they nonetheless subject to distinct doctrinal principles (like in the United States)?[4] This final chapter explores these—complex—questions. Section I starts with an analysis of the legal structure of the customs union; and we shall see there that the Court has indeed injected (strong) 'national' and (weak) 'federal' elements into this aspect of the EU common market. With regard to internal taxation, on the other hand, the Union has—in principle—remained loyal to the international market model. For it has continued to review national tax measures (almost) exclusively within the—isolated—normative frame of each single Member State. This

[1] For the other three fundamental freedoms, the Treaty did not textually provide for two distinct constitutional regimes, and it therefore seemed that if fiscal measures were included, they would be governed to the same extent as regulatory measures. For a discussion of fiscal measures within the three 'other' freedoms see Section II(2/b) of this chapter.

[2] This chapter understands 'fiscal' measures in a broad sense to include all pecuniary charges demanded by (national) public authorities generally.

[3] On the GATT treatment of customs barriers, see: Chapter 1, Section II(2/a) of this volume.

[4] On the distinct constitutional principles here, see: Chapter 2, Section II of this volume.

international perspective respects the—internal—fiscal 'sovereignty' of the Member States; and the Court's 'international' approach to dual taxation here contrasts strikingly with its 'federal' treatment of dual regulation after *Cassis*.

But let us tread slowly and approach each fiscal regime in turn.

I. Customs Duties: A National Market Model

Customs duties are the traditional weapon of the mercantilist State.[5] They are employed to 'protect' domestic goods and to financially nourish State resources. Under ordinary international law, such customs duties are not per se prohibited.[6] But 'based upon a customs union', the European Union did—from the very start—adopt a stricter stance:

> The Union shall comprise a customs union which shall cover all trade in goods and which shall involve *the prohibition between Member States* of customs duties on imports and exports and of all charges having equivalent effect, and the adoption of a common customs tariff in their relations with third countries.[7]

The EU 'customs union', as defined here, forms an integral part of the EU 'common market'. It thereby has two dimensions: the *elimination* of all internal customs barriers was to be complemented by the *creation* of a common external tariff for goods coming from third States. And while the external aspect of the customs union shall not interest us here,[8] the central prohibition with regard to internal customs can today be found in Article 30 TFEU. It states:

> Customs duties on imports and exports and charges having equivalent effect shall be prohibited between Member States. This prohibition shall also apply to customs duties of a fiscal nature.

The prohibition applies to customs on imports and exports equally; and it also appears to be an absolute one. The central question therefore simply is this: what are customs duties and charges having equivalent

[5] On the philosophy of mercantilism, see: Chapter 1, Section I(1) of this volume.

[6] We saw in Chapter 1, Section II(2) that the GATT, while committed to tariff reductions, perceives customs duties as the sole legitimate instrument of trade protectionism.

[7] Article 28(1) TFEU (emphasis added).

[8] For a very general treatment, see: R. Schütze, *Foreign Affairs and the EU Constitution*, Chapter 12, Section 1.

effect?[9] We shall analyse this question first and subsequently explore whether Article 30—despite the lack of textual indications or any additional provisions—allows for any implied exceptions and derogations.

1. *General Aspects: Customs Duties and Equivalent Charges*

With no express definition in the EU Treaties, the European Court has defined the concept of 'customs duty' in line with traditional international law. Yet Article 30 also expressly extended the prohibition to all 'charges having equivalent effect to customs duties' (CEECD);[10] and this wording betrayed 'a general intention to prohibit not only measures which obviously take the form of the classic customs duty'.[11] In *Commission v Italy*,[12] the Court catholically defined a CEECD as 'any charge which, by altering the price of an article exported, has the same restrictive effect on the free circulation of that article as a customs duty'.[13] The purpose of the charge would here be totally irrelevant because Article 30 simply 'ma[de] no distinction based on the purpose of the duties and charges the abolition of which it requires'.[14]

But would Article 30 nonetheless require a *protectionist* effect? Despite a brief flirtation with the idea,[15] the Court has long ago chosen not to go down that path. The mere existence of any—pecuniary—burden on goods when crossing a national frontier is thus enough to establish a restricting effect. This constitutional choice was made in *Statistical Levy*.[16]

[9] For early literary discussions, see: R. Barents, 'Charges of Equivalent Effect to Customs Duties'; as well as: F. Wooldridge and R. Plender, 'Charges Having an Effect Equivalent to Customs Duties: A Review of the Cases'; N. Vaulont, 'Die Vereinfachung der Verfahren und Förmlichkeiten im innergemeinschaftlichen Warenverkehr im Lichte der Rechtsprechung des Europäischen Gerichtshofs zum Verbot der Erhebung von Abgaben zollgleicher Wirkung'; J. Kohler, *Abgaben zollgleicher Wirkung im Recht der Europäischen Gemeinschaften*.

[10] Textually, this was not too dissimilar to the GATT wording. For according to Article II:1(b) GATT, the GATT also demands that goods 'be exempt from *all other duties or charges of any kind* imposed on or in connection with the importation in excess of those imposed on the date of this Agreement or those directly and mandatorily required to be imposed thereafter by legislation in force in the importing territory on that date' (emphasis added).

[11] Joined Cases 2 and 3/62, *Commission v Luxembourg and Belgium*, 432.

[12] Case 7/68 *Commission v Italy*, 423. [13] Ibid., 429. [14] Ibid.

[15] Joined Cases 2 and 3/62, *Commission v Luxembourg and Belgium*, 433; see also: Joined Cases 52 and 55/65, *Germany v Commission*, 170: 'For this reason the disputed charges have a discriminatory effect on the imported products, which, however small it may be, is equivalent to that of a customs duty.'

[16] Case 24/68, *Commission v Italy (Statistical Levy)*.

Italy had imposed a levy on goods leaving (or entering) Italy for the purpose of collecting statistical data. Since the levy applied universally to all goods crossing the national border, Italy understandably argued that the measure could not constitute a CEECD 'since any protection of domestic production or discrimination is eliminated'.[17] The Court respectfully disagreed:

In prohibiting the imposition of customs duties [and CEE], the Treaty does not distinguish between goods according to whether or not they enter into competition with the products of the importing country. Thus, the purpose of the abolition of customs barriers is not merely to eliminate their protective nature, as the Treaty sought on the contrary to give general scope and effect to the rule on the elimination of customs duties and charges having equivalent effect, in order to ensure the free movement of goods.

It follows from the system as a whole and from *the general and absolute nature of the prohibition of any customs duty applicable to goods moving between Member States that customs duties are prohibited independently of any consideration of the purpose for which they were introduced and the destination of the revenue obtained therefrom.*[18]

The Court thus clarified that the European Treaties outlawed *all* customs duties and equivalent charges—including restrictions devoid of a protectionist effect.[19] And, as a consequence, the Court teleologically defined a CEECD as follows:

[A]ny pecuniary charge, however small and whatever its designation and mode of application, which is imposed unilaterally on domestic or foreign goods by reason of the fact that they cross a frontier, and which is not a customs duty in the strict sense, constitutes a charge having equivalent effect ... even if it is not imposed for the benefit of the State, is not discriminatory or protective in effect and if the product on which the charge is imposed is not in competition with any domestic product.[20]

This definition centres Article 30 on an absolute restriction test: any pecuniary charge that hinders intra-Union trade would be prima facie prohibited.[21]

[17] Ibid., para. 12. [18] Ibid., paras. 6–7 (emphasis added). [19] Ibid., para. 9.

[20] Ibid., paras. 6–9 (emphasis added).

[21] In a small number of cases, the Court flirted with the idea of incorporating non-pecuniary obstacles into the notion of a charge having equivalent effect, see: Joined Cases 37–8/73, *Sociaal Fonds voor de Diamantarbeiders v NV Indiamex and Feitelijke Vereniging De Belder*, paras. 6–7 (emphasis added): 'The elimination of such charges is designed to promote the free movement of goods within the [Union]. It must therefore be sufficiently comprehensive to include the abolition of all pecuniary, *administrative or other obstacles*, for the purpose of achieving a unified market between the Member States.' See also: Case 63/74, *Cadsky SpA v Istituto nazionale per il Commercio Estero*.

And expressly rejecting a *de minimis* threshold, even the smallest of effects would matter.[22] Yet importantly, the scope of Article 30 appeared to be conceptually limited to charges on goods crossing a *national* frontier. This confined the absolute prohibition to measures that are *distinctly* applicable to imports; and, by attacking solely (external) border measures, Article 30 seemed to perfectly fit into a (modern) international law framework. For even if it went beyond the substantive level of the GATT obligations with regard to customs duties, the provision did not touch the (internal) sovereignty of a State over indistinctly applicable measures. Exploring this classic reading of Article 30 in the next subsection, we shall see however that this international law reading was eventually challenged by a string of cases dealing with equally applicable regional frontier charges.

a. Goods Crossing an External Border: An International Reading

The Court has traditionally tied the restriction rationale underlying Article 30 to a very specific category of measures. Customs duties (and equivalent charges) are here defined as 'national' border charges. Article 30 thus only outlaws national measures that impose a charge when goods cross a *national* frontier—that is, when they are 'imported' into a Member State. In the words of the Court:

> The prohibition, in trade between Member States, of all customs duties and of all charges having equivalent effect refers to all charges *demanded on the occasion or by reason of importation* which, imposed specifically on imported products and not on similar domestic products, alter their cost price and thus produce the same restrictive effect on the free movement of goods as a customs duty.[23]

And again:

> The concept of charges having an effect equivalent to customs duties on imports is directed to any charge exacted *at the time or because of import*, which, specifically affecting an imported product to the exclusion of a similar domestic product, has the same restrictive effect on the free movement of goods as a custom duty.[24]

[22] Case 24/68, *Commission v Italy (Statistical Levy)*, para. 14: 'The very low rate of the charge cannot change its character with regard to the principles of the Treaty[.]'

[23] Case 29/72, *Marimex*, para. 6 (emphasis added). This definition was made in the context of Article 22 of Regulation 805/68 whose first paragraph (legislatively) prohibited 'the levying of any customs duty or charge having equivalent effect'.

[24] Case 39/73, *Rewe-Zentralfinanz GmbH v Direktor der Landwirtschaftskammer Westfalen-Lippe*, para. 3 (emphasis added).

Customs duties and CEEs are therefore characterized as measures that are—by definition—*distinctly* applicable to imports (or exports). They apply *specifically* to 'imports' or 'exports' because only these, and not domestic goods, need to cross the national frontier. Fiscal measures that indistinctly apply to imported and domestic goods, on the other hand, cannot be considered custom duties or equivalent charges. Not applying distinctly to imports, they are not *border* measures but constitute *internal* taxation.[25]

The distinction between a 'border' charge and an 'internal' tax can however sometimes be difficult. The GATT solution here distinguishes between whether or not the internal tax or charge applies 'to an imported product and to the like domestic product'.[26] And in its past jurisprudence, the European Court of Justice has—*mutatis mutandis*—followed this suggestion. In *Statistical Levy*,[27] the Court thus held:

> [T]he concept of a charge having equivalent effect does not include taxation which is imposed in the same way within a State on similar or comparable domestic products, or at least falls, in the absence of such products, within the framework of general internal taxation, or which is intended to compensate for such internal taxation within the limits laid down by the Treaty.[28]

Where a State can prove that a similar tax is imposed in a similar way on a similar domestic product, the fiscal charge will thus fall outside the scope of Article 30. And even where there is no specific domestic product to compare with, the Court has excluded fiscal duties from the scope of Article 30 when they form part of a general framework of internal taxation. Yet the Court has insisted that fiscal charges claimed to form part of a general system of internal taxation must be 'applied systematically in accordance with the same criteria to domestic products and imported products alike'.[29]

[25] Case 25/67, *Firma Milch-, Fett- und Eierkontor GmbH v Hauptzollamt Saarbrücken*. See also: Case 193/85, *Cooperativa Co-Frutta Srl v Amministrazione delle finanze dello Stato*, para. 9: 'The essential feature of a charge having an effect equivalent to a customs duty which distinguishes it from an internal tax therefore resides in the fact that the former is borne solely by an imported product as such whilst the latter is borne both by imported and domestic products.'

[26] 1947 GATT, Annex I, Ad Article III states: 'Any internal tax or other internal charge, or any law, regulation or requirement of the kind referred to in paragraph 1 which applies to an imported product and to the like domestic product and is collected or enforced in the case of the imported product at the time or point of importation, is nevertheless to be regarded as an internal tax or other internal charge, or a law, regulation or requirement of the kind referred to in paragraph 1, and is accordingly subject to the provisions of Article III.'

[27] Case 24/68, *Commission v Italy (Statistical Levy)*. [28] Ibid., para. 11.

[29] Case 29/72, *Marimex v Italian Finance Administration*, para. 7. The Court has interpreted the requirement of an application of the 'same criteria' strictly. In Case 132/78, *Denkavit Loire*

Especially in its dealings with 'compensatory' taxes, the Court has been very strict: 'If such compensation were permitted, every State, by virtue of its sovereignty in its own domestic affairs, could in this manner compensate the widest variety of tax burdens imposed on any product and this practice would open an irreparable breach in the principles of the Treaty.'[30]

In conclusion, the European legal order has traditionally limited the scope of Article 30 to fiscal charges that are 'borne solely by a product which crosses a frontier';[31] and the classic—international—reading of Article 30 has thereby insisted that this frontier is a 'national' frontier. The European Court has consequently held that all charges that are 'equally imposed' on imported and domestic products would fall outside the scope of Article 30.[32]

v France, the Court had to deal with a French health measure that generally imposed a financial charge on meat. However, the calculation base of the charge differed depending on whether the meat had been slaughtered on French territory or whether it had been imported. The Court held that such a differential system would not apply the 'same criteria' to domestic and imported products (ibid., para. 8): '[I]n order to relate to a general system of internal dues, the charge to which an imported product is subject must impose the same duty on national products and identical imported products at the same marketing stage and that the chargeable event giving rise to the duty must also be identical in the case of both products. It is therefore not sufficient that the objective of the charge imposed on imported products is to compensate for a charge imposed on similar domestic products—or which has been imposed on those products or a product from which they are derived—at a production or marketing stage prior to that at which the imported products are taxed. To exempt a charge levied at the frontier from the classification of a charge having equivalent effect when it is not imposed on similar national products or is imposed on them at different marketing stages or, again, on the basis of a different chargeable event giving rise to duty, because that charge aims to compensate for a domestic fiscal charge applying to the same products—apart from the fact that this would not take into account fiscal charges which had been imposed on imported products in the originating Member State—would make the prohibition on charges having an effect equivalent to customs duties empty and meaningless.'

30 Joined Cases 2–3/62, *Commission v Luxembourg and Belgium (Gingerbread)*, 433.

31 Joined Cases C-441–2/98, *Michaïlidis v Idryma Koinonikon Asfaliseon (IKA)*, para. 22. See also: Case C-221/06, *Stadtgemeinde Frohnleiten and Gemeindebetriebe Frohnleiten GmbH v Bundesminister für Land- und Forstwirtschaft, Umwelt und Wasserwirtschaft*, para. 28: 'In the light of that definition and as regards the characteristics of the Altlastenbeitrag, it should be noted that all long-term depositing of waste is in principle subject to payment of that levy, whether the waste comes from Austria or another Member State. A levy such as the Altlastenbeitrag is not therefore charged because a border of the Member State which imposed that levy has been crossed.'

32 Joined Cases 2–3/62, *Commission v Luxembourg and Belgium (Gingerbread)*, 434. The Court has however clarified that even if there is a—formally—indistinctly applicable charge, the latter will not apply equally to domestic and imported goods where the charge is used to exclusively support domestic products. See only: Case 77/72, *Capolongo v Azienda Agricole*, paras. 13–14: '[W]hen such a financial charge or duty is intended exclusively to support activities which

b. Goods Crossing an Internal Border: Towards a National Reading

Article 30 traditionally hinged on the fact that only *foreign* goods would—as imports—cross a *national* border, and any charge imposed on that external border-crossing would therefore, by definition, specifically apply to imports.

But what about situations, where a charge is imposed on the crossing of a *regional* border *within* a Member State? Would regional charges also be caught by Article 30? Under the international model, this should *not* be the case when the charge equally applies to imported and domestic products. For once the absolute restriction test in Article 30 is extended from distinctly to indistinctly applicable measures, any fiscal charge imposed on any frontier-crossing within the national territory would be outlawed; and this would transform Article 30's underlying philosophy from an international to a national one. Surprisingly, in a string of cases decided in the last two decades, the Court appears to have accepted that transformation.

A first case here is *Legros*, which dealt with a 'regional' customs charge that was levied when German motor vehicles were imported into La

specifically profit taxed domestic products, it can follow that the general duty levied according to the same criteria on the imported product and the domestic product nevertheless constitutes for the former a net supplementary tax burden, whilst for the latter it constitutes in reality a set-off against benefits or aids previously received ... Consequently, a duty within the general system of internal taxation applying systematically to domestic and imported products according to the same criteria, can nevertheless constitute a charge having an effect equivalent to a customs duty on imports, when such contribution is intended exclusively to support activities which specifically benefit the taxed domestic product.' The Court subsequently interpreted this exception restrictively by insisting that an equally applicable tax that is part of the general tax system will constitute a charge having equivalent effect 'only if such a duty, which is limited to particular products, had the sole purpose of financing activities for the specific advantage of the taxed domestic products so as to make good, wholly or in part, the fiscal charge imposed upon them' (Case 77/76, *Cucchi v Avez*, para. 16).

The case law has however become fairly complex in this area, see: Case C-234/99, *Nygård v Svineafgiftsfonden, and Ministeriet for Fødevarer, Landbrug og Fiskeri*, para. 23: 'It is in this regard settled case-law that if the advantages stemming from the use of the revenue from a charge forming part of a general system of internal charges applying systematically to national products processed and marketed on the national market and to products exported in an unprocessed state fully offset the burden borne by the national product processed and marketed on the national market when it is placed on the market, that charge constitutes a charge having an effect equivalent to a customs duty, contrary to Articles [28 and 30] of the Treaty. On the other hand, if the advantages accruing to the taxed national products processed and marketed on the national market from the use of the revenue generated by the charge offset only partially the burden borne by those products, such a charge will constitute a breach of the prohibition of discrimination laid down by Article [110] of the Treaty.'

Réunion—an island in the Indian Ocean that constitutes an overseas *département* of France.[33] The 'dock dues' imposed were thereby levied on all goods—including French goods—with the exception of products produced within the region.[34] The question for the Court was therefore whether a charge levied 'in one region of the national territory of a Member State and affecting in the same manner goods from the rest of the national territory' could fall under Article 30.[35] The French government denied that such a regional charge could ever constitute a CEECD, since it was not distinctly applicable to imports into (metropolitan) France.[36] But the Court rejected this view. Emphatically invoking '*the unity of the [Union] customs territory*', it found that a regional charge 'constitutes an obstacle to the free movement of goods which is at least as serious as a charge levied at the national frontier'.[37]

What exactly did that mean? Had the Court consciously transformed Article 30 into a 'national' customs union clause? The Court subsequently clarified its jurisprudence in *Lancry*.[38] The judgment is worth quoting at length:

> The unity of the [Union] customs territory is undermined by the establishment of a regional customs frontier just the same, whether the products on which a charge is levied by reason of the fact that they cross a frontier are domestic products or come from other Member States. Furthermore, the obstacle to the free movement of goods created by the imposition on domestic products of a charge levied by reason of their crossing that frontier is no less serious than that created by the collection of a charge of the same kind on products from another Member State.
>
> *Since the very principle of a customs union covers all trade in goods, as provided for by Article [28 TFEU], it requires the free movement of goods generally, as opposed to inter-State trade alone, to be ensured within the Union.* Although Article [28 et seq.] makes express reference only to trade between Member States, that is because it was assumed that there were no charges exhibiting the features of a customs duty in existence within the Member States. Since the absence of such charges is an essential precondition for the attainment of a customs union covering all trade in goods, it follows that they are likewise prohibited by Article [30].[39]

[33] Case C-163/90, *Administration des Douanes et Droits Indirects v Léopold Legros and others*.

[34] Ibid., para. 4. [35] Ibid., para. 10. [36] Ibid., para. 14.

[37] Ibid., paras. 16–17 (emphasis added).

[38] Joined Cases C-363, 407–11/93, *Lancry SA v Direction Générale des Douanes and others*.

[39] Ibid., paras. 27–9 (emphasis added).

The Court here unequivocally held that regional charges could violate Article 30 even when imposed—indistinctly—on imported and domestic goods. But this jurisprudential line nonetheless remained—partly—ambivalent as to the legality of charges *exclusively* imposed on domestic products.[40] According to a 'federal' reading of Article 30, such 'purely internal' charges should not be caught;[41] yet according to a fully fledged 'national' market model, the unity of the Union's customs territory would of course equally demand their abolition.

What model would the Court prefer here? The constitutional ambivalence appears to have been resolved in *Simitzi*.[42] The Court was asked to assess 'ad valorem charges levied by a Member State on goods entering one region of its territory *solely from other regions of the same State* and on goods despatched from one region *solely to other regions of the same State*';[43] and it indeed found—expressly referring to *Lancry*—that '[t]he same reasoning must apply in the case of a charge levied on goods despatched from one region to other regions of the same State'.[44] And in a fourth case, the Court finally clarified that its 'national' concept of CEECD applied to import as well as export charges,[45] and that 'the size of the territorial administrative authority which levied the tax is [also] immaterial'.[46]

[40] Ibid., para. 30: 'Secondly, the situation does not appear to be of a kind where all the components are wholly confined to one Member State. As the French Government has correctly pointed out, the levying of charges exhibiting the features of dock dues could be classified as a purely internal situation only if the dues were levied exclusively on products from the same Member State. It is not disputed that dock dues apply to all products entering the overseas department concerned, irrespective of their origin. It would accordingly be inconsistent to hold, on the one hand, that dock dues constitute charges having equivalent effect in so far as they are levied on goods from other Member States and to concede, on the other, that those dues do not constitute charges having equivalent effect where they are levied on goods from metropolitan France.'

[41] On the phenomenon of 'reverse discrimination' as an integral part of the federal model, see: Chapter 4, Section I(1/a) of this volume.

[42] Joined Cases C-485–6/93, *Simitzi v Kos*.

[43] Ibid., para. 24 (emphasis added).

[44] Ibid., para. 26. See also: Case C-293/02, *Jersey Produce Marketing Organisation Ltd v States of Jersey and Jersey Potato Export Marketing Board*. In the latter case, the Court added a hypothetical argument as to why these purely internal charges are affecting intra-Union trade (ibid., para. 65): '[E]ven though the 2001 Act covers, according to its wording, only potatoes despatched to the United Kingdom for consumption there, that does not rule out the possibility that such potatoes, once within the United Kingdom, might then be re-exported to other Member States, with the result that the contribution in question may be levied on goods which, after having passed through the United Kingdom in transit, are in fact exported to other Member States.'

[45] Case C-72/03, *Carbonati Apuani Srl v Comune di Carrara*.

[46] Ibid., para. 28.

This jurisprudence undoubtedly points towards a 'national' model that is completely disconnected from *inter*-State trade. For even if an international trade rationale can still explain why regional charges on *foreign* imports are of a discriminatory nature,[47] an international reading of Article 30 is simply unable to outlaw regional charges imposed on *domestic* products. A national market philosophy is thus at work when Article 30 is used 'to obtain a declaration that a charge imposed on whisky transported from Scotland, not to Lyon but to London, or on San Daniele ham transported from Friuli, not to Stuttgart but to Sardinia, is unlawful'.[48] And while this 'national' interpretation of Article 30 to (purely) internal charges has been heavily contested by various Advocates General,[49] the Court has consistently brushed aside the argument that Article 30 is confined to trade 'between Member States'.[50] It has, on the contrary, counterclaimed that '[t]he very principle of a customs union, as provided for by Article [28 TFEU], *requires the free movement of goods to be ensured within the Union generally, not in trade between Member States alone*'.[51]

To textually support this reading of Article 30—an interpretation that contradicts the very wording of the provision—the Court has found it helpful to point to the 'national' definition of the European internal market as 'an area without internal frontiers' in Article 26(2) TFEU.[52] The argument however encounters insurmountable historical and systematic hurdles.[53] The—unspoken—teleological reasons behind the Court's choice

[47] Advocate General Jacobs in Case C-163/90, *Administration des Douanes et Droits Indirects v Léopold Legros and others*, para. 33: 'As the Commission rightly points out, discrimination on the basis of regional origin constitutes partial discrimination on the basis of nationality, since the region concerned forms part of the national territory of a Member State. To put the point another way, goods which originate in other Member States inevitably suffer less favourable treatment.'

[48] Advocate General Tesauro in Joined Cases C-363, 407–11/93, *Lancry SA v Direction Générale des Douanes and others*, para. 21.

[49] Ibid., para. 27: 'To summarize the points that I have developed, where goods from one Member State pass from one region to another in the same Member State the basic and essential condition for the application of Article [28] et seq. of the Treaty is not satisfied.' See also Advocate General Maduro in Case C-72/03, *Carbonati*, para. 46: 'the customs union is first and foremost a system for free movement between Member States, not a system for the crossing of internal frontiers'.

[50] See only: Case C-72/03, *Carbonati*, para. 21.

[51] Ibid., para. 22 (emphasis added).

[52] Ibid., para. 23.

[53] For an excellent elaboration of this point, see: Advocate General Leger in Case C-293/02, *Jersey Potatoes*, paras. 127–34. The Advocate General concludes (ibid., para. 134): 'Thus, the term 'internal frontiers' must be taken to mean inter-State frontiers (in the context of trade between Member States, within the [Union]), to the exclusion of intra-State frontiers (in the

in favour of a national interpretation of Article 30 may however be twofold. First, there seems to be a fear that '[i]f regional authorities remained free to impose such charges, the free movement of goods within the [Union] could be completely disrupted' in light of the 'innumerable regional frontiers which exist within the [Union]'.[54] And the Court may, secondly, have felt that there exists a social contradiction in the idea of 'a single market in which barriers to trade between Portugal and Denmark are prohibited, whilst barriers to trade between Naples and Capri are immaterial'.[55] But both of these arguments can be countered.[56] The Court has nevertheless—so far—struck to its teleological guns.

2. *Special Aspects: Third-Country Goods and Justifications*

a. Third-Country Goods and Direct Imports into the Union

The benefits of Article 30 not only apply to Member State goods.[57] The Treaties indeed expressly extend them to 'products coming from third countries which are in free circulation in Member States'.[58] Under Article 29, third-country goods are considered to be 'in free circulation in a

context of trade within one and the same Member State) and in contrast to external frontiers (in the context of trade between Member States and non-member countries).'

[54] Advocate General Jacobs in Case C-163/90, *Legros*, para. 26. But should the task of creating a 'national' market not be a national task? Should the European Union create the 'national' markets of its Member States?

[55] Advocate General Tesauro in Joined Cases C-363, 407–11/93, *Lancry*, para. 28: 'An experienced lawyer will also notice the paradox of a single market in which barriers to trade between Portugal and Denmark are prohibited, whilst barriers to trade between Naples and Capri are immaterial.' Various Advocate Generals and the Court thus seem to be motivated by a desire to eradicate reverse discrimination, see only: Advocate General Leger in Case C-293/02, *Jersey Potatoes*, para. 113: 'That analysis [in *Lancry*], it seems, reflects the concern of the Court to avoid contributing to the emergence of reverse discrimination, in that, following the delivery of its judgment (if the latter had established a difference of classification of that kind), domestic products would have been subject to less favourable treatment than products imported from other Member States.'

[56] It all depends on one's (market) philosophical perspective, and some have therefore argued in favour of a 'federal' reading of Article 30. See the excellent analysis by A. Tryfonidou, 'Resolving the Reverse Discrimination Paradox in the Area of Customs Duties: The *Lancry* Saga', 334: '[I]f, indeed, the Court's main concern in the *Lancry* saga was to address the issue of reverse discrimination, over-extending the scope of Article 30 TFEU by including situations that are unrelated to the aim of that provision was, with respect, not the right way to do so.'

[57] For an extensive discussion of this point in the context of Article 34, see: Chapter 5, Section I(1) of this volume.

[58] Article 28(2) TFEU.

Member State' once 'the import formalities have been complied with and any customs duties or charges having equivalent effect which are payable have been levied *in that State*'.

What exactly did this formulation mean? Was it implicitly based on the idea that, within a customs union, all customs matters were to be centrally harmonized by the Union; or did Article 29 operate even in the absence of a Union customs code? And if the latter, did the formulation imply that Member States remained free to erect fiscal barriers for direct imports of third-country goods from outside the Union, yet once a first national customs border had been successfully crossed these goods were entitled to move freely in all other Member States? This—federal reading—of Article 29 is proposed by its wording, which—taken by its black letters—suggests that the customs rules of the State of entry will have to be mutually recognized by all other Member States. And despite the exclusive competence of the Union over the 'customs union' and its 'common commercial policy',[59] the Union legal order has indeed—for a long time—emphasized these federal elements within Article 29 TFEU. The Union has thus traditionally deferred to the law of the first-entry Member State; and, as a corollary, Member States were relatively free to impose CEECDs (or customs formalities) on direct imports from third States.

A good illustration of this federal solution is offered by *Sociaal Fonds voor de Diamantarbeiders*.[60] The case concerned a national charge that had been levied on the import of rough diamonds coming from third countries. The Union's common customs tariff had been introduced by Regulation 950/68 and the question arose 'to what extent the Member States may introduce or maintain, after 1 July 1968, charges having an effect equivalent to customs duties, levied on goods imported directly from third countries, and under what conditions they may be required to eliminate them'.[61] The lengthy answer by the European Court of Justice was as follows:

> [T]he customs union involves the establishment of a single customs tariff for the whole [Union], as envisaged at [30–3 TFEU]. This common tariff is intended to

[59] Article 31 TFEU equivocally states: 'Common Customs Tariff duties shall be fixed by the Council on a proposal from the Commission.' And according to Article 3(1)(a) and (e) TFEU, the Union enjoys an exclusive competence for the 'customs union' as well as its 'common commercial policy'.

[60] Joined Cases 37–8/73, *Sociaal Fonds voor de Diamantarbeiders v NV Indiamex et Association de fait De Belder*.

[61] Ibid., para. 3.

achieve an equalization of customs charges levied at the frontiers of the [Union] on products imported from third countries, in order to avoid any deflection of trade in relations with those countries and any distortion of free internal circulation or of competitive conditions...

The Common Customs Tariff was introduced, for the [Union] as originally constituted, by Regulation No. 950/68 of the Council, which came into force on 1 July 1968. Although that Regulation does not expressly allow for the elimination or equalization of charges other than customs duties as such, it is nevertheless clear from its objective that under it Member States are prohibited from amending, by means of charges supplementing such duties, the level of protection as defined by the Common Customs Tariff ... It follows therefore that subsequent to the introduction of the Common Customs Tariff all Member States are prohibited from introducing, on a unilateral basis, any new charges or from raising the level of those already in force. *As regards charges already in existence, prior evaluation by the [Union] authorities is necessary in order to establish their incompatibility with the Treaty and the obligation to eliminate them. It follows that such charges may only be considered to be incompatible with [Union] law pursuant to provisions adopted by the [Union].*[62]

The judgment presented a nuanced solution with regard to the powers left to the Member States vis-à-vis third-country goods. In the absence of a constitutional prohibition for CEECD for direct imports from third countries, the case was governed by Union legislation in the form of the Common Customs Tariff Regulation. And since the latter only outlawed *newly* introduced CEECDs, the elimination of already existing customs barriers vis-à-vis third-country goods was left to the political discretion and rhythm of the (future) Union legislature. For direct imports, there was thus—in the absence of Union legislation—no absolute prohibition on *existing* customs barriers.

This constitutional lenience towards external customs barriers was confirmed in *Simmenthal*.[63] The Italian authorities had levied charges in respect of health inspections to which consignments of frozen beef, imported from a third country, had been subjected. In the course of a preliminary ruling, the question arose whether these charges constituted an illegal CEECD, and whether the same principles that characterized the Court's jurisprudence under Article 30 would also apply to direct imports from third States. The Court did not think so:

[62] Ibid., paras. 8–10, 12–13, and 18–20 (emphasis added).

[63] Case 70/77, *Simmenthal SpA v Amministrazione delle finanze.*

Where the elimination of charges having an effect equivalent to customs duties is applied to trade with third countries, its objectives and legal basis are different from those which underlie and justify the prohibition of such charges in intra-[Union] trade. In so far as intra-[Union] trade is concerned, the prohibition is laid down in Article [28 TFEU] itself, and is unconditional and absolute because it is designed to establish free movement of goods within the [Union].

On the other hand, in so far as trade with third countries is concerned, the question whether it is necessary to abolish, maintain, amend or introduce charges having equivalent effect must be related both to the requirements of the common commercial policy and to the requirements, consequent upon the introduction of the Common Customs Tariff, of harmonization of conditions of importation from third countries ... *It follows from the same considerations that the prohibition is not absolute in so far as trade with third countries is concerned, and that when they impose that prohibition the Council or, where appropriate, the Commission may make exceptions or derogations from it.*[64]

The Court consequently held that the constitutional principles governing Article 30, developed for Member State goods, were *not* applicable to imports from third countries. Instead of an absolute and unconditional prohibition, Union law did allow pecuniary charges in addition to the (harmonized) Union customs duties. Yet the Court still insisted that 'the intrinsic effect of such charges on the relevant trade with third countries must be uniform in all the Member States';[65] and it therefore explored to what extent the Union had also harmonized the area with regard to health inspections at the external borders of the European Union.[66]

b. *Exemptions and Justification(s): Two Objective 'Justifications'*

The prohibition of customs duties within the Union always faced an absolute silence on possible justifications. The Treaties indeed did not—unlike the GATT—list any exemptions to customs barriers to trade in goods.

Was this a deliberate constitutional choice? The unavailability of the Union's justificatory clause in Article 36 for fiscal restrictions was clearly confirmed in *Commission v Italy (Art Treasures)*.[67] Italy had tried to defend a charge on the export of goods with artistic or historical value by pointing

[64] Ibid., paras. 21–3 and 26 (emphasis added).

[65] Ibid., para. 27.

[66] Ibid., paras. 29–55.

[67] Case 7/68, *Commission v Italy (Art Treasures)*. For the text of Article 36 and its interpretation, see: Chapter 5, Section II(2) of this volume.

to the relevant legitimate interests that could justify restrictions on quantitative restrictions. Yet the Court rejected this reasoning. Exceptions to the free movement of goods had to be interpreted restrictively; and with regard to Article 36 this meant that it 'is not possible to apply the exception laid down in the latter provision to measures which fall outside the scope of the prohibitions referred to in the chapter relating to the elimination of quantitative restrictions between Member States'.[68] Article 36 was thus confined to *regulatory* restrictions and could not be extended to *fiscal* charges.[69] And since there existed no specific justifications in the Treaty for measures falling into Article 30, the Court concluded that the provision 'does not permit of any exceptions'.[70]

The Court has however subsequently recognized two very specific *implied* exceptions.

The first exception relates to the situation where a fiscal charge constitutes consideration for a service rendered.[71] In *Statistical Levy*,[72] the Italian government thus argued that its statistical data for imports and exports benefited individual traders, and that this commercial advantage 'justifies their paying for this public service' as a *quid pro quo*.[73] The Court indeed accepted the abstract idea;[74] yet it gave it an extremely

[68] Case 7/68, *Commission v Italy (Art Treasures)*, 430.

[69] The reason that the Court gave for the non-availability of justifications for customs duties is that the latter would not be suitable to protect the legitimate interests involved (ibid.): 'Finally, the fact that the provisions of Article 36 which have been mentioned do not relate to customs duties and charges having equivalent effect is explained by the fact that such measures have the sole effect of rendering more onerous the exportation of the products in question, without ensuring the attainment of the object referred to in that article, which is to protect the artistic, historic or archaeological heritage.'

[70] Case 24/68, *Commission v Italy (Statistical Levy)*, para. 10; and see also: Case 2/69, *Sociaal Fonds voor de Diamantarbeiders v S.A. Ch. Brachfeld*, para. 19/21.

[71] For the GATT solution here, see: Article II:2: 'Nothing in this Article shall prevent any [Member] from imposing at any time on the importation of any product: ... (c) fees or other charges commensurate with the cost of services rendered.' And see also Article VIII:1(a) GATT: 'All fees and charges of whatever character (other than import and export duties and other than taxes within the purview of Article III) imposed by [Members] on or in connection with importation or exportation shall be limited in amount to the approximate cost of services rendered and shall not represent an indirect protection to domestic products or a taxation of imports or exports for fiscal purposes.'

[72] Case 24/68, *Commission v Italy (Statistical Levy)*.

[73] Ibid., para. 15.

[74] Ibid., para. 11: 'Although it is not impossible that in certain circumstances a specific service actually rendered may form consideration for a possible proportional payment for the service in question, this may only apply in specific cases which cannot lead to the circumvention of the provisions of Article [30] of the Treaty.'

restrictive interpretation. And since, in the present case, the statistical information was only 'beneficial to the economy as a whole', the advantage was 'so general' that the charge could not be regarded 'as the consideration for a *specific* benefit'.[75] A border charge could therefore only be justified if it was consideration for a *specific* service benefiting *individual* traders. This line of argument was confirmed in *Bresciani*.[76] The Court here held that compulsory health inspections were not a specific service for individual importers; and it also found it of no relevance that the charge at issue was proportionate to the costs of the compulsory health inspections, since the inspections were conducted in the general public interest and should consequently be financed by the public purse.[77]

The second—implied—exception from the absolute prohibition of customs charges are charges that a Member State levies as compensation for frontier checks *that are required by European Union law*. The rationale behind this exception is that the Member States here act on behalf of the Union, and in a manner that facilitates the free movement of goods. For example, in *Bauhuis*,[78] the Court had to deal with a Union law that required veterinary and public health inspections by the exporting Member State so as to make multiple frontier inspections by the importing Member State(s) unnecessary. Finding such health inspections to be not unilaterally imposed by a Member State but reflecting 'the general interest of the [Union]',[79] the Court thus held that they would not hinder intra-Union trade in goods. Since the Member States here act as the decentralized Union administration,[80] national charges for these 'Union' inspections were legal. The conditions for

[75] Ibid., para. 16 (emphasis added). See also Case 39/73, *Rewe-Zentralfinanz eGmbH v Direktor der Landwirtschaftskammer Westfalen-Lippe*, esp. para. 4.

[76] Case 87/75, *Bresciani v Amministrazione Italiana delle Finanze*.

[77] Ibid., para. 10: 'Nor, in determining the effects of the duty on the free movement of goods, is it of any importance that a duty of the type at issue is proportionate to the costs of a compulsory public health inspection carried out on entry of the goods. The activity of the administration of the State intended to maintain a public health inspection system imposed in the general interest cannot be regarded as a service rendered to the importer such as to justify the imposition of a pecuniary charge. If, accordingly, public health inspections are still justified at the end of the transitional period, the costs which they occasion must be met by the general public which, as a whole, benefits from the free movement of [Union] goods.'

[78] Case 46/76, *Bauhuis v The Netherlands*.

[79] Ibid., para. 29.

[80] On executive federalism and the duty of the Member States to indirectly administer EU law, see: R. Schütze, *European Constitutional Law*, Chapter 9, Section 4.

this '*Bauhuis* justification' were subsequently developed in *Commission v Germany*.[81]

II. Internal Taxation: An International Market Model

With regard to fiscal barriers, the prohibition of customs duties and the prohibition of discriminatory taxation are two sides of the same coin. In the Union legal order, Article 110 TFEU is designed to complement Article 30 TFEU:

> Article [110] supplement[s], within the system of the Treaty, the provisions on the abolition of customs duties and charges having equivalent effect. [Its] aim is to ensure free movement of goods between the Member States in normal conditions of competition by the elimination of all forms of protection which result from the application of internal taxation which discriminates against products from other Member States.[82]

Due to their complementary roles, the material scopes of Articles 30 and 110 are meant to be fundamentally different. As we saw earlier, the former was traditionally designed to catch national measures that impose a charge on goods crossing the *external* (national) frontier, whereas Article 110 was to apply when foreign goods are subject to *internal* taxation. Like two sides of the same coin, the two prohibitions were thus bound together yet mutually exclusive.[83] And this difference in their thematic

[81] Case C-18/87, *Commission v Germany*, esp. para. 8: '[S]uch fees may not be classified as charges having an effect equivalent to a customs duty if the following conditions are satisfied: (a) they do not exceed the actual costs of the inspections in connection with which they are charged; (b) the inspections in question are obligatory and uniform for all the products concerned in the [Union]; (c) they are prescribed by [European] law in the general interest of the [Union]; (d) they promote the free movement of goods, in particular by neutralizing obstacles which could arise from unilateral measures of inspection adopted in accordance with Article 36 of the Treaty.'

[82] Case 193/85, *Cooperativa Co-Frutta Srl v Amministrazione delle finanze dello Stato*, para. 25. See also: Case 252/86, *Bergandi v Directeur général des impôts*, para. 17.

[83] Case 57-65, *Lütticke GmbH v Hauptzollamt Sarrelouis*, 211: 'Article[] [30] on the one hand and Article [110] on the other cannot be applied jointly to one and the same case. Charges having an effect equivalent to customs duties on the on hand and internal taxation on the other hand are governed by different systems.' The Court would confirm this in 1975 in Case 94/74, *IGAV v ENCC*, para. 13: 'One and the same scheme of taxation cannot, under the system of the Treaty, belong simultaneously to both categories mentioned, having regard to the fact

'object' also seemed to imply a fundamental difference with regard to the constitutional test applicable within each prohibition. Article 30 was originally based on a (*absolute*) restriction test for *distinctly* applicable measures, while Article 110, on the other hand, was centered on a (*relative*) discrimination test for *indistinctly* applicable measures. This discrimination rationale within Article 110 was clearly informed by the international philosophy set out in Article III:2 GATT; yet, as we shall see later, the Court has, in the past sixty years, come to accept islands of fiscal federalism here too. But would the Court go as far as limiting double taxation within the European internal market? And, in particular: would the—federal—idea of mutual recognition apply here too? Let us explore these questions in turn.

1. *Discriminatory Taxation and the Free Movement of Goods*

Article 110 deals with *indistinctly* applicable measures—that is, measures that may apply to foreign *and* domestic goods. It is therefore not formulated as an absolute prohibition but instead reads:

> [1] No Member State shall impose, directly or indirectly, on the products of other Member States any internal taxation of any kind in excess of that imposed directly or indirectly on similar domestic products.
>
> [2] Furthermore, no Member State shall impose on the products of other Member States any internal taxation of such a nature to afford indirect protection to other products.

The text of the provision makes clear that it only applies to taxes on *goods*—that is, indirect taxes.[84] And by focusing on 'products of other Member States', Article 110 also clearly suggested that third-country goods—even those in free circulation within the Union—would *not* benefit from the provision. Yet despite strong textual and systemic considerations,[85] the

that the charges referred to in Article [30] must be purely and simply abolished whilst, for the purpose of applying internal taxation, Article [110] provides solely for the elimination of any form of discrimination, direct or indirect, in the treatment of the domestic products of the Member States and of products originating in other Member States.' And see also: Case C-78/90, *Compagnie Commerciale de l'Ouest and others v Receveur Principal des Douanes de La Pallice Port*, para. 22: 'The provisions on charges having equivalent effect and those on discriminatory internal taxation cannot be applied together. The scope of each of those provisions must therefore be defined.'

[84] Case 20/76, *Schöttle & Söhne OHG v Finanzamt Freudenstadt*.

[85] For some of the systemic considerations, see Chapter 3, Section I of this volume.

Court has subsequently come to find that Article 110 would apply to third-country goods in free circulation.[86] And, again against the clear wording of Article 110 (and despite a specific provision governing exports),[87] the Court has equally 'clarified' that Article 110 also applied to taxes on goods destined for exportation.[88]

[86] Case 193/85, *Co-Frutta*, paras. 25–6: 'It is true that, unlike the wording of Article [28] of the Treaty, which expressly refers to products coming from third countries which are in free circulation in Member States, Article [110] refers only to products "of other Member States". However, as the Court has consistently held, the first and second paragraphs of Article [110] supplement, within the system of the Treaty, the provisions on the abolition of customs duties and charges having equivalent effect. Their aim is to ensure free movement of goods between the Member States in normal conditions of competition by the elimination of all forms of protection which result from the application of internal taxation which discriminates against products from other Member States. Accordingly, Article [110] must guarantee the complete neutrality of internal taxation as regards competition between domestic products and products imported from other Member States. Article [110] cannot be interpreted in a manner contrary to the aim indicated above. Under Article [28] (1) of the [FEU] Treaty the [Union] is to be based upon a customs union which is to cover all trade in goods and the adoption of a common customs tariff. As the Court pointed out in its judgment of 15 December 1976 (Case 41/76 *Donckerwolcke* [1976] ECR 1921), according to Article [28](2) the provisions adopted for the liberalization of intra-[Union] trade apply in identical fashion to products originating in Member States and to products coming from third countries which are in free circulation in the [Union] in accordance with the requirements laid down by Article [29]. In that connection the Court has made it clear that, as regards the free movement of goods within the [Union], products which are in free circulation are definitively and wholly assimilated to products originating in Member States.'

[87] Article 111 TFEU states: 'Where products are exported to the territory of any Member State, any repayment of internal taxation shall not exceed the internal taxation imposed on them whether directly or indirectly.' The provision thus allows—but does not require—Member States to refund internal consumer taxes when goods are exported.

[88] Case 142/77, *Statens Kontrol med ædle Metaller v Larsen*, paras. 21–5 (emphasis added): 'The wording of Article [110] refers only to the discriminatory application of systems of internal taxation to products imported from other Member States. The application of the same systems of taxation to exports is referred to in Articles [111–112] from the point of view of the repayment of excessive taxation which may distort conditions of trade within the common market. It follows from a comparison of those provisions that the aim of the Treaty in this field is to guarantee generally the neutrality of systems of internal taxation with regard to intra-[Union] trade whenever an economic transaction going beyond the frontiers of a Member State at the same time constitutes the chargeable event giving rise to a fiscal charge within the context of such a system. It therefore seems necessary to interpret Article [110] as meaning that the rule against discrimination which forms the basis of that provision also applies when the export of a product constitutes, within the context of a system of internal taxation, the chargeable event giving rise to a fiscal charge. *It would in fact be incompatible with the system of the tax provisions laid down in the Treaty to acknowledge that Member States, in the absence of an express prohibition laid down in the Treaty, are free to apply in a discriminatory manner a system of internal taxation to products intended for export to other Member States.*'

According to the structure of Article 110, the provision outlaws two types of national taxes. Paragraph 1 declares illegal all national taxes that *discriminate* against foreign goods; and discrimination here means that 'similar' foreign goods are treated dissimilarly. Paragraph 2 then covers a second variant of fiscal protectionism. Strictly speaking, it is not based on a discrimination rationale, because its scope is wider than outlawing the dissimilar treatment of 'similar' goods.[89] Yet by prohibiting the 'indirect protection to other products', the better view regards Article 110(2) as outlawing all general forms of discrimination; and the relationship between the two paragraphs may thus best be described as one of *lex specialis* to *lex generalis*.[90]

a. *Paragraph 1: Discrimination against 'Similar' Foreign Goods*

Article 110 (1) prohibits foreign goods to be taxed 'in excess of' similar domestic goods. This outlaws internal taxes that fiscally disadvantage imported products.[91] This might occur through direct or indirect means;[92] and it may take place through direct or indirect discrimination. Direct

[89] On the two distinct tests for Article 110(1) and 110(2) TFEU, see text at n.116 below.

[90] Case 193/85, *Co-Frutta*, para. 19: '[W]here the requirement of similarity prescribed by the first paragraph of Article [110] is not fulfilled, the second paragraph of that article is intended to cover all forms of indirect tax protection in the case of products which, without being similar within the meaning of the first paragraph of Article [110], are nevertheless in competition, even partial, indirect or potential competition, with each other.'

[91] The Court has clarified that, in line with the clear wording of Article 110, the latter does not capture reverse discrimination—that is, a situation where a Member States fiscally disadvantages its own products. See only: Case 86/78, *SA des grandes distilleries Peureux v directeur des Services fiscaux de la Haute-Saône et du territoire de Belfort*, para. 32: 'Although Article [110] prohibits any Member State from imposing internal taxation on products imported from other Member States in excess of that on national products, it does not prohibit the imposition on national products of internal taxation in excess of that on imported products.'

[92] The reference to goods being 'directly or indirectly' taxed was to clarify that the provision catches taxes on the finished product as well as taxation imposed on prior manufacturing stages. This was established, albeit in the context of Article 111, in Case 45/64, *Commission v Italy*, 866: 'As used in Article [111], the expression "directly" must be understood to refer to taxation imposed on the finished product, whilst the expression "indirectly" refers to taxation imposed during the various stages of production on the raw materials or semi-finished products used in the manufacture of the product.'

discrimination takes place where national taxes *legally* disadvantage foreign goods by—for example—imposing a higher tax rate than that for domestic goods.[93] Indirect discrimination occurs where the same national tax formally applies to both foreign and domestic goods, but materially imposes a *heavier* fiscal burden on the former.[94]

An excellent illustration of an indirectly discriminatory tax can be seen in *Commission v France*.[95] The Commission had brought enforcement proceedings against France on the ground that its differential tax on light-tobacco and dark-tobacco cigarettes violated Article 110. Having found that the two types of cigarettes were 'similar',[96] the Court moved on to address the issue of discrimination and here found as follows:

> Although [the French tax] does not establish any formal distinction according to the origin of the products, it adjusts the system of taxation in such a way that the cigarettes falling within the most favourable tax category *come almost exclusively from domestic production whereas almost all imported products come within the least advantageous category*. Those features of the system are not nullified by the fact that a very small fraction of imported cigarettes come within the most favourable category whereas, conversely, a certain proportion of domestic production comes within the same tax category as imported cigarettes. *It appears, therefore, that the system of taxation is designed in such a way as to benefit a typical domestic product and handicaps imported cigarettes to the same extent*.[97]

The judgment brilliantly explicates the concept of indirect discrimination (and also confirmed that fiscal measures may not be justified by reference to the express justifications reserved for regulatory measures in Article 36 TFEU).[98] Where similar goods were treated dissimilarly, a violation of Article 110 had occurred.

[93] See Case 57/65, *Lütticke GmbH v Hauptzollamt Sarrelouis*; as well as Case 148/77, *Hansen & Balle v Hauptzollamt de Flensburg*.

[94] On this point, see my discussion of Case 112/84, *Humblot v Directeur des services fiscaux*, in the text at n. 104.

[95] Case C-302/00, *Commission v France (Dark Tobacco)*.

[96] Ibid., paras. 22 et seq.

[97] Ibid., para. 30 (emphasis added).

[98] Ibid., paras. 32–3: 'Without explicitly invoking Article [36], the French Government argues that [the French tax system] is conducive to the protection of human health and life. In this regard, it is sufficient to point out that Article [36] of the [FEU] Treaty must be interpreted strictly and thus cannot be understood as authorising measures of a different nature from the quantitative restrictions on imports and exports and measures having equivalent effect laid down by Articles [34 and 35 TFEU].'

The central key to Article 110(1) thus lies in the concept of 'similarity'. For only where imported and domestic goods are similar will the provision require equal fiscal treatment. When are domestic and foreign goods *similar?* Early on, the Court clarified that similarity is wider than identity,[99] and that similarity relates to comparability.[100] Comparability here means that two goods 'have similar characteristics and meet the same needs from the point of view of consumers'.[101] However, are 'whisky' and 'cognac' comparable drinks?[102] In a series of cases, the Court was asked to establish criteria to determine when two products are 'similar'—and when they are not. The Court has thereby endorsed a 'broad interpretation of the concept of similarity' that will nonetheless take account of 'objective' differences between two seemingly similar products.[103]

An excellent illustration of this approach is *Humblot.*[104] Monsieur Humblot had acquired a (German) Mercedes car in France. The car possessed 36 CV (fiscal horsepower) and he had to pay a special tax imposed by the French Revenue Code, which distinguished between a progressive annual tax for cars up to 16 CV and a single special tax for cars above this rate. The special tax was nearly five times higher than the highest rate of the general progressive tax. And as France did not produce any cars above 16 CV, the question arose whether the special tax was 'in excess of' the national tax on domestic goods. But are small (French) cars comparable to big (German) cars? The French government defended its internal tax regime by arguing that 'the special tax is charged solely on luxury vehicles,

[99] See: Case 148/77 *Hansen & Balle*, para. 19: 'The application of that provision is based not on a strict requirement that the products should be identical but on their "similarity".'

[100] See: Case 168/78, *Commission v France (Whisky v Cognac)*, para. 5.

[101] Case 45/75, *Rewe-Zentrale des Lebensmittel-GroBhandels GmbH v Hauptzollamt Landau/Pfalz*.

[102] Case 168/78, *Commission v France (Whisky v Cognac)*.

[103] Case 243/84, *John Walker v Ministeriet for Skatter og Afgifter*, para. 11. 'The Court endorsed a broad interpretation of the concept of similarity in its judgments ... and assessed the similarity of the products not according to whether they were strictly identical, but according to whether their use was similar and comparable. Consequently, in order to determine whether products are similar it is necessary first to consider certain objective characteristics of both categories of beverages, such as their origin, the method of manufacture and their organoleptic properties, in particular taste and alcohol content, and secondly to consider whether or not both categories of beverages are capable of meeting the same needs from the point of view of consumers.'

[104] Case 112/84, *Humblot v Directeur des services fiscaux*.

which are *not similar*, within the meaning of the first paragraph of Article [110] to cars liable to the differential tax'.[105] The Court disagreed. For while it acknowledged the power of the Member States to 'subject products such as cars to a system of road tax which increases progressively in amount depending on an *objective criterion*, such as the power rating',[106] the French tax system did not do so and thus (indirectly) discriminated against foreign cars.[107]

What 'objective' criteria may however be used fiscally to distinguish between seemingly similar products? This question is—misleadingly—called the question of 'objective justification'.[108] What stands behind this misnomer is the idea that, while a national tax system must be neutral towards foreign goods, it can nevertheless discriminate between goods 'on the basis of objective criteria'.[109] Thus, where a Member State discriminates on the basis of a social or regional policy objective, such a public policy objective will not amount to protectionist discrimination. The discrimination is here 'justified' by 'objective' criteria that distinguish two products. The Court has consquently held, in the context of a differential tax system for alcoholic beverages:

> [I]n the absence of any unification or harmonization of the relevant provisions, [Union] law does not prohibit Member States from granting tax advantages, in the form of exemption from or reduction of duties, to certain types of spirits or to certain classes of producers. *Indeed, tax advantages of this kind may serve legitimate economic or social purposes, such as the use of certain raw materials by the distilling industry, the continued production of particular spirits of high quality, or the continuance of certain classes of undertakings such as agricultural distilleries.* However, according to the requirements of Article [110], such preferential systems must be extended without discrimination to spirits coming from other Member States.[110]

This position was confirmed in *Commission v France (Natural Sweet Wines).*[111] The Commission had brought proceedings against a French tax

[105] Ibid., para. 9. [106] Ibid., para. 12.

[107] While the Court was coy with regard to the exact violation, the case appears to acknowledge a partial violation of Article 110(1) in para. 14. For a subsequent case on the—reformed—French car tax system, see Case 433/85, *Feldain v Directeur des services fiscaux du département du Haut-Rhin*.

[108] Case 21/79, *Commission v Italy (Regenerated Oil)*. The term is used ibid., para. 16: 'objectively justified'.

[109] Case 243/84, *John Walker v Ministeriet for Skatter og Afgifter*, para. 23.

[110] Case 148/77, *Hansen & Balle*, paras. 16–17 (emphasis added).

[111] Case 196/85, *Commission v France (Natural Sweet Wines)*.

scheme that exempted naturally sweet wines from the higher consumption duty on liqueur wines. The French government defended this differential treatment by pointing to the fact that 'natural sweet wines are made in regions characterized by low rainfall and relatively poor soil, in which the difficulty of growing other crops means that the local economy depends heavily on their production'.[112] This regional policy objective gave preferential treatment to a 'traditional and customary production' over similar goods resulting from industrial production. And this 'objective' criterion was not discriminating against foreign goods,[113] for the differential treatment is here not related to the 'nationality' of the good but to objective factors independent of the domestic or foreign origin of the products concerned. These objective factors must however be perfectly projected onto imported goods.[114] If this is not the case or where the Court finds that behind seemingly 'objective' factors hides a 'national dimension', it will hold the national tax to be materially discriminatory.[115]

b. Paragraph 2: Protection against 'Competing' Foreign Goods

Even when an internal tax does not discriminate against 'similar' foreign products, it might still fall within the second paragraph of Article 110. For in the words of the Court:

> The second paragraph of Article [110] is complementary to the first. It prohibits the imposition of any internal taxation which imposes a higher charge on an

[112] Ibid., para. 9.

[113] Ibid., para. 10. See also: Case C-132/88, *Commission v Greece*, as well as Case C-213/96, *Outokumpu Oy*.

[114] Case 127/75, *Bobie Getränkevertrieb GmbH v Hauptzollamt Aachen-Nord*. If a Member State thus affords special advantages to some products, such as beer produced in small breweries, it needs to extend them to imported beers; see ibid., para. 10: 'If therefore a Member State has elected to apply to home-produced beer a graduated tax calculated on the basis of the quantity which each brewery produces in one year, the first paragraph of Article [110] is only fully complied with if the foreign beer is also taxed at a rate, the same or lower, applied to the quantities of beer produced by each brewery during the period of one year.' However, Member States are not obliged to apply the most favourable tax rate, within a differentiated tax system, to all imports. Only imports that fulfil the 'objective' criteria of the lower tax band will benefit from it.

[115] In the words of A. Easson, 'Fiscal Discrimination: New Perspectives on Article 95 of the EEC Treaty', 544: 'What was found offensive, in the "spirits" cases, was not that vodka was taxed more heavily than aquavit, or whisky more heavily than brandy, but that the tax systems in question were characterised by the fact that those products of essentially domestic manufacture came within the most favourable tax categories and almost all of those which were imported were subject to higher taxation, that is to say there existed an effective discrimination which possessed a "national dimension".'

imported than a domestic product which competes with the imported product, although it is not similar to it within the meaning of the first paragraph of Article [110]. The prohibition also applies in the absence of direct competition where the internal taxation subjects the imported product to a specific fiscal charge in such a way as to protect certain activities distinct from those used in the manufacture of the imported product. However, the said second paragraph is only applicable when the various economic relationships envisaged by it are not merely fortuitous, but lasting and characteristic.[116]

Strictly speaking, the rationale behind Article 110(2) is broader than a prohibition on discriminatory taxation. (For the idea of discrimination implies treating similar goods dissimilarly, and where there are no similar domestic products, there cannot be discrimination.[117]) Yet the better way is to see Article 110(2) as an extension of the—indirect—discrimination rationale in Article 110(1). Its reach is simply wider when outlawing all internal taxes that grant 'indirect protection' to domestic goods. For the provision here targets national taxes that *generally disadvantage foreign goods*. The Court has however held that such indirect protection can only occur when domestic goods are *in competition* with imported goods.[118] And Article 110(2) consequently requires two elements to be fulfilled before a

[116] Case 27/67, *Fink-Frucht GmbH v Hauptzollamt München-Landsbergerstrasse*, Summary Point 5. On the two distinct tests for Article 110(1) and 110(2) TFEU, see ibid., 233: 'Whereas the first paragraph of Article [110] only prohibits taxation in so far as it exceeds a clearly defined level, the prohibition laid down in the second paragraph is based on the protective effect of the taxation in question to the exclusion of any exact standard of reference. A tax must therefore be considered as incompatible with the Treaty if it is capable of having the effect referred to above.' The Court will consequently start its analysis with the first variant in Article 110, and only where the goods are found not to be 'similar' will it move to the residual variant in para. 2. For unlike the second paragraph of the provision, Article 110(1) presumes the discrimination to be protectionist.

[117] Case 184/85, *Commission v Italy (Bananas)*. Article 110(2) thus solves the problem of—exotic—products, where there may be no similar domestic products.

[118] Case 27/67 *Fink-Frucht*, 232: 'In addition to the prohibition imposed in the first paragraph of Article [110], the second paragraph of the same article forbids the imposition on imported products of any form of taxation "of such a nature as to afford indirect protection to other products". Such protection would occur in particular if internal taxation were to impose a heavier burden on an imported product than on a domestic product with which the imported product is, by reason of one or more economic uses to which it may be put, in competition, even though the condition of similarity for the purposes of the first paragraph of Article [110] is not fulfilled.' Where this is not the case, Article 110(2) will indeed not apply; see Case C-47/88, *Commission v Denmark*; as well as Case C-383/01, *DeDanskeBilimportører v Skatteministeriet, Toldog Skattestyrelsen*.

national tax is found to hinder the free movement of goods. The national law will tax *competing* goods differently; and, secondly, this differentiation generally protects *national* goods and thus indirectly 'discriminates' against foreign goods.

When will foreign and domestic goods be in competition? Within Article 110(2), the Court has generally adopted a flexible approach. This can be seen in *Commission v United Kingdom (Beer & Wine)*.[119] The Commission had brought infringement proceedings against Great Britain in the belief that its tax regime for wine granted indirect protection to British beer. The excise tax on wine was indeed significantly higher than that on beer, and as Britain produced very little wine but a lot of beer, the suspicion of indirect protectionism arose. Britain counterclaimed that there was no competitive relationship between beer and wine, and that there could thus be no such protectionist effect. Not only were the two products 'entirely different' with regard to their production and price structure,[120] the goods would hardly ever be substituted by consumers.[121] The Court was not impressed with this line of argument, and espoused a dynamic understanding of product substitution:

> In order to determine the existence of a competitive relationship under the second paragraph of Article [110], it is necessary to consider not only the present state of the market but also the possibilities for development within the context of the free movement of goods at the [Union] level and the further potential for the substitution of products for one another which may be revealed by intensification of trade, so as fully to develop the complementary features of the economies of the Member States in accordance with the objectives laid down by Article [3] of the [EU] Treaty ... For the purpose of measuring the degree of substitution, it is impossible to restrict oneself to consumer habits in a Member State or in a given region. In fact, those habits, which are essentially variable in time and space, cannot be considered to be a fixed rule; the tax policy of a Member State must not therefore crystallize given consumer habits so as to consolidate an advantage acquired by national industries concerned to comply with them.[122]

[119] Case 170/78, *Commission v United Kingdom (Beer & Wine, Interim Judgment)*.

[120] Ibid., para. 13.

[121] Ibid.: 'As regards consumer habits, the Government of the United Kingdom states that in accordance with long-established tradition in the United Kingdom, beer is a popular drink consumed preferably in public-houses or in connexion with work; domestic consumption and consumption with meals is negligible. In contrast, the consumption of wine is more unusual and special from the point of view of social custom.'

[122] Ibid., paras. 6 and 14.

The Court here brilliantly attacked the chicken-and-egg problem within Article 110(2). Indeed, two goods might not presently be in competition *because* of the artificial price differences created by internal taxation. The British argument that its tax policy only reflected a social habit in which beer was mass-consumed, while wine was an 'elitist' drink, disregarded the fact that the social habit might itself—at least partly—be the product of a—national—fiscal policy. And once this fiscal policy disappeared, beer and wine *could* be in competition. This *dynamic* understanding of product substitutability acknowledges the ability of fiscal regimes to *dynamically* shape consumer preferences. And in stepping out of a purely national frame, the Court here added a federal 'flavour' to Article 110.

Once a foreign product has been found to be in competition with a domestic product, the Court will—secondly—investigate whether the national tax regime generates a protectionist effect. In the above case, the Court indeed found that the significantly higher tax burden on wine would afford protection to domestic beer.[123] (Importantly, Article 110(2) will however not demand fiscal equality between competing products. It only demands that the fiscal difference *is not inspired by national protectionism*.[124]) And in another case involving 'drinks in Luxembourg',[125] the Court considered a clear protectionist effect to exist where 'an essential part of domestic production' came within the most favourable tax category whereas competing products—'almost all of which [were] imported from other Member States'—were subject to higher taxation.[126]

2. *Double Taxation and 'Fiscal Sovereignty'*

Must a Member State of the European Union acknowledge the existence of its sister 'sovereigns' outside its territory; or can it ignore all fiscal burdens

[123] Case 170/78, *Commission v United Kingdom (Beer & Wine, Final Judgment)*, para. 27.

[124] A fiscal relation between beer and wine of 1:5 was thus held to be 'protective'.

[125] G. Rodrigues Iglesias, 'Drinks in Luxembourg: Alcoholic Beverages and the Case Law of the European Court of Justice'.

[126] Case 168/78, *Commission v France (Whisky v Cognac)*, para. 41. In its subsequent jurisprudence, the Court has nonetheless tried to establish a more nuanced economic analysis to determine when a protectionist effect is present and when not. Cf. Case C-167/05, *Commission v Sweden (Beer & Wine)*; and A. J. Easson, *Taxation in the European Community*, 62: 'An examination of the Court's jurisprudence suggests that, where the products subject to the higher tax are exclusively, or almost exclusively, imported, then the tax will be considered to be protectionist in nature ... By contrast, where a substantial proportion of the more heavily taxed products are of domestic manufacture the tendency has been to hold that the system is valid.'

already imposed on a good entering into its jurisdiction? Despite endeavours of international coordination,[127] the classic international law solution allows each State to disregard all 'external' fiscal events. While internal taxation must not discriminate against imports, the jurisdictional frame within which discrimination is assessed is always the host State one; and from inside this domestic frame, a 'double burden' resulting from a second State's taxing powers simply cannot be perceived. Would this international 'blind spot' towards double taxation also be part of the EU common market?

The fiscal regime created by the 1957 Rome Treaty had been drafted to align the European 'common market' with the international taxation model. Article 110 TFEU reflected the (international) discrimination rationale in Article III GATT, while Article 111 TFEU only *permitted* each Member State to reimburse internal taxes for exports—yet it did *not compel* them to do so.[128] With regard to fiscal matters, the Union legal order thus appeared to respect the—internal—'fiscal sovereignty' of the Member States, and in particular their choice of 'all connecting factors for tax jurisdiction'.[129] But should the EU internal market not confront double taxation in the same way as it has come to control double regulation? Would the—parallel—existence of twenty-eight different sovereignties not spell the end of intra-Union trade?

This final section explores whether the Union has moved away—or not—from its international origins towards a more federal model for internal tax measures.[130] We shall see that the Union has generally remained loyal to the international law fold. The Court has thus held that double taxation on goods falls outside the prohibitive sphere of Article 110; and in the absence of a specific prohibition on double taxation, and '[a]lthough the abolition of such effects is doubtless[ly] desirable in the interests of the freedom of

[127] International coordination efforts have established the 'destination' principle for indirect taxes, according to which only the country of destination should impose consumer taxes. However, this is a choice left to each State. For direct taxation, see: OECD Model Convention with Respect to Taxes on Income and on Capital, https://www.oecd.org/ctp/treaties/2014-model-tax-convention-articles.pdf.

[128] This was expressly confirmed by the Court in Case 27/74, *Demag v Finanzamt Duisburg-Süd*, where it held that a Member State is not obliged to exonerate internal taxes under Article 111—thus giving rise to the possibility of double taxation.

[129] B. J. M. Terra and P. J. Wattel, *European Tax Law*, 884.

[130] On the question of double taxation in the European Union generally, see: A. Rust (ed.), *Double Taxation within the European Union*; D. Gutmann, 'How to Avoid Double Taxation in the European Union?'; as well as G. Kofler and R. Mason, 'Double Taxation: A European "Switch in Time"?'.

movement of goods', such an abolition can 'only result from the harmonization of the national systems under Article [113] or possibly Article [115] of the Treaty'.[131] The Union control of double taxation—unlike double regulation—consequently seemed to be confined to the sphere of positive integration. The exception to this rule is Value Added Tax (VAT) to which we shall turn next.

a. Indirect Taxation: The Special Case of Value Added Tax

The dominance of the international model for internal taxes in the EU common market appears to be suspended for one particularly important indirect tax: VAT. In the past, the Court here seems to have adopted an alternative solution.

This alternative approach started with *Schul I*—a case decided only three years after *Cassis*.[132] The case concerned the sale of a second-hand sports boat. The boat had been purchased in France, where value added tax at the rate of 17.6 per cent had duly been paid. It was subsequently exported into the Netherlands, where the Dutch revenue authorities levied an additional value added tax of 18 per cent on the sales price. This was the normal—indistinctly applicable—rate applied within the Netherlands, and it therefore seemed that no discrimination had taken place. The applicant in the main action nonetheless brought proceedings against the Dutch tax authorities on the ground that 'the levying of value-added tax on the importation of products from another Member State supplied by a private person *gives rise to an overlapping of taxes*'.[133]

Would the double imposition of VAT violate European law? Having first explored the 'common system' of value added tax adopted by the Union legislature,[134] the Court found that the latter was not applicable to the present situation.[135] The analysis would therefore have to concentrate on the

[131] Case 142/77, *Statens Kontrol med ædle Metaller v Larsen*, para. 34. This was confirmed in Case C-72/92, *Scharbatke GmbH v Federal Republic of Germany*; Case C-234/99, *Nygård v Svineafgiftsfonden, and Ministeriet for Fødevarer, Landbrug og Fiskeri*; as well as Case C-517/04, *Koornstra & Zn. vof v Productschap Vis.*

[132] Case 15/81, *Gaston Schul Douane Expediteur BV v Inspecteur der Invoerrechten en Accijnzen, Roosendaal.*

[133] Ibid., para. 7 (emphasis added).

[134] By the time of the case, the Union had already established a common coordination system through the adoption of Union harmonization measures on the basis of Articles 111 and 115 TFEU (ibid., para. 9).

[135] Ibid., paras. 8–15.

constitutional principles within the negative integration sphere—and here in particular, Article 110 TFEU. Would the latter contain the (federal) principle of mutual recognition or would the coordination of national fiscal systems exclusively depend on European legislation? The Member States *as well as the Union institutions* passionately pleaded that only the political process could solve the question of double taxation.[136] The Court however offered a nuanced solution, which must be quoted at some length:

> [A]t the present stage of [Union] law the Member States are free, by virtue of Article [110], to charge the same amount on the importation of products as the value-added tax which they charge on similar domestic products. Nevertheless, this compensation is justified only in so far as the imported products *are not already burdened with value-added tax in the Member State of exportation since otherwise the tax on importation would in fact be an additional charge burdening imported products more heavily than similar domestic products.* That view derives in the first place from the terms of Article [110] of the Treaty which prohibits not only the direct but also the indirect imposition of internal taxation on products from other Member States in excess of that on similar domestic products. That prohibition would not be complied with if imported products could be subject to the value-added tax applicable to similar domestic products without account being taken of the proportion of value-added tax with which those products are still burdened at the time of their importation.
>
> *Such an interpretation accords with the need to take account of the objectives of the Treaty which are laid down in Articles 2 and 3 [TEU] among which appears, in the first place, the establishment of a common market. The concept of a common market as defined by the Court in a consistent line of decisions involves the elimination of all obstacles to intra-[Union] trade in order to merge the national markets into a single market bringing about conditions as close as possible to those of a genuine internal market ...* Consequently, it is necessary also to take into account the value-added tax levied in the Member State of exportation for the purpose of determining the compatibility with the requirements of Article [110 TFEU] of a charge to value-added tax on products from another Member State supplied by private persons where the supply of similar products within the territory of the Member State of importation is not so liable.[137]

[136] Ibid., para. 25: 'The Member States which have taken part in these proceedings, the Council and Commission contend that the elimination of the overlapping of taxes within the [Union], however desirable it may be, can be achieved only by means of the gradual harmonization of the national taxation systems under Article [113] or [115] of the Treaty and not by applying Article [110]. In support of that argument it was alleged that the overlapping of taxes is a corollary of the fact that the Treaty, by reserving power in relation to internal taxation to the Member States, has allowed tax frontiers to remain.'

[137] Ibid., paras. 31–4 (emphasis added).

The Court here seemed to insist—in line with the federal philosophy underlying *Cassis de Dijon*—that even in the absence of Union legislation, Article 110 could apply to situations in which obstacles to trade were created by the parallel existence and concurrent exercise of national tax powers.[138] But did this mean that Article 110 outlawed double taxation as such; or, had the Court simply suggested that a Member State, while being allowed to tax again, had to take into account the tax already levied? The judgment, sadly, pointed in both directions.[139] Did the Court thus outlaw double taxation or only the cascading effect of double taxation? Doubts remained. Luckily, a second reference was soon made. Yet the judicial principles underlying *Schul II* were not much clearer.[140] And sensing a formidable political opportunity, the Commission energetically drew up its own conclusions and, like in the aftermath of *Cassis de Dijon*, adopted a 'Commission Communication' concerning the consequences of the two *Schul* cases.[141] The Commission here held:

In essence, the conclusions which the Commission draws from the judgments of the European Court in the *Schul* cases are that the double imposition of VAT on goods exported from one Member State to another is contrary to [Union] law and to the achievement of a genuine common market ... The Court was called upon to clarify the position on a number of points in Case 47/84 (Gaston Schul). In its decision of 21 May 1985, it laid down the method for calculating the VAT due on the importation by a private person of used goods which had already borne VAT in the Member State of export. The method laid down was as follows:

(a) the taxable amount is constituted either by the price of the goods less the residue of the VAT paid in the exporting Member State which is still incorporated

[138] Ibid., para. 38: 'Nevertheless although the establishment of a system of complete neutrality in the field of competition involving full remission of tax on exportation is indeed a matter for the [Union] legislature, so long as such a system is not established Article [110] of the Treaty prevents an importing Member State from applying its system of value-added tax to imported products in a manner contrary to the principles embodied in that article.'

[139] In one part, we read that 'the *amount* of value-added tax payable on importation must be reduced by the residual part of the value-added tax of the Member State of exportation which is still contained in the value of the product when it is imported' (ibid., para. 34, emphasis added); while other parts of the judgment suggest that the Court wished to outlaw the inclusion of the first tax in the calculation of the price base for the second tax.

[140] Case 47/84, *Staatssecretaris van Financiën v Gaston Schul Douane-Expediteur BV*.

[141] Commission Communication on the Decisions of the European Court of Justice of 5 May 1982 and 21 May 1985 (the *Gaston Schul* cases) relating to the importation by an individual of used goods purchased in another Member State from an individual, OJ 1986 C 13/2.

in that price or, in the absence of such a price, by the customs value, which is a VAT-free value;

(b) the rate of tax is the rate applicable to supplies for consideration effected within the territory of the country of importation;

(c) *the amount of VAT resulting from the application to the taxable amount at (a) of the rate at (b) shall be reduced by the residue of the VAT paid in the exporting Member State*;

(d) the residue of VAT in the exporting Member State is:

- either the amount of VAT actually paid in that State less the percentage by which the value of the goods has diminished, if the value of the goods has in fact diminished between the last VAT payment and their importation, or
- the full amount of VAT actually paid in that State where the value of the goods has increased since the last VAT payment.[142]

This interpretation of the judgment—especially point (c)—appeared to introduce the idea of mutual recognition within Article 110.[143] For a second taxing State would not only have to eliminate any cascading effects; it could potentially be required to reduce the amount of tax due by the amount of tax already paid in a first Member State.

Has the Court accepted the Commission lead? In its subsequent jurisprudence, the Court has indeed partly projected a *Cassis*-like solution to internal tax measures. In *Drexl*,[144] a German national working and residing in Italy had bought a second-hand car in Germany and subsequently imported it into Italy. Not having paid the required 18 per cent value added tax charged upon importation, Drexl was prosecuted with 'smuggling' by

[142] Ibid., 2–3 (emphasis added).

[143] D. Weber, 'In Search of a (New) Equilibrium between Tax Sovereignty and the Freedom of Movement Within the EC', 592, has argued that, in tax cases, the principle of mutual recognition should rather be called the principle of mutual acceptance: '[T]he ECJ has recognized the right of each of the Member States to levy its own tax. It is thus not so that the Member State of importation may not levy tax because the Member State of exportation has already levied tax. This would amount to mutual recognition. The ECJ merely observed that the double taxation that occurs is a restriction of the freedom of movement. The state of importation has simply to accept the taxation in the state of exportation (by giving a credit). Under the principle of mutual acceptance, a Member State may apply its own tax system and may thus levy additional tax ... From *Gaston Schul* one can see that the ECJ does not ask that the host Member State not levy any tax at all (thus recognizing taxation in the origin state). It only asks that the tax levied in the origin state be granted a credit.'

[144] Case 299/86, *Criminal proceedings against Rainer Drexl*.

the Italian authorities; and in his defence he argued that 13 per cent value added tax had already been paid in Germany. Thus the question before the Court was this: would Article 110 allow Italy to charge the full 18 per cent of the—adjusted—net value of the car; or would the Court insist that, since the German tax had already been paid, Italy would have to deduce it from the amount of Italian tax due? Clarifying its previous jurisprudence, the Court advocated the second solution:

> [T]he amount of value-added tax payable on importation must be calculated by taking into account the amount of value-added tax paid in the Member State of exportation which is still contained in the value of the product in such a way that that amount is not included in the taxable amount *and is in addition deducted from the value-added tax payable on importation.*[145]

The judgment provided a strong signal that the international law principle, according to which each Member State could exercise its fiscal sovereignty, without regard to its sister States, had come to an end for the EU common market. Unmitigated double taxation, imposed on imports from other Member States, could violate Article 110.[146] This *Cassis*-like approach severely challenged the idea that the exclusive frame of analysis within Article 110 'is the system of taxation chosen by each Member State ... which constitutes the [sole] point of reference'.[147] But since the wording of Article 110 speaks unequivocally of discrimination, the Court felt textually forced to root its—new—federal approach in a Union-wide notion of (material) discrimination.[148]

145 Ibid., para. 12 (emphasis added).

146 By contrast, in the subsequent decision in Case C-165/88, *ORO Amsterdam Beheer BV and Concerto BV v Inspecteur der Omzetbelasting Amsterdam*, the Court clarified that its *Schul* jurisprudence did not outlaw double taxation on second-hand goods as such but only double taxation following the importation of a good, see ibid., para. 18: 'First of all, it should be noted that, although in its judgments of 5 May 1982 and 21 May 1985 in the two *Gaston Schul* cases, cited above, to which reference is made by the plaintiffs in the main proceedings and by the Commission, the Court held that the imposition of VAT on the importation of goods supplied by a private person from another Member State, where no VAT was levied on a transaction of the same type within the territory of the State of importation, was incompatible with [Union] law, that ruling was not based on a general principle prohibiting tax cumulation but on Article [110] of the Treaty, which prohibits internal taxation which discriminates against imported goods.'

147 Case 127/75, *Bobie Getränkevertrieb GmbH v Hauptzollamt Aachen-Nord*, para. 9.

148 For this point, see already: R. Barents, 'Recent Case Law on the Prohibition of Fiscal Discrimination under Article 95', 656: 'First, to apply this provision to the problem of double taxation, which in legal terms means the result of a disparity between differing national

In sum: for VAT on goods, the Union has adopted a federal model; and *Schul* has consequently—like *Cassis de Dijon*—been decried as 'one of the most extreme examples of judicial legislation by the Court'.[149] This federalization of Article 110 is however confined to an area in which a comprehensive system of Union *legislation* already coordinates most aspects anyway.[150] For all other internal taxes, by contrast,[151] the international model—allowing for double taxation—appears to continue.[152] This can equally be seen with regard to the other three fundamental freedoms.

b. Beyond Goods: The Rise and Fall of the Federal Model

Unlike the case for goods and Article 110, the EU Treaties contained no other special prohibition on discriminatory taxation; and the remaining three fundamental freedoms were moreover silent on their application to fiscal measures. The Union, nonetheless, quickly clarified that direct taxation could fall within the scope of the free movement of workers provisions;[153]

tax legislation, required that this provision had to be interpreted as a prohibition of material discrimination.'

[149] A. J. Easson, *Taxation in the European Community*, 40.

[150] On this point, see: B. J. M. Terra and P. J. Wattel, *European Tax Law*, Chapter 6; as well as M. Lang, 'Double Taxation and EC Law', 11: 'The European Union has made a lot of progress in harmonizing tax law as far as indirect taxes are concerned. Almost every issue in the VAT field is dealt with by [EU] directives ... Direct taxation is not harmonized at all.'

[151] See only: Case C-234/99, *Nygård v Svineafgiftsfonden*; as well as Case C-517/04, *Koornstra & Zn. vof v Productschap Vis.*

[152] Cf. W. Schön, 'Der freie Warenverkehr, die Steuerhoheit der Mitgliedstaaten und der Systemgedanke im europäischen Steuerrecht—Teil II: Das Verbot diskriminierender und protektionistischer Abgaben und das Problem der Belastung "exotischer" Waren', 353: '[Artikel 110] schützt im Grundsatz nicht vor steuerlichen Doppelbelastungen. Daher verstößt der nationale Gesetzgeber, der die für den Export bestimmte und für den heimischen Markt produzierte Ware gleichmäßig steuerlich erfaßt, auch dann nicht gegen [Artikel 110], wenn die exportierte Ware im Bestimmungsland erneut steuerlich erfaßt wird. [Artikel 111] gestattet dem Herkunftsstaat in diesen Fällen zwar die Rückerstattung der Abgabenbelastung, erzwingt sie jedoch nicht.'

[153] See only: Regulation 1612/68 on Freedom of Movement for Workers within the Community (1968) OJ (English Special Edition), 475; esp. Article 7 (emphasis added): '(1). A worker who is a national of a Member State may not, in the territory of another Member State, be treated differently from national workers by reason of his nationality in respect of any conditions of employment and work, in particular as regards remuneration, dismissal, and should he become unemployed, reinstatement or re-employment; (2). He shall enjoy the same social and *tax advantages as national workers.*'

and this extension has been confirmed for all other fundamental freedoms.[154]

But if the three remaining freedoms covered *regulatory* as well as *fiscal* measures simultaneously, did this not imply that both types of measures would be governed by the same constitutional principles? Would the Court therefore apply its restriction-based approach, developed for regulator measures,[155] equally to fiscal measures? Or, has the Court established different principles for these measures by—for example—insisting on an (international) discrimination test *à la Keck*? The second solution would find strong systemic support from the free movement of goods, where—as we saw—the Treaty expressly distinguished between regulatory and fiscal measures; and where the Court has accepted a different market model for each type of measure.

aa. Direct Taxation: A (Short) Flirt with the Federal Model

The Court originally developed its fiscal jurisprudence in close alignment with its case law governing regulatory matters.[156] And it thus seemed that the move from an international to a federal model would also apply to internal taxation.

Even with regard to the (then) relatively underdeveloped fourth freedom, the freedom of capital, the Court has therefore found that it may

[154] For persons, see only: Case C-204/90, *Bachmann v Belgium*; Case C-279/93, *Finanzamt Köln-Altstadt v Schumacker*; as well as Case C-80/94, *Wielockx v Inspecteur der Directe Belastingen*. The services provisions cover, like the free movement of persons provisions, 'regulatory' as well as 'fiscal' measures; see e.g. Case C-134/03, *Viacom Outdoor Srl v Giotto Immobilier*; as well as Case C-544/03, *Mobistar SA v Commune de Fléron*. For the capital provisions, see only: Case C-439/97, *Sandoz GmbH v Finanzlandesdirektion für Wien, Niederösterreich und Burgenland*; and Case C-513/04, *Kerckhaert and Bernadette Morres v Belgische Staat*.

For the extensive literature on taxation and free movement in this context, see only: S. Kingston, 'The Boundaries of Sovereignty: The ECJ's Controversial Role Applying Internal Market Law to Direct Tax Measures'; M. J. Graetz and A. C. Warren, 'Dividend Taxation in Europe: When the ECJ Makes Tax Policy'; J. Snell, 'Non-Discriminatory Tax Obstacles in Community Law'; K. Banks, 'The Application of the Fundamental Freedoms to Member State Tax Measures: Guarding against Protectionism or Second-Guessing National Policy Choices?'; M. Isenbaert, *EC Law and the Sovereignty of the Member States in Direct Taxation*; C. H. J. I. Panayi, *European Union Corporate Tax Law*.

[155] For a—very—brief summary of the evolution of the three other fundamental freedoms, see the *Conclusion* (II) in this volume.

[156] For an excellent analysis of the early case law here, see: K. Banks, 'The Application of the Fundamental Freedoms to Member State Tax Measures'.

cover *non*-discriminatory fiscal restrictions. In *Sandoz*,[157] the Court dealt with Austrian legislation imposing a stamp duty of 0.8 per cent on any loan. Sandoz challenged the national measure by claiming that the imposition of a stamp duty 'constituted an obstacle to the free movement of capital between a borrower residing in Austria and a lender established in another Member State which was likely to deter the borrower from turning to such a lender'.[158] The Austrian Finance Minister objected that the national law 'did not discriminate against lenders established in a Member State other than that of the borrower'.[159] Yet the Court held that this was irrelevant. The national law '*deprive[d] residents of a Member State of the possibility of benefiting from the absence of taxation which may be associated with loans obtained outside the national territory*'. And since the stamp duty was '*likely to deter [national] residents from obtaining loans from persons established in other Member States*', it constituted a restriction to capital movement under Article 63 TFEU.[160]

Did this mean that the fundamental freedoms for persons, services, and capital would adopt a restriction test that went beyond discrimination? And, in particular, what about non-discriminatory national measures that were seen to hinder free movement not because they themselves discriminated but where an obstacle to trade arose due to the existence of multiple tax burdens? Would a dual fiscal burden through double taxation be compatible with EU internal market law? After some doubts, the Court has provided a clear—negative—answer. In *Kerckhaert*,[161] a Belgian resident

[157] Case C-439/97, *Sandoz GmbH v Finanzlandesdirektion für Wien*. See also: T. Horsley, 'The Concept of an Obstacle to Intra-EU Capital Movement', 165: 'The ruling in *Sandoz* represents, in the area of direct taxation, the high-water mark in the Court's review of non-discriminatory national rules as obstacles to intra-EU movement.'

[158] Case C-439/97, *Sandoz*, para. 14.

[159] Ibid., para. 15.

[160] Ibid., para. 19 (emphasis added). For a similar formulation, see Case C-478/98, *Commission v Belgium*, para. 18: 'Measures taken by a Member State which are liable to dissuade its residents from obtaining loans or making investments in other Member States constitute restrictions on movements of capital within the meaning of that provision.' And for 'obstacle' language in the context of direct taxation, see: Case C-385/00, *F. W. L. de Groot v Staatssecretaris van Financiën*, para. 115: '[Union] law contains no specific requirement with regard to the way in which the State of residence must take into account the personal and family circumstances of a worker who, during a particular tax year, received income in that State and in another Member State, except that the conditions governing the way in which the State of residence takes those circumstances into account must not constitute discrimination, either direct or indirect, on grounds of nationality, or an obstacle to the exercise of a fundamental freedom guaranteed by the Treaty.'

[161] Case C-513/04, *Kerckhaert and Morres v Belgische Staat*. For an extensive discussion of the case, see G. Kofler and R. Mason, 'Double Taxation: A European "Switch in Time"?', 74 et seq.

received dividends from a French company. These dividends had been taxed at the rate of 15 per cent in France, yet they were equally subject to Belgian income tax at the rate of 25 per cent—without the possibility of having the French tax 'set off' against the Belgian tax. The applicants argued that, since their 'French' dividends were taxed twice, the Belgian tax legislation constituted a restriction on the free movement of capital that fell foul of Article 63 TFEU.

Would the (unmediated) dual taxation of capital violate the free-movement principle behind the internal market? In the context of regulatory barriers to goods, the answer after *Cassis de Dijon* is crystal clear: the dual regulation by the home and the host State violates free-movement law—unless it is justified by means of imperative requirements of the public interest. Yet the Court rejected the extension of this federal philosophy and insisted that European Union law only prohibited fiscal discriminations within the host State's tax system:

It is true that discrimination may consist not only in the application of different rules to comparable situations but also in the application of the same rule to different situations. However, in respect of the tax legislation of his State of residence, the position of a shareholder receiving dividends is not necessarily altered, in terms of that case-law, merely by the fact that he receives those dividends from a company established in another Member State, *which, in exercising its fiscal sovereignty*, makes those dividends subject to a deduction at source by way of income tax. In circumstances such as those of the present case, the adverse consequences which might arise from the application of an income tax system such as the Belgian system at issue in the main proceedings *result from the exercise in parallel by two Member States of their fiscal sovereignty.*

It must be recalled, in that regard, that conventions preventing double taxation such as those envisaged in [ex-]Article 293 EC are designed to eliminate or mitigate the negative effects on the functioning of the internal market resulting from the coexistence of national tax systems referred to in the preceding paragraph. *[Union] law, in its current state and in a situation such as that in the main proceedings, does not lay down any general criteria for the attribution of areas of competence between the Member States in relation to the elimination of double taxation within the [Union] ... Consequently, it is for the Member States to take the measures necessary to prevent situations such as that at issue in the main proceedings by applying, in particular, the apportionment criteria followed in international tax practice.*[162]

[162] Case C-513/04, *Kerckhaert and Morres v Belgische Staat*, paras. 19–23 (emphasis added). Ex-Article 293 EC has since been repealed. It envisaged the conclusion of international agreements between Member States to 'abolish double taxation within the Community'. For an

In this fundamentally important judgment, the Court clearly discarded the idea of 'fiscal' mutual recognition.[163] Fiscal measures dealing with direct taxation would only be subject to a discrimination test; and 'discrimination' meant discrimination *within the host State tax system* and therefore did not include the negative consequences arising from dual taxation by different Member States. Following *Bobie* in the context of indirect taxes,[164] the Court thus insisted that discrimination needed to be exclusively assessed on the basis of one (!) national system. All adverse consequences flowing from the imposition of the—second but neutral—Belgian tax were thus discarded, as they simply resulted 'from the exercise in parallel by two Member States of their fiscal sovereignty'.[165]

The Court has repeated this solution—also for the freedom of establishment—in *Test Claimants (II)*:

> [S]ince European Union law, as it currently stands does not lay down any general criteria for the attribution of areas of competence between the Member States in relation to the elimination of double taxation within the European Union, each Member State remains free to organise its system for taxing distributed profits, provided, however, that the system in question does not entail discrimination prohibited by the FEU Treaty.[166]

Within the European 'common market', an individual may thus have to pay inheritance tax twice—when two Member States greedily insist on imposing their fiscal 'sovereignty'.[167] And the Court has expressly confirmed that the Member States are 'not obliged therefore to adapt their own tax systems to the different systems of tax of the other Member States in order, inter alia, to eliminate the double taxation arising from the exercise in parallel by those Member States of their fiscal sovereignty'.[168] With regard to direct taxation, consequently, the Court has rejected the 'federal'

analysis of the provision, see: R. Schütze, 'European Law and Member State Agreements: An Ambivalent Relationship?', 120.

[163] J. Snell, 'Non-Discriminatory Tax Obstacles in Community Law', 360: 'The judgment in *Kerckhaert* is a clear statement of principle. International double taxation is not contrary to the Treaty free movement rules. A country can apply an even-handed tax to all income, regardless of the fact that the same income has already been taxed in another Member State.'

[164] Case 127/75, *Bobie Getränkevertrieb GmbH v Hauptzollamt Aachen-Nord*.

[165] Case C-513/04, *Kerckhaert and Morres v Belgische Staat*, para. 20.

[166] Case C-35/11, *Test Claimants in the FII Group Litigation v Commissioners of Inland Revenue and the Commissioners for Her Majesty's Revenue & Customs*, para. 40

[167] Case C-67/08, *Block v Finanzamt Kaufbeuren*.

[168] Ibid., para. 31.

model and instead prefers a—modern—'international' model that is based on the internal sovereignty of the Member States.

bb. Double Taxation: A 'Federal' Most-Favoured-Nation Clause?

In the absence of Union legislation providing general criteria for the apportionment of direct taxes within the EU internal market, it is therefore exclusively in the hands of the States to—themselves—eliminate double taxation. Within this international model, Member States have done this via bilateral—international—tax treaties.[169]

Has the Union here nonetheless imposed 'federal' limits on these international agreements? In particular, does the prohibition of discrimination on grounds of nationality require bilateral treaties to be 'multilateralized'?[170] The argument has been made,[171] but critics have invoked the reciprocity principle as a limit to extending the benefits granted under a bilateral treaty.[172] In the past, the Court has tended to defend the international market model against the idea of a 'federal' most-favoured nation (MFN) clause.[173] This was most famously

[169] Case C-513/04, *Kerckhaert and Morres v Belgische Staat*, paras. 21–2. On the status of these double taxation agreements in the Union legal order, see R. Schütze, 'European Law and Member State Agreements: An Ambivalent Relationship?', 150 et seq.

[170] C. Tietje, 'Die Meistbegünstigungsverpflichtung im Gemeinschaftsrecht', 399.

[171] Ibid, 406, 412–3: 'Im folgenden wird sich unter systematischen und teleologischen Gesichtspunkten zeigen, daß es sich bei einer Meistbegünstigungsverpflichtung eben doch um eine Form der Nichtdiskriminierung handelt und die Verpflichtung zur Meistbegünstigung im Falle bestehender inter-se Abkommen im Gemeinschaftsrecht daher nach [Artikel 18 AEUV] zu beurteilen ist ... Diesem Ergebnis zufolge können sich Unionsbürger auf [Artikel 18 AEUV] berufen, um sich einer Ungleichbehandlung aufgrund unterschiedlicher Regelungen in Doppelbesteuerungsabkommen oder auf sie bezogener Personenkontrollen nach dem zweiten Schengener Übereinkommen zu erwehren.'

[172] In this sense see E. Kemmeren, 'The Termination of the "Most Favoured Nation Clause" Dispute in Tax Treaty Law and the Necessity of a Euro Model Tax Convention', 147–8: 'The basis for this point of view is found in the special nature of a bilateral tax treaty between a Member State and another State, whether this State is a Member State or not. Such an agreement is the result of a negotiating process between both states by which the rights and obligations are laid down on the basis of the reciprocity principle. Such a treaty underlies a (well-) provided balance, also with respect to the financial consequences'. And see also: K. Vogel, D. Gutmann, and A Paula Dourado, 'Tax Treaties between Member States and Third States: "Reciprocity" in Bilateral Tax Treaties and Non-Discrimination in EC Law', 87: 'Such a way of reasoning relies on the aforementioned idea that a tax treaty is a coherent set of rules established by two contracting parties with conflicting interest. It assumes that those Contracting Parties have reached an economic balance through negotiation. The consequence of this approach to tax treaties is that their structure should not be jeopardised on the basis of hazardous comparisons with the situation of third State residents.'

[173] Case C-204/90, *Bachmann v Belgium*.

confirmed in *D*.[174] A German national here claimed that the Dutch law on wealth tax was discriminatory and thus violated the freedom of capital; yet the Dutch measure differentiated on objective grounds and was thus held to be not discriminatory. However, there existed a bilateral Convention between Belgium and the Netherlands for the avoidance of double taxation of income and property; and under Article 25(3) of that Convention, a person resident in Belgium would have been entitled to allowances and other tax benefits that the Netherlands granted to its own residents.

Would Union law require the *Dutch* authorities to treat a *German* national like a *Belgian* national? While admitting that 'there are situations where the benefits under a bilateral convention may be extended to a resident of a Member State which does not have the status of party to that convention',[175] the present case concerned the question whether a non-resident can be compared to another non-resident who received special treatment under a double taxation convention. For the Court, this was a different situation and from here it held as follows:

> Similar treatment with regard to wealth tax in the Netherlands of a taxable person, such as Mr D., resident in Germany and a taxable person resident in Belgium, presupposes that those two taxable persons are regarded as being in the same situation. It is to be remembered that, in order to avoid the same income and assets being taxed in both the Netherlands and Belgium, Article 24 of the Belgium-Netherlands Convention allocates powers of taxation between those two Member States and Article 25(3) lays down a rule under which natural persons resident in one of those two States are entitled in the other to the personal allowances which are granted by it to its own residents. *The fact that those reciprocal rights and obligations apply only to persons resident in one of the two Contracting Member States is an inherent consequence of bilateral double taxation conventions. It follows that a taxable person resident in Belgium is not in the same situation as a taxable person resident outside Belgium so far as concerns wealth tax on real property situated in the Netherlands. A rule such as that laid down in Article 25(3) of the Belgium-Netherlands Convention cannot be regarded as a benefit separable from the remainder of the Convention, but is an integral part thereof and contributes to its overall balance*.[176]

The refusal to extend the benefits of a bilateral agreement between two Member States to other Union citizens (that were not resident in

[174] Case C-376/03, *D v Inspecteur van de Belastingdienst/Particulieren/Ondernemingen buitenland te Heerlen*. See more generally: K. Engsig-Sørensen, 'The Most-Favoured-Nation Principle in the EU'.

[175] Case C-376/03, *D*, para. 55.

[176] Ibid, paras. 59–62 (emphasis added).

either State) will thus not violate the EU non-discrimination principle. International cooperation can legitimately bring two (or more) Member States closer to each other without automatically violating EU internal market law. International tax conventions will thus remain *bilateral* conventions; as the Union legal order has not imposed a general 'most-favoured-nation' obligation on its Member States.

Conclusion

What is the constitutional regime governing fiscal measures in the European 'common market'? For goods, the EU Treaties had specifically set up a dual regime that distinguished between customs duties and internal taxation. The former was meant to outlaw *border* measures that imposed a charge on goods crossing a (external) frontier while the latter would outlaw *internal* taxes that were discriminatory. These constitutional regimes were two sides of the same coin: the prohibition on customs duties was to apply to national measures that *distinctly* apply to imports, while the provision on internal taxation outlawed *indistinctly* applicable measures that fiscally discriminated against foreign goods. The two central prohibitions can today be found in Articles 30 and 110 respectively; and, as we have seen, they were both originally based on an international market model.

Has this changed over the past six decades? The Court has indeed injected 'national' elements into its customs law when it extended the absolute prohibition on 'national' customs duties to 'regional' customs. This extension not only means that indistinctly applicable customs charges may now fall into the scope of Article 30;[177] the Court has even held that regional charges that exclusively apply to domestic goods would still undermine the 'unity' of the Union's customs territory. This dissociation of Article 30 from international (external) borders has given the provision a 'national' frame. With regard to third-country goods, on the other hand, the Court has recognized 'federal' elements within the provision. For Union law here—in the absence of Union secondary law on customs and commercial matters—deferred to the law of the first-entry State, while imposing

[177] For a recent confirmation, see only: Case C-254/13, *Orgacom BVBA v Vlaamse Landmaatschappij*.

a—federal—duty on the other Member States to mutually recognize that decision.

With regard to Article 110, on the other hand, the Court has solidly built on the international GATT frame. Article 110 continues to only insist on the 'neutrality' of the host State in tax matters and therefore embodies a relative—international law—standard.[178] 'In particular, it does not provide a basis for censuring the excessiveness of the level of taxation which the Member States might adopt for particular products, in the absence of any discriminatory or protective effect.'[179] Under this international model, the Member States are consequently only prevented from adopting discriminatory measures.[180] This acknowledgement of the internal 'fiscal sovereignty' of the Member States contrasts with the rejection of regulatory sovereignty under all fundamental freedoms. (The exception to this rule is value added tax, where the Court accepts a *Cassis*-like approach to double taxation. But this is a small exception to the fiscal exceptionalism generally recognized under European law.)

The philosophical reason behind this exceptionalism has been said to be the different nature of fiscal measures. For even when fiscal measures pursue regulatory interests, their primary function is to collect revenue; and whereas all Member States may benefit from the public interest regulation of one of its sisters, they will not necessarily benefit from the latter's fiscal coffers.[181] In the fiscal sphere, it is therefore not the *disparities* between fiscal

[178] On this 'relativism' of Article 110, see only: A. Easson, *Taxation in the European Community*, 63: 'One rather striking conclusion that emerges from the "classification" cases is that fiscal rules that are prohibited in one Member State could be perfectly legally applied in another State. For example, Germany would be permitted to tax spirits made from fruit and from cereals, beer and wine, large and small cases, in a way that Denmark, the United Kingdom and France are not allowed to, since Germany produces significant quantities of products in each category.'

[179] Case C-47/88, *Commission v Denmark*, para. 10. The Court has nonetheless allowed for a limit, albeit in the context of the free-movement provisions, to this relative logic; see only: Case C-98/14, *Berlington Hungary Tanácsadó és Szolgáltató kft and others v Magyar Állam*.

[180] S. Kingston, 'The Boundaries of Sovereignty', 309: '[I]t would seem that the discrimination-based approach is, for now, winning the day, with the Court using a discrimination analysis[.]' See also: B. J. M. Terra and P. J. Wattel, *European Tax Law*, 904: 'Mutual recognition does not work in direct tax matters, as there is no EU rule telling us which jurisdiction should recognize which jurisdiction's subjection to tax. This sets direct tax cases apart from cases on (mutual recognition of) legal personality of companies incorporated elsewhere, professional diploma's product safety requirements, phytosanitary checks, etc.'

[181] In this sense also: J. Snell, 'Non-Discriminatory Tax Obstacles in Community Law', 365: 'The collection of revenue by one State in no way protects the revenue interest of another. The collection of taxes by country B does not benefit the Treasury of country A.' This is in

systems that create obstacles to trade but the very *existence* of parallel fiscal systems. The Court's distinct treatment of double taxation, when compared to double regulation, can thus—partly—be justified. Yet it should not be justified by reference to the antiquated idea of fiscal sovereignty. For it is hard to accept why a federal market that has long abandoned the idea of the regulatory 'sovereignty' of the Member States must pay homage to the fiscal 'sovereignty' of the latter.

In this—federal—spirit, there are no 'constitutional' problems in attacking double taxation within the European market.[182] On the contrary, 'the fact that a taxable event might be taxed twice is the most serious obstacle there can be to people and their capital crossing internal borders'.[183] And while there are—surely—great(er) practical problems in reducing double taxation, as opposed to double regulation, there is definitely something wrong when two (or more) States simultaneously impose corporate or inheritance tax on the same taxable event within a *common* market. The European Court should here take some lessons from its American counterpart.[184] For even if the latter has not

my view the single most important difference between regulatory and fiscal measures; and it is therefore—fundamentally—mistaken to assume a complete assimilation between the two (contra J. H. H. Weiler, 'Epilogue: Towards a Common Law of International Trade', 210–11).

[182] For scholars in favour of prohibiting double taxation within the EU internal market, see only: W. Schön, 'Europäische Kapitalverkehrsfreiheit und Nationales Steuerrecht'; and G. Kofler and R. Mason, 'Double Taxation: A European "Switch in Time"?'. For the opposite view see: D. Weber, 'In Search of a (New) Equilibrium Between Tax Sovereignty and the Freedom of Movement Within the EC', 614–15: 'The idea is often put forward in the literature that the principle of mutual recognition should also be applied by the ECJ to direct taxes. If this principle were to be applied, disparities would also be seen as a restriction of the freedom of movement. This idea should, in my opinion, be left for what it is. Mutual recognition applied to direct taxation entails that one of the two Member States entirely or partially must give up its taxation rights (taxation in the other Member State is "recognized") so that the disadvantage arising from a disparity (for example, double taxation) can be removed. This would mean that the ECJ would have to make a choice as to which Member State has the power to tax a certain item of income (residence state or source state?) ... It is inherent to the sovereignty to levy tax that the exercise of this sovereignty is not dependent on the taxation of another Member State. A Member State may make its own choices on how it wants to structure its tax sovereignty and, in doing so, is not dependent on any other state whatsoever (if this were not the case, the state would not be sovereign).'

[183] Advocate General Ruiz-Jarabo Colomer, Case C-376/03, *D v Inspecteur van de Belastingdienst/Particulieren/Ondernemingen buitenland te Heerlen*, para. 85.

[184] In this sense also: J. Snell, 'Non-Discriminatory Tax Obstacles in Community Law', 364: '[T]he European Court of Justice could have drawn lessons from the case law of the US Supreme Court, which insists that each state tax only that portion of revenues from interstate activity that reasonably reflects the in-state component of the activity.'

allowed itself to judicially create—in the absence of federal legislation—a unitary tax apportionment regime, it has nonetheless—and rightly—insisted that each State is only entitled to its 'fair' share. This solution may not completely eliminate the fiscal exceptionalism within the EU common market but it does incorporate a federal limit on the taxing powers of the States.

CONCLUSION

Europe's Gemeinweg *towards a Federal Market*

This book has tried to bring—forgotten or foreign—ways of thinking about 'common' markets to an analysis of the European Union and the structure of its law. Its comparative and conceptual approach thereby hoped to offer a complementing alternative to the common law 'methodology' that reduces the life of law to experience(s) without logic.[1] For even if there is no single philosophy that explains the structure of European internal market law, to portray the evolution of the latter as a succession of pragmatic compromises is as banal as it is misleading.[2] Yet many a common law scholar

[1] On the weaknesses and strengths of (English) common law thinking, see: P. S. Atiyah, *Pragmatism and Theory in English Law*; and see also: G. Radbruch, *Der Geist des Englischen Rechts und die Anglo-Amerikanische Jurisprudenz*.

[2] For a fresh and explicit celebration of British common law pragmatism, see: G. Davies, 'The Court's Jurisprudence on Free Movement of Goods: Pragmatic Presumptions, not Philosophical Principles', 26–7 (emphasis added): '[T]he Court has shown a consistent and entirely appropriate indifference to the grand philosophical scheme of things, about which there is not that much for a lawyer to say ... The big ideational framework of the market is a done deal, and what the case law on free movement does, and seems to do, is not to develop or challenge this, but to translate it into pragmatic presumptions and rules which can be used by lawyers and courts. *The rules and principles stated by [the] Court are far better understood as embodying a series of compromises, perceptions of fact, and pragmatic approximations which aim to deal with the problems of evidence, workload, and legal clarity, rather than as on ongoing monologue about market philosophy.*'

Oh, you common lawyers! Oh, you procedural 'realists'! Are we truly to believe that those procedural problems fully 'determine' the substantive outcome without any judicial 'philosophy'—what a dirty word—partly determining whether an 'international' or 'supranational' solution is favoured? Did the *International Fruit* Court not have a judicial philosophy; and what about *Cassis*; and what about *Keck* and *Italian Trailers*? Should these cases really be reduced 'to deal with problems of evidence, workload, and legal clarity'? This common-law-realist view is, in my opinion, fundamentally mistaken in two ways. First, it minimizes the moments in which Constitutional Courts very consciously reflect on which *direction* or 'philosophy' to choose; and, secondly, it disregards the power of unconscious constitutional choices in which a particular market philosophy, once adopted, is 'embedded' by the normative power of facticity. The task of an academic scholar is, in both cases, to identify these conscious or unconscious philosophical

continues to partake in an orgy of case law in which the author mechanically presents one case after the other—without any serious attempt to reduce the empirical 'diversity' to a level where *some* conceptual 'unity' occurs.[3] And, sadly, a marked absence of normative 'constructivism' can also be detected in recent 'contextual' approaches to the subject.[4] However:

choices and, if need be, to constructively critique them. This is of course not to say that the Court exclusively and constantly thinks about which market philosophy to adopt; nor will it always adopt judicial decisions in line with its (current) market philosophy.

[3] This is a general feature of much contemporary British EU law scholarship—seen, of course, from my 'Continental' point of view. For a recent criticism of the—overly—'empirical' approach to EU internal market law, see: S. Enchelmaier, 'Four Freedoms, Ever More Principles'.

[4] For an interesting attempt to 'contextualize' the fundamental freedoms by exploring sociological and procedural aspects, see now: P. Caro de Sousa, *The European Fundamental Freedoms: A Contextual Approach*. The book primarily explores the institutional (procedural) 'context' to specific judicial decisions and therefore comes close to the common law 'realist' approach discussed in n. 2 And as regards doctrinal constructivism, de Sousa uncritically defers to the three models developed by Miguel Maduro—discussed in the 'Introduction'.

A second excellent attempt to 'contextualize' EU internal market law has very recently been made by Clemens Kaupa. His *The Pluralist Character of the European Economic Constitution*, published shortly before I completed this manuscript, insists on a research programme that attempts to historically reconstruct important moments in the evolution of the European economic constitution (a 'contextual' choice that I fully share, see my *Framing Dassonville: Text and Context in European Law*); yet I beg to differ with regard to a number of—fundamental—assumptions and conclusions, the most important of which is probably this: even if one assumes a 'pluralist' or 'open' position in that 'the Union's legal framework cannot be held to constitute a comprehensive choice in favour of any specific ideological position' (ibid., 2), does that mean that there is no—normative—evolution, say, from a less to a more liberal constitution? Of course there exist 'multiple historical, political and economic narratives that shape the dominant understanding of the European economic constitution' (ibid., 4), but does this mean that it is wrong to claim 'that internal market law exhibits some form of increasing normative bias against national regulation' (ibid., 164)? Personally, I think Kaupa's denial here arises, ironically, from his acceptance of the traditional—but historically inaccurate—*Dassonville–Cassis–Keck* story and the (consequently wrong) idea that the sole 'doctrinal tool to establish the substantive meaning of the Treaty freedom provisions in relation to the specific situation in question is proportionality balancing' (ibid., 189). According to the evidence offered in this book, this view is hard to accept. For once one agrees that the philosophy underlying Article 34 TFEU has progressively changed from an international to a federal (or even national) rationale, the very scope of Article 34 assumes a 'substantive' meaning. And again: depending on which market model the Court applies, there are different types of proportionality standards that normatively pre-commit the substantive result under a rule of reasonableness, Article 36 TFEU or imperative requirements; and it is therefore, in my view, seriously mistaken to argue that the 'doctrinal system developed' by the Court 'remains agnostic as to the weight to be assigned to the various interests concerned' (ibid., 196). Does it not make a difference whether Germany has to justify the imposition of its product standard on French goods against a presumption that its (host State) standard is *generally* legitimate as opposed to the post-*Cassis* presumption that the home State standard is *generally* legitimate? The existence of these

it is even more disheartening to see the 'philosophers' of European law portray the construction of the European market in simplistic 'creationist' terms that—wrongly—hold that the Court heroically embraced a 'national' market philosophy in *Dassonville*.[5] This 'idealistic' reading of Article 34 is utterly dissociated from all historical, sociological and jurisprudential contexts and must be rejected as a complete folly.[6]

The most promising way to 'understand' the foundation and evolution of European internal market law is thus to steer a synthetic middle course between (common law) empiricism and (civil law) idealism. *For all constitutional thought without content is empty; all case law without constitutional concepts is blind!* In light of this methodological 'programme', the following *Conclusion* will first present and evaluate the results encountered above in the context of the free movement of goods and, in a second step, offer a generalizing silhouette beyond goods so as to indicate an overall solution for the structure of the entire European common/internal market.

I. Summary and Evaluation

The empirical and conceptual history of the EU common market, offered in this book, compared the evolution of that market against the—respective—market structures created by international and American law. We saw in Chapter 1 how modern States originally tried to protect their—freshly

substantive legality presumptions is not just a procedural matter on the 'burden of proof'; it is a matter of normative pre-commitment. So, while I agree—of course—with Kaupa that there is a 'plurality' of different constitutionally possible meanings for Article 34 TFEU, to point to the 'indeterminate' and 'pluralist' content of Article 34 for its own sake proves, in my view, nothing. In fact, any deep contextual analysis here contains the (American) 'realist' danger of postmodernistically undercutting all constructive attempts to identify normative models that—albeit changing—structure the law of the internal market. What, in my view, is therefore important is to try and 'make sense'—and relate—the various 'hegemonic' narratives that have come to give normative meaning to Article 34; and this is what this book has tried to do.

[5] The most famous illustration here is J. H. H. Weiler's 'Epilogue: Towards a Common Law of International Trade'. How this fairy tale became a respectable point of departure for many an international and European trade law scholar remains a mystery to me. But even the best of internal market scholars have fallen under its spell, see only: C. Barnard, *The Substantive Law of the EU: The Four Freedoms*, 75 and 79.

[6] For a particular discussion of the Weiler 'interpretation' see: R. Schütze, *Framing Dassonville: Text and Context in European Law*, Chapter 6.

constituted—national markets against foreign competition. This mercantilist philosophy would only slowly give way to a philosophy of free trade and the idea of an international division of labour. The rise of free trade agreements in the nineteenth century, brutally interrupted by two World Wars, experienced a renaissance in the twentieth century through the rise of multilateral trade organizations. The most important of these global organizations today is the World Trade Organization, which administers the General Agreement on Tariffs and Trade (GATT). The latter contains a number of provisions that generally structure international trade in goods, and here in particular a prohibition on quantitative restrictions and a general prohibition on discrimination. These international law instruments commit States to binding international rules that limit their *external* sovereignty, while they generally respects the *internal* sovereignty States enjoy over their own 'internal' market.

This international coordination contrasts with the construction of the US American market during the nineteenth and twentieth centuries. Chapter 2 analysed the structure of this American 'common' market in some detail. The principal constitutional tool here was the (dormant) Commerce Clause, which outlaws State measures that discriminate or excessively burden interstate trade. And by prohibiting non-discriminatory measures that apply to 'inter-State' and 'intra-State' trade equally, the Supreme Court has embraced a 'national' market model. Yet the Commerce Clause also continues to host a number of 'international' and 'federal' elements: not only is the principal test under the Commerce Clause an anti-discrimination test designed to root out 'economic protectionism',[7] the jurisprudence on fiscal barriers revealed a federal approach to (dual) taxation.

What about the legal structure of the European common market? Part II explored this question in four separate chapters. Chapter 3 gave an overview of the Union's constitutional tools for the creation of its common market. Historically, the central provision here has been Article 34 TFEU—the European equivalent of the (American) dormant Commerce Clause. Article 34 outlaws quantitative restrictions on imports (and all measures having an equivalent effect). Originally borrowed from international trade law, the provision was transformed in the course of its—turbulent—evolution from an 'international' to a 'federal' market-building tool. This transformation was primarily achieved through *Cassis de Dijon*.

[7] See generally Chapter 2 of this volume; and in particular: D. H. Reagan, 'The Supreme Court and State Protectionism: Making Sense of the Dormant Commerce Clause'.

The famous judgment replaced the *principle* of host State control with the *principle* of home State control; and this replacement had fundamental repercussions for the *internal* sovereignty of all (host) States. For the latter lose their 'sovereign' rights to regulate 'their' markets with regard to foreign products, and thus a part of their internal sovereignty.

How deep would the federal model cut into the internal sovereignty of the Member States? Chapters 4 and 5 explored the general and special aspects of the federal market model. While originally confined to the category of product requirements, the Court soon tried to expand the *Cassis* 'logic' to selling arrangements. This expansion however collapsed into a national market philosophy that the Court was ultimately unable to control. With *Keck*, the international law idea of discrimination thus returned to Article 34 for this category of measures; but this retreat did not prevent the Court from also developing a new jurisprudential line on consumer-use restrictions that centred on a (national) market-access test. The post-*Keck* jurisprudence is therefore characterized by the coexistence of three major jurisprudential principles for 'internal' measures: the *international* principle of discrimination, the *federal* principle of mutual recognition, and the *national* principle of market access. How exactly these three principles will relate to each other remains to be seen but it is hoped that the Court will ultimately adopt a consistent and coherent approach to Article 34.[8] But as we saw in Chapter 5, some special considerations do apply to trade in third-country goods and export restrictions under Article 35. (Importantly, however, the limited scope of Article 35 must not be seen as an aberration but constitutes an integral part of the federal solution under Article 34.)

The Union has thus *generally* moved from an international to a federal market model.[9] The specific exception here relates to fiscal measures. This fiscal affairs exception was discussed in Chapter 6. In line with the dual regime set up by the Treaties, we distinguished between customs duties and internal taxation; and while the former regime (now) embraces a national market philosophy, the latter has remained loyal to an international law structure. For under

[8] For an analysis of this need for coherence, see: N. Nic Shuibhne, *The Coherence of EU Free Movement Law: Constitutional Responsibility and the Court of Justice*.

[9] But to repeat: the thesis advanced in this book is not absolute. It did not claim that there were no elements of a federal market model in the early phases of the Union, nor that there are no elements of an international market model at present. The book—like its predecessor—makes a relative claim: the *predominant* market philosophy underlying the structure of European law has changed from one philosophy to the other.

Article 110, the Member States continue to enjoy internal fiscal 'sovereignty'; and this anachronistic and antagonistic position seriously challenges the very purpose behind any 'common' market—that is, 'to merge the national markets into a single market bringing about conditions as close as possible to those of a genuine internal market'.[10] This lesson was learnt some time ago by the US Supreme Court. Realizing that fifty cumulative fiscal burdens would invariably bring interstate commerce to an end, American jurisprudence thus insists on a 'fair apportionment' between the States. Each State here retains a part of its fiscal sovereignty; yet the Union limits this portion to what fairly reflects each State's 'added value' to interstate trade.

In conclusion: the European Union has continuously moved away from the GATT solution to a market that is 'in between' international and national law. This 'federal' market comprises elements from all three types of market models, yet the normative centre of the EU internal market lies today closer to the national than to the international end of the spectrum. While the non-discrimination principle continues to offer a basic (minimum) threshold, the principles of mutual recognition and free market access go far beyond the international level of market liberalization. Figure 9 tries to locate each of the central provisions on goods on a spectrum from international to national law. Importantly, even if Articles 34 and 30 contain clear elements of a national model, the European Court of Justice should *not* construct these articles as individual rights to trade; and it should, in my view, continue to resist a reading of Article 16 EU Charter—protecting the 'freedom to conduct a business'—that would go beyond the fundamental freedoms.[11] The Union should indeed never engage in the (American)

[10] Case 15/81, *Gaston Schul Douane Expediteur BV v Inspecteur der Invoerrechten en Accijnzen, Roosendaal*, para. 33.

[11] Article 16 EU Charter states: 'The freedom to conduct a business in accordance with Union law and national laws and practices is recognised.' Importantly, while all EU fundamental rights primarily address the Union, they can also apply to national laws where the national measures fall within the scope of EU law, cf. R. Schütze, *European Constitutional Law*, Chapter 12, Section 4. Moreover, the Court has emphasized time and again that Article 16 EU Charter is not an absolute right and would therefore be subject to limitations (cf. Case C-101/12, *Schaible v Land Baden-Württemberg*); and it has equally clarified that the relationship between the free-movement provisions and Article 16 EU Charter will be dominated by the former, cf. Case C-367/12, *Sokoll-Seebacheresp*, paras. 20–3: 'First of all, it should be noted that the referring court raises questions about the interpretation not only of Article 49 TFEU, relating to the freedom of establishment, but also of Article 16 of the Charter setting out the freedom to conduct a business. Article 16 of the Charter provides that "[t]he freedom to conduct a business in accordance with European Union law and national laws and practices is

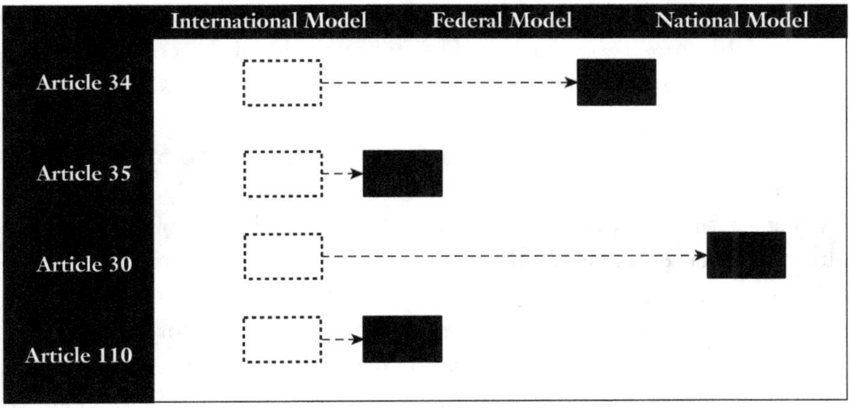

Figure 9. Results: market models and Treaty provisions on goods

'economic due process' philosophy that characterized past jurisprudence under the Fourteenth Amendment.

Overall, then, in combining international and national elements, the European internal market has clearly moved to a federal middle ground. But should European constitutionalism embrace the federal structure of its common market; or, would it be better governed by an international or national market philosophy? Leaving aside reactionary 'international law' sirens,[12] much of the debate has centred on the relative advantages of the federal and the national market model. The essential question here is this: should the free-movement provisions be confined 'to liberalise *intra*-[Union] trade'; or should they be intended 'to encourage the unhindered pursuit of commerce in individual Member States'?[13] Within a federal model, the Union confines its market-building philosophy to the

recognised". Thus, when identifying the scope of the freedom to conduct a business, Article 16 of the Charter refers specifically to European Union law. That reference to European Union law must be understood as meaning that Article 16 of the Charter refers, inter alia, to Article 49 TFEU, which guarantees the fundamental freedom of establishment. In those circumstances and given that the questions referred concern the freedom of establishment only, the national legislation at issue in the main proceedings should be assessed with regard to Article 49 TFEU alone.' For a recent look at Article 16 of the Charter, see: R. Babayev, 'Private Autonomy at Union Level: On Article 16 CFREU and Free Movement Rights'.

[12] Most prominently here: J. H. H. Weiler, 'Epilogue: Towards a Common Law of International Trade'.

[13] Advocate General Tesauro, Case C-292/92, *Hünermund and others v Landesapothekerkammer Baden-Württemberg*, para. 1.

elimination of obstacles to trade that arise from the *diversity* of State regulations within a *common* market. The national model, by contrast, insists that '[i]f an obstacle to inter-state trade exists, it cannot cease to exist simply because an identical obstacle affects domestic trade';[14] and it therefore disregards the distinction between *inter*-State and *intra*-State obstacles to trade.

What are the—respective—(dis)advantages of each solution? The federal solution preserves some regulatory 'pluralism' that is traditionally identified with federal unions in general and the European Union in particular. Pluralism allows distinct national communities to express their own politico-economic philosophy. They can live 'their' traditions and they can identify 'their' values within 'their' markets. Yet the federal solution equally means that each State should, in principle, respect and recognize the national solutions of all the other Member States of the Union. For unlike the international model, the various State markets are not simply *coordinated*; they are *integrated* markets. They are thereby integrated in a dual sense. They are integrated into the 'common' European market but, more importantly still, each State market must also (partially) integrate the other States' regulatory regimes within its national market. The shift from the international model to the federal model therefore comes with a (partial) loss of internal sovereignty and the intensification of regulatory competition. This regulatory competition can propel progress and choice; yet regulatory competition may also lead to 'revere discrimination' and a 'race to the bottom'; and it thus itself generates competitive distortions within the common market.

By contrast, the national model insists that the same commercial conditions apply everywhere. Regulatory or fiscal plurality is replaced by a single economic constitution that sets a unitary 'national' standard of constitutionality. Within this model, the full advantages of economic scale and scope are exploited. Theoretically, the choice in favour of a national model should thereby not precondition the degree of market regulation. For 'national' uniformity can be achieved through negative or positive integration (and where the latter is pursued according to the French or German standard, the regulatory intensity of the Union market would doubtlessly be above the British standard). However, where market integration is primarily pushed through negative integration, without being complemented by positive harmonization,

[14] Advocate General Jacobs, Case C-412/93, *Société d'Importation Edouard Leclerc-Siplec v TF1 Publicité SA and M6 Publicité SA*, para. 39.

the national model entails the danger of 'establish[ing] a market without rules'.[15] Within such a unitary economic constitution, the EU Treaties' free-movement provisions would assume an 'individualistic' interpretation that approximates the (American) 'economic due process' jurisprudence under the Fourteenth Amendment. The Court here leaves its role as—relative—arbitrator between competing 'sovereignty' claims of the Member States and becomes the—absolute—judge of the politico-economic choices within Europe. This may raise serious legitimacy questions.[16]

Each of the two solutions—the federal and the national model—consequently contain advantages and disadvantages. The choice of which model is to prevail will—of course—primarily depend on what kind of economic constitution one wants.[17] Substantively, the European Economic Constitution should best be a mixed constitution. It should combine the regulatory autonomy of *Nation* States with limitations on that autonomy, which follow from their being *Member* States of the European Union.[18] For the Union judiciary, in particular, this means that it must find a balance between (national) centralization and (international) decentralization. The European common market should thus combine European unity

[15] Advocate General Tizzano, Case C-442/02, *CaixaBank France v Ministère de l'Économie, des Finances et de l'Industrie*, para. 63. And see also: C. Joerges, 'The Market without the State? The "Economic Constitution" of the European Community and the Rebirth of Regulatory Politics'.

[16] In the remarkably frank words of Justice Black of the US Supreme Court (*Ferguson v Skrupa*, 372 US 726 (1963), 731): 'We refuse to sit as a "superlegislature to weigh the wisdom of legislation," and we emphatically refuse to go back to the time when courts used the Due Process Clause "to strike down state laws, regulatory of business and industrial conditions, because they may be unwise, improvident, or out of harmony with a particular school of thought." Nor are we able or willing to draw lines by calling a law "prohibitory" or "regulatory." Whether the legislature takes for its textbook Adam Smith, Herbert Spencer, Lord Keynes, or some other is no concern of ours.' For an in-depth discussion of these legitimacy questions, see the *Epilogue*.

[17] Importantly, speaking of the European Economic 'Constitution' does not mean subscribing to German ordoliberalism or American economic due process! On the (German) idea of an 'European Economic Constitution' and the place of the common market within it, see only: J. Basedow, *Von der deutschen zur europäischen Wirtschaftsverfassung*; W. Mussler, *Die Wirtschaftsverfassung der Europäischen Gemeinschaft im Wandel: Von Rom nach Maastricht*; and for discussions in English see: W. Sauter, 'The Economic Constitution of the European Union'; as well as: J. Baquero Cruz, *Between Competition and Free Movement: The Economic Constitutional Law of the European Community*. Importantly, the concept of 'economic constitution' has remained 'pluralistic' and contested (cf. J. M. Luczak, *Die Europäische Wirtschaftsverfassung als Legitimationslement europäischer Integration*, 24).

[18] For an interesting new account of the transformation from Nation States to Member States, see: C. Bickerton, *European Integration: From Nation-States to Member States*.

with national diversity. Its structure should reflect the structure of the European Union writ large.[19]

II. Beyond Goods

The EU internal market comprises 'an area without internal frontiers in which the free movement of goods, *persons*, *services* and *capital* is ensured'.[20] And while the free movement of goods has—for a long time—determined the scope and depth of market integration,[21] the three other freedoms have gradually caught up in the course of the last three decades. The three remaining freedoms have thereby also moved away from the international law solution that outlawed only direct or indirect forms of discrimination;[22] and today they all embrace a federal market structure.

With regard to the free movement of persons, the Treaties historically distinguish between workers and self-employed persons. The former are dealt with in Article 45 TFEU, which refers to 'the abolition of *any*

[19] R. Schütze, 'On "Federal"' Ground: The European Union as an (Inter)national Phenomenon'; and for a more detailed analysis see—in the future—my *From International to Federal Union: The Changing Structure of European Law*.

[20] Article 26(2) TFEU (emphasis added).

[21] C. Blumann (et al), *Commentaire Mégret. Introduction au marché intérieur—Libre circulation des marchandises*, 7.

[22] With regard to indirect discrimination, see only: Case 152/73, *Sotgiu v Deutsche Bundespost*; and Case 71/76, *Thieffry v Conseil de l'ordre des avocats à la cour de Paris*. For an express rejection of the idea of obstacles arising from disparities within the 'early' case law of the Court, see: Case C-177/94, *Perfili*, para. 17 (emphasis added): 'However, the Court has consistently held that, in prohibiting every Member State from applying its law differently on the ground of nationality, within the field of application of the Treaty, Articles [18, 49, 56] *are not concerned with any disparities in treatment which may result, between Member States, from differences existing between the laws of the various Member States*, so long as they affect all persons subject to them in accordance with objective criteria and without regard to their nationality.' For an analysis of the 'early' case law with regard to the free movement of persons, see only: E. Johnston and D. O'Keeffe, 'From Discrimination to Obstacles to Free Movement: Recent Developments Regarding the Free Movement of Workers 1989–1994'; and now also: A. Tryfondidou, 'The Notions of "Restriction" and "Discrimination" in the Context of the Free Movement of Persons Provisions: From a Relationship of Interdependence to One of (Almost Complete) Independence', 392: '[U]nder the Court's original approach, the notion of "restriction" was defined and limited by the concept of "discrimination" and, accordingly, only discriminatory restrictions on free movement could, originally, amount to a violation of the relevant provisions.'

discrimination based on nationality between workers of the Member States as regards employment, remuneration and other conditions of work and employment'. Despite this express reference to discrimination, the Court has nonetheless come to accept that *non*-discriminatory measures could fall within the scope of the provision. The famous confirmation of that possibility is *Bosman*.[23] The case concerned a professional football rule according to which another club could not employ a football player unless the latter paid a transfer or training fee. This was a non-discriminatory rule that applied to nationals and non-nationals alike.[24] Nevertheless, the Court found that 'those rules [were] likely to restrict the freedom of movement'[25] and that they therefore 'constitute[d] an obstacle to freedom of movement for workers',[26] because they *'directly affect[ed] players' access to the employment market in other Member States'*.[27]

This rejection of the international model has also occurred for the freedom of establishment under Article 49 TFEU, and a good illustration here is *Gebhard*.[28] The case involved a German lawyer who had practised law in Italy under the title 'avvocato' without being formally admitted to the Italian Bar. This had violated the relevant national rules on the organization of the legal profession. And while the Court unambiguously testified to their 'non-discriminatory' character, the national rules were still found to violate Article 49 because they were 'liable to hinder or make less attractive' the freedom of establishment.[29] This market-access formula potentially included all types of regulatory barriers and could even be mistaken for a 'national' reading of Article 49. The Court however limited the provision's negative ambit to national measures that hindered '[a]ccess to the market' of *foreign* establishments;[30]

[23] Case C-415/93, *Union royale belge des sociétés de football association ASBL v Jean-Marc Bosman*.

[24] Ibid., para. 98. [25] Ibid., para. 99. [26] Ibid., para. 100.

[27] Ibid., para. 103 (emphasis added). On this point, see also Case C-176/96, *Lehtonen et al. v Fédération royale belge des sociétés de basket-ball*, paras. 49–50.

[28] Case C-55/94, *Gebhard*.

[29] Ibid., para. 37.

[30] Case C-442/02, *CaixaBank France v Ministère de l'Économie, des Finances et de l'Industrie*, para. 14; as well as Case C-400/08, *Commission v Spain*, para. 64: 'In that context, it should be borne in mind that the concept of "restriction" for the purposes of Article [49 TFEU] covers measures taken by a Member State which, although applicable without distinction, affect access to the market for undertakings from other Member States and thereby hinder intra-[Union] trade.' For an analysis of the case law on persons in light of the market-access test, see E. Spaventa, *Free Movement of Persons in the European Union: Barriers to Movement in Their Constitutional Context*, Chapter 5.

and it thus seemed to still subscribe to a 'federal' model of negative integration.[31]

What about the free movement of services under Article 56 TFEU? The Court in *Säger* confirmed that Article 56 went beyond discrimination.[32] Drawing on the principle of mutual recognition, the Court here held that the provision would capture all national rules that were 'liable to prohibit or otherwise impede the activities of a provider of services established in another Member State *where he lawfully provides similar services*'; [33] yet it ultimately insisted that non-discriminatory measures must 'affect access to the market' and 'thereby hinder intra-[Union] trade'.[34] The question that has been hotly debated in the past is whether Article 56 contains—like Article 34—a *Keck*-like exception.[35] For while not having expressly transferred the idea of 'selling arrangements' to services, the Court has nonetheless excluded from the scope of Article 56 'measures, the only effect of which is to create additional costs in respect of the services in question and which affect in the same way the provision of services between Member States and that within one Member State'.[36] The better view however sees this statement simply as a—federal—reminder that the trade-hindering effect must be greater for *inter*-State trade than for *intra*-State trade.

Finally, what about the free movement of capital under Article 63 TFEU? While certainly a latecomer, the fact that the fourth freedom could also cover non-discriminatory capital restrictions was confirmed

[31] For the opposite conclusion, see: E. Spaventa, 'From "Gebhard" to "Carpenter": Towards a (Non-)Economic European Constitution', 765: 'In *Gebhard*, the Court leaves economic agnosticism to espouse a notion of liberal market economy.'

[32] Case C-76/90, *Säger v Dennemeyer*. [33] Ibid., para. 12.

[34] Case C-518/06, *Commission v Italy & Finland*, para. 64.

[35] The argument had been advanced in Case C-384/93, *Alpine Investments BV v Minister van Financiën*, but the Court distinguished the national measure at issue from a selling arrangement (ibid., para. 36: 'Such a prohibition is not analogous to the legislation concerning selling arrangements held in *Keck and Mithouard* to fall outside the scope of Article [34] of the Treaty'). According to some authors, the distinction between product requirements and selling arrangements cannot be transposed to the field of services, while others have argued that the Court may eventually accept an extension of *Keck* to the freedom to provide services (cf. M. Maduro, 'The Sage of Article 30 EC Treaty: To be Continued'). For an extensive discussion of these issues, see: J. Luís da Cruz Vilaça, 'On the Application of *Keck* in the Field of Free Provision of Services', 25; as well as: D. Doukas, 'Untying the Market Access Knot: Advertising Restrictions and the Free Movement of Goods and Services'.

[36] Case C-544/03, *Mobistar SA v Commune de Fléron*, para. 31.

in *Sandoz*.[37] The Court here dealt with Austrian legislation imposing a stamp duty of 0.8 per cent on any loan. Sandoz challenged the national measure by claiming that the imposition of a stamp duty 'constituted an obstacle to the free movement of capital between a borrower residing in Austria and a lender established in another Member State which was likely to deter the borrower from turning to such a lender'.[38] The Austrian Finance Minister objected that the national law '*did not discriminate against lenders established in a Member State other than that of the borrower*'.[39] The Court however held that this was irrelevant. The national law 'deprive[d] residents of a Member State of the possibility of benefiting from the absence of taxation which may be associated with loans obtained outside the national territory'; and since the stamp duty was 'likely to deter [national] residents from obtaining loans from persons established in other Member States', it constituted a restriction to capital movement under Article 63 TFEU.[40]

In sum: all three remaining fundamental freedoms have followed the free movement of goods and embraced a federal model (even with some 'national' elements). And like for goods, there also exists a fiscal 'exception' within the other market freedoms.[41] Interestingly, outside the free movement of goods, the Court appears to have never expressly endorsed a category approach à la *Keck*. It thus does not seem to review different types of regulatory measures against different doctrinal tests but—instead—generally tests all national measures against the principles of non-discrimination, mutual recognition and market access. And while the Court has not yet come to expressly acknowledge the coexistence of all three market principles *à la Ker-Optika*, it nonetheless seems to implicitly endorse a unitary

[37] Case C-439/97, *Sandoz GmbH v Finanzlandesdirektion für Wien*. According to Horsley, 'The Concept of an Obstacle to Intra-EU Capital Movement', 165 '[t]he ruling in *Sandoz* represents, in the area of direct taxation, the high-water mark in the Court's review of non-discriminatory national rules as obstacles to intra-EU movement'.

[38] Case C-439/97, *Sandoz*, para. 14. [39] Ibid., para. 15.

[40] Ibid., para. 19. For a similar formulation, see: Case C-478/98, *Commission v Belgium*, para. 18: 'Measures taken by a Member State which are liable to dissuade its residents from obtaining loans or making investments in other Member States constitute restrictions on movements of capital within the meaning of that provision.' For a brilliant criticism of these rulings, see: K. Banks, 'The Application of the Fundamental Freedoms to Member State Tax Measures: Guarding against Protectionism or Second-Guessing National Policy Choices?'.

[41] The exceptional status of fiscal measures, even for the three 'other' freedoms, has already been discussed in Chapter 6, Section II(2/b) of this volume.

approach here.[42] In the words of a distinguished commentator, the Court has indeed '*never replaced* the discrimination test by the restriction test' but always 'used a formula that seems to indicate that it is the discrimination test that is *generally* applicable, whereas the restriction test becomes applicable only in specific cases'.[43] However, like for goods, the question remains whether a violation of one of the three substantive principles is a *necessary* condition. Indeed, the Court has not yet decisively clarified if the *Dassonville*-like formula of 'national measures liable to hinder or make less attractive the exercise of fundamental freedoms' constitutes a (purely) jurisdictional formula or operates as an (independent) substantive criterion.[44]

These questions deserve to be analysed—though not by me!—in the future.

[42] See only: Case C-357/10, *Duomo and others*, para. 36: 'It is settled case-law that Article [56 TFEU] requires not only the elimination of all discrimination against service providers established in another Member State on the ground of their nationality but also the abolition of any restriction, even if it applies without distinction to national providers of services and to those of other Member States, when it is liable to prohibit, impede or render less attractive the activities of a service provider established in another Member State where it lawfully provides similar services. In the same vein, the Court has also held that Article [56] precludes the application of any national rules which have the effect of making the provision of services between Member States more difficult than the provision of services purely within a Member State.' On the distinction between the 'category approach' and the 'unitary approach' within the context of the free movement of goods and Article 34, see: Chapter 4, Section II(4) of this volume.

[43] W. H. Roth, 'The European Court of Justice's Case Law on Freedom to Provide Services: Is *Keck* Relevant?', 6 (emphasis added).

[44] For the *Dassonville*-line formula, see only Case C-55/94, *Gebhard v Consiglio dell'Ordine degli Avvocati e Procuratori di Milano*, para. 37. For a case, where the Court appears to use the formula as an independent substantive test, see: Case C-169/07, *Hartlauer Handelsgesellschaft mbH v Wiener Landesregierung and Oberösterreichische Landesregierung*, esp. para. 34: 'A national rule under which the establishment of an undertaking from another Member State is subject to the issue of a prior authorisation constitutes a restriction within the meaning of Article [49], since it is capable of hindering the exercise by that undertaking of freedom of establishment by preventing it from freely carrying on its activities through a fixed place of business.'

EPILOGUE

Courts and Free Markets—The Legitimacy Question

'Common markets cannot simply be *opened*, they must be *established*'.[1] The establishment of a common market is thereby always the result of a—centralizing—will. But who should create (trans-)national markets: the *central* legislature or the *central* judiciary? We saw above that for the European Union, the centralizing will that created the European market was predominantly a *judicial* will.[2]

Did this make the creation of the European market *ipso facto* undemocratic and illegitimate? The answer depends on the perspective and model we choose. Within an international model, democratic legitimacy will be primarily imparted by the (national) parliamentary consent of each Member State to conclude an international free trade agreement, and as long as the latter does not affect the internal 'sovereignty' of a State there will be no 'democratic deficit' here. Within a federal model, this—simple and straightforward—legitimacy story cannot be told. For as soon as the internal sovereignty of a State is permanently curtailed, a second source of legitimacy will be needed.[3] And this is even more so within a national model (yet under an 'economic-due-process' version of that model, there is potentially a liberal source of legitimation: the idea of an individual right to free trade).

How can one legitimate the creation of the European common market; and is there a correlation between the various judicial readings of the

[1] P. Reuter, *La Communauté Européenne du Charbon et de l'Acier*, 142 (emphasis added).

[2] For a comparative perspective here, see: M. Egan, *Single Markets: Economic Integration in Europe and the United States*.

[3] It will, I am afraid, definitely not be the international law '*Grundnorm*' of *pacta sunt servanda*.

free-movement provisions and the question of legitimacy? This *Epilogue* wishes to—retrospectively—raise this important question by looking at past and present attempts to legitimize the words and deeds of the European Court of Justice.

I. 'We, the *Other* Court'

Twenty years ago, an interesting—and swiftly famous—answer to the legitimacy question was offered by Miguel Poiares Maduro. Heavily influenced by the 'representation-reinforcing theory of judicial review', developed by J. H. Ely,[4] and ingeniously entitled *We the Court*,[5] his book developed a complex web of arguments that is not always easy to disentangle. Its central premise is however clearly expressed as follows:

> [T]hough the case law of the Court of Justice has led to deregulation, this is so only from a national perspective and does not correspond to a neo-liberal construction of the European Constitution by the Court of Justice. *Instead, the outcome of the decisions of the European Court of Justice in the review of national and [Union] legislation fits within a 'European majority policy'*. The Court's approach to the European Economic Constitution has revealed a peculiar type of activism: defined in this book as *majoritarian activism*. The broad scope given to market integration rules (notably Article [34]) in the review of national regulations was not intended to control the degree of public intervention in the market but to bring about harmonization among national rules through the judicial process.[6]

On a *descriptive* level, the book therefore argued that the jurisprudence of the Court of Justice had been seriously misunderstood when identified with neo-liberal deregulation—a phenomenon that Maduro equates with the US American idea of 'economic due process'. For instead of protecting minority economic rights against national (democratic) regulation, the European Court showed a '*majoritarian* activism'. And again in the words of the author:

> Contrary to the traditional conception of judicial activism addressed to the protection of minorities against the democratic majority will, European

[4] J. H. Ely, *Democracy and Distrust: A Theory of Judicial Review*, esp. 181. Maduro did however not directly draw on Ely but absorbed the latter's ideas only indirectly via his intellectual hero Neil Komesar, whose *Imperfect Alternatives: Choosing Institutions in Law, Economics, and Public Policy* dedicated a substantial section to a reading of Ely's famous book.

[5] M. Poiares Maduro, *We the Court: The European Court of Justice and the European Economic Constitution*. For a more extensive review of this book, see: R. Schütze, 'Judicial Majoritarianism Revisited: "We, the Other Court?"'.

[6] Ibid., 2 (emphasis added).

> judicial activism can better be described as majoritarian activism: promoting the rights and policies of the larger European political community (the majority) against the 'selfish' or autonomous (depending on the point of view) decisions of national polities (the minorities) ... What the Court does when it considers Article [34] is not to impose a certain constitutional conception of public intervention in the market, but to compensate for the lack of [Union] harmonisation. *This is why the regulatory balance set by the Court normally corresponds to the view of the Commission, and to the legislation in the majority of Member States ... Its yardstick is what the Court identifies as the European Union majority policy, in this way subjecting States regulations to harmonisation in the Court.*[7]

The judicial review of State legislation by the Court is consequently characterized as 'a kind of [Union] *legislative* process', in which the Court operates as a super-legislature that judicially harmonizes diverse national rules '*in accordance with an "ideally drafted" representation of all States' interest*'.[8]

Importantly, and this is the main *normative* premise of Maduro's argument: while majoritarian activism is generally good, unlimited 'majoritarian activism' is nevertheless not always the best solution for the European common market. '[T]he majoritarian approach followed by the Court in the review of State measures under Article [34] is insufficient and inadequate, since it focuses exclusively, on problems within the States' regulatory process and ignores all other institutional malfunctions that may be present in the judicial, [Union] and market process.'[9] The Court—even when adopting a European majority view—would thus overstep its mandate whenever it generally assessed all national legislation in light of the Union majority view. For the Court of Justice 'should not second-guess national regulatory choices, but should instead ensure that there is no under-representation of the interests of nationals of other Member States in the national political process'.[10] Thus, only where national measures are 'suspect' of being tainted by a corrupted (national) political process should the Court come into action.

[7] Ibid., 11 and 78 (emphasis added).

[8] Ibid., 78 (emphasis added).

[9] Ibid., 104.

[10] Ibid., 173. And see also ibid., 158: 'There has been a general acceptance of the different levels of discretion employed by the Court in its case law. In doing so, they have failed to address the institutional choice inherent in the replacement of a State's assessment of the costs and benefits of a measure by the Court's assessment of those costs and benefits. Nor have they broached the question of the European Economic Constitution that should underlie any interpretation of Article [34] and its review of market regulation.'

What are we to make of this *descriptive* account and its *normative* critique? Hardly ever has a thesis spread so quickly and so widely within European academic circles.[11] And yet, already on a *descriptive* level, serious doubts must be in order. Leaving aside the unhistorical and unsystematic discussion of the various classical readings of Article 34,[12] what are we to make of

[11] The judicial majoritarianism thesis has had an enormous influence on academic writings on the internal market (cf. C. Barnard, *The Substantive Law of the EU: The Four Freedoms*, esp. 175 and 182) and on the role of the Court in the European Union more generally (cf. A. Stone-Sweet, *The Judicial Construction of Europe*, esp. 135 and 141).

[12] I continue to find 'We the Court' a very hard nut to crack! Its internal structure has a baroque curvature; and its multiple arguments are, more often than not, underdeveloped and unrelated. Two particular issues come to my mind. First, when Maduro discusses the 'classical readings' of Article 34 in Chapter 2, he distinguishes three readings according to three tests: a discrimination test, a balancing (cost–benefit) test, and typological tests that combine elements of the two previous tests according to the types of measures involved. But is that really the best way to categorize the different tests in Article 34, especially if—as he claims—the Court actually follows a judicial majoritarianism? And where does the principle of mutual recognition fit in here; and where is a 'historical' or evolutionary analysis of the case law? Can *Dassonville* and *Cassis* really be reduced to 'establishing the foundations of a cost/benefit analysis (a balance test) under Article [34]' (ibid., 52)?

Secondly, how do these various tests correlate with the three models of market integration that Maduro constructs? It will be recalled (see: 'Introduction' of this volume, n. 14), that Maduro refers to three 'alternative' models of the European Economic Constitution in Chapter 4 of his book: a centralized model, a competitive model, and a decentralized model. And while this is not the place to (again) balance the pros and cons of the labels as such, how does he link these 'theoretical' models to the 'practical' tests? We are told that '[t]he disputes over Article [34] and European regulation are basically disputes over these different constitutional models and the different legitimacy they presuppose' (ibid., 109); so, how do they link up to the judicial readings of Article 34? The centralized model is expressly linked to the idea of judicial majoritarianism; that is (presumably), the cost–benefit model. By contrast, the decentralization model is identified with anti-protectionism and thus (presumably) the anti-discrimination test. Finally, what about the 'competitive model'? We are here told that it is informed by the 'economic due process' idea (ibid., 110), but apparently it is equally linked with 'mutual recognition' and the 'new approach to harmonisation' (ibid., 131). But there is nothing to worry about all these ambivalences because none of these models is meant to be an (idealized) empirical model! As the author tells us so frankly on the last page: 'At this point, no particular model has been adopted. Instead, the future of the European Economic Constitution probably lies in an ongoing discourse involving these different models.' What a cheeky—yet admirable—way out!

In my reading Maduro only allows for two tests under Article 34: a discrimination test (correlated with anti-protectionism and the decentralized model) and a balancing test. However, importantly, since balancing tests are not operative at the scope level but the justification level, they are seen as part and parcel of all models—including the decentralized model (cf. ibid., 163: 'In effect, anti-protectionist theories are complemented by balance tests. In such cases, anti-protectionism is not the sole criterion used in reviewing State measures, but it is the first: if a State measure is found to be protectionist, it will then be submitted to cost/benefit analysis. As a consequence, the anti-protectionist test does not prevent the balance test, but limits its use by the Court: the proportionality of a measure will only be assessed if that

the claim that the Court consistently follows the majority view among the Union Member States?

Empirically, this is simply unproven.[13] For unlike the US Supreme Court (in certain contexts),[14] the Court of Justice never expressly engages

measure is discriminatory or protectionist.') Maduro here—wrongly, I think—believes that the justification level will always imply a balancing test. Such an understanding of the evolution of Article 36 and imperative requirements however glosses over the two possible theoretical conceptions for proportionality discussed in Chapter 5, Section II(2/b) of this volume.

[13] Maduro lists a number of cases, where he feels that the Court expressly follows a majoritarian methodology. For an extremely rare case where the Court seems to have done so, see: Case C-126/91, *Schutzverband gegen Unwesen in der Wirtschaft e.V. v Yves Rocher*, para. 18: 'Furthermore, a comparative examination of the laws of the Member States shows that information and protection of the consumer can be ensured by measures which are less restrictive of intra-[Union] trade than those at issue in the main proceedings.' However, more often, the Court simply points to differences in the legislation of some (!) Member States, cf. Case C-241/89, *SARPP v Chambre syndicale des raffineurs et conditionneurs de sucre de France and others*, para. 30: 'Moreover, that obstacle to intra-[Union] trade is the result of a disparity between the national legislative schemes. The documents before the Court show that although French law prohibits any statements alluding to the word "sugar" or to the physical, chemical or nutritional properties of sugar in the advertising of artificial sweeteners, such statements are allowed in other Member States.' And within this second scenario, the Court often confines its 'comparative' methodology to the two Member States involved, see only: Case C-362/88, *GB-INNO-BM v Confédération du commerce luxembourgeois*, para. 9: 'It is apparent from the documents before the Court that the advertising of sales offers involving a price reduction and stating the duration of the offer and the prices previously charged is prohibited by the Luxembourg legislation but permitted by the provisions in force in Belgium.' Indeed, in the absolutely great majority of cases, the Court simply compares the host state legislation against the home state legislation. The precise empirical record on the influence of comparative law on the Court is however hard to establish. According to A. Stone-Sweet, *The Judicial Construction of Europe*, having looked at all Article 34 cases up to 1997, in only half of the cases did the Court find that the national legislation violated the internal market provisions. But what does that mean? Surprisingly, this seasoned political scientist here simply takes Maduro's word as proof that judges systematically (!) engage in majoritarian activism (ibid., 135). However, having re-read all the cases on Article 34 and 35 TFEU myself, I simply cannot find any traces of the 'systematic' judicial majoritarianism that Maduro claims to have discovered.

[14] On the judicial practice of 'State counting' as a form of judicial majoritarianism in the United States, as well as its many problems, see: R. M. Hills, Jr., 'Counting States'. The famous example of judicial majoritarianism is the Eighth Amendment ('Excessive bail shall not be required, nor excessive fines imposed, nor cruel and unusual punishments inflicted'), where the Supreme Court uses State counting to see if there is a 'national consensus'—for example with regard to the death penalty (cf. *Stanford v Kentucky*, 492 US 361 (1989) as well as *Roper v Simmons*, 543 US 551 (2005)). Judicial majoritarianism is here unambiguously explicit (ibid., at 561): 'The evidence of national consensus against the death penalty for juveniles is similar, and in some respects parallel, to the evidence *Atkins* held sufficient to demonstrate a national consensus against the death penalty for the mentally retarded. When *Atkins* was decided, 30 States prohibited the death penalty for the mentally retarded. This number comprised

in the type of 'State counting' that Maduro suggests.[15] The Court indeed hardly ever engages in any significant comparative law exercise,[16] and even if there is an 'in-built' comparative dimension within every transnational court,[17] that comparison will most of the time be severely

12 that had abandoned the death penalty altogether, and 18 that maintained it but excluded the mentally retarded from its reach. By a similar calculation in this case, 30 States prohibit the juvenile death penalty, comprising 12 that have rejected the death penalty altogether and 18 that maintain it but, by express provision or judicial interpretation, exclude juveniles from its reach. See Appendix A, *infra* ... A majority of States have rejected the imposition of the death penalty on juvenile offenders under 18, and we now hold this is required by the Eighth Amendment.'

Very few American constitutional scholars have recognized State counting outside this context, but see: C. B. Lain, 'The Doctrinal Side of Majority Will'; as well as her excellent earlier 'The Unexceptionalism of "Evolving Standards"', esp. at 400: '[T]he discussion above is not meant to suggest that the Supreme Court *always* polls the States in its constitutional decision-making, or even that it does so most of the time. In the end, the frequency, and formality, with which the Court polls the States depends on the constitutional context. In some areas—substantive due process protection of fundamental rights comes to mind—the doctrine is just as patently majoritarian and formally entrenched as "evolving standards". In other areas—equal protection is a nice example—the doctrine is majoritarian not as stated, but as applied, and the state polling is more sporadic.'

[15] Sadly, we are not even told what 'majoritarianism' is! How, then, do we count? Do we count States as political entities, or do we count State populations? If we add up the smallest fifteen States within the EU, we reach about 61 million—that is, slightly higher than the size of Italy, but still lower than the respective (!) populations of France, Germany, and the United Kingdom. Should the Court thus follow a majority of States representing 12 per cent of the Union population and impose that result on the super-majority of 88 per cent of the Union population? Is that democratic majoritarianism? By contrast, if the Court were to count State populations, the four biggest Member States would represent more than 50 per cent of the Union population. Alas, should the Court impose the will of these four against the will of the remaining twenty-four States? Is that democratic majoritarianism? Or, does Maduro suggest that the Court actually uses the qualified (double) majority in the Council?

[16] For an academic analysis of the few contexts in which the Court does sometimes expressly use comparative law, see: P. Pescatore, 'Le Recours, dans la jurisprudence de la Cour de Justice des Communautés Européennes, à des normes déduites de la comparaison des droit des États Membres'; as well as: K. Lenaerts, 'Interlocking Legal Orders in the European Union and Comparative Law'.

[17] K. Lenaerts, 'Interlocking Legal Orders in the European Union and Comparative Law', 874: 'It is striking that the case law of the Court of Justice and the [General Court] contains remarkably few express references to comparative law ... The relatively rare judgments of the Court of Justice and the [General Court] in which comparative law comes to the fore may be said to constitute merely "the tip of the iceberg." This is not surprising. As an international institution, the [Union] judicature is "naturally" brought to adopt a comparative approach for different reasons: the members of the Court of Justice and the [General Court] have their roots in different legal cultures, the texts and notions to be

truncated and unrepresentative.[18] Moreover: conceptually, majoritarian activism cannot have any place in the context of 'border' measures; but even with regard to product requirements, is it really indicative of 'majoritarianism' when one State's legislation is struck down because no other State has exactly the same rule?[19] And with all due respect, is it not too simplistic to argue that '[i]n cases where no overview of national legislation is given, it is still possible to find other elements of a majoritarian approach' because the Court here follows the Commission?[20] For even if it were empirically correct to argue that the Court regularly 'follows' the Commission,[21] should we blindly assume that the Commission always wishes to act as a 'virtual' Council? Prior to the Maastricht Treaty,[22] this may have been a rational institutional strategy within the *positive* integration sphere. But what incentivizes the Commission to do this outside the legislative process in the sphere of *negative* integration? Why should the *supranational* Union executive, whose very mandate is based on the idea that it is *not* to represent the Member States, act as if it represented a *State* majority in a sphere of *negative* integration? The 'intuition' that the Commission 'instinctively' adopts the State majority view—as opposed to a progressive State minority—simply requires proof, hard proof.

interpreted are multilingual and most of the cases brought before the [Union] judicature are anchored in a precise national context.'

[18] From a 'realist' perspective, there is of course not only one—'the'—Court but the Court has allowed its chambers to operate as fully fledged 'miniature' courts whose decisions have the same legal value as decisions of the 'Full Court'. And since the absolutely great majority of all cases are decided by chambers of three or five judges, only three (or five) jurisdictions will be directly represented in the deliberations. Thus, even assuming an implicit comparative approach à la Lenaerts, the question then is: are three (or five) judges representative of the majority of the Member States?

[19] M. Maduro, *We the Court*, 72: 'These are cases regarding State regulation of traditional national products, or of specific national traditions concerning the composition or presentation of products. Here, we see a minoritarian interest—one State's tradition—as opposed to the majoritarian interest, which takes the form of the interest of all other Member States not sharing or conforming to that tradition. In all the cases found by the author in this area, the Court struck down the national regulation.'

[20] Ibid., 73.

[21] For a remarkable empirical analysis of this point, see: B. Kilroy, 'Integration through Law: The ECJ and Governments in the EU'.

[22] After the 1992 Treaty on European Union, concluded at Maastricht, the European Parliament gradually rose to become a co-legislator with the Council. To obtain a qualified majority within the Council would, henceforth, only be one worry of the Commission, as it now also needed to obtain a majority in the first (!) chamber of the EU legislator.

But leaving the descriptive *non sequitur* aside, is there not an enormous—normative—appeal in the judicial majoritarianism thesis? The answer depends on the *type* of activity the Court is undertaking and the *type* of national measure reviewed. Where the Court engages in a market-*building* activity, a judicial majoritarian solution is definitely misplaced when it comes to *border* measures. For if the Court would here follow a majoritarian approach, it would simply condone—in light of Europe's protectionist past—national practices that were traditionally followed by the majority—if not all—of the Member States.[23] But even when it comes to the review of product requirements or selling arrangements, should the Court always follow the majority view; or are there areas in which a 'subsidiarity' solution should apply within Article 34? Put differently, should there be pockets of national 'sovereignty' in which a majoritarian judicial review should not invade? My answer to this question is: yes; and I believe that the normative critique of an unlimited judicial majoritarianism offered by *We the Court* is here right—yet it is right for the wrong reasons.

For what alternative solution did Maduro propose? Inspired by the Court's *Keck* judgment,[24] his constitutional alternative appears quite intuitive. Wrongly, but understandably, assuming that the *Keck* Court signalled a 'mov[e] from a market building to a market maintenance approach in the area of [the] free movement of goods',[25] his suggestion is that the Court should reduce the scope of Article 34 by focusing its energy on 'suspect' national measures. Suspect measures are national measures that do not deal with cross-national interests; and they are defined, in the author's own words, as follows:

It is suggested that the Court of Justice should not second-guess national regulatory choices, but should instead ensure that there is no under-representation of the interests of nationals of other Member States in the national political process. As it will not be possible for the Court of Justice to carry out case by case assessments to identify such representative malfunction in the national political process, tests must be designed to identify suspect measures.

[23] The same reasoning applies, mutatis mutandis, to fiscal measures where it is simply not the disparity of national rules but their parallel existence that creates obstacles to intra-Union trade. Conveniently, Maduro leaves fiscal measures out of his analysis.

[24] Maduro started his PhD in 1991 and defended it in 1996; with the *Keck* judgment given at the end of 1993. Much of the Maduro thesis is thus a *Keck*-inspired thesis.

[25] M. Maduro, *We the Court*, 99.

In this regard, it is possible to individuate two types of interests affected by national measures which interfere with the free movement of goods: cross-national interests and national interests. For the former, the interests affected are uniform throughout the [Union]. For the latter, the interests affected diverge throughout the [Union]. If the interests regulated by a national measure are equal in the different Member States, then there is no suspicion of over-representation of national interests or under-representation of the interests of nationals of other Member States. That is the case with many national measures regulating market circumstances, which may explain the bias in their favour illustrated in *Keck*.[26]

Maduro's proposal here reveals itself as an attempt to generalize the *Keck* solution beyond selling arrangements. In essence: 'if a national measure regulates uniform or cross-national interests it will not *prima facie* fall under Article [34]'; and, '[i]n this case, a national measure should only be submitted to a balance test by the Court if it is shown to be discriminatory'.[27] The *Keck* solution should thus be applied to all national measures that are untainted by a national 'bias'; and national bias is defined as a result of an 'institutional malfunction' of national parliaments:

Even in a context of optimal diversity (in which the goal is efficient State regulation) the States' political processes present representative problems in the regulation of the common market. Regulatory decisions are made taking into account national interests. Interests of nationals of other Member States are not normally taken into account. Even when national legislation is not enacted with protectionism intents or does not discriminate against foreign nationals, the institutional structure of the States' regulatory process tends, in any case, to favour home interests ... This results in what may be called national bias and is an essential component of the test to be proposed[.][28]

But are not all *national* measures coloured by a *national* bias? The only way out of this definitional cul-de-sac is for Maduro to refer to the idea of 'virtual representation'.[29] In enacting national laws that concern 'cross-national'

[26] Ibid., 173–4. [27] Ibid., 174. [28] Ibid., 148.

[29] In the European internal market context, this argument had first been made by W.-H. Roth, 'Wettbewerb der Mitgliedstaaten, oder Wettbewerb der Hersteller', 87–8: 'Die zwischen [Artikel 34 und 35 AEUV] differenzierte Rechtsprechung des Gerichtshofs mag seine Erklärung in—unausgesprochenen—Annahmen über den Ablauf politischer Entscheidungsprozesse in den Mitgliedstaaten finden. Für die Abschaffung von Regelungen der Importstaaten mit marktabschottender Wirkung gibt es in aller Regel keine hinreichend einflussreiche Lobby in den Importstaaten: Verbraucher, denen die Marktöffnung zugute käme, können (trotz der Existenz von Verbraucherverbänden) ihre Interessen zumeist nicht hinreichend artikulieren. Hingegen werden inländische Wirtschaftsteilnehmer (Industrie, Handel) ihren Einfluß in nachhaltiger Weise geltend machen, um einen Fortbestand (oder

interests, a *national* parliament is presumed to be 'virtually' representing the interests of all *European* citizens because these interests are evenly distributed within the Union; and as a result, a non-discriminatory national measure that deals with a 'cross-national' interest should fall outside the scope of negative integration and thus outside the purview of the Court. In this conception, Article 34 derives its legitimation, unlike an economic due process conception, not from the fact that it grants an *economic* fundamental right but—on the contrary—a *political* fundamental right.[30]

What are we to make of this theoretical conception of judicial legitimacy in general, and Maduro's practical test in particular? The *theoretical* idea that a Court can neutralize the counter-majoritarian difficulty by adopting an 'antitrust' orientation that concentrates on the malfunctioning of the political process is surely interesting.[31] However, the process–substance

gar die Neueinführung) marktabschottender Regelungen zu erreichen ... Bei den den Export belastenden Maßnahmen liegen die Dinge in der Regel anders: Die wirtschaftlichen Akteure (mit Einfluß auf die Entscheidungsprozesse) sind durchweg an einem ungehinderten Export interessiert.' This is—ingeniously—used to explain the difference in the jurisprudence between Articles 34 and 35 TFEU.

[30] M. Maduro, 'Reforming the Market or the State? Article 30 and the European Constitution: Economic Freedom and Political Rights', 72–3 (emphasis added): 'However, not reading the European Economic Constitution as a neo-liberal programme does not mean that Article [34] cannot be seen as a fundamental economic freedom ... I agree that a European Constitution does require a body of fundamental economic rights or freedoms (limiting, if necessary, public intervention in the market) in parallel to those normally found in national constitutions. However, this is not the role in which I would cast Article [34] ... My proposal, however, goes beyond a "rule of competences" conception of Article [34]. *By attributing to it a role of correction of national political processes vis-à-vis representation of the nationals of other Member States, I maintain a fundamental rights conception of the free movement rules ... Free movement rules will be a political fundamental right, not an economic fundamental right.*'

[31] J. H. Ely, *Democracy and Distrust*, 102–3: 'The approach to constitutional adjudication recommended here is akin to what might be called an "antitrust" as opposed to a "regulatory" orientation to economic affairs—rather than dictate substantive results it intervenes only when the "market", in our case the political market, is systematically malfunctioning ... Our government cannot fairly be said to be "malfunctioning" simply because it sometimes generates outcomes with which we disagree, however strongly (and claims that it is reaching results with which "the people" really disagree—or would "if they understood"—are likely to be little more than self-deluding projections). In a representative democracy value determinations are to be made by our elected representatives, and if in fact most of us disapprove we can vote them out of office. Malfunction occurs when the process is undeserving of trust, when (1) the ins are choking off the channels of political change to ensure that they will stay in and the outs will stay out, or (2) though no one is actually denied a voice or a vote, representatives beholden to an effective majority are systematically disadvantaging some minority out of simple hostility or a prejudiced refusal to recognize commonalities of interest, and thereby denying that minority

distinction for judicial review is an unworkable one.[32] And the democracy-centred rationale behind process-constitutionalism loses much of its strength in a *federal* context. For within federal contexts, judicial review cannot be reduced to an institutional choice between a (*un*democratic) court and a (democratic) parliament. Courts here arbitrate between the regulatory claims of the *democratic* majority of the Union and the *democratic* majority of a State. But worse, Maduro's attempt to portray the European Court as the protector of the European demos by outlawing State legislation on the ground that the State people did not virtually represent the broader European public is not just a convoluted way to conceive the problem, it simply begs the question![33] True, the US Supreme Court has at times subscribed to the idea,[34] but the idea of 'virtual representation' is—in my view—a 'constitutional stupidity'.[35] For 'to establish local governments designed to respond to local needs and then question actions by those governments because of a lack of national perspective would be almost perversely incongruous'.[36]

the protection afforded other groups by a representative system. Obviously our elected representatives are the last persons we should trust with identification of either of these situations.'

32 L. Tribe, 'The Puzzling Persistence of Process-Based Theories'.

33 In this sense: W. H. Roth, 'The European Court of Justice's Case Law on Freedom to Provide Services: Is *Keck* Relevant?', 9: '[T]he representative malfunction argument is based on the assumption that if the under-representation of interests of people from other Member States were corrected in the national political process, the outcome of the decision-making process would be different, protecting the interests of people residing out-of-state. It is submitted that this kind of analysis begs the question: if people residing out-of-state were indeed represented in the national political process, it is by no means clear whether their voice would be heard if they held just a minority view.'

34 See only Justice Stone in *South Carolina State Highway Dept. v Barnwell*, 303 US 177 (1938), 184—footnote 2: 'Underlying the stated rule has been the thought, often expressed in judicial opinion, that when the regulation is of such a character that its burden falls principally upon those without the State, legislative action is not likely to be subjected to those political restraints which are normally exerted on legislation where it affects adversely some interests within the State.'

35 On 'constitutional stupidities' generally, see: W. N. Eskridge and S. V. Levinson, *Constitutional Stupidities, Constitutional Tragedies*.

36 E. M. Maltz, 'How Much Regulation Is Too Much? An Examination of Commerce Clause Jurisprudence', 80. See also: L. Tribe, *American Constitutional Law*, 1054: 'Economic localism cannot be characterized as a symptom of breakdown in local democratic processes. Because this defect is routine rather than exceptional, this model of review serves not as a brake on judicial scrutiny of state laws, but as a directive to the courts to review and invalidate a wide range of quite ordinary legislative measures.' Probably the strongest and most thorough critique of the virtual representation idea has come from D. H. Regan, 'The Supreme Court and State Protectionism: Making Sense of the Dormant Commerce Clause', 1164: 'The *Carolene Products* theory assumes that out-of-state interests really ought to be represented—the theory assumes it is a defect in our system that the system denies foreigners representation, as it is a

What are we to make of the *practical* test suggested? Professor Maduro draws the dividing line between measures that pursue a 'cross-national' as opposed to a national interest by stating that the former are 'uniform throughout the [Union]' so that 'there is no suspicion of over-representation of national interest and under-representation of the interests of nationals of other Member States'.[37] What are these uniform interests? Is a use restriction of jet skies or a speed limit on a busy commercial artery a cross-national interest that is uniform throughout the Union? Does a Finnish trade union represent worker interests in other Member States? And what about the alcohol content in fruit-liqueurs: cross-national or national? Maduro's test boils down to a regressive tautology; and while tautologies can be wonderful poetic devices, they hardly help in the solution of theoretical and practical constitutional problems. In any event, if one did adopt a process-based theory of judicial review, should we not rather suspect political malfunction when *national* parliaments deal with *cross*-national interests? And, by the way, how does Article 35 and fiscal measures fit into Maduro's theory? Questions over questions—and no answers in sight!

In conclusion, while *We the Court* presents a highly original argument by a brilliant young *thésard*,[38] the 'majoritarian activism' thesis remains empirically unproven, theoretically weak, and—at least in the version offered by Maduro—practically unworkable.

II. 'Policy Building' and the Court

Where does this leave us with regard to the legitimacy of the judicial creation of the EU common market? Since the Court is doing more than being the passive mouth of (international) law, are there external legitimizing elements to justify what the Court is doing?

defect if racial minorities or women are unrepresented or represented ineffectively. But that assumption is not warranted. Non-representation of foreign interests follows from the simple fact that there are separate States; and the existence of separate States, while it might be a defect in an ideal political system, can hardly be treated as a defect in ours.'

37 M. Maduro, *We the Court*, 173–4.

38 Based on his EUI thesis, Maduro's book was the first to 'theorize' the case law on the internal market. This was a remarkably original and laudable endeavour that still deserves much praise today.

In modern societies, legitimizing elements may be offered by democratic,[39] liberal,[40] economic (or other) normative theories.[41] And in light of the previous section, we should completely abandon the attempt to portray the *judicial* creation of the 'federal' European market as *in itself* a democratic process. When *Cassis de Dijon* was decided, it was undoubtedly 'undemocratic': the move from an international to a federal model was a 'constitutional moment' that could not have been envisaged, in advance, by the national parliaments of the Member States when signing the original Treaties.[42] And unlike the US Constitution, we cannot indirectly attribute (federal) democratic legitimacy on the basis that the Union legislature could have overturned all judicial interpretations thanks to the power of 'congressional consent'.[43] But faced with a choice between an *undemocratic* common market and *no* common market, the Court simply chose the former option—and, as we shall see below, rightly so.

Importantly, democratic legitimacy is of course not the only accepted source of legitimacy in modern societies. In addition to input-oriented legitimacy, there also exists output-oriented legitimacy:

> Input-oriented democratic thought emphasizes 'government *by the people*'. Political choices are legitimate if and because they reflect the 'will of the people'—that is, if they can be derived from the authentic preferences of the members of a community. By contrast, the output perspective emphasizes 'government *for the people*'. Here, political choices are legitimate if and because they effectively promote the common welfare of the constituency in question.[44]

Both forms of legitimacy are often complementary in modern societies; and output legitimacy is—equally often—entrusted to counter-majoritarian institutions, which 'derive[] legitimacy from [their] capacity to solve problems requiring collective solutions'.[45] And if one accepts that

[39] See only: J. H. Ely, *Democracy and Distrust.*

[40] See only: R. Dworkin, *Taking Rights Seriously.*

[41] See only: R. Posner, *The Economics of Justice.*

[42] One avenue to escape from this undemocratic predicament is to extend the time-frame and to argue that the federalization of the common market was retrospectively democratized when the Member States signed the Single European Act. However, democracy is generally seen as an *ex ante* legitimizing device for future decisions; yet, I shall return to the *ex post* democratic legitimacy theme later.

[43] For in the EU legal order, the judicial interpretation of Article 34 is hierarchically *above* Union legislation. On the US doctrine of congressional consent, see Chapter 2, Section I (2/a) of this volume.

[44] F. Scharpf, *Governing in Europe*, 6.

[45] Ibid., 11.

counter-majoritarian institutions play a significant social role, the idea that a vital interest is protected against the will of the democratic majority is not so hard to swallow.[46] The protection of *liberal* interests against the tyranny of the majority is thus an important constitutional 'output' that modern societies are meant to offer; and with the rise of complex national economies, many States have also come to accept that there are advantages—for all—of transferring complex macroeconomic choices to technocratic and independent institutions, such as Central Banks.

The core problem with any liberal or economic justification theory, however, is that they prioritize *individual* over *collective* values. For even if output legitimacy is defined in utilitarian terms as a government *for the people*, this 'republican' form of output legitimacy regularly collapses into a liberal legitimation narrative. The reason for this normative instability is rooted in the fact that republican conceptions of output legitimacy must—and often cannot—justify a *common* conception of the 'common good'.[47]

[46] Let me have this point summed up brilliantly by someone else: 'The whole point of having an unelected judiciary is its ability to serve as a check on majority rule, which is why the Supreme Court's counter-majoritarian capacity undergirds almost every normative theory of judicial review. Explicit majoritarian doctrine renders this role a virtual impossibility, for a check on majority will that depends on majority will is hardly a check at all' (C. B. Lain, 'The Unexceptionalism of "Evolving Standards"', 417).

In Britain, counter-majoritarian institutions have, literally and metaphorically, had a terrible press in the past. And we seem to live in an era where the deification of the legal 'sovereignty' of the Westminster Parliament leads Britain's politicians to call for a protection against such known 'evils' as 'Strasbourg human rights' and 'Brussels supranationalism'! All of this reminds me of Giovanni Sartori's witty commentary on the British 'constitution' (cf. 'Constitutionalism: A Preliminary Discussion', 854): '[A]s I was trying recently to sort out the juridical features of present-day dictatorial systems, it occurred to me that some English constitutional textbooks would be of great help. "No higher law and limitless legislative power," "fusion of powers," "no special protection for fundamental rights," etc.—all these principles applied very nicely to dictatorships. What is more, the very definition given in Wheare's textbook, "The British Constitution is the collection of legal rules and non-legal rules which govern the government in Britain," appeared to be—but for the terms, "British" and "Britain"—the most fitted to describe dictatorial constitutions. (For "rules" applies to any kind of rule—including the rule of rulership—and the specification "non-legal rules" just gives the final touch of perfection to the concept of unchecked, uncontrolled and absolute exercise of power.) I have not made the experiment the other way around, that is, using the apologetic writings on dictatorial constitutions in order to get highlights on the virtues of the English one: but my guess is that, again changing but one word (the geographic referent), the English constitution would come out in brighter colors following this procedure than it appears, e.g. to the reader of Jennings' *The Law and the Constitution*.'

[47] For while many of us would agree that *some* economic prosperity is a commonly shared value, it will be much harder to find such a non-metaphysical 'republican' conception beyond a basic overlapping consensus within society. Having two cars, instead of one, may thus be

A similar problem affects a third legitimating source for the European project that has been suggested. Doubting that 'outcome legitimacy explains all or perhaps even most of the mobilizing force of the European construct', Joseph Weiler has proposed 'that at the conceptual level there is a third type of legitimation',[48] which 'has been decisive to the legitimacy of Europe and to the positive response of both the political class and citizens at large'.[49] What is this third type of legitimation? For the star 'philosopher' of European law, it is political 'messianism' in that 'the justification for action and its mobilizing force derive not from process, as in classical democracy, or from result and success, *but from the ideal pursued, the destiny to be achieved, the 'Promised Land' waiting at the end of the road*'.[50] What is the ideal or destiny behind this form of 'telos legitimacy'; and how did it manifest itself? Citing the Schuman Declaration as the 'manifesto of political messianism',[51] the answer is the following:

> Peace, at all times an attractive desideratum, would have had its appeal in purely utilitarian terms. But it is readily apparent that in the historical context in which the Schuman Plan was put forward the notion of peace as an ideal probes a far deeper stratum ... The dilemma posed was an acute example of the alleged tension between Grace and Justice which has taxed philosophers and theologians through the ages—from William of Ockham (pre-modern), Friedrich Nietzsche (modernist) and the repugnant but profound Martin Heidegger (post-modern) ... At a deeper level it managed to tap into the two civilizational pillars of Europe: the Enlightenment and the heritage of the French Revolution and the European Christian tradition. Liberty was already achieved with the defeat of Nazi Germany ... But here was a project, encapsulated in the Schuman Declaration, which added to the transnational

a central value within a consumerist manifesto but not necessarily a common value within a republican constitution. On the distinction between materialist and post-materialist values and their respective roles within modern societies, see: R. Inglehart, *The Silent Revolution: Changing Values and Political Styles Among Western Publics*; and more recently: 'Changing Values among Western Publics from 1970 to 2006.'

[48] Professor Weiler has republished the argument about eight times in the past fifteen years. I shall concentrate on what I consider to be the last and longest treatment of the issue, namely: 'In the Face of Crisis: Input Legitimacy, Output Legitimacy and the Political Messianism of European Integration'. Weiler originally developed his 'messianic' argument in the mid-1990s as a reaction to the 'crisis' following the 1992 Maastricht Treaty, and subsequently revived the argument in the early 2010s in reaction to the financial crisis.

[49] Ibid., 831–2. [50] Ibid., 832 (emphasis added).

[51] Ibid. For a much more mundane functionalist reading of the Schuman Declaration, see: A. Milward, *The Re-Construction of Western Europe, 1945–1951*, 475: 'The Schuman Plan was called into existence to save the Monnet Plan.' For a (brief) extract of the Schuman Plan, see Chapter 3, 'Introduction' of this volume.

level both equality and fraternity ... The Schuman Plan was also a call for forgiveness, a challenge to overcome an understandable hatred. In that particular historical context the Schumanian notion of peace resonated with, was evocative of, the distinct teaching, imagery and values of the Christian call for forgiving one's enemies, for love, for grace—values so recently consecrated in their wholesale breach. The Schuman Plan was in this sense, evocative of both confession and expiation, and redolent with the Christian belief in the power of repentance and renewal and the ultimate goodness of humankind.[52]

It is hard to distil much sense from this preachy pop-philosophy,[53] but its essence seems to be this: Instead of *real* peace and *real* prosperity—as existing outputs—the *promise* of these outputs (and of course, all the substantive 'goodies' of the Enlightenment *and* Catholic philosophy harmoniously combined) are what legitimized the European project in the past. What are the empirical and normative credentials of this third source of legitimacy? Empirically, it is hard to believe that the 'Union' ideal—peace and prosperity *through integration*—was generally accepted outside the small circles of Union mandarins.[54] The European project, in the early

[52] J. H. H. Weiler, 'In the Face of Crisis: Input Legitimacy, Output Legitimacy and the Political Messianism of European Integration', 834–5.

[53] No one has better ridiculed the tendency to hagiographize Schuman and the other 'saints' of EU law than A. Milward. In a chapter dedicated to 'The lives and teachings of the European saints' in his *The European Rescue of the Nation State*, 318–19, we thus read: 'The historiography of European integration is dominated by legends of great men. Most histories emphasize the role of a small band of leading statesmen with a shared vision. For the [Union]'s supporters they have become saints, men who held fast to their faith in European unity and through the righteousness of their beliefs and the single-mindedness of their actions overcame the doubting faithlessness of the world around them. Monnet, Schuman and Spaak are honoured above others in the calendar ... On the one side had stood the believers, on the other the heathen opposition. The history of the [Union] was a struggle between the forces of light and darkness ... Widely held though it is, this is a view which entirely misrepresents the historical significance of the early fathers ... [And] [f]rom the traces they did leave it is none the less possible to arrive at an understanding of their role in integration unobscured by any received theology or the account of fabulists.' For a fresh look at the hagiography issue, see: Y. Karagiannis, 'The Origins of the Common Market: Political Economy vs. Hagiography'. One of the crucial points, within both Milward's and Karagiannis's accounts, is the emphasis on the external influence coming from the United States—a matter inexcusably missing from the Weiler fable.

[54] The political messianism behind the Schuman Declaration did not marshal enough legitimating resources—even at the level of the national elites!—for the (failed) European Defence Community or the (failed) European Political Community, which were after all, all about peace (and supranationality). The only type of 'telos' ideology in the 1950s was probably offered by (classic) federalism, which—by wrongly insisting on reproducing a federal State—dramatically declined by the end of the 1950s. The dominating elite 'philosophy' thereafter became neo-functionalism and, with it, the emphasis changed to output legitimacy. And for a

decades, was a 'journey to an unknown *destination*';[55] and even if there was a 'permissive consensus' towards European integration, there existed 'no clues at all as to *what* it [was] about the system that [was] attractive and *why*'.[56] But more importantly: normatively, the 'theory' of political messianism

much more 'intergovernmental' reading of the early European integration project recall the—blatantly exaggerated (and therefore funny)—debate between Sir Humphrey and 'his' Minister:

> JIM HACKER: 'Europe is a community of nations, dedicated towards one goal.'
> SIR HUMPHREY: 'Oh, ha ha ha.'
> JIM HACKER: 'May we share the joke, Humphrey?'
> SIR HUMPHREY: 'Oh Minister, let's look at this objectively. It's a game played for national interests, it always was. Why do you suppose we went into it?'
> JIM HACKER: 'To strengthen the brotherhood of Free Western nations.'
> SIR HUMPHREY: 'Oh really. We went in to screw the French by splitting them off from the Germans.'
> JIM HACKER: 'So why did the French go into it then?'
> SIR HUMPHREY: 'Well, to protect their inefficient farmers from commercial competition.'
> JIM HACKER: 'That certainly doesn't apply to the Germans.'
> SIR HUMPHREY: 'No no, they went in to cleanse themselves of genocide and apply for readmission to the human race.'

That this wonderful caricature from the British TV Series *Yes, Minister* was not too far from the truth after all, see only: S. Hoffmann, *The European Sisyphus: Essays on Europe, 1964–1994*, 32.

What about the broader 'masses'? Weiler is here ambivalent. On the one hand he alludes to a broad social legitimacy, yet on the other hand, he tells us in the context of the Maastricht Treaty that 'Maastricht was greeted by the *typical* indifference with which the elite-driven European construct was habitually met'; and '[t]hat, indeed, *has always been the Achilles Heel of the European construct*—the question whether the undoubtedly noble project enjoys popular legitimacy' (Weiler, In the Face of Crisis, 826 (emphasis added)). Personally, I could believe that there was an 'idealistic' legitimizing force that was even widely shared, but it was, in my view, not a force towards a positive 'goal' in the future but rather a negative force that pushed people away from the blind nationalism so devastating in the earlier part of the twentieth century. But if that is the case, the legitimacy source that Weiler wishes to describe does not lie in the future but in the past. The same was true for many a 'real-existing-socialist' State—perhaps the other famous 'messianic' project within the second half of the twentieth century. For on a mass level, the latter was not socially legitimated by a belief in a 'class-free' society and apply-pie for everybody; it primarily drew its legitimizing force from the fight against fascism. And this form of legitimacy is not 'messianic'—it is not based on some distant workers' paradise in the future. Once this change of perspective is accepted, it is also easier to explain why this source of legitimacy gradually disappears the more we move away from the past. For Weiler, on the other hand, the reason lies in the very 'phenomenology' or 'ontology'—or both?—of any messianic project: if it fails, it fails; and if it succeeds, it will become a victim of its own success.

[55] A. Shonfield, *Europe: Journal to an Unknown Destination* (emphasis added).

[56] L. N. Lindberg and S. A. Scheingold, *Europe's Would-Be-Polity*, 39—quoted in C. Schrag-Sternberg, *The Struggle for EU Legitimacy: Public Contestation, 1950–2005*, 14. In the words of the author of this remarkable monograph, ibid. 23: 'The obvious argument underpinning the post-national discourse was that European integration constituted the antithesis to war and to

occupies—as the ideational counterpart of materialist output legitimacy—a clearly 'eudaemonist' position. It assumes the existence of a 'common good' through a self-fulfilling tautology: the pursuit of a conception of the common good is 'justified' by the very idea of what 'is' the common good. So, political messianism may perhaps *explain* the missionary zeal of (paternalistic) 'angels', but it simply cannot provide a *justification* theory for a 'people of devils'.

Is there anything, then, that can legitimate the judicial creation of the European common market—without recourse to liberal or eudaemonist values? I think there is, and my answer to this question draws on Kant's social contract theory. Social contract theories typically locate their legitimating potential in the *past*. (A constitution is thus legitimate when it derives from a *past* decision of the people; and the common law—this eternal customary law—is legitimate simply because it 'is' from the *past*.) But not all social contract theories do locate their legitimizing narrative in the past; and the most famous illustration of a *future*-oriented social contract theory is that of Immanuel Kant.[57] The latter ingeniously replaces the idea of a single (past) act of legitimation with the idea of a legitimating process towards (inter) national order. A decision is thus 'legitimate' whenever it contributes to the realization of a—future—social contract;[58] and, as long as an act progressively moves in this direction, all present injustices are justified by a 'permissive law' that is itself normatively rooted in a postulate of practical reason.[59]

Can such a *progressive* social contract theory offer a *new* legitimatizing narrative to European integration? It can hardly be disputed that, within modern States, input and output legitimacy have increasingly been disjointed by a process of social globalization and economic interdependence.[60]

nationalism, which itself had been discredited by the two world wars'. Accordingly, the predominant discourse was not one of ideals, destiny or goals, but it was functionalist thinking that was 'underlying the Communities' system as well as official discourses' (ibid. 44). I could not agree more.

[57] For an excellent overview here see: C. Langer, *Reform nach Prinzipien: Untersuchungen zur politischen Theory Immanuel Kants*; as well as W. Kersting, *Die Politische Philosophie des Gesellschaftsvertrags*, Chapter 6.

[58] C. Langer, *Reform nach Prinzipien*, 56: 'Der einmalige Akt der Legitimation wird verzeitlicht zu einem unendlichen Prozeß der annähernden Verwirklichung der Idee des Vertrags.'

[59] On the Kantian notion of the 'permissive law', see R. Brandt, 'Das Erlaubnisgesetz, oder: Vernunft und Geschichte in Kants Rechtslehre'; as well as: R. Schütze: 'The "Unsettled" Eighteenth Century: Kant and his Predecessors'.

[60] See only: D. Held and A. McGrew, *The Global Transformations Reader: An Introduction to the Globalization Debate*.

'Nation-states can no longer secure the boundaries of their own territories, the vital necessities of their populations, and the material preconditions for the reproduction of their societies by their own efforts.'[61] The regulatory ideal of a social contract, and the legitimating power of democracy, can consequently only be saved once public decisions regain their ability to positively regulate private (economic) actors; and with the nation State having simply lost 'boundary control' over the economy,[62] such *public* regulation of *private* interests will increasingly only be possible at the supranational level. In light of today's 'disorganised capitalism',[63] there is thus a postulate of practical reason that demands to recreate democratic processes above the nation State:

> If one does not want to resign oneself to [the fact that governmental functions shift to the level of transnational governance], while nevertheless having to acknowledge that the growing dependence of nation states on the systemic constraints of an increasingly interdependent world society is irreversible, then *the political necessity of extending democratic procedures beyond national borders imposes itself. This necessity is a logical implication of the idea of a democratic civil society influencing its own conditions of existence*: 'if a system is more democratic to the extent that it permits citizens to govern themselves on matters that are important to them, then in many circumstances a larger system would be more democratic than a smaller one, since its capacity to cope with certain matters—defence and pollution, for example—would be greater.'[64]

Thus, the simple idea is this: in light of the dramatic decline of nation States to legislate *effectively* in a globalized economy, there is a clear need to extend political capacities—and with it the potential for democratic self-agency—to a supranational level. Democratic input legitimacy is here

[61] J. Habermas, *The Divided West*, 176.

[62] One illustration of this loss of 'public' power vis-à-vis 'private' power is the intense corporate tax competition that has resulted from globalization and thereby weakened the modern welfare state (cf. D. Rodrik, *The Globalization Paradox*, 193: 'There has been a remarkable reduction in corporate taxes around the world since the early 1980s. The average for the member countries of the OECD countries, excluding the United States, has fallen from around 50% in 1981 to 30% in 2009.'). And in light of events that happened recently: which national government on the European Continent would still dare—especially in light of strong US American 'concerns'—to ask a multinational corporation, like 'Apple', to repay €13 billion in (unpaid) taxes (see *Financial Times*, 30 August 2016)? And how did it ever come to a situation—to quote the Austrian Chancellor in this context—that 'Amazon' and 'Starbucks' pay less tax than a Viennese (!) café or sausage stand (*The Independent*, 3 September 2016)? How is that—morally—justifiable?

[63] C. Offe, *Disorganized Capitalism: Contemporary Transformations of Work and Politics*.

[64] J. Habermas, *The Crisis of the European Union*, 16 (emphasis added, quoting R. Dahl).

linked to output legitimacy. For if democracy is the ability to collectively decide on certain *outputs*, it loses its core meaning when the very ability to positively determine these outputs is lost. If nation States therefore cannot regulate *multi*-national companies, a postulate of practical reason demands that there shall be a *multi*-national legislator. This supranational legislator will, of course, formally be less close to its citizens, yet it may still be substantially more 'legitimate' because of its 'system capacity' and its consequent ability to regain the power to translate the collective wishes of the people into the social sphere.[65] This dialectical trade-off between input and output legitimacy took place when (direct) democracy was 'translated' from its city context to that of the nation State;[66] and, in light of the social

[65] This relationship between 'citizen effectiveness' and 'system capacity' is explored in R. Dahl and E. Tufte, *Size and Democracy*, Chapter 2. And in order to illustrate their point, let me use the (hypothetical) dialogue between 'Jean-Jacques' (Rousseau) and 'James' (Madison) offered in R. Dahl, *Democracy and Its Critics*, 204–5. When Jean-Jacques claims that 'it is necessarily the case that the greater the number of citizens, the smaller the weight of each citizen in determining the outcome', James responds: 'My dear Jean-Jacques, I fear your goddess has abandoned you. If it were true that a smaller system must always be more democratic than a larger, then the most democratic system would consist of one person, which is absurd.' And, surprisingly, Jean-Jacques admits: 'Let us say that a system is more democratic to the extent that it permits citizens to govern themselves on matters that are important to them. Then in many circumstances a larger system would be more democratic than a smaller one, since its capacity to cope with certain matters—pollution, fiscal and monetary policy, unemployment, social security, defense, and so on—would be greater. On this view a unit large enough to deal with matters of importance to the people concerned will always be more democratic than any smaller unit.'

In my view, it is therefore utterly mistaken to consider the EU as a doomed democratic project because it will, in democratic terms, always diminish democracy when measured against 'national democracy'. This view has been relentlessly propagated by Joseph Weiler, whose negative position is essentially this (J. H. H. Weiler, 'The Constitution of Europe', 264): 'Even if the Union were to replicate in its system of governance the very same institutional set-up found in its constituent states, there would be a diminution in the specific gravity, in the political weight, in the level of control of each individual within the redrawn political boundaries.' But for Weiler the 'democratic deficit' of the Union goes further in that the 'Community and Union governance and [Union] institutions have a perverse effect on th[e] principal democratic processes within the Member States' (ibid., 266). This exclusively negative view does not, of course, do any justice to the capacity-enhancing potential of elevating democratic government to the supranational level. But these issues are, for our philosopher, only 'bread and circus' issues.

[66] Contra, G. Majone, *Dilemmas of European Integration: The Ambiguities and Pitfalls of Integration by Stealth*, 188: 'It is worth remembering that the idea of the primacy of the territorial state has the same origin as the idea of democracy, namely in the Greek polis.' This utterly unhistorical and un-sociological view misleads this famed political scientist into reifying the nation State in quasi-Hegelian terms (ibid: 'the absolute primacy of the territorial state over all competing principles of social cohesion').

realities of 'our' global times, a similar 'translation' needs to be made to rescue (representative) democracy by placing it into a new supranational context.[67]

What does this mean for the European Court of Justice? Once we accept that, within the twenty-first century, the nation State increasingly loses its claim to be the 'natural' unit for questions of justice and that the 'spheres of justice' must be expanded (as a postulate of practical reason) to allow for the *public* regulation of *private* interests operating transnationally, this postulate may 'justify' the European Court of Justice's judicial activism in establishing a federal market.[68] For the Court can be seen as creating the *legal preconditions* in which a *future* supranational democracy may work. By creating a common market, the Court 'forces' reluctant States to leave their 'sovereign' freedom and to accept a 'civil law' above States. Seen in this light, '[t]he gradual limitation of national sovereignty is part of a slow and painful forward march of humanity'.[69] The judicial creation of the common market—normatively tainted from a national perspective—now appears as a *progressive* force that transforms Europe from a 'social' community into a 'legal' community that can—finally—be legitimized once it turns itself into a 'political' community.[70] The Court's task here is to *prepare* the ground for this supranational political agency. It is not just a *market*-builder but also a *polity*-builder. For by announcing an *exeundum e statu naturali*, it invites the Member States, and their peoples, to enter into a new 'social contract'.[71]

[67] In the words of D. Held, *Democracy and the Global Order: From the Modern State to Cosmopolitan Governance*, 143: 'The transformation of politics which has followed in the wake of the growing interconnectedness of states and societies and the increasing intensity of international networks requires a re-examination of political theory as fundamental in form and scope as the shift which brought about the conceptual and institutional innovations of the modern state itself.' We indeed need a—new—theory of democracy beyond the nation State.

[68] Ideally, of course, this task should have been achieved through the national peoples acting directly, or—as international law requires—indirectly through their States. But one can hardly expect State *institutions* to be eager to curb their own powers. The European judiciary is here a necessary avant-garde catalyst in the transformation of Europe. On the conception of the avant-garde in the global justice context, see: L. Ypi, *Global Justice and Avant-Garde Political Agency*.

[69] Lord Cockfield, *The Guardian* (11 November 1988), cited by A. Milward, *The European Rescue of the Nation State*, 2.

[70] On the coming into existence of such a political community, see: A. Giddens, *Turbulent and Mighty Continent: What Future for Europe*.

[71] The 'invitation' to abandon (international) decision-making within the political realm, offered by the Court since 1979, was indeed taken up by the Member States after the Single

This Kantian reading of European integration locates—like political messianism,[72] albeit not in the folkloristic Weiler version—the legitimizing potential of European integration in the future. Yet unlike the eudaemonist position implicit in any 'political' messianism, it sees the 'telos' or future 'output' of European integration not in the promise of particular substantive values but in the creation of a *legal* constituency in which a future *political* constituency can work. In this light, the judicial activism of the Court may—surprisingly—even be justified on 'democratic' grounds. But unlike Maduro's idea of (virtual) democratic representation of *existing* majorities,[73] the democratic justification here lies in the *future*.

For this future-oriented social contract argument to work, a fundamental precondition must however be fulfilled: whenever the Court goes beyond the international market model, there must be the *possibility* of subsequent Union legislation. Thus, wherever the common market

European Act. This development disproves, empirically, one of the greatest—in the dual sense of the term—mistakes in the history of European legal scholarship: the 'equilibrium thesis' proposed in 1981 by Joseph Weiler ('The Community System: The Dual Character of Supranationalism'), which received its celebrated format in Weiler's 'The Transformation of Europe', in *The Constitution of Europe*, 10). While this cannot be the place to discuss the thesis in any detail, it suffices to highlight that it was not only disproved by—subsequent—history but that it was conceptually flawed from the start. For what the thirty-year-old Weiler did not realize was that—after 1979—the decisional 'intergovernmentalism' within the 'political' branches of the Union was simply 'replaced' by the decisional supranationalism offered by the judicial branch. (Strikingly, the 'Transformation of Europe' does not mention *Cassis de Dijon* once! What would we say of a history of the twentieth century that did not mention the United States?) Indeed, after 1979, it was hard, if not impossible, to insist on a negative correlation between normative and decisional supranationalism in the sense that the more 'legal' European law got (through direct effect and supremacy), the more the Member States would politically 'control' the decision-making process. This view simply does not take account of the sphere of negative integration—the more important sphere within the early European Union. For when the Court 'decides' on the scope—not the nature—of Article 34 TFEU, it takes a substantive decision, which will—hopefully—be implemented by the national courts *without the national legislature or executive having any political 'control' over this judicial decision*. For an extensive discussion of the relationship between 'normative' and 'decisional' supranationalism in general, and the Weiler 'equilibrium thesis' in particular, see: R. Schütze, *From International to Federal Union: The Changing Structure of European Law*.

[72] For the classic study of political messianism, see: J. L. Talmon, *Political Messianism: The Romantic Phase*.

[73] This is an absolutely fundamental difference between my position and Maduro's book. For Maduro, the Court of Justice's jurisprudence on Article 34 TFEU 'is' legitimate as it reflects a democratic majority (whatever he means by that) within the EU. By contrast, my reading is that the Court's jurisprudence on Article 34 TFEU 'may' be legitimate in the future if the judicial decision is subsequently followed by a democratic decision of the Union legislator.

expands, the Union's legislative powers (and activities) must also expand into ever-wider fields. For only through a European-wide public act is the promise of democratic self-'constitution' redeemed. These 'public' acts should be legislative acts; for it is here that the European 'demos' primarily comes into being through a reflective process of parliamentary self-constitution.[74]

The relationship between negative and positive integration, while not discussed in this book, thus becomes absolutely vital. Because the expansion of Article 34 TFEU not only demands an expansion of the legislative powers for the Union;[75] the move from an international to a federal model within the sphere of negative integration *normatively* also demands a corresponding move in the sphere of positive integration. For only this second step can legitimate *ex post facto* the 'constitutional' decision to leave the 'state of nature' that existed under 'ordinary' international law. And, in any event, is the whole point of creating a European 'domestic' market not the hope of regaining the ability to 'domesticate' that market; that is: to tame the wild forces of globalization by supranational public rules?

What is the status quo of this politico-constitutional transformation of the European Union? The central problem within the positive integration sphere today is not so much the (constitutional) competence structure of the Union but its (legislative) decision-making structure. For unlike the

[74] Leaving the ambivalent Renan thought aside, this idea was probably first clearly expressed by the Weimar scholar Rudolf Smend, see: *Staatsrechtliche Abhandlungen*, 155: 'Im parlamentarischen Staat ist das Volk nicht schon an sich politisch vorhanden ... sondern es hat sein Dasein als politisches Volk, als souveräner Willensverband in erster Linie vermöge der jeweiligen politischen Synthese, in der es immer von neuem überhaupt als staatliche Wirklichkeit existent wird.'

And see now also: S. Benhabib, *Another Cosmopolitanism*, 33: '[T]he paradox of democratic legitimacy has a corollary that has been little noted: every act of self-legislation is also an act of self-constitution. "We, the people" who agree to bind ourselves by these laws, are also defining ourselves as a "we" in the very act of self-legislation.' And for a similar point see J. Habermas: 'The ethical-political self-understanding of citizens in a democratic community must not be taken as an historical-cultural a priori that makes democratic will-formation possible, but rather as flowing contents of a circulatory progress that is generated through the legal institutionalization of citizens' communication. This is precisely how national identities were formed in modern Europe. Therefore it is to be expected that the political institutions to be created by a European constitution would have an inducing effect.' See J. Habermas, 'Remarks on Dieter Grimm's "Does Europe Need a Constitution?"', 306.

[75] I have explored this expansion and the corresponding move from dual to cooperate federalism in: R. Schütze, *From Dual to Cooperative Federalism: The Changing Structure of European Law.*

decisional capacities of the judicial branch, the decisional capacities of the other branches have, in comparison, remained underdeveloped; and, despite significant progress since *Cassis de Dijon*,[76] the *decisional* asymmetry between negative and positive integration can only completely disappear once the Union drops all out-dated international law remnants.

But this is a story for another time. It will be told in the third—and last—volume on the changing structure of European law.

[76] On the post-1979 rise of the European Parliament and the post-1979 decline of unanimity voting in the Council in the history of European integration, see: R. Schütze, *European Constitutional Law*, Chapter 1; as well as my (future) *From International to Federal Union: The Changing Structure of European Law*.

BIBLIOGRAPHY

Abel, A., '*The Commerce Clause in the Constitutional Convention and in Contemporary Comment*' (1940–1) 25 Minnesota Law Review 432

Accominotti, O. and Flandreau, M., 'Bilateral Treaties and the Most-Favored-Nation Clause: The Myth of Trade Liberalization in the Nineteenth Century' (2008) 60 World Politics 147

Ankersmit, L., 'What if Cassis de Dijon Were Cassis de Quebec?: The Assimilation of Goods of Third Country Origin in the Internal Market' (2013) 50 Common Market Law Review 1387

Appleby, J. O., *Economic Thought and Ideology in Seventeenth-Century England* (Princeton, 1978)

Armstrong, K., 'Mutual Recognition', in C. Barnard and J. Scott (eds.), *The Law of the Single European Market: Unpacking the Premises* (Hart, 2002), 225

Arnull, A., 'What Shall We Do on Sunday?' (1991) 16 European Law Review 112

Atiyah, P. S., *Pragmatism and Theory in English Law* (Stevens, 1987)

Babayev, R., 'Private Autonomy at Union Level: On Article 16 CFREU and Free Movement Rights' (2016) 53 Common Market Law Review 979

Bairoch, P. and Burke, S., 'European Trade Policy, 1815–1914', in P. Mathias and S. Pollard (eds.), *The Cambridge Economic History of Europe*, Volume 8: *The Industrial Economies: The Development of Economic and Social Policies* (Cambridge University Press, 1989), 1

Balassa, B., *The Theory of Economic Integration* (Allen & Unwin, 1961)

Ballard, R. G., '"Dormant" No More: The Supreme Court Wakens the Dormant Commerce Clause in *Granholm v Heald*' (2006) 41 Wake Forest Law Review 303

Banks, K., 'The Application of the Fundamental Freedoms to Member State Tax Measures: Guarding against Protectionism or Second-Guessing National Policy Choices?' (2008) 33 European Law Review 482

Baquero Cruz, J., *Between Competition and Free Movement: The Economic Constitutional Law of the European Community* (Hart, 2002)

Barents, R., 'Charges of Equivalent Effect to Customs Duties' (1978) 15 Common Market Law Review 415

——'New Developments in Measures having Equivalent Effect' (1981) 18 Common Market Law Review 271

——'Recent Case Law on the Prohibition of Fiscal Discrimination under Article 95' (1986) 23 Common Market Law Review 641

Barnard, C., 'Sunday Trading: A Drama in Five Acts' (1994) 57 Modern Law Review 449

—— 'Derogations, Justifications and the Four Freedoms: Is State Interest Really Protected', in C. Barnard and O. Odudu (eds.), *The Outer Limits of European Law* (Hart, 2009), 273

—— *The Substantive Law of the EU: The Four Freedoms* (Oxford University Press, 2016)

Basedow, J., *Von der deutschen zur europäischen Wirtschaftsverfassung* (Mohr Siebeck, 1992)

Baumann, P., 'Common Organizations of the Market and National Law' (1977) 14 Common Market Law Review 303

Beck, R., 'The New Jurisprudence of the Necessary and Proper Clause' (2002) University of Illinois Law Review 581

Benhabib, S., *Another Cosmopolitanism* (Oxford University Press, 2008)

Berardis, G., 'The Common Organization of Agricultural Markets and National Price Regulations' (1980) 17 Common Market Law Review 539

Béraud, R. C., 'Les Mesures d'effet équivalent au sens des articles 30 et suivants du Traité de Rome' (1968) 4 Revue Trimestrielle de Droit Europeén 265

Bickerton, C., *European Integration: From Nation-States to Member States* (Oxford University Press, 2012)

Biklé, H. W., 'The Silence of Congress' (1927) 41 Harvard Law Review 200

Bittker, B. I. and Denning, B. P., 'The Import–Export Clause' (1998) 68 Mississippi Law Journal 521

Blumann, C. et al., *Commentaire Mégret. Introduction au marché intérieur—Libre circulation des marchandises* (Université de Bruxelles, 2015)

Bonn, F., 'Les Entraves techniques aux échanges communautaires' (1969) Revue du Marché Commun, 369–87

Bosher, J. F., *The Single Duty Project: A Study of the Movement for a French Customs Union in the Eighteenth Century* (Athlone Press, 1964)

Brace, R. M., 'The Anglo-French Treaty of Commerce of 1786: A Reappraisal' (1947) 9 The Historian 151

Brandt, R., 'Das Erlaubnisgesetz, oder: Vernunft und Geschichte in Kants Rechtslehre', in R. Brandt (ed.), *Rechtsphilosophie der Aufklärung* (de Gruyter, 1982), 233

Braudel, F., *Civilization and Capitalism: 15th–18th Century*, Volume III: *The Perspective of the World* (Collins Sons & Co., 1984)

Bronz, G., 'The International Trade Organization Charter' (1949) 62 Harvard Law Review 1089

—— 'An International Trade Organization: The Second Attempt' (1955–6) 69 Harvard Law Review 440

Búrca, G. de, 'The Principle of Proportionality and its Application in EC Law' (1993) 13 Yearbook of European Law 105

Calvin, P., *Securing the World Economy: The Reinvention of the League of Nations, 1920–1946* (Oxford University Press, 2013)

Cannizzaro, E., 'Producing "Reverse Discrimination" through the Exercise of EC Competences' (1997) 17 Yearbook of European Law 29

Caro De Sousa, P., 'Through Contact Lenses, Darkly: Is Identifying Restrictions to free Movement Harder than Meets the Eye? Comment on *Ker-Optika*' (2012) 37 European Law Review 79

—— *The European Fundamental Freedoms: A Contextual Approach* (Oxford University Press, 2015)

Catchpole, L. and Barav, A., 'The Public Morality Exception and the Free Movement of Goods: Justification of a Dual Standard in National Legislation?' (1980) 1 Legal Issues of European Integration 1

Chalmers, D., 'Repackaging the Internal Market: The Ramifications of the *Keck* Judgment' (1994) 19 European Law Review 385

Clercq, A. de (ed.), *Recueil des Traités de la France*, Volume 1: *1713–1802* (Pedone-Lauriel, 1880)

Close, G., 'Harmonisation of Laws: Use or Abuse of the Powers under the EEC Treaty' (1978) 3 European Law Review 461

Clough, S. B., *France: A History of National Economics, 1789–1939* (Octagon Books, 1970)

Coenen, D. T., 'Business Subsidies and the Dormant Commerce Clause' (1998) 107 Yale Law Journal 965

Condliffe, J. B., *The Commerce of Nations* (Norten, 1950)

Conrad, C. R., *Processes and Production Methods (PPMs) in WTO Law: Interfacing Trade and Social Goals* (Cambridge University Press, 2011)

Cooke, F. H., 'The Pseudo-Doctrine of the Exclusiveness of the Power of Congress to Regulate Commerce' (1911) 20 Yale Law Journal 297

Crandall, S. B., 'The American Construction of the Most-Favored-Nation Clause' (1913) 7 American Journal of International Law 708

Crosskey, W. W., *Politics and the Constitution in the History of the United States*, Volume 1 (University of Chicago Press, 1953)

Cushman, B., 'Formalism and Realism in Commerce Clause Jurisprudence' (2000) 67 University of Chicago Law Review 1089

Cushman, R. E., 'The National Police Power under the Commerce Clause of the Constitution (I)' (1918–19) 3 Minnesota Law Review 289

Dahl, R., *Democracy and Its Critics* (Yale University Press, 1991)

Dahl, R. and Tufte, E., *Size and Democracy* (Stanford University Press, 1974)

Dam, K. W., 'Regional Economic Arrangements and the GATT: The Legacy of a Misconception' (1963) 30 University of Chicago Law Review 615

—— *The GATT: Law and International Economic Organization* (University of Chicago Press, 1970)

Dashwood, A., 'Hastening Slowly: The Communities' Path Towards Harmonization', in H. Wallace et al. (eds.), *Policy Making in the European Communities* (Wiley, 1977), 273

Dashwood, A., '*Cassis de Dijon*: The Line of Cases Grows' (1981) 6 European Law Review 287

Dautricourt, C. and Thomas, S., 'Reverse Discrimination and Free Movement of Persons under Community Law: All for Ulysses, Nothing for Penelope?' (2009) 34 European Law Review 433

Davies, G., 'The Court's Jurisprudence on Free Movement of Goods: Pragmatic Presumptions, not Philosophical Principles' (2012) 2 European Journal of Consumer Law 25

Dawes, A., 'A Freedom Reborn? The New Yet Unclear Scope of Article 29 EC' (2009) 34 European Law Review 639

Day, D. S., 'Revisiting *Pike*: The Origins of the Nondiscrimination Tier of the Dormant Commerce Clause Doctrine' (2004) 27 Hamline Law Review 45

Defossez, A., 'L'histoire d'une divergence et d'une possible reconciliation. L'article 29 CE' (2009) Cahiers de Droit Européen 409

Denning, B. P., 'Confederation-Era Discrimination against Interstate Commerce and the Legitimacy of the Dormant Commerce Clause Doctrine' (2005–6) 94 Kentucky Law Journal 37

—— 'Reconstructing the Dormant Commerce Clause Doctrine' (2008) 50 William and Mary Law Review 417

Diamond, P., 'Dishonourable Defences: The Use of Injunctions and the EEC Treaty—Case Study of the Shops Acts 1950' (1991) 54 Modern Law Rewiew 72

Dietz, S. and Streinz, T., 'Das Marktzugangskriterium in der Dogmatik der Grundfreiheiten' (2015) 50 Europarecht 50

d'Oliveira, H. U. J., 'Is Reverse Discrimination Still Possible under the Single European Act?', in *Forty Years On: The Evolution of Postwar Private International Law in Europe* (Kluwer, 1990), 71

Doukas, D., 'Untying the Market Access Knot: Advertising Restrictions and the Free Movement of Goods and Services' (2006–7) 9 Cambridge Yearbook of European Legal Studies 177

Dowling, N. T., 'Interstate Commerce and State Power' (1940–1) 27 Virginia Law Review 1

Dunham, A. L., *The Anglo-French Treaty of Commerce of 1860* (University of Michigan Press, 1930)

Dworkin, R., *Taking Rights Seriously* (Bloomsbury, 2011)

Early, A. R. and Weitzman, R. G., 'A Century of Dissent: The Immunity of Goods Imported for Resale from Nondiscriminatory State Personal Property Taxes' (1975) 7 Southwestern University Law Review 247

Easson, A., *Tax Law and Policy in the EEC* (Sweet & Maxwell, 1980)

—— 'Fiscal Discrimination: New Perspectives on Article 95 of the EEC Treaty' (1981) 18 Common Market Law Review 521

—— *Taxation in the European Community* (Athlone Press, 1993)

Eeckhout, P., *The European Internal Market and International Trade: A Legal Analysis* (Clarendon Press, 1994)

Egan, M., *Constructing a European Market: Standards, Regulation and Governance* (Oxford University Press, 2001)

—— *Single Markets: Economic Integration in Europe and the United States* (Oxford University Press, 2015)

Ehring, L., 'De Facto Discrimination in World Trade Law: National and Most-Favored-Nation Treatment—or Equal Treatment?', Jean Monnet Working Paper 12/01 (http://jeanmonnetprogram.org/archive/papers/01/013201.html)

Ely, J. H., *Democracy and Distrust: A Theory of Judicial Review* (Harvard University Press, 1980)

Enchelmaier, S., '"Moped Trailers", "Mickelsson & Roos", "Gysbrechts": The ECJ's Case Law on Goods Keeps on Moving' (2010) 29 Yearbook of European Law 190

—— 'Four Freedoms, Ever More Principles' (2016) 36 Oxford Journal of Legal Studies 192

Engsig-Sørensen, K., 'The Most-Favoured-Nation Principle in the EU' (2007) 34 Legal Issues of Economic Integration 315

Epiney, A., *Umgekehrte Diskriminierungen: Zulässigkeit und Grenzen der discrimination à rebours nach europäischem Gemeinschaftsrecht und nationalem Verfassungsrecht* (Heymans, 1995)

Erler, G., *Grundprobleme des internationalen Wirtschaftsrechts* (Schwartz, 1956)

Eskridge, W. N. and Levinson, S. V., *Constitutional Stupidities, Constitutional Tragedies* (New York University Press, 1998)

Eule, J. N., 'Laying the Dormant Commerce Clause to Rest' (1982) 91 Yale Law Journal 425

Fernandez, J. M. and O'Leary, S., 'Judicial Exceptions to the Free Provision of Services' (1995) 1 European Law Journal 308

Fichte, J. G., *The Closed Commercial State* (Suny Press, 2012)

Francis, A. D., 'John Methuen and the Anglo-Portuguese Treaties of 1703' (1960) 3 The Historical Journal 103

Frankfurter, F., 'Taney and the Commerce Clause' (1936) 49 Harvard Law Review 1286

Fremuth, M., '"Cassis de Dijon": Zu der dogmatischen Einordung zwingender Erfordernisse' (2006) 41 Europarecht 866

Freund, P. A., 'Foreword' to T. R. Powel, *Vagaries and Varieties in Constitutional Interpretation* (Columbia University Press, 1956)

Friedmann, W. G., *The Changing Structure of International Law* (Stevens, 1964)

Giddens, A., *Turbulent and Mighty Continent: What Future for Europe* (Polity, 2014)

Gillingham, J., *Coal, Steel, and the Rebirth of Europe, 1945–1955: The Germans and French from Ruhr Conflict to Economic Community* (Cambridge University Press, 1991)

Gormley, L., 'Quantitative Restrictions and Measures Having Equivalent Effect' (1981) 6 European Law Review 454

—— 'Actually or Potentially, Directly or Indirectly? Obstacles to the Free Movement of Goods' (1989) 9 Yearbook of European Law 195
—— 'Reasoning Renounced? The Remarkable Judgment in *Keck and Mithouard*' (1994) 5 European Business Law Review 63
—— 'The Definition of Measures Having Equivalent Effect', in A. Arnull et al., (eds.), *Continuity and Change in EU Law: Essays in Honour of Sir Francis Jacobs* (Oxford University Press, 2008), 189
—— 'Free Movement of Goods and Their Use: What Is the Use of It?' (2011) 33 Fordham International Law Journal 1589
—— 'Inconsistencies and Misconceptions in the Free Movement of Goods' (2015) 40 European Law Review 925
Graetz, M. J. and Warren, A. C., 'Dividend Taxation in Europe: When the ECJ Makes Tax Policy' (2007) 44 Common Market Law Review 1577
Graf, M., *Der Begriff 'Maßnahmen gleicher Wirkung wie mengenmäßige Einfuhrbeschränkungen' in dem EWG-Vertrag* (Heymanns, 1972)
Greaves, R., 'Advertising Restrictions and the Free Movement of Goods and Services' (1998) 23 European Law Review 305
Groeben, H. von der et al. (eds.), *Kommentar zum EWG- Vertrag* (Nomos, 1974)
Grotius, H., *The Freedom of the Seas* (Oxford University Press, 1916)
Gutmann, D, 'How to Avoid Double Taxation in the European Union?', in I. Richelle et al. (eds.), *Allocating Taxing Powers within the European Union* (Springer, 2013), 63
Habermas, J., 'Remarks on Dieter Grimm's "Does Europe Need a Constitution?"' (1995) 1 European Law Journal 303
—— *The Divided West* (Polity, 2006)
—— *The Crisis of the European Union* (Polity, 2013)
Hallstein, W., *Europe in the Making* (Allen and Unwin 1972)
Hamilton, A., *Report on the Subject of Manufacturers* (Cosimo Classics, 2007)
Hamilton, A., Madison, J., and Jay, J., *The Federalist*, ed. T. Ball (Cambridge University Press, 2003)
Hanf, D., '"Reverse Discrimination" in EU Law: Constitutional Aberration, Constitutional Necessity, or Judicial Choice?' (2011) 18 Maastricht Journal of European and Comparative Law 29
Harryvan A. G. and Harst, J. van der (eds.), *Documents on European Union* (St Martin's Press, 1997)
Hay, P., 'The European Common Market and the Most-Favored-Nation Clause' (1961–2) 23 University of Pittsburgh Law Review 661
Heinzerling, L., 'The Commercial Constitution' (1995) Supreme Court Review 217
Held, D., *Democracy and the Global Order: From the Modern State to Cosmopolitan Governance* (Stanford University Press, 1996)
Held, D. and McGrew, A., *The Global Transformations Reader: An Introduction to the Globalization Debate* (Polity Press, 2003)

Hellerstein, W., 'State Taxation and the Supreme Court: Towards a More Unified Approach to Constitutional Adjudication' (1977) 75 Michigan Law Review 1426

—— 'State Taxation of Interstate Business: Perspectives on Two Centuries of Constitutional Adjudication' (1987–8) 41 Tax Law 37

—— 'Is "Internal Consistency" Foolish?: Reflections on an Emerging Commerce Clause Restraint on State Taxation' (1988) 87 Michigan Law Review 138

Henderson, W. O., 'The Anglo-French Commercial Treaty of 1786' (1957) 10 The Economic History Review 104

—— *The Zollverein* (Cass & Company, 1959)

Hertslet, L., *A Complete Collection of the Treaties and Conventions and Reciprocal Regulations at Present Subsisting between Great Britain and Foreign Powers*, Volume XI (Her Majesty's Stationary Office, 1864)

Hills, R. M.Jr , 'Counting States' (2009) 32 Harvard Journal of Law & Public Policy 17

Hoffmann, S., *The European Sisyphus: Essays on Europe, 1964–1994* (Westview Press, 1995)

Hornbeck, S., 'The Most-Favored-Nation Clause' (1909) 3 American Journal of International Law 395

Horsley, T., 'The Concept of an Obstacle to Intra-EU Capital Movement', in N. Nic Shuibhne and L. W. Gormley (eds.), *From Single Market to Economic Union: Essays in Memory of John A. Usher* (Oxford University Press, 2012), 155

Hudec, R. E., *The GATT Legal System and World Trade Diplomacy* (Butterworth Legal Publishers, 1990)

Hume, D., *Essays, Moral, Political, and Literary* (1742), II.V.16 'Of the Balance of Trade' (http://www.econlib.org/library/LFBooks/Hume/hmMPL28.html#Part II, Essay V, 'Of the Balance of Trade')

Iliasu, A. A., 'The Cobden-Chevalier Commercial Treaty of 1860' (1971) 14 The Historical Journal 67

Inglehart, R., *The Silent Revolution: Changing Values and Political Styles Among Western Publics* (Princeton University Press, 1977)

—— 'Changing Values among Western Publics from 1970 to 2006' (2008) 31 West European Politics 130

Ipsen, H. P., *Europäisches Gemeinschaftsrecht* (Mohr, 1972)

Irwin, D. A., *Against the Tide: An Intellectual History of Free Trade* (Princeton University Press, 1998)

—— 'The Aftermath of Hamilton's "Report on Manufactures"' (2004) 64 The Journal of Economic History, 800

—— *Trade Policy Disaster: Lessons from the 1930s* (MIT Press, 2011)

Irwin, D. A., Mavroidis, P. C., and Sykes, A. O., *The Genesis of the GATT* (Cambridge University Press, 2009)

Isenbaert, M., *EC Law and the Sovereignty of the Member States in Direct Taxation* (IBFD Publications, 2010)

Jackson, J. H., 'The General Agreement on Tariffs and Trade in United States Domestic Law' (1967–8) 66 Michigan Law Review 249

—— *World Trade and The Law of the GATT* (Bobbs-Merrill, 1969)

Jansson, M. S. and Kalimo, H., '*De Minimis* Meets "Market Access": Transformations in the Substance—and the Syntax—of EU Free Movement Law?' (2014) 51 Common Market law Review 523

Joerges, C., 'The Market without the State? The "Economic Constitution" of the European Community and the Rebirth of Regulatory Politics' (1997) 1 European Integration Online Papers (http://papers.ssrn.com/sol3/papers.cfm?abstract_id=302710)

Johnston, E. and O'Keeffe, D., 'From Discrimination to Obstacles to Free Movement: Recent Developments Regarding the Free Movement of Workers 1989–1994' (1994) 31 Common Market Law Review 1313

Joliet, R., 'EEC Law and Appellations of Origin: The Scotch Whisky Case' (1975) 38 Modern Law Review 200

—— 'Der freie Warenverkehr: Das Urteil *Keck und Mithouard* und die Neuorientierung der Rechtsprechung' (1994) 43 Geweberblicher Rechtsschutz und Urheberrecht (Internationaler Teil) 979

Kaczorowska, A, '*Gourmet* Can Have His *Keck* and Eat It!' (2004) 10 European Law Journal 479

Karagiannis, Y., 'Origins of the Common Market: Political Economy vs. Hagiography' (2016) 54 Journal of Common Market Studies 233

Kaupa, C., *The Pluralist Character of the European Economic Constitution* (Hart, 2016)

Keesling, F. M., '*Michelin Tire Corporation v Wages*: The Demise of the Original Packaging Doctrine' (1977–8) 50 Southern California Law Review 719

Kemmeren, E., 'The Termination of the "Most Favoured Nation Clause" Dispute in Tax Treaty Law and the Necessity of a Euro Model Tax Convention' (1997) 6 EC Tax Review 146

Kersting, W., *Die Politische Philosophie des Gesellschaftsvertrags* (Wissenschaftliche Buchgesellschaft, 1996)

Kilroy, B. A., 'Integration Through Law: ECJ and Governments in the EU' (University of California, unpublished thesis)

Kindleberger, C. P., 'The Rise of Free Trade in Western Europe, 1820–1875' (1975) 35 Journal of Economic History 20

Kingston, S., 'The Boundaries of Sovereignty: The ECJ's Controversial Role Applying Internal Market Law to Direct Tax Measures' (2006–7) 9 Cambridge Yearbook of European Legal Studies 287

Kofler, G. and Mason, R., 'Double Taxation: A European "Switch in Time"?' (2007) 14 Columbia Journal of European Law 63

Kohler, J., *Abgaben zollgleicher Wirkung im Recht der Europäischen Gemeinschaften* (Duncker & Humblot, 1978)

Komesar, N., *Imperfect Alternatives: Choosing Institutions in Law, Economics, and Public Policy* (University of Chicago Press, 1997)

Kon, S. D., 'Aspects of Reverse Discrimination in Community Law' (1981) 6 European Law Review 75

Koutrakos, P., 'On Groceries, Alcohol and Olive Oil: More on Free Movement of Goods after *Keck*' (2001) 26 European Law Review 391

Lain, C. B., 'The Unexceptionalism of "Evolving Standards"', 57 (2009–10) UCLA Law Review 365

—— 'The Doctrinal Side of Majority Will' (2010) Michigan State Law Review 775

Lampe, M., 'Explaining Nineteenth-Century Bilateralism: Economic and Political Determinants of the Cobden–Chevalier Network' (2011) 64 Economic History Review 644

Lang, M., 'Double Taxation and EC Law', in R. S. Avi-Yonah et al. (eds.), *Comparative Fiscal Federalism: Comparing the European Court of Justice and the US Supreme Court's Tax Jurisprudence* (Kluwer, 2008), 11

Langer, C., *Reform nach Prinzipien: Untersuchungen zur politischen Theory Immanuel Kants* (Klett-Cotta, 1998)

Lawson, G. and Granger, P. B., 'The "Proper" Scope of Federal Power: A Jurisdictional Interpretation of the Sweeping Clause' (1993–4) 43 Duke Law Journal 267

Lenaerts, K., 'Interlocking Legal Orders in the European Union and Comparative Law' (2003) 52 International and Comparative Law Quarterly 873

Lianos, I., 'In Memoriam *Keck*: The Reformation of the EU Law on the Free Movement of Goods' (2015) 40 European Law Review 225

Lindberg, L. N. and Scheingold, S. A., *Europe's Would-Be-Polity* (Prentice-Hall, 1970)

List, F., *National System of Political Economy*, Volume 2: *The Theory* (Cosimo Classics, 2005)

Loewenheim, U., 'Die Beseitigung Nichttarifärer Handelsschranken im Innergemeinschaftlichen Handel unter besonderer Berücksichtigung der gewerblichen Schutzrechte und des Urheberrechts: Deutscher Landesbericht', in: *The Elimination of Non-Tariff Barriers with Particular Reference to Industrial Property Rights Including Copyright* (FIDE, 1982), 4.1

Luczak, J. M., *Die Europäische Wirtschaftsverfassung als Legitimationslement europäischer Integration* (Duncker & Humblot, 2009)

Luís da Cruz Vilaça, J., 'On the Application of *Keck* in the Field of Free Provision of Services', in M. Andenas and W. H. Roth (eds.), *Services and Free Movement in EU Law* (Oxford University Press, 2003), 25

Machlup, F., *A History of Thought on Economic Integration* (Macmillan Press, 1977)

Maduro, M., 'Reforming the Market or the State? Article 30 and the European Constitution: Economic Freedom and Political Rights' (1997) 3 European Law Journal 55

—— 'The Saga of Article 30 EC Treaty: To be Continued' (1998) 5 Maastricht Journal of European and Comparative Law 298

—— *We the Court: The European Court of Justice and the European Economic Constitution* (Hart, 1998)

—— 'The Scope of European Remedies: The Case of Purely Internal Situations and Reverse Discrimination', in C. Kilpatrick and T. Novitz (eds.), *The Future of Remedies in Europe* (Hart, 2000), 117

—— 'Revisiting the Free Movement of Goods in a Comparative Perspective', in: Court of Justice of the European Union, *The Court of Justice and the Construction of Europe: Analysis and Perspectives on Sixty Years of Case Law* (Asser, 2013), 485

Majone, G. *Dilemmas of European Integration: The Ambiguities and Pitfalls of Integration by Stealth* (Oxford University Press, 2005)

Maltz, E. M., 'How Much Regulation Is Too Much? An Examination of Commerce Clause Jurisprudence' (1981) 50 George Washington Law Review 47

Marx, F., *Funktion und Grenzen der Rechtsangleichung nach Art.100 EWG-Vertrag* (Carl Heymanns, 1976)

Masclet, J. C., 'Les Articles 30, 36 et 100 du traité C.E.E. à la lumière de l'arrêt "Cassis de Dijon"' (1980) 16 Revue Trimestrielle de Droit européen 611

Mattera, A., 'L'Arrêt "Cassis de Dijon". Une nouvelle approche pour la réalisation et le bon fonctionnement du marché intérieur' (1980) 23 Revue du Marché Commun 505

—— 'De l'arrêt "Dassonville" à l'arrêt "Keck". L'obscure clarté d'une jurisprudence riche en principes novateurs et en contradictions' (1994) Revue du Marché Unique Européen 117

Mavroidis, P., *Trade in Goods* (Oxford University Press, 2012)

Melloni, M., *The Principle of National Treatment in the GATT: A Survey of the Jurisprudence, Practice and Policy* (Bruylant, 2005)

Metzger, S. D., 'United States Foreign Trade: Past, Present and Future' (1961) 6 Villanova Law Review 503

Millarg, E., 'Anmerkung zum Urteil in der Rs. 120/78' (1979) Europarecht 417

Milward, A., *The Re-Construction of Western Europe, 1945–1951* (University of California Press, 1984)

—— *The European Rescue of the Nation State* (Routledge, 2000)

Mitchell, A. D. and Lockhart, N. J. S., 'Legal Implications for PTAs under the WTO', in S. Lester et al. (eds.), *Bilateral and Regional Trade Agreements: Commentary and Analysis*, Volume 1 (Cambridge University Press, 2016), 81

Montesquieu, C. de, *The Spirit of the Laws* (Cambridge University Press, 1989)

Morini-Comby, J., *Mercantilisme et protectionnisme. Essai sur les doctrines interventionnistes en politique commerciale du XVe au XIXe siècle* (Librairie Félix Alcan, 1930)

Mortelmans, K., 'Article 30 of the EEC Treaty and Legislation Relating to Market Circumstances: Time to Consider a New Direction?' (1991) 28 Common Market Law Review 115

—— 'The Common Market, the Internal Market and the Single Market, What's in a Market?' (1998) 35 Common Market Law Review 101

Mosler, H., 'Der Vertrag über die Europäische Gemeinschaft für Kohle und Stahl' (1951–2) 14 Zeitschrift für ausländisches öffentliches Recht und Völkerrecht 1

Mun, T., *England's Treasure by Forraign Trade* (Macmillan, 1895 [1664])

Mussler, W., *Die Wirtschaftsverfassung der Europäischen Geimeinschaft im Wandel: Von Rom nach Maastricht* (Nomos, 1998)

Nakhimovsky, I., *The Closed Commercial State: Perpetual Peace and Commercial Society from Rousseau to Fichte* (Princeton University Press, 2011)

Neumann, J. and Türk, E., 'Necessity Revisited: Proportionality in World Trade Organization Law After *Korea—Beef*, *EC—Asbestos* and *EC—Sardines*' (2003) 37 Journal of World Trade 199

Nic Shuibhne, N., 'Free Movement of Persons and the Wholly Internal Rule: Time to Move On?' (2002) 39 Common Market Law Review 731

—— *The Coherence of EU Free Movement Law: Constitutional Responsibility and the Court of Justice* (Oxford University Press, 2013)

Nolde, B., 'Droit et technique des traités de commerce' (1924) 3 Collected Courses of the Hague Academy of International Law 291

Offe, C., *Disorganized Capitalism: Contemporary Transformations of Work and Politics* (Polity, 1985)

Oliver, P., 'Further Reflections on the Scope of Articles 28–30 (Ex 30–36) EC' (1999) 36 Common Market Law Review 783

—— 'Of Trailers and Jet Skis: Is the Case Law on Article 34 TFEU Hurtling in a New Direction?' (2010) 33 Fordham International Law Journal 1423

Oliver, P. et al., *Free Movement of Goods in the European Union* (Hart, 2010)

Oliver, P. et al., 'Free Movement of Goods', in C. Barnard and S. Peers (eds.), *European Union Law* (Oxford University Press, 2014), 325

Ophüls, C. F., 'Die Geltungsnormen des Europäischen Gemeinschaftsrechts', in B. Aubin et al. (eds.), *Festschrift für Otto Riese* (C. F. Müller, 1964), 1

—— 'Staatshoheit und Gemeinschaftshoheit: Wandlungen des Souveränitätsbegriffs', in *Recht im Wandel: Festschrift 150 Jahre C. Heymanns Verlag* (Heymanns, 1966), 519

Oppenheim, L., *International Law: A Treatise*, Volume 1: *Peace* (Longman, Greens and Co., 1912)

Ortino, F., *Basic Legal Instruments for the Liberalisation of Trade: A Comparative Analysis of EC and WTO Law* (Hart, 2004)

Panayi, C. H. J. I., *European Union Corporate Tax Law* (Cambridge University Press, 2013)

Papadopoulou, R. E., 'Situations purement internes et droit communautaire: un instrument jurisprudentiel à double fonction ou une arme à double tranchant?' (2002) 38 Cahiers de Droit Euopéen 95

Parry, A. and Hardy, S., *EEC Law* (Sweet & Maxwell, 1973)

Pescatore, P., *The Law of Integration: Emergence of a New Phenomenon in International Relations, Based on the Experience of the European Communities* (Sijthoff, 1974)

—— 'Le Recours, dans la jurisprudence de la Cour de Justice des Communautés Européennes, à des normes déduites de la comparaison des droit des États Membres' (1980) 32 Revue Internationale de Droit Comparé 337

—— 'La Carence du législateur communautaire et le devoir du juge', in G. Lüke, G. Ress, and M. R. Will (eds.), *Rechtsvergleichung, Europarecht und Staatenintegration: Gedächtnisschrift für Léontin-Jean Constantinesco* (Heymanns, 1983), 559

Pickup, D. M. W., 'Reverse Discrimination and Freedom of Movement for Workers' (1986) 23 Common Market Law Review 135

Pinder, J., 'Positive and Negative Integration: Some Problems of Economic Union in the EEC' (1968) 24 The World Today 88

Posner, R., *The Economics of Justice* (Harvard University Press, 1981)

Postan, M., 'The Trade of Medieval Europe: The North', in E. Miller, C. Postan, and M. M. Postan (eds.), *The Cambridge Economic History of Europe*, Volume II: *Trade and Industry in the Middle Ages* (Cambridge University Press, 1987), 168

Powell, T. R., 'Current Conflicts between the Commerce Clause and State Police Power, 1922–1927 (II)' (1928) 12 Minnesota Law Review 470

—— 'Notes: State Taxation of Imports: When Does an Import Cease to Be an Import?' (1944–5) 58 Harvard Law Review 858

Pufendorf, S., *De Jure Naturae et Gentium Libri Octo*, Volume 2, translation of the 1688 edn (Clarendon Press, 1934)

Radbruch, G., *Der Geist des Englischen Rechts und die Anglo-Amerikanische Jurisprudenz* (LIT, 2006)

Rawlings, R., 'The Eurolaw Game: Some Deductions from a Saga' (1993) 20 Journal of Law and Society 309

Regan, D. H., 'The Supreme Court and State Protectionism: Making Sense of the Dormant Commerce Clause' (1985–6) 84 Michigan Law Review 1091

—— 'The Meaning of "Necessary" in GATT Article XX and GATS Article XIV: The Myth of Cost–Benefit Balancing' (2007) 6 World Trade Review 347

Reich, N., 'Competition between Legal Orders: A New Paradigm of EC Law' (1992) 29 Common Market Law Review 861

—— 'The "November Revolution" of the European Court of Justice: *Keck*, *Meng* and *Audi* Revisited' (1994) 31 Common Market Law Review 459

Reid, E., 'Regulatory Autonomy in the EU and WTO: Defining and Defending' (2010) 44 Journal of World Trade 877

Reuter, P., *La Communauté européenne du Charbon et de l'Acier* (Librairie générale de droit et de jurisprudence, 1953)

—— *Organisations européennes* (Presses Universitaires de France, 1965)

Ricardo, D., *The Principles of Political Economy and Taxation* (Dover Publications, 2004)

Ritter, C., 'Purely Internal Situations, Reverse Discrimination, *Guimont*, *Dzodzi* and Article 234' (2006) 31 European Law Review 690

Rodrigues Iglesias, G., 'Drinks in Luxembourg: Alcoholic Beverages and the Case Law of the European Court of Justice', in D. O'Keeffe (ed.), *Judicial Review in European Union Law: Liber Amicorum in Honour of Lord Slynn of Hadley* (Kluwer, 2000), 523

Rodrik, D., *The Globalization Paradox* (Oxford University Press, 2012)

Röpke, W., *International Order & Economic Integration* (Reidel Publishing Company 1959)

Roth, W.-H., 'Wettbewerb der Mittgliedstaaten oder Wettbewerb der Hersteller? Plädoyer für eine Neubestimmung des Art. 34 EGV' (1995) 159 Zeitschrift für das gesamte Handelsrecht und Wirtschaftsrecht 78

—— 'The European Court of Justice's Case Law on Freedom to Provide Services: Is *Keck* Relevant?', in M. Andenas and W. H. Roth, *Services and Free Movement in EU Law* (Oxford University Press, 2002), 1

—— 'Exports of Goods and Services within the Single Market: Reflections on the Scope of Article 29 and 49 EC', in T. Tridimas and P. Nebbia (eds.), *European Union Law for the Twenty-First Century*, Volume 2: *Internal Market and Free Movement Community Policies* (Hart, 2004)

Rust, A. (ed.), *Double Taxation within the European Union* (Kluwer, 2011)

Sartori, G., 'Constitutionalism: A Preliminary Discussion' (1962) 56 American Political Science Review 853

Sauter, W., 'The Economic Constitution of the European Union' (1998) 4 Columbia Journal European Law 27

Scharpf, F., *Governing in Europe* (Oxford University Press, 1999)

Scheuner, U., 'Die völkerrechtlichen Grundlagen der Weltwirtschaft in der Gegenwart' (1953) 2 Verhandlungen des 40. Deutschen Juristentags 19

Schmeder, W., *Die Rechtsangleichung als Integrationsmittel der Europäischen Gemeinschaft* (Carl Heymanns, 1978)

Schön, W., 'Europäische Kapitalverkehrsfreiheit und Nationales Steuerrecht', in W. Schön (ed.), *Gedächtnisschrift für Brigitte Knobbe-Keuk* (Schmidt, 1997), 743

—— 'Der freie Warenverkehr, die Steuerhoheit der Mitgliedstaaten und der Systemgedanke im europäischen Steuerrecht—Teil II: Das Verbot diskriminierender und protektionistischer Abgaben und das Problem der Belastung "exotischer" Waren' (2001) 36 Europarecht 341

Schrag-Sternberg, C., *The Struggle for EU Legitimacy: Public Contestation, 1950–2005* (Palgrave, 2013)

Schütze, R., *From Dual to Cooperative Federalism: The Changing Structure of European Law* (Oxford University Press, 2009)

—— 'On "Federal" Ground: The European Union as an (Inter)national Phenomenon' (2009) 46 Common Market Law Review 1069

—— 'Federalism as Constitutional Pluralism: Letter from America', in M. Avbelj and J. Kommarek (eds.), *Constitutional Pluralism in the European Union and Beyond* (Hart, 2012), 185

—— 'European Law and Member State Agreements: An Ambivalent Relationship?', in R. Schütze, *Foreign Affairs and the EU Constitution* (Cambridge University Press, 2014), 120

—— *European Constitutional Law* (Cambridge University Press, 2015)

—— 'Of Types and Tests: Towards a Unitary Doctrinal Framework for Article 34 TFEU?' (2016) 41 European Law Review 826

—— 'Tax Barriers to Intra-Union Trade: American "Federalism", European "Internationalism"?' (2016) 35 Yearbook of European Law 382

—— 'Judicial Majoritarianism Revisited: "We, the Other Court"?' (2018) 43 European Law Review (forthcoming)

—— 'The "Unsettled" Eighteenth Century: Kant and his Predecessors', in R. Schütze and M. Gehring, *Governance and Globalisation: International Problems—European Solutions?* (Cambridge University Press, forthcoming)

—— *Framing Dassonville: Text and Context in European Law* (Cambridge University Press, in preparation)

—— *From International to Federal Union: The Changing Structure of European Law* (in preparation)

Schulze, R. and Hoeren, T. (eds.), *Dokumente zum Europäischen Recht*, Volume 1: *Gründungsverträge* (Springer, 1999)

Schwarzenberger, G., 'The Principles and Standards of International Economic Law' (1966) 117 Collected Courses of the Hague Academy of International Law 1

—— *Economic World Order?* (Manchester University Press, 1970)

—— 'Equality and Discrimination in International Economic Law' (1971) 25 Yearbook of World Affairs 163

Sedler, R. A., 'The Negative Commerce Clause as a Restriction on State Regulation and Taxation: An Analysis in Terms of Constitutional Structure' (1985) 31 Wayne Law Review 885

Seidel, M., 'Aktuelle Probleme der Rechtsangleichung gemäß Art.100 EWG-Vertrag' (1967) 2 Europarecht 202

—— 'Der EWG-rechtliche Begriff der "Maßnahmen gleicher Wirkung wie eine mengenmäßige Beschränkung"' (1967) 20 Neue Juristische Wochenschrift 2081

Semmel, B., *The Rise of Free Trade Imperialism* (Cambridge University Press, 2008)

Setser, V. G., 'Did Americans Originate the Conditional Most-Favored-Nation Clause?' (1933) 5 Journal of Modern History 319

Shonfield, A., *Europe: Journey to an Unknown Destination* (Penguin, 1973)
Slot, P. J., *Technical and Administrative Obstacles to Trade* (Sijthoff, 1975)
Smend, R., *Staatsrechtliche Abhandlungen und andere Aufsätze* (Duncker & Humblot, 2010)
Smith, A., *An Inquiry into the Nature and Causes of the Wealth of Nations*, ed. K. Sutherland (Oxford University Press, 1993) (and see also http://www.econlib.org/library/Smith/smWN16.html)
Snell, J., 'Non-Discriminatory Tax Obstacles in Community Law' (2007) 56 International and Comparative Law Quarterly 339
Snyder, R. C., *The Most Favoured-Nation Clause* (King's Crown Press, 1948)
Spaventa, E., 'On Discrimination and the Theory of Mandatory Requirements' (2002) 3 Cambridge Yearbook of European Legal Studies 457
—— 'From "Gebhard" to "Carpenter": Towards a (Non-)Economic European Constitution' (2004) 41 Common Market Law Review 743
—— *Free Movement of Persons in the European Union: Barriers to Movement in their Constitutional Context* (Kluwer, 2007)
—— 'Leaving "Keck" Behind?: The Free Movement of Goods after the Rulings in "Commission v Italy" and "Mickelsson and Roos"' (2009) 34 European Law Review 914
—— 'The Outer Limit of the Treaty Free Movement Provisions: Some Reflections on the Significance of *Keck*, Remoteness and *Deliège*', in C. Barnard and O. Odudu (eds.), *The Outer Limits of European Union Law* (Hart, 2009), 245
Starkowski, R., *Die Angleichung technicher Rechtsvorschriften und industrieller Normen in der Europäischen Wirtschaftsgemeinschaft* (Duncker & Humblot, 1973)
Steiner, J., 'Drawing the Line: Uses and Abuses of Article 30 EEC' (1992) 29 Common Market Law Review 749
Stödter, R., 'Völkerrecht und Weltwirtschaft' (1950–1) 13 Zeitschrift für ausländisches öffentliches Recht und Völkerrecht 67
Stone-Sweet, A., *The Judicial Construction of Europe* (Oxford University Press, 2004)
Strauss, D. A., 'Why Was *Lochner* Wrong?' (2003) 70 University of Chicago Law Review 373
Szydło, M., 'Export Restrictions within the Structure of Free Movement of Goods: Reconsideration of an Old Paradigm' 47 (2010) Common Market Law Review 753
—— 'How to Reconcile National Support for Renewable Energy with Internal Market Obligations? The Task for the EU Legislature after *Ålands vindkraft* and *Essent*' (2015) 52 Common Market Law Review 489
Talmon, J. L., *Political Messianism: The Romantic Phase* (Secker & Warburg, 1960)
Taussig, F. W., *The Tariff History of the United States* (Elibron Classics, 2005)
Terra, B. J. M. and Wattel, P. J., *European Tax Law* (Kluwer, 2012)
Tietje, C., 'Die Meistbegünstigungsverpflichtung im Gemeinschaftsrecht' (1995) 30 Europarecht 398

Tinbergen, J., *International Economic Integration* (Elsevier Publishing, 1965)
Tribe, L., 'The Puzzling Persistence of Process-Based Theories' (1980) 89 Yale Law Journal 1063
——*American Constitutional Law* (Foundation Press, 2000)
Tridimas, T. and Nebbia, P., *European Union Law for the Twenty-First Century*, Volume 2: *Internal Market and Free Movement Community Policies* (Hart, 2004)
Tryfonidou, A., 'The Outer Limits of Article 28 EC: Purely Internal Situations and the Development of the Court's Approach through the Years', in C. Barnard and O. Odudu (eds.), *The Outer Limits of European Law* (Hart, 2009), 197
——*Reverse Discrimination in EC Law* (Kluwer, 2009)
—— 'Resolving the Reverse Discrimination Paradox in the Area of Customs Duties: The *Lancry* Saga' (2011) 22 European Business Law Review 311
——'The Notions of "Restriction" and "Discrimination" in the Context of the Free Movement of Persons Provisions: From a Relationship of Interdependence to One of (Almost Complete) Independence' (2014) 33 Yearbook of European Law 385
Tushnet, M., 'Rethinking the Dormant Commerce Clause' (1979) Wisconsin Law Review 125
Ulmer, P., 'Zum Verbot mittelbarer Einfuhrbeschränkungen im EWG Vertrag' (1973) 19 Aussenwirtschaftsdienst des Betriebs-Beraters 349
Usher, J., 'The Effects of Common Organisations and Policies on the Powers of a Member State' (1977) 2 European Law Review 428
Ustor, E., 'First Report on the Most-Favoured-Nation Clause' (1969) 2 Yearbook of the International Law Commission 157
Vattel, E. de, *The Law of Nations* (Johnson & Co., 1883)
Vaulont, N., 'Die Vereinfachung der Verfahren und Förmlichkeiten im innergemeinschaftlichen Warenverkehr im Lichte der Rechtsprechung des Europäischen Gerichtshofs zum Verbot der Erhebung von Abgaben zollgleicher Wirkung' (1977) 12 Europarecht 1
VerLoren Van Themaat, P., 'Bevat Artikel 30 van het EEG-Verdrag slechts een non-discriminatie-beginsel ten aaanzien van invoerbeperkingen?' (1967) Sociaal-Economische Wetgeving 632
Vignes, D., 'La Clause de la nation la plus favorisée et la pratique contemporaine. Problèmes posés par la Communauté économique européenne' (1970) 130 Collected Courses of the Hague Academy of International Law 207
Viner, J., 'The Most-Favored-Nation Clause in American Commercial Treaties' (1924) 32 Journal of Political Economy 101
——*Studies in the Theory of International Trade* (Kelley, 1975)
——*The Customs Union Issue* (Oxford University Press, 2014)
Vogel, K., Gutmann, D., and Paula Dourado, A., 'Tax Treaties between Member States and Third States: "Reciprocity" in Bilateral Tax Treaties and Non-Discrimination in EC Law' (2006) 15 EC Tax Review 83

Vogelaar, T. W., 'The Approximation of the Laws of Member States under the Treaty of Rome' (1975) 12 Common Market Law Review 21

Waelbroeck, D., *Les Règlementations nationales de prix et le droit communautaire* (Université de Bruxelles, 1975)

Wagenbaur, R., 'Das Verbot steuerlicher Diskiminierung' (1969) 4 Europarecht 27

Weatherill, S., 'After *Keck*: Some Thoughts on How to Clarify the Clarification' (1996) 33 Common Market Law Review 885

—— 'Recent Case Law Concerning the Free Movement of Goods: Mapping the Frontiers of Market Deregulation' (1999) 36 Common Market Law Review 51

—— 'Free Movement of Goods' (2012) 61 International and Comparative Law Quarterly 541

—— *EU Consumer Law and Policy* (Elgar, 2013)

Weber, D., 'In Search of a (New) Equilibrium between Tax Sovereignty and the Freedom of Movement Within the EC' (2006) 34 Intertax 585

Weiler, J. H. H., 'The Community System: The Dual Character of Supranationalism' (1981) 1 Yearbook of European Law 267

—— *The Constitution of Europe: 'Do the New Clothes Have an Emperor?' and Other Essays on European Integration* (Cambridge University Press, 1999)

—— 'Epilogue: Towards a Common Law of International Trade', in J. H. H. Weiler (ed.), *The EU, The WTO and the NAFTA* (Oxford University Press, 2000), 201

—— 'In the Face of Crisis: Input Legitimacy, Output Legitimacy and the Political Messianism of European Integration' (2012) 34 Journal of European Integration 825

—— 'Editorial: On My Way Out—Advice to Young Scholars II: Career Strategy and the Publication Trap' (2015) 26 European Journal of International Law 795

Wellinghausen, W., 'Anmwerkung zu EuGH, Slg. 1974, 837 ("Dassonville")' (1975) 10 Europarecht 319

Wennerås, P. and Bøe Moen, K., 'Selling Arrangements, Keeping *Keck*' (2010) 35 European Law Review 387

Weyer, H., 'Freier Warenverkehr, rein innerstaatliche Sachverhalte und umgekehrte Diskriminierung' (1998) 33 Europarecht 435

White, E. L., 'In Search of the Limits to Article 30 of the EEC Treaty' (1989) 26 Common Market Law Review 235

Wilcox, C., *A Charter for World Trade* (Macmillan, 1949)

Williams, N. R., 'Why Congress May Not "Overrule" the Dormant Commerce Clause' (2005) 53 UCLA Law Review 153

Williams, N. R. and Denning, B. P., 'The "New Protectionism" and the American Common Market' (2009) 85 Notre Dame Law Review 247

Winham, G. R., *The Evolution of International Trade Agreements* (University of Toronto Press, 1993)
Winkel, K., 'Die Vereinbarkeit staatlicher Preislenkungsmaßnahmen mit dem EWG-Vertrag' (1976) 45 Neue Juristische Wochenschrift 2048
Wittgenstein, L., *Tractatus Logico-Philosophicus* (Routledge, 2001)
Woods, L., 'Consistency in the Chambers of the ECJ: A Case Study on the Free Movement of Goods' (2012) 31 Civil Justice Quarterly 340
Wooldridge, F. and Plender, R., 'Charges Having an Effect Equivalent to Customs Duties: A Review of the Cases' (1978) 3 European Law Review 101
Wyatt, D., 'Quantitative Restrictions and Measures Having Equivalent Effect' (1981) 6 European Law Review 185
Ypi, L., *Global Justice and Avant-Garde Political Agency* (Oxford University Press, 2012)
Zebel, S. H., 'Fair Trade: An English Reaction to the Breakdown of the Cobden Treaty System' (1940) 12 The Journal of Modern History 161
Zeiler, T. W., *Free Trade, Free World: The Advent of GATT* (University of North Carolina Press, 1999)

INDEX

Notes: Page numbers in **bold** denote detailed/extended analysis. *n* = footnote. *f* = figure.